# SUPER STOCK

## DRAG RACING THE FAMILY SEDAN

### BY LARRY DAVIS

**CarTech**®

# CarTech®

CarTech®, Inc.
39966 Grand Avenue
North Branch, MN 55056
Phone: 651-277-1200 or 800-551-4754
Fax: 651-277-1203
www.cartechbooks.com

© 2010 by Larry Davis

Edit by Steve Hendrickson
Layout by Dennis Jenkins

ISBN 978-1-934709-48-1
Item No. CT495

Library of Congress Cataloging-in-Publication Data

Printed in China
10 9 8 7 6 5 4 3 2 1

**Front Cover:**

*The manufacturers go head to head at the 1968 NHRA Winternationals. Dodge was well represented with the Dick Landy team which numbered at least four cars, while Ford including the Russ Davis Ford team headed by Gas Ronda. This is the run for the SS/EA trophy, in which the Landy Dodge Dart was victorious over Ronda's Cobra Jet Mustang, 12.01 to 12.02. (Match Race Madness)*

**Title Page:**

*Bill Jenkins puts it to Charles Rogers' SS/AA 426 1965 Plymouth A 990 in round two of the Super Stock Eliminators. "Grumpy's" Camaro has a 375 horsepower, 396-ci Semi-Hemi Chevy and a 4-speed transmission, and was the only car entered in SS/C, winning the class with a solo run of 14.79. (Author's Collection)*

**Dedication:**

*Dave Strickler waves at the camera as he returns to the pits at York US Dragway in 1968. This version of* Old Reliable *was a Z-28 with a 302-ci small-block Chevy rated very conservatively at 290 horsepower. Dave used this combination to win in the SS/J class. The orange screamer turned an unreal 11.57 en route to the World Championship victory in October 1968, much to the chagrin of the Hemi-Dart and Barracuda drivers. (Author's Collection)*

**Back Cover:**

*Dick Landy's SS/B Hemi Dodge charges off the line at the 1968 NHRA National Drags held at Indianapolis Raceway Park. The Chrysler Clinic teams of Sox & Martin in Plymouth and Dick Landy's Dodges had so many cars entered that Chrysler had to draft other name drivers to handle all the cars. Dick Landy was assisted by his son, Mike, as well as Butch Leal, "The California Flash." (Match Race Madness)*

OVERSEAS DISTRIBUTION BY:

Brooklands Books Ltd.
P.O. Box 146, Cobham, Surrey, KT11 1LG, England
Phone: 01932 865051 • Fax: 01932 868803
www.brooklands-books.com

Brooklands Books Aus.
3/37-39 Green Street, Banksmeadow, NSW 2109, Australia
Phone: 2 9695 7055 • Fax: 2 9695 7355

# THE MANY THANKS GO TO ...

This book has been a labor of love; and a lot more "labor" than I thought it would be. With the constant pushing by my wife, Sue, and my daughter, Kris, it has finally come to fruition. Now Sue can have her kitchen and spare room back.

The prime mover on this labor of love has been my best friend of almost 40 years — Larry Brinkley. "Brink" and I have been car buddies forever. We built model cars together; we built real cars together. I was at his wedding and he was at mine. At one time, we even thought about getting married in the back of an El Camino at the strip. But Bonnie and Sue vetoed that idea.

It was about then that Brink bought *Old Reliable II*. The first thing he did was contact Dave Strickler with questions on how to validate that it was indeed the real deal. It was! Then he asked Dave about photos so we could begin restoration. "Sure," Dave said, "I'll put a batch of stuff together for you." That was early Spring 1984. One month later, Dave Strickler passed away. The following Christmas, Brink got a phone call from Susie Strickler. She had found Brink's letter with Dave's stuff, and was going to send the color slides of the car to Brink. Not only was the restoration of *Old Reliable* under way, but I now had photos in color of Strickler's cars for the book.

Brink also contacted NHRA about photos of the car. It was then that we met a gentleman named Leslie Lovett. Les was somewhat of a curator of the NHRA photo collection in Los Angeles. Within a week, Brink had photos of Strickler at the '62 Nationals. When I contacted Mr. Lovett and told him about my project, he was more than willing to help. A few photo packages passed back and forth between NHRA and my mailbox, mostly Z-11 material from early 1963. Then the book was placed on the back burner again. Mr. Lovett passed away recently, and he will definitely be missed. He knew the NHRA archives inside and out.

Brink and I are both pack rats and never throw anything away. So when he bought Dave Strickler's *Old Reliable II* and started restoring it, we brought a bunch of stuff out of storage. It was then that I got the idea to do this book. Reaching back into both our memories, and the storage cabinets full of books, magazines, pit passes, and pictures (we even have an Amalie Oil sign that we "liberated" at the Nationals in '66), I saw that I had the beginnings of a book. Then I found my old slides taken at strips all over the Midwest between 1964 and 1971.

The problem was that I didn't have a publisher. My regular publisher (I write aviation books) wouldn't handle it. It didn't have wings or guns! The book lay dormant for about 10 years, just gathering material and dust. Then I met Dave Arnold of Specialty Press. He wanted me to write some aviation books for his company. At a meeting in Columbus one Saturday afternoon, he informed Sue and I that he was there for a car parts convention. He had just started a publishing company called CarTech® Inc.

BINGO! The light went on. I mentioned the idea I had for a book on super stock racing. He thought about it for about ten minutes, asking all kinds of questions. Then said YES! Once I had a definite commitment from Dave, I was off and running trying to find anyone who could and would help. I thought, this should be easy, everyone was there at the strip in the '60s, and everyone had a camera. Boy was I wrong.

Yes, they were all there. However, they were racing and didn't have time to take pictures; or they took pictures they thought weren't worthy of publication; or worse, they had bunches of stuff but weren't willing to help in any way. Believe me there were a lot of the latter types. The book was dead in the water again, and it gathered dust for a couple of years.

Then Brink started thinking about some of the guys we knew. "How about Tom Schiltz?" Brink asked. He said that Tom had been (still is) a photographer with NHRA. When I contacted Tom, he was very receptive to the idea and turned over several albums of color photos that he took in the 1962 - 1969 era. Now I had enough to really get started.

I began to search everywhere for photos and contacts. At a local swap meet, I met a gentleman named Jack Bleil. He had a lot of photos and was the first to offer open-ended help. Jack also put me in contact with a couple of other photo guys, including Bob Plumr of Drag Racing Memories. Bob was another gentleman who offered help without question. He had bought the old Gold Dust photo collection of Skip Norman. Skip had offered me some help in the early days of this project, but then got out of the business in one of the "dead times" for the book and we lost touch with each other.

It was Bob Plumr who put me in touch with "The Man" when it comes to super stock history. His name is Joel Naprstek, aka RACECARART. Joel is a walking encyclopedia of knowledge. He has touched base with most of the big name drivers, and quite a few little guys too, who raced the super stock and match race circuit of the 1960s. If I needed a question answered, or a photo of some car or driver, Joel knew the answer or pointed me in the right direction. I can't thank Joel enough for all his help.

One of the people Joel put me in touch with is a young man, in his early 20s, named Raj Reddi. Raj is in love with the early super stocks, especially the Z-11 Chevrolets. He had collected a bunch of photos of the West Coast drivers and cars and was willing to loan them to me. Raj also put me in touch with Terry Prince and Russ Griffith. Terry had been associated with Don Nicholson in the very early '60s, had a few photos of his cars, and a wonderful story about those early days of drag racing in Southern California. Russ Griffith was a track photographer at Puyallup Raceway in Washington. Russ supplied a batch of photos that he had taken in 1964–1965.

When the idea for the book had first come to mind, I had tried contacting anyone I could find who might have some memorabilia. One of those guys was Brent Hajek. Brent is a collector of those old super stockers and FX cars. He called me one night and offered his entire photo collection — some 200 photos of old drag cars in the 1963–1966 era. I readily accepted. Brent filled in many gaps in the Ford story.

Along the way, Joel put me in touch with a great many people. Robert Genat, a book writer in his own right, sent several shots his brother had taken at Detroit Dragway in the early '60s, plus some gorgeous color of the restored *Melrose Missile* and Tom Jacobsen's *Old Blue* 409 Biscayne. John Lacko had been a photographer at

US 131 Dragway in the mid-1960s. He had a catalog of photos from his collection that he made available.

Joel also put me in touch with an internet site — the gas-fx line. It was through that website that I met a large group of people who had the same interest that I did — old gassers and super stockers. This led me to Charlie Morris, who knows Fords as well as anyone; Marv Smith, a historian on Atlanta racing; Glenn Miller and Pete Garramone, who were track photographers; Ken Andruss, who was around Dragway 42 at the same time that I was; Grady Bryant, who was partners with the legendary Dickie Harrell; and Tom Molyneaux, who has his own memorabilia site — DragRaceVideo.

Through various people at the manufacturers I was able to contact Mr. Jim Wangers of Royal Pontiac, and Mr. Al Eckstrand, the famous "Lawman." Both of these gentlemen granted interviews and supplied photos for the book.

To everyone who helped in any little way (and there were about 100 of you) or anyone who just kept saying, "Keep at it!", MANY, MANY THANKS!

If you are interested in obtaining any of the photos in this book, contact me and I will put you in touch with the owners of the photos.

*Super Stock* is the story of an era in automotive history, an era that will never be seen again. I lived it and loved it. Enjoy the book!

*Still Cruisin'*
*Larry Davis*
*September 2001*

# DEDICATION

This book is dedicated to Dave Strickler, who is no longer with us but who was responsible for much of the history that is written in this book. Dave, you are gone but will never be forgotten.

*Smokin' 'em off the line at the '69 Nationals! The author's second Chevy II was built for Super Stock/F class, but was really just a street machine. However, when it was running right, it ran in the high 12s; Dick Landy's SS/F Dodge was running in the mid-11s. Note the nine Dragway 42 win stickers in the rear window. (NHRA)*

# CHAPTER ONE

# FULL THROTTLE CRUISIN'

**I**can still remember one day in mid-June 1962, when I walked into Hillman's Record Store to check on the latest releases. I always came in on Tuesday afternoon after the mailman delivered new records. I asked Viv if anything had come in and she handed me a stack of new 45s. About midway through the stack was a new single by some West Coast guys called the Beach Boys. Viv said it was really getting a push and was quite good.

As I checked out the "A" side ("Surfin' Safari") and thought about spending the 49 cents for the new song. I turned it over to check the "B" side. The title was a simple three-digit number, "409". To most people it would have meant nothing at all, but to me, a die-hard Chevrolet man, it stood for the hottest thing to hit the streets anywhere — the Chevrolet 409 cubic inch Turbo-fire engine rated at 409 horsepower.

That ended the purchase debate. I plunked down the 51 cents (tax you know!), took it straight home, and popped it on my little RCA 45 rpm record player. There it was, a song about a car; not just any car, this was about "a 4-speed, dual-quad, Positraction 409." Super stock drag racing had hit the radio in a big way. That record didn't leave my turntable for the next three months — not until the Beach Boys released the song about a Sting Ray beating a 413 Dodge!

I first began drag racing, i.e. street racing, almost from the moment I got my driver's license. First with my mom's 1953 Ford flathead, stick shift (3 on a tree); then with the 1957 Plymouth convertible that followed. It didn't take me very long to go through both of those cars. Neither was ready for a constant diet of jackrabbit, tire-smoking starts, and full-throttle cruises through every gear. The flathead Ford actually fared better in the daily grind of boulevard racing. It finally bit the dust when a guy went through a stop sign and I hit him broadside.

The Plymouth, which my wife dearly loved, was finished after about 6 months. It had the 318 engine with a two-barrel carb, and a PowerFlite two-speed automatic transmission. The PowerFlite transmission was definitely not made for the way I was driving it. The car ran great, but after two transmission failures it was time to move on.

It was then that I got my first super stock car; well, I thought it was my first! We traded the Plymouth on a red, 1960 Chevrolet Impala convertible, powered by a 250 horsepower, 348 cubic-inch Turbo-thrust V-8. It was a stick shift (again 3 on a tree), with a standard open rear end (non-limited slip). The window sticker was a real shock — $3,197.85 with radio, heater, and white sidewall tires. I had wanted to get a '61 Impala 2-door hardtop that the dealer had in stock. It was powered by a 350 horsepower, 348ci engine, and had a 4-speed transmission and Positraction rear end. A really awesome car at the time, but my dad vetoed that one and I had to settle for the convertible.

The '60 convertible was quite fast on the street. Fast enough to get me several tickets for speeding and reckless operation when the cops saw me smoking the rear tires as I left the drive-in! The car needed modifications before it would be right. Those GM engineers sure didn't realize that the car was meant to be drag raced.

The first thing that went was the "3 on a tree." Chevrolet column shift linkage was prone to locking up, i.e., the bushings in the steering column would work loose enough to have the shift levers jam between low and second gear. You had to stop, open the hood, and wedge a screwdriver down between the levers and pry them apart; very embarrassing in the middle of a race. In went a Corvette floor shift and linkage. A hole was cut in the floor with a cutting torch and the gorgeous red "salt and pepper" carpet was opened with a razor blade to allow the shifter handle to poke through. It was crude but effective.

(Capitol Records)

*This red '60 Impala convertible with the big engine, a 250 horse, 348 Chevy, 4 speed, and 4.11 Positraction rear end was the author's first super stocker. It had all the latest go-fast equipment, including Moon disc hubcaps, '59 Caddy tail lights, and Moon Eyes decal in the windshield.* (Author's Collection)

was possible to burn them off in a two-week period, if the racing was good, but you could get them replaced for three bucks whenever they got bald! I went through about 6 pairs of Bucrons.

I could now hold my own with almost everything on the street. Of course, Bill Foster's '60 Impala hardtop beat me all the time, but he was running the 350-horse engine that became available late in the 1960 model run. Fords were no problem (except for Dave Domenic's T-Bird-powered '54 Ford). Neither were the Mopars of that era. Several big Pontiacs known as "Indians" or "Ponchos," started showing up in '61, and that made the street scene untenable.

I tried the local strip action at Magnolia Drag Strip, but I didn't have the right combination to win the class. Plus my driving skill left a little to be desired, especially off the starting line. However, after my first trip down the quarter mile at Magnolia, known affectionately as "The Swamp," I was bitten by the competition bug. If I couldn't race and win, then I could certainly watch or hang around with the guys who were racing and winning. Magnolia was my first venture into the land of super stock drag racing.

At The Swamp I learned all about things like classes, coming off the line (known otherwise as "out of the chute" or "gate"), how to increase your horsepower without making radical changes to the engine, which gears were best for my combination, what the best times were that I had to beat, and of course, how to cheat and not get caught! By then, my super stocker had been relegated to the lowest

Next came the exhaust. Now everyone knows that engines don't breathe when running through restrictive, sound-deadening factory mufflers. I'd had full-length lakes pipes on the Plymouth but that was a custom car. The Impala was a race car! I opted for the latest in street exhaust systems — a set of 2-inch galvanized plumber's pipes, welded right at the elbow where the header pipe bent to go into the mufflers.

For normal use, these were closed using threaded pipe caps. They weren't bad but they had a nasty habit of vibrating loose and falling off at the wrong times, like when a car is coming from the opposite direction and you're under full throttle. Bang! Off goes the cap onto the street at 50+ mph, ricocheting off the blacktop and through the oncoming car's grille. No, I didn't stop to collect my lost cap! I just drove to the nearest hardware store and bought another one.

Transmissions and rear ends were the next problem. By the time I made the right change, I had gone through seven 3-speed transmissions and three rear-end assemblies. Finally I bought a 4 speed and a 4:11 Positraction rear end. The 4 speed was $288.00, while the Positraction unit was $110.00. My friend, Larry Brinkley, "Brink," worked at the Ewing Chevrolet Parts Department, and we fast became very knowledgeable in removing and rebuilding both transmissions and rear ends.

Tires were a never-ending problem. The stock 800x14 tires were bald within months, and they simply had no traction. On went the best racing rubber available at the time — a pair of 850x14 Atlas Bucrons that were made of very soft butyl rubber. Surprisingly, these tires really did have good bite, but they also wore out very fast. It

*Larry Brinkley, AKA "Mr. 409," has worked at Ewing Chevrolet for over 36 years. According to the author, there isn't anything Brinkley doesn't know about the great years of Chevrolet, '55 through '64. Brinkley now owns a large piece of Super Stock history, having acquired and restored the original* Old Reliable II, *the '62 409 Chevy that Dave Strickler won SS/S with at the 1962 Nationals.* (Author's Collection)

class, C Stock. My best times were in the low 15-second range; not bad, just not competitive.

By this time the street action was really getting out of hand. In late '61, Chevrolet introduced the 409. Those '61 engines were relatively mild, having only a single four barrel and rated at only 360 horsepower. Yet, they were awesome when compared with the familiar 350-horse 348s. They were also very rare and only one guy in town had one, which he had built from over-the-counter parts.

By 1962, the 409 was king of the street. With high-compression heads and dual quads, the '62 409 was rated at a whopping 409 horses. They were plentiful. It seemed like everyone had one. Every time the Beach Boys sang, another 409 would pull up next to you. My convertible just wasn't getting the job done anymore.

Not only that, the hot rod industry was really taking off in our area of Northeastern Ohio. Everyone was building something, and they all ended up on the street. Imagine pulling up to a traffic light and looking over to the right to see a dark blue '49 Packard sedan with really huge dump tubes coming right through the bottom of the front fenders. That was Dave Koffel's E/G national record holder. He and Susie used to drive it to and from the grocery store and drive-ins on the weekends!

The ultimate was seeing a true all-out factory drag team race on the street. It happened on a Friday night in the Summer of 1962. Brink and I pulled into the Waterloo Drive-In on this particular

*Magnolia Drag Strip return road in 1961, which wasn't even paved. You sat in this line waiting for a time slip, which you put in the front window to show you had a real race car as you paraded through the local drive-in restaurant.* (Author's Collection)

*The Magnolia Drag Strip Summer 1961 Top Eliminator run-off between Blaine Shiveley's Chrysler-powered dragster and Bob Janson's Headless Horseman, '32 Ford roadster with the engine in the passenger compartment, and the driver in the engine compartment looking through the Plexiglas grille. Just behind the roadster is the author's '60 Impala, waiting for its turn on the track. Note the flagman in the grass to the left of the dragster. He was afraid to stand between the cars!* (Bob Janson)

night to find the place buzzing with excitement. "What's up?" we asked. "There's going to be a match race tonight," was the answer.

The first to arrive was a big super stock Pontiac complete with dealership lettering and "SS/S" painted on the doors. The driver unhooked the tow bar and pushed the big Poncho into a food stall, ordered a coke, and set about getting the car ready to race. He opened the headers, changed the street tires for super stock cheater slicks, made some minor adjustments, closed the hood, and waited.

Next in was the local hero and his '62 Plymouth. The Fury hardtop had one of the new 413 Chrysler engines with the short cross-ram intake mounting two four barrels. It was one of the Torqueflite cars. It being the primary car for his family, he simply drove it in rather than tow it. He too, backed into a stall, opened the hood and trunk, and started to get ready for the race — opened the header caps, changed the tires, and got some ice from the restaurant to cool the engine down a bit.

When everything was ready, the two drivers met inside where a mutual friend held the stakes — $500.00 — a lot of money for the time. Then it was time to race. Both drivers jumped into their cars, fired up, and left by the back entrance onto Aurora Boulevard, across Whipple Road, and into the back of the Country Fair Shopping Center parking lot. Then it was out onto West Tuscarawus Street and wait for the light. The crowd was anxious and moved out to the curb.

The two cars pulled up to the traffic light heading west — Plymouth in the curb lane, Pontiac in the center. As we looked down West Tuscarawus, we could see several police cruisers along the way. Generally, police didn't allow street racing. However, this race was between a local guy and a factory team racer. The police were just as curious as the spectators and this time they were actually going to help keep the normal traffic from interfering with the race. As the light started to change, we could hear the RPMs rising until both engines were screaming. GREEN! The Pontiac launched very hard, getting about a car-length lead on the Plymouth. As they flashed past, we could see that the Pontiac was holding its lead. Winner of Round One — Pontiac.

We watched as both cars proceeded west and turned around in the parking lot of Central Catholic High School. Now they pulled back onto West Tuscarawus and waited at the Woodlawn light. Again, we heard the RPMs rise and watched as both cars launched at the Green. This time the end of the 1/4 mile was very near to us in the restaurant. Plymouth! The race was tied and everyone was screaming wildly.

The two super stockers pulled back into the restaurant parking lot and backed into their stalls. The hoods were opened, and plenty of ice from the restaurant manager cooled down the cars for the final. The Pontiac driver made a couple of minor adjustments. The Plymouth driver just kept putting ice on the intake and radiator.

After about a 40 minute wait, it was time. Both drivers again met and talked. Then it was back into the cars, out the back gate of the restaurant, and up through the shopping center lot to wait for a red light at Whipple Road. Both cars then pulled out onto West Tuscarawus. Just to make things even, they switched lanes, with the Pontiac taking the curb lane this time. They waited for the light.

GREEN! Both cars came out dead even. As they passed the restaurant, we couldn't tell who was in the lead. At the 1/4 mile spot, the "judge" blinked his flash light — curb lane and Pontiac! The cars turned around again and returned to the restaurant. The Pontiac driver collected his 500 bucks, hooked up his tow bar and left. A lot of money changed hands between patrons of the restaurant that night. It was my first glimpse at a match race. It wouldn't be my last.

Shortly after that scene on the streets of Canton, Ohio, I decided to get something that would run with anything on the street. It was October 1962, I had a good job, and was living at home. At the newsstand I picked up a copy of *Car Life* magazine and there it was, my next car — a bright red '63 Corvette Sting Ray convertible. Since this was my money, I chose the options and we ordered it from the hot rod dealer in the area — Dutch Folk Chevrolet in Akron. The sticker price was an outrageous $4,337.15!

Six weeks later, it was in and waiting for me to pick up. Bright red, white convertible top, radio, and go-fast equipment. Powered by a 340 horsepower, 327ci Corvette engine, my 'Vette had a 4-speed, close ratio transmission, and 4:11 Positraction rear end. After the usual break-in period (I think I waited 3 days before pushing the RPMs over 6500!), I hit the streets to take on all comers.

The one time we actually went to the strip, the car turned a 13.07 ET on a national record of 13.05 in B/SP class. That was with closed exhausts and street tires. There was a standing joke about riding with me in that car. If I hit a good 2nd gear, the glove box door would pop open and 'puke' everything out onto the passenger. Everyone said it

*The Corvette was the ultimate street machine in 1963 and the author owned one. The author's '63 roadster had all the stuff to make it go: 340 horse engine, 4 speed, and 4.11 Positraction. Plus, the author added all the trim items that made the car cool: all-white frame, fenderwells, and floor; Rader Wheels, and no front bumper (extra weight, you know!). Everyone in town knew that red 'Vette, including all the cops. (Author's Collection)*

was because I was pulling the wheels off. I knew it was because the car was just torquing and the door latch was probably loose, but it made the reputation of the car even more fearful.

### SUUUNNNDAAAYYY!!!

The voice on the radio screamed it out. "See the biggest names in drag racing! Don Nicholson, The Ramchargers, The Golden Commandos, Dave Strickler and *The Old Reliable*, Arnie 'The Farmer' Beswick, and local favorite, Arlen Vanke. They'll be there! Where? At Dragway 42 for the *Drag News* Super Stock Invitational this SUUUNNNDAAAYYY! Be there or be square!"

It was the great Summer of 1963 and the biggest names in super stock drag racing were coming to town, or at least to the local strip. Throughout late 1962 and early 1963, the drive-in and garage news was all about which was the best — Chevy, Ford, Pontiac, Dodge or Plymouth. This Sunday (and many Sundays throughout the rest of the Summer) it would be settled, but never for long. As soon as one of the manufacturers would win, the other companies would either build a bigger engine or make a significant change to bring them back into competition.

Sunday, July 7, 1963, was special. *Drag News*, the national drag racing newspaper and voice of the American Hot Rod Association, was hosting a Super Stock Invitational at Dragway 42, West Salem, Ohio. *Drag News* had a "Mr. Stock Eliminator" list and all the biggest names fought for first place on the list in match races at strips all over the country. This battle for the first name on the list was ongoing throughout the entire year of 1963, and was much more accurate than the single-meet Stock Eliminator titles. It was possible, and indeed probable, for a driver to defend his number one standing 30-40 times in a season.

During the weekend of July 6-7, 1963, everyone who was anyone was at Dragway 42 to battle for the title. "Dyno Don" Nicholson was there with his whole team (he was #1 on the *Drag News* List). "Fast Eddie" Schartman and Hubert Platt were there too. Dave Strickler brought *Old Reliable IV*. Frank Sanders had the Rudolph Chevrolet car. Mike Lenke towed in from California with the Bourgeois & Wade Impala. Six Z-11 Chevrolets at one strip! Few of the fans had ever seen <u>one</u> Z-11.

Pontiac was represented by both of Arnie Beswick's wicked Tempests, Arlen Vanke and Jim Wangers and the Royal Pontiac. The Ramchargers were there with two cars. The Golden Commandos had three! Bill "Maverick" Golden and Bill Hanyon had towed in all the way from Los Angeles. Local drivers like Wes Koogle and his *Original Dependable* Dodge, Bill Abraham, and a host of others made up the field.

It was a wild weekend. Brink, Tom Schiltz, and I talked our way into the best seat in town for the entire weekend of racing — on top of the Dragway 42 timing tower — with a movie camera, shooting all

*Tom Schiltz, Brinkley, and the author were all on top of the Dragway 42 tower at the* Drag News *Invitational. Tom had a still camera, the author had an 8mm movie camera.* (Tom Schiltz)

*Dragway 42 pit pass.* (Author's Collection)

the action right on the starting line. That film has some of the best racing ever seen. On one section, I scanned the staging lanes just prior to the actual races; count 'em, five Z-11 Chevys, with Dyno Don making burnouts in the staging lanes.

When the meet was over there was a new number one on the *Drag News* list — Arnie "The Farmer" Beswick and his *Mrs. B's Grocery Getter* '63 Tempest wagon. "The Farmer" beat the Ramchargers, Arlen Vanke, Maverick, and his other car, *Mr. B's Run-About* Tempest coupe for the title. However, that wasn't all the racing. Arlen Vanke defeated Hubert Platt's *Georgia Shaker* Z-11 for his spot on the *Drag News* list. Then Platt turned around and set a new record for A/FX at 11.93 seconds. It was the most unforgettable weekend that I had ever experienced, to that date.

In the Winter of '63 - '64, just as I was about to get the Corvette ready for the '64 drag season, with headers and slicks making it a real race car, I got an unexpected letter from Uncle Sam. So I went into the Army, ending up at a nice little country estate called Fort Bragg, North Carolina; I wasn't alone. There were several guys from the Cleveland area, as well as Pittsburgh, and we were all looking for some racing action.

We found it nearby at a pair of drag strips that were little more than blacktop paths in the middle of a corn field. Here I would be introduced to southern-style match racing. Our first stop was at Fayetteville Drag Strip, just outside of Fort Bragg. It was incredible! A blacktop strip between some trees, in the middle of a farmer's field.

No lights, no starting system. Since the strip had no lights, the race cars had to have working headlights. There was, however, a win indicator system of sorts. It was the same as my home strip at Magnolia. There were two guys at the finish end of the 1/4 mile watching the end of the race. Each held binoculars to see which car finished first. Whichever lane was the winner, the guy on that side of the strip would turn on a large light.

The first time I went to Fayetteville Drag Strip was in the early winter of 1964. Now you must remember that we did have a really first-class drag strip back home — Dragway 42, an officially sanctioned NHRA strip, complete with Christmas tree starting system and automatic win lights and clocks. The cars raced about 200 feet away from the crowd, with guard rails between the cars and the crowd.

Fayetteville, on the other hand, didn't even have rest rooms. My first time there, we watched Ronnie Sox's '64 A/FX Comet take on four local cars: the *Hemi Hannah* Plymouth, Billy West, Melvin Yow driving the O.B. Hewett match race Hemi-Dodge, and an unlettered, unfinished '63 Plymouth. Few of these cars were legal super stockers in any sense of the word. The '63 Plymouth had no bumpers or hood, no headlights, and a gutted interior. Yet, it was allowed to run in stock class against Sox's Comet. It was, "Run What Ya Brung!"

Safety? There was no such thing at Fayetteville. The crowd stood right on, I mean physically *on,* the starting line, between and beside the race cars. The track itself was a strip of blacktop, maybe 20 feet wide, that went off into the night about 2,000 feet. Between the race

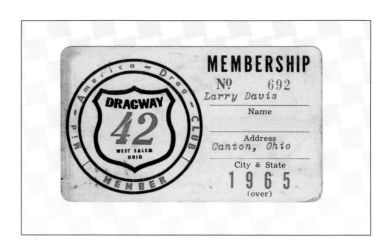

*Dragway 42 membership card.* (Author's Collection)

cars and the crowd was the safety of a chicken wire fence. I remember one night when Dyno Don Nicholson brought his big Hemi-Comet to Fayetteville. I stood at about the 500 foot mark, leaning on the fence as the cars went by, close enough that I could reach out and touch that big red Comet whizzing past at over 100 mph!

The other southern strip I visited was Piedmont Drag Strip near Greenville, North Carolina. It actually was several steps above Fayetteville, but still not what anyone could classify as a sanctioned drag strip. Piedmont was wider and longer than Fayetteville. Except for the starting line, this strip actually did have some safety standards, with guard rails to keep the fans away. It even had a toilet!

The strip itself, went off into the wooded area, which kept most of the fans safely back from the finish line. Which was a good thing whenever one of those southern-style stockers got out of control, which happened often. Lee Malkemes lost control of Hubert Platt's old *Georgia Shaker* Thunderbolt, rolling it several times near the end of Piedmont. At Fayetteville, the crash would probably have been disastrous, but even Piedmont was far from safe.

In 1965, when Ronnie Sox came to Piedmont with his altered wheelbase Plymouth funny car, the *Paper Tiger*, running an injected Hemi, the race had to be shortened from 1/4 mile to 1/8th mile due to the extremely high speeds the cars were attaining. The stopping area was just too short for the safety of the drivers, and as always, the starting line area was crowded with fans. You could literally have your hand on Sox's big Plymouth as he left the starting line with the front wheels three feet in the air! Such were the ways of southern-style super stock racing.

When I returned home in 1965, things were happening quickly in the world of drag racing: Strips were highly successful with many big meets, GM was introducing new factory hot rods like the Z-16 Chevelle and V-8 Chevy II, Funny Cars had arrived, and all my friends had race cars. I was still a part of it, albeit a spectator for the

*Match racing, southern style. Billy West's Plymouth against Melvin Yow's match-race Dodge at Fayetteville Drag Strip, near Fort Bragg, NC. The spectators stood on the starting line, in between the cars, and just a few off the track the entire 1,320 feet. It was loud, dangerous, and a lot of fun!* (Author's Collection)

most part. Brink had been attending the NHRA Nationals for quite a few years by 1965. I had attended none, although I had been to the *Drag News* Stock Car Invitationals, the Detroit Nationals, and quite a few NHRA sanctioned Regional and Points Meets. In 1965, the Nationals came to me.

NASCAR held its Nationals at Dragway 42 in 1965. Not only was I in attendance, I was entered. I entered the new 'Vette that I had purchased after getting out of the Army. It was one of the new big-block Corvettes, powered by a 425 horse, 396ci Chevrolet Semi-Hemi. The car ran good, when it ran, but it had trouble staying together and was broken when the NASCAR Nationals came to Dragway 42. So, with entry in hand, Brink and I put together a quick entry. We took Mom's '64 Valiant coupe, a 6-cylinder Torqueflite hardtop, added a cut-out to the exhaust system, put a few decals on the windows, and went racing. The NASCAR officials didn't care, they just wanted entries. So it was that we went from AA/SP to M/SA. Guess what — we won!

In late 1965, I traded the big 'Vette for an economy car, a Chevy II. My dad was ecstatic! He didn't realize it was one of the L79 option Chevy IIs, with a 350 horsepower, 327ci Corvette engine. That car was both the most fun and the scariest ride I have ever known. It went like hell, but had no brakes. It didn't matter because you had about 1,000 feet to stop at Magnolia before you went into the swamp; 2,000 feet at Quaker City and Dragway 42. I won several trophies with the Chevy II, but the most fun was on the street. It was common knowledge that you didn't mess with that brown

*Summer 1966 and the author has just returned from Quaker City Drag Strip where he won A/Stock class over a field of 421 Pontiacs, 427 Fords, and the vaunted 426 Street Hemis. Using a basically stock factory engine, with slicks, open headers, and a change to a 4.88 Positraction, the Chevy II would run in the 12-second bracket, at 112+ mph. (Author's Collection)*

Chevy II. One of the local guys bought a new dark blue Plymouth, equipped with the 4-speed Street Hemi. The first thing he did was come looking for me. It was match race time on Cleveland Avenue.

The first night, I beat him so bad in first gear that I quit. Race over. He took the car back to the dealership to get it set up. A week later, we

*Over Labor Day 1966, the author made his first venture to the NHRA National Drags in Indianapolis. Larry Brinkley (walking behind the Nomad) was entered with his G/Stock '56 Nomad, which was towed to Indy with a Chrysler owned by the author's dad. This is the Sundial Motel, where they stayed. The motel's owners didn't like the racers tuning cars at 2 a.m. with open exhaust headers. (Author's Collection)*

raced again, same results. Again, he took it back for further tuning. Same result. He didn't understand that he was giving up about 800 pounds, plus my gearing (4.88:1) gave me a hell of a hole shot. Back to the dealer, then up to the drive-in. "Where's Davis?" When he found me he said, "If I don't beat you tonight, the car will be for sale tomorrow." I went home and got the Chevy II, opened the headers, checked the tire pressure, and went down to the drive-in. The race was over in first gear, as usual, but this time I held it through second and well into third. The result — about 6 car lengths and pulling away. "For Sale: 1966 Belvedere I, 426 Hemi engine, 4 speed. Call———."

In 1966 I attended my first NHRA Nationals. It was the wildest six-day party I'd ever attended. Brink was entered with his G/Stock '56 Nomad. That meant I got in free, almost. The entry fee was $25.00, which included you, your car, and two pit crew! Six days of the best drag racing anywhere, and it cost me a whole 5 bucks!

We towed the Nomad to Indy using my dad's new Chrysler. I left him my beater, a '57 Chevy station wagon. The Chevy II was too wild for him to drive. We stayed on the east side of town at a little motel called the Sundial. It was quiet for 357 days of the year. Then

*The parking lot of the 500 Shopping Center was used for Tech Inspection at the Nationals. Everyone waited in line to get to inspection and weigh-in. It was "Hurry up and wait!"* (Author's Collection)

the Nationals came, and hot rodders filled the Sundial parking lot. In fact, hot rodders filled the whole town. Any non-racing tourists were driven out by the loud tuning of cars which happened all day and night, well into the early morning hours.

Our second day in Indy, we took the Nomad for tech inspection and classification. It was held in the parking lot of the 500 Shopping Center, about a mile from the strip. I don't know how any of those merchants survived the week. There were thousands of race cars filling their parking lot. Plus tow cars and just plain spectators. It was like being back in the Army — "hurry up and wait!" The line for inspection was as long as the shopping center, and it took the better part of the day to get weighed in and checked. Unless you were first in line, you didn't have much chance of getting to the strip for a few time trials runs.

Back at the motel, we had supper, and started looking for things to do. Another member of Brink's pit crew was Skip McEwen. Skip told us to pile into his car; he knew where the action was. Downtown we went, right in the heart of Indianapolis. We pulled up at a traffic light and Skip parked. I couldn't understand why we parked in that place as there was nothing but a Howard Johnson Motor Lodge. Within a few minutes, I understood.

Out of the clear night came a loud roar, obviously an engine with open exhausts — a very powerful engine. As we looked across at the motel parking lot, a red early '40s Willys coupe pulled out of the parking lot. It had this ominous scoop poking through the hood. Its doors were lettered and the roof said it all — A/Gas Supercharged!

The Willys pulled onto the street, straightened the front wheels, and let it rip! Right down through the middle of town. The driver

only went about a block and a half, then shut it down and coasted to a stop, turned around and went back into the Howard Johnson parking lot. Wow! About 10 minutes later we heard another loud roar. This time it was a small, very sleek, dark blue dragster, and not one of the little guys either. This one had a blown Chrysler Hemi in it. Like the Willys, the rail driver pulled onto the street, straightened the front wheels, and hammered it. Again, about two blocks down he shut it off and popped the parachute! The push car came out and pushed him back to the motel.

Holy Cow! Where were the cops? Well, they were there the whole time, watching the action with the rest of us. It seemed that all the major hot dogs stayed at this Howard Johnson, and they tuned their cars during the night, using the Indianapolis street as a test track. We watched the whole scene for about three hours before going back to our mundane Sundial for some rest.

The next day, and every day for the next five days, was pretty much the same. Go to the strip, make a few time trial runs, make some adjustments, and tour the pits to watch the big boys do their thing. We collected any and everything that the race sponsors gave away — spark plugs by the sets; T-shirts by the armful; decals; Hurst

*Larry Brinkley's G/Stock Nomad,* RealLemon, *waits to make a run at the '66 Nationals. Brink's 225 hp Nomad had all the latest goodies for the class: .060-inch overbore, Hurst shifter, Stahl Headers, Elk's Head Service heads, Traction Masters, and M&H Racemasters. The car ran in the 14s, which was good enough to win at local strips, but not at the Nationals.* (Author's Collection)

shifters (if you caught the Hurst guy in a good mood); oil by the case. All for the $25 entry fee.

You could even have your carburetor completely rebuilt by one of the manufacturers that had a booth there. If you broke something, the Hurst people had a complete fix-it shop to help with any problem. The Hurst Shifty Doctor would completely rebuild your shifter if you were having problems of any kind. The only thing they didn't give away were tires, unless you were a really big name driver. However, you could buy the tires at a very cheap price; just make sure you wore their decal if you won.

At night it was a repeat of previous nights. The days were long and hot; and the nights were short but filled with excitement. When it came time to actually race, our excitement remained at a high level despite Brink losing in the first round.

*The sign that you were really a big time racer — you had a fancy tow car to take your race car to the track. The author bought a '67 El Camino to tow his Chevy II. Note that the Chevy II now has big M&H Racemaster Super Stock tires and, of course, the ultimate street advertisement: "Caution — Race Car In Tow." (Author's Collection)*

Of course, after you lost on Saturday, you could still watch the Nationals unfold over the next two days. After all, your crew pit passes were good for all six days of the Nationals. All too soon, it was Monday and the Nationals were over. As we headed back for Ohio, I made up my mind that I would be at the '67 Nationals, and not just as a spectator either. I would be entered!

By 1967, my A/S Chevy II had been turned into a B/Modified Production beast. Over the winter of '66, we pulled the reasonably stock 327 out and sent it to the machine shop. It was bored to 333ci, then reassembled with loose tolerances. Crane heads and camshaft (also an Iskendarian and Crower) were used in place of the factory 350 hp units. On top went a new Edelbrock cross-ram intake, sporting a pair of 600 cfm Holley 4 barrels. Mallory supplied the spark, and M/T headers completed the package. A Schieffer clutch assembly was used. In the rear we pulled the old 4.88:1 gears and installed

5.13:1. Since the car was in B/MP, we were limited to 7" tires, and I went with M&H Racemasters — on the street!

I have a lot of memories regarding that Chevy II. One is the first time we put fire into the engine after the B/MP rebuild. Brink was behind the wheel and cranking the starter to build oil pressure. I was watching the oil pressure gauge. When it approached 50 pounds, Bobby plugged in the coil, Brink hit the throttle, and the engine fired right now! It was very loud in the garage with the open headers. As I watched the oil gauge, I was stunned to see the needle go way over to "SW"! Looking up at the tach, I read 9300 rpm!

"What the hell? Shut it down!" I looked at Brink, then at Bobby, who was inappropriately holding the throttle springs in his hand. When Brink hit the throttle, both carbs went full open because the springs came off their mounts. We reached 9300 rpm on an engine that was slightly over 5 seconds old! We tore it down and checked the bearings. Everything was OK, but boy, would that engine rev after that!

I entered the '67 NHRA Nationals in B/MP. The car ran close to the record, about 11.75. I had reason to believe that I could win. However, two things conspired to end that dream. First, "Dandy Dick" Landy showed up with one of the previous year's Clinic cars, modified for B/MP. He came off the trailer at 11.16! Still, everyone had a chance, between foul starts and breaking out at the finish, as long as you made the class call.

I didn't! The class was scheduled to run at 10 am. We got up at 7 am, hooked up and went to breakfast. Plenty of time to get to the

*Here, at Dragway 42, is the author running for the M/SA trophy in his mother's '64 Valiant, 6-cylinder Torqueflite. He wanted to enter his big 'Vette in AA/Sports, but it was broke. He put a cut-out on the Valiant exhaust, added some speed decals, and went racing. Guess what — he won! (Author's Collection)*

strip and make the 10 am call. We arrived at about 9:15 am. As I'm towing past the staging lanes, I see Landy's Dodge and several other B/MP cars waiting at the line. NHRA had called the class an hour early. I complained but was the ultimate loser of the "If you snooze, you lose!" rule.

I skipped 1968 at the Nationals as my new job at the fire department kept me pretty busy for the entire last half of the year. Besides, I didn't have anything to run as I had sold the Chevy II. I built another 'Vette for the street and had my '67 El Camino that I used to tow the Chevy II, but neither remotely resembled a race car. In early 1969, I bought another 350 hp '66 Chevy II and built it for SS/F. It ran pretty good, turning in the 12s at over 117 mph but it wasn't competitive.

It did, however, get me an entry into the '69 Nationals. Who was the main competition again? Dandy Dick Landy. There seemed to be factory-backed Clinic cars in almost every class. Brink and I took turns driving the car, but it wasn't even close to the competition. Landy won the class, of course. It left a very bitter taste in my mouth for sanctioned drag racing. I figured, if the factory guys were so greedy that they had to win every class, what chance did I, the little guy, have of winning. That was the end of my racing career, except for an occasional joust with a GTO or Mustang on the street.

Today, I have a nice, old '62 Chevy Impala SS hardtop. It's nothing big, just a 250 hp, 327 small block, with a 4 speed and Positraction. Yet, it's plenty for the street. Besides, I have a nice 4-speed, dual-quad, Positraction, 409 in the garage ready to drop in whenever the bug hits me. Maybe this Summer, I'll show those new Camaros and Mustangs what a real super stock machine looks like. Brink? He bought a piece of SS/S history — Dave Strickler's *Old Reliable II*, and completely restored it to what it looked like in late 1962. No, it's not for sale!

*The author's maroon Impala SS and Brinkley's* Old Reliable *at the Ewing Chevrolet Car Show in 1988. Brinkley bought the old Strickler SS/S class winner in 1984, then completely restored it to what it was after the '62 Nationals. (Author's Collection)*

# CHAPTER TWO

# 1955–1960 — THE BEGINNING

**I**n the early 1950s, most Americans were enjoying "the good life." It was truly the "Happy Days" era. Just like the television show, girls dressed in pony tails and poodle skirts while guys wore white socks and dress shirts. Hoodlums wore jeans, T-shirts, and leather jackets. The average household income was slightly over $6,000.00/year. Dwight D. Eisenhower became president in 1952 on a campaign to end the fighting in Korea. He was popular with the people and was re-elected in 1956. Rock and Roll was in its infancy, and popular hangouts were local drive-in restaurants, eating in Dad's car of course. There were literally no drugs and violent crime was rare. People left their houses and cars unlocked without fear. The most common task of a small city police officer was making sure no kids stayed out too late at night.

It was June, 1950 when the first known drag strip came to life. It was established at Orange County Airport, near Santa Ana, California. Initially, the strip didn't even have any class breakdowns. It was simply "run what you brung" every Sunday; and run them they did — coupes, roadster, pipe rails called dragsters, and stockers.

About a year later, the National Hot Rod Association (NHRA) was founded. It took three years before the first racing classes were established by this new organization. The classes included the all-out cars or 'HOT' classes for dragsters, competition coupes and roadsters, and other home-built vehicles. The other classes were the Open Gas Coupe and Sedan classes, for modified engines installed in stock bodied cars and stockers — lots of stockers.

There were flathead V-8 Fords of all eras. Chevy cars and trucks were powered by an overhead-valve inline 6 cylinder engine. In 1951, Chrysler had the hemispherical head V-8 of 331 cubic inches (a far cry from the monster motors that it would evolve into). Pontiacs had flathead inline 6s and 8s, Buicks had overhead valve straight 8s, while Oldsmobile and Cadillac both had V-8s with overhead valves.

The hottest stockers were usually the Fords, at least until the overhead V-8s came out. Light in weight, the flathead Ford V-8 put out plenty of horsepower compared with the inline 6- and 8-cylinder engines of the competition. Also, Ford had many options to make a stocker go quicker, such as lower rear end ratios and overdrive transmissions.

By 1954, the horsepower race had already started to heat up. Ford introduced the 239 cubic inch overhead valve V-8. Chevrolet countered with multiple carburetors and introduction of the Corvette, which was also powered by the inline 6. Even Hudson had a multiple carb, high-performance engine that was available at the dealer — the same engine that was winning at oval tracks throughout the South. The race for super stock had begun. It was Olds, with first the 303ci, then 324ci overhead valve V-8, and up to 165 horsepower, that was the hottest stocker at the drag strip.

In 1955, Rock and Roll made its debut with the big noise coming from a movie soundtrack, *Blackboard Jungle,* which featured Bill Halcy singing "Rock Around the Clock." Later in the year, a young truck driver shook up the music world with his wild gyrating antics and music: Elvis Presley. In just a few months he would be crowned the King of Rock and Roll, although other performers such as Little Richard and Chuck Berry would dispute that.

*Another early '50s car with V-8 power was the Cadillac. Garrott's Pure Oil sponsored this '51 Caddy for M/S class at Magnolia Drag Strip in 1965. The Caddy was turning ETs in the high 17-second bracket, but was never competitive on a national level. (Bruce Baker)*

*This 1954 Oldsmobile of Wayne and Mark Dorey competed in M/Stock at York US 30 Dragway. The '54 Oldsmobile engine, with 303 cubic inches and 165 horsepower, was virtually the same car that Arnie Beswick drove to victory at the 1955 and 1956 NHRA Nationals. (Lee Menszak)*

*Early Oldsmobiles were competitive well into the 1960s. Sam Shinabery's Marble Muncher '52 Oldsmobile, sponsored by Chesrown Olds in Columbus, Ohio, was the winner in N/S at the '67 Springnationals. (Author's Collection)*

It was this year that NHRA finally had enough organization and recognition throughout the nation to begin holding regional drag championships. The manufacturers fueled the fire in the stock classes by developing high horsepower combinations for family cars available at <u>any</u> dealership in the nation. The NHRA Stocker rules were simple: No modifications other than with factory available equipment. Both standard shift and automatics ran in the same class. The exhaust system must be complete in every way, with the spent gases routed through a complete exhaust system. Tires one size larger than stock were permitted, but the tread had to be at least 1/8" in depth.

Ford sought to unseat the Chevrolet Corvette as the nation's only sports car, by introducing the Ford Thunderbird in 1955. The T-Bird was powered by a high-performance 272ci V-8 that offered 198 horsepower with a single four-barrel carb. However, most of the T-Bird engine options were now available in any of the regular Ford car line, with either a 3-speed standard transmission, commonly called a 3-speed stick, or with the Ford-O-Matic automatic transmission.

Chevrolet introduced the first of the legendary small-block V-8 series of engines — a 265 cubic inch, overhead valve V-8 that offered up to 195 horsepower with a four-barrel carb, dual exhausts, and a solid lifter camshaft that would rev over 6000 rpms. All the 265ci engines were available in any body style, including the '55 Corvette, and could be ordered with either the 3-speed stick, with or without overdrive, and a 2-speed Powerglide automatic transmission.

Pontiac also came out with an overhead valve V-8 in 1955, the 287ci V-8 that was rated at 180 horsepower with a single two-barrel carb as the only carburetor setup available. However, besides using the standard General Motors 3-speed stick as in the Chevrolets, the bigger Pontiac had a decided advantage with automatic classes in

having the 4-speed Hydra-Matic, the same transmission used by Oldsmobile. Oldsmobile increased the cubic inches of its standard V-8 from 303ci to 324ci, with 202 horsepower available to remain the hot stocker through 1955.

*Certainly one of the more famous early Chevy stockers was the* Monster Mash *'55 campaigned by first, Bill Spanakas, then John Marteney. Built and prepared by Jenkins Competition, the car was a terror not only in I/Stock class, but also for Little Stock Eliminator wherever it raced, turning times in the high 14s. Spanakas held the National Record for I/S speed at 94.63 mph in 1965. (Author's Collection)*

The Chrysler camp had multiple entries in the stocker field, headed by the big Chrysler 300. The 300 owned the NASCAR circuit using a 331ci hemi-head engine rated at 300 horsepower. For drag racing, Dodge offered a 270ci Red Ram hemi-head V-8 in a lighter weight sedan, which was rated at 193 horsepower. Plymouth offered a 259ci V-8 rated at 177 horsepower, but it didn't have hemi heads.

By the late Summer of 1955, NHRA had the classes and competition to conduct the first National Drag Championship. It was held at Great Bend, Kansas over the Labor Day weekend in September 1955. There were twelve divisions in the hot categories, each one broken down by cubic-inches-to-weight ratio into four hot classes.

In Stock Division, there were just four classes, A, B, C, and D Stock; broken down by factory advertised horsepower-to-weight ratio. The big Chrysler entries headed the top class — A Stock. B Stock was filled with the lighter weight Olds sedans and the Chevys and Fords with the new high horsepower V-8s. C Stock had the heavyweights such as Hudson and Cadillac, or the lower horsepower, heavier Pontiac and Olds convertibles and station wagons. D Stock was the home of the flathead Fords and straight 6- and 8-cylinder Chevys and Pontiacs.

When the first NHRA Nationals was over, the fastest stocker was a '54 Olds sedan tuned and driven by a farmer from Morrison, Illinois. His was a name that would by synonymous with Pontiac super stock drag cars for decades to come: Arnie "The Farmer" Beswick. Beswick's '54 Olds turned a speed of exactly 80 mph to win B Stock. Ken Peck's '53 Ford flathead won D Stock with a speed of 67.41 mph. No elapsed time was recorded for stockers.

It's interesting to note that at this time, there was so little media interest in stocker classes that no NHRA National Records were kept. In fact, *Hot Rod* Magazine coverage of the Nationals listed all the class winners <u>except</u> Stock classes. When listing the various official rules and classes, *Hot Rod* also listed every class except Stock. This lack of official interest in Stock classes would remain until 1960, even though the stockers would be the most prevalent class at every drag strip on every Sunday.

## 1956

In 1956, the horsepower race heated up greatly, but the results were the same. Ford upped the cubic inches of the Thunderbird V-8 from 272ci to first 292ci, then to 312ci, and added a two four-barrel carburetor option that resulted in a whopping 260 horsepower. Chevy countered with a hotter solid lifter camshaft, high compression heads with bigger valves, and a two four-barrel carburetor intake. The top of the line combination pulled 245 horsepower out of the little 265ci V-8.

The Chrysler camp offered two new sport sedans — the Dodge D-500 and the Plymouth Fury. The Dodge had a 315ci hemi-head Red Ram V-8 that offered up to 260 horsepower. The Plymouth Fury pulled 240 horsepower out of the bigger 303ci standard overhead valve V-8. Pontiac offered a variety of carburetor and high-per-

*Dick and Bob Reffert campaigned Biggy and Itchy's* Stovebolt '56 Chevy *in G/S. The* Stovebolt *was powered by a 271ci (.030 overbored 265ci engine) '56 Chevy, with high-compression heads, solid-lifter cam, and two Carter four-barrel carburetors. Racing at the NASCAR Nationals in 1965, the car was classed as FF/S, but was NHRA classed as G/Stock. (Author's Collection)*

formance options in 1956, including a 285 horsepower, two four-barrel equipped 316ci V-8. Olds opened up the 303ci engine to 324ci which gave up to 240 horsepower.

*Typical racing action in the lower classes, this was a match between a '56 Pontiac street stocker and the professionally set up Sunday-only stocker. The '56 Pontiac had one of the 216 horsepower, four barrel, 316 cubic-inch V-8s, with a Hydra-Matic transmission. It probably had exhaust cutouts and soft rubber tires. (Jack Bleil)*

The Stock rules and classes remained virtually the same at NHRA strips — A Stock through D Stock. Even though the Stock classes continued bringing in the most entrants, thus generating the most revenue per division, the major associations and the print media continued to be indifferent. While the major publications like *Hot Rod* and *Motor Trend* covered the big events, they again completely ignored the Stock classes. National Records were still not kept for Stock classes. The 1956 NHRA Nationals were again held at Great Bend, Kansas. The '54 Olds sedan of Arnie "The Farmer" Beswick was the repeat top stocker at the meet.

*Sedan Deliverys were quite popular in the '60s due mostly to the fact that they could be equipped with the 4-speed Hydra-Matic transmission, which was optional in the Chevy truck line. Wayne Jessel's Yoo Hoo Too held the National Record for G/SA running a 225 hp Chevy and the Hydra-Matic. (Author's Collection)*

*The first of Jere Stahl's many race-prepared stockers at Cecil County Drag Strip, Maryland, in May 1964. Sponsored by Cordia Chevrolet in York, Pennsylvania, Stahl's G/S wagon was the most feared Junior Stocker of the era. It held the National Record at 13.57 and 101.23 mph, which was quicker than cars classed as high as D/S! Extra long collectors on the exhaust headers were a trademark of Jere Stahl. (Joel Naprstek)*

## 1957

Tension in the world increased in 1957 when Russia launched the first satellite, *Sputnik I*, clearly taking the lead in the arms race. Russian missiles could strike the United States with impunity. People dug bomb shelters in their back yards and schools taught children what to do in case of atomic attack. Huge sirens were installed atop buildings to warn of incoming Soviet bombers.

A more positive excitement was stirring in the world of stock car drag racing. Several items were introduced including fuel injection, four-speed manual transmissions, and superchargers. For the first time, NHRA offered a new class for these new options — Super Stock.

At Chevrolet, the 265ci was bored out to 283 cubic inches. High-compression heads were added with larger valves. The legendary Duntov solid lifter camshaft, commonly known as the 270 cam, was made available; and the whole package was topped off with a pair of Carter WCFB four-barrel carburetors or the brand new Rochester fuel injection unit that mechanically metered the gas. With the dual-quad setup, the package was rated at 270 horsepower, but with the Rochester fuel injection, the rating was 283 horsepower. This was the first engine to offer one horsepower per cubic inch — 283 horses from 283 inches. The 283 was also offered with a number of lower compression heads and hydraulic lifter camshafts, with horsepower ratings between 185 and 250 with fuel injection.

A 4-speed manual transmission was available in the Corvette only. Both the 2-speed Powerglide and 3-speed Turboglide automatic transmissions were available. However, any solid lifter, high-performance engine was available only with a manual transmission,

either 3 or 4 speed. This option would remain the same until 1965 when the Turbo-Hydra-Matic became available. There were some '57 Chevys that were ordered with a 4-speed transmission, which was simply placed in the trunk at the factory, awaiting dealer installation.

At Ford, the standard V-8 became 312ci. With a solid-lifter cam and dual four-barrel carbs, the high-performance 312 was rated at 265 horsepower. The big news at Ford was the introduction of the McCullogh VR-57 supercharger that forced air into a single enclosed Holley four-barrel carburetor. This combination brought the horsepower of the 312 up to 300, and made the Ford competitive with the Chevys. Although the engines were known as Thunderbird V-8s, they were available throughout the entire Ford line. Still, Ford suffered from a lack of a 4-speed manual transmission, which Chevy had available. Ford would not have a 4-speed transmission available until 1961.

At Pontiac, the engine was opened up to 347ci and topped off with a pair of high-compression heads and a hotter hydraulic lifter camshaft. With a single four barrel, the top Pontiac engine option was rated at 317 horsepower. Transmissions included the standard 3-speed stick and the 4-speed Hydra-Matic. Olds had a similar program with the 371ci engine and J-2 option with three two-barrel carburetors rated at 312 horsepower. However, the added weight of luxury accessories made the Olds too heavy to be competitive in Super Stock.

The Chrysler entries were again the Dodge and Plymouth. The Dodge D-500 now had the 354ci Hemi equipped with dual quads and high-compression heads, rated at 340 horsepower. The Plymouth Fury had a 350ci wedge-head engine with 10:1 compression ratio and dual four barrels. The Fury V-800 engine was rated at 290 horsepow-

*One of the most consistent winners at the '66 Nationals was the* Jolly Green Giant, *a '57 Chevy station wagon driven by Ken Gunning out of Philadelphia. The Gunning Brothers entry not only won the H/S class, but also held the National Record at 13.73. (Author's Collection)*

er. Coupled with the new 3-speed Torqueflite automatic transmission, the Dodges and Plymouths were very competitive.

At NHRA, the greater horsepower of the new engine combinations forced a revision of the Stock classes. One important addition was the top category, which for the first time was designated Super Stock. The 270 and 283 horsepower Chevys, the 270 horsepower Pontiacs, and the 300 horsepower, supercharged '57 Fords all competed in Super Stock. One thing that was not allowed was use of the 4-speed transmission by drivers of '57 Chevys, since the 4 speed was only available in the Corvette. This was later changed by NHRA.

The competition was fierce in Stock classes all over the country. Sponsored cars began showing up in the Stock classes at various strips, although it was usually something like "Smith's Exxon" or "Joe's Speed Shop." The manufacturers and dealers for the most part, still had not gotten officially involved in drag racing, even though they were heavily involved in the NASCAR circuit.

NHRA now offered six Stock classes: S/S, A/S, B/S, C/S, D/S, and E/S, but still there were no official records kept for Stock classes. The classes were broke down by horsepower to weight: S/S, 0 – 12.59 lbs./hp; A/S, 12.60 – 14.99; B/S, 15.00 – 16.99; C/S, 17.00 – 20.99; D/S, 21.00 – 26.99; E/S, 27.00 and up. There was still no breakout for automatic transmissions, and the stock class rules remained the same as they had been in 1955 — stock meant absolutely factory stock, no open exhausts, no bigger tires, no suspension changes. Any change whatsoever dropped your car into Gas Class, period.

Big Bad Ford *was a '57 Ford campaigned by the Naprstek Brothers in F/S in the summer of 1963. Powered by a 300 horsepower, McCullogh supercharged 312ci Thunderbird V-8, Art, Joel, and Kenny drove the car every day and raced on the weekends. The Ford turned 13.60s at places like Dover, New York and Atco Dragway, New Jersey — with a 3-speed stick and Bucron tires.* (Joel Naprstek)

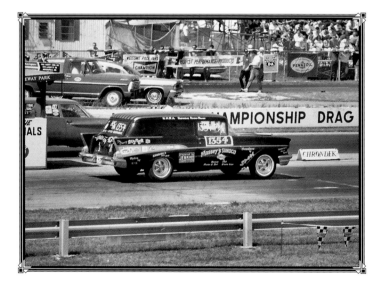

Earl Krutz *brought his '57 Chevy sedan delivery, The Cherry Buster III, to the '67 Nationals with a share of the National Record for H/SA. Sedan Deliveries and El Caminos were another favorite, but only because under NHRA rules they were allowed to run any truck transmission available — including the 4-speed Hydra-Matic.* (Author's Collection)

The Holt Brothers *out of Cleveland, Ohio, campaigned this '57 Chevy in E/S class. Built and prepared by Hart Automotive, the fuel-injected '57 sedan had a 4-speed transmission. NHRA liberalized the rules in the early 1960s to allow any '57 or newer Chevy to use the Corvette 4-speed transmission.* (Author's Collection)

Because of their availability and relative inexpensive cost (both in purchase price and operating cost), the Chevys dominated the entry lists. Yet, it was a Pontiac that would win the Nationals. The '57 Nationals were held at the Oklahoma State Fairgrounds over Labor Day weekend, which had become standard for NHRA. When the meet was over, John Zink, a Tulsa, Oklahoma native, drove his 270 horsepower '57 Pontiac Star Chief to the first-ever Super Stock title with a top speed of 93.60 mph. Guess who won the B/S title again — Arnie "The Farmer" Beswick. The legend was growing.

*At the 1969 Nationals, several cars were running out of the Stahl Engineering stables, including this '57 Chevy driven by LaVerne Benner. From the looks of the car, it would appear that the crew has replaced the driveshaft u-joint, which was prone to breakage under high RPM starts with slicks. (Jack Bleil)*

## 1958

On January 31, 1958, the United States put its first satellite into orbit, bringing the arms race just a little closer. The music world was brought into the fray when Elvis was drafted in March. Despite all the world's troubles, super stock racing was thriving and the horsepower race was on.

Car engines were becoming bigger, not just in horsepower but also in cubic inch displacement. Everyone knows that bigger is always better. Pontiac increased its cubes from 347 to 370. Olds jumped a full 25 inches, from 371 to 394. Pontiac improved its top-of-the-line performance engines by adding a three two-barrel carb setup and the Rochester fuel injection system, the same unit as installed on Chevrolet's 283. The top horsepower for Pontiac was 310 on the injection engine, and 300 on the triple carb engine. The '58 J-2 Olds with three two-barrels offered 312 horsepower. Both makes still used the 4-speed Hydra-Matic and standard 3-speed manual transmissions.

At Chrysler, both Dodge and Plymouth increased cubic inches and horsepower to keep up with the other manufacturers, but the Dodge no longer used the hemi-head engine. The Dodge D-500 had a 361 cubic inch motor that was shared with the Plymouth Fury Golden Commando V-8. The D-500 with two four-barrel carbs was rated at 320 horsepower. Dodge also jumped on the fuel injection band wagon, offering a similar Rochester unit in the D-500 rated at 333 horsepower. The Plymouth Fury, while sharing the same basic engine as the Dodge D-500, was rated at only 305 horsepower with dual quads.

Ford introduced two completely new engines — a 332ci and 352ci engine. Both were based on the same block, but the 352ci version had a longer stroke. For the high-performance option, the 352ci engine could be had with high-compression heads at 10.2:1, and was topped with a single four-barrel carb. Gone was the supercharger option from 1957. The hot 352ci Thunderbird engine was rated at 300 horsepower. However, as most Ford mechanics were to find out, the 300 horsepower was very elusive.

Chevrolet introduced the first of the new "W" engines — the 348ci Turbo-thrust V-8 that would ultimately become legend in the early 1960s both at the strips and on the radio. The 348 was a totally new design from the venerable small-block 283, and very different from every other engine of the era. The compression chamber was not in the cylinder head as all other engines were. The 348ci engine had the compression chamber in the cylinder bore.

The 348 heads had the valves staggered as opposed to straight across from each other as on all other engine types, save for the Chrysler hemi-head. This staggered valve arrangement created an indented area in the head shape between the exhaust ports, resulting

*Another consistent trophy winning '58 Pontiac was* Black Magic, *driven by Mary Ann Foss. Running out of Belville, Ohio, Mary Ann won D/SA class in 1964 with a time of 14.24 at 98.68 mph, with a car built entirely by her husband. In 1966, Mary Ann graduated to a '65 Plymouth Hemi S/SA car called the* Go-Hummer. *Originally campaigned by Wes Koogle as* The Original Dependable. *(Author's Collection)*

*In 1960, the '58 Pontiac of Jerry Maycuck was usually the winner of both S/S and Top Stock at Erie Dragway. The car was equipped with the tri-power version of the 370ci Trophy engine, and held the Erie Dragway strip record for S/S at 14.00 and 105 mph. (Jack Bleil)*

in the characteristic scalloped head and valve cover shape. In 1958, Chevrolet high-performance options included a solid-lifter camshaft, with a single four-barrel carb on an aluminum intake manifold. This "Police Option" 348 Super Turbo-thrust V-8 put out 305 horsepower. With the 3 two-barrel option, the horsepower went up to 315.

One of the additional performance items that was made readily available for the first time in a passenger car, was the Borg Warner T-10 4-speed manual transmission, still only available as a dealer-installed option. With Positraction and one of the low rear-end ratios, which were available down to 5.38:1, the '58 Chevy was a potent package for Super Stock. All these high-performance options were available either direct from the factory as Regular Production Options (RPOs), or could be purchased over the parts counter at any dealership. Cost: a 4 speed was $188.00, while a 4.56 Positraction rear end was $114.00.

With all these improvements in performance, there would still be no super stock war in 1958; at least not in NHRA races. NASCAR had a winter meet that included drag racing for the first time. It was held at Flagler Beach Airport, Florida between February 14th and 22nd. While all the local strips were holding big stocker meets all over the nation, NHRA put a damper on the whole super stock program. At the 1958 National Championship Drags, again held at Oklahoma City Fairgrounds Drag Strip, NHRA imposed a 500 car entry limit. That's 500 cars total for both Hot and Stock classes. Since there were far more than 500 cars applying for entry into the Hot car categories, NHRA decided to <u>eliminate</u> the stock categories entirely from the '58 Nationals. However, the super stock war would pick up where it left off in 1959.

## 1959

War was a common theme in 1959. Communism set in as Fidel Castro took control of the Cuban government. North Vietnam controlled the rebellion in South Vietnam, and in July the first U.S. soldiers were killed when acting as "advisors" at a compound near Saigon.

This year also saw the deaths of three of the biggest names in Rock and Roll: Buddy Holly, Ritchie Valens, and J.P. "Big Bopper" Richardson. Their airplane crash stunned the music world and left it forever changed.

Big changes occurred in the world of automakers as well. Attempting to garner some of the new economy car market away from Volkswagen, automakers introduced the Ford Falcon, Chevrolet Corvair, and Chrysler Valiant.

This also was the year when the factory horsepower ratings really started to take off. The Chevrolet 348 Super Turbo-thrust V-8 had a new solid lifter high-lift camshaft and higher compression heads. The new heads upped the compression ratio from 9.5:1 in the 1958 315 hp engine, to 10.5:1. New high-dome pistons combined with the new heads upped the compression ratio of the 335 hp engine to 11.25:1. The 335 horsepower Biscayne sedan, equipped with a close ratio 4 speed (now factory-installed as a regular production option) and 4.56:1 rear gears and Positraction, was quite competitive with the high-performance Pontiac. With three two-barrel carburetors, the new engine was initially rated at 315 horsepower, but a new camshaft increased that to 335 hp before the end of the '59 model season.

*Harold Ramsey towed his fuel-injected '57 Chevy from Wilmington, Delaware, to the '59 Nationals at Detroit Dragway to compete in Super Stock class. Running against much bigger engines like the 348 Chevy and 389 Pontiac, Ramsey flawlessly shifted the 3-speed transmission (the 4 speed hadn't been approved by NHRA yet) and walked off with not only S/S class but also Stock Eliminator, with a time of 14.94 and a speed of 92.30 mph. (Jack Bleil)*

Pontiac extended the stroke 1/4", and with the existing 4.0625 bore, it took the cubic inches out to 389. With a hotter camshaft and three two-barrel carbs, the Trophy 420-A engine was rated at 345 horsepower, and 330 horsepower with a single four barrel. The Pontiac was still only available with the Hydra-Matic and 3-speed standard transmission. Although Oldsmobile increased the bore of its high-performance engine from 371ci to 394ci, offering 315 horsepower with a single four-barrel carb, the Olds had simply become too heavy to compete and dropped out of the drag race picture entirely.

The Dodge and Plymouth camps made their cars more reliable, while not increasing the horsepower significantly. Plymouth increased cubic inches from 350ci in 1958 to 361ci in 1959. The 361ci Golden Commando V-8 put out 305 horsepower using a single four barrel.

Dodge shared the new Chrysler B-block wedge engine with the bigger Chrysler cars like the DeSoto and Chrysler 500 series. The new wedge-head engine had 383 cubic inches, with a 10:1 compression ratio, a solid lifter camshaft, and two four-barrel carbs. It was rated at 345 horsepower, and was easily the most competitive of the two Chrysler Corporation entries. With the new Torqueflite transmission, the Dodges started to make people at the strips sit up and take notice. However, NHRA rules still had both stick and automatic cars competing against one another in the same class, and at this time, the standard transmission cars clearly held the advantage.

Ford decided to refine what it had. The 352ci Thunderbird V-8 remained basically the same as it had been in 1958, with 300 horsepower using a single four-barrel carb. The '59 Ford was substantially heavier than the '58, and, as with Oldsmobile, Ford dropped out of the drag race competition.

It was in 1959 that the dealerships started to join in the action on the drag strips. Dealerships like Royal Pontiac in Royal Oak, Michigan, started backing teams comprised of their own salesmen and mechanics. Still, the vast majority of the stockers were wrenched and driven by the everyday person who just stopped in the dealership and bought the fastest thing the manufacturer could put together at the factory. However, the Royal '59 Pontiac was originally built to race the NASCAR high back tracks, and didn't race on the drag strip until 1960.

NHRA took notice of the increased popularity in the stockers and added a Stock Eliminator title (plus a Middle and Sports Eliminator) to its 1959 Nationals list of eliminators. Stock Eliminator would match up the 50 fastest stockers, regardless of what class they were in. For the first time, the Nationals were held outside the Corn Belt area of the United States, as NHRA moved it to Detroit Dragway, right outside Motor City.

Even with all the gigantic changes in the super stock motors (the big cubic inches, wild cams, and multiple carb setups), it was a small-block Chevy that took home the first Stock Eliminator title. Harold Ramsey's '57 Chevrolet sedan from Wilmington, Delaware won the Super Stock class and was NHRAs first Stock Eliminator. The little 150 sedan, equipped with the 283 horsepower, fuel-injected engine, turned 14.94 at 92.30 mph to win S/S class, and 15.55 on the Stock Eliminator run. The black 210 Chevy sedan was almost factory stock, and did NOT have a 4 speed. The motor had never been out of the car. Ramsey did install a 4.56:1 Positraction rear end, Hedman headers, and a set of Atlas Buchon tires.

George Chaltin's '57 Ford took the A/Stock class win at 15.16. A new team entered a wild looking '49 Plymouth in C Altered class. It was powered by an early vintage Chrysler Hemi with a high-rise intake manifold that had been designed by the team. The team was made up of a bunch of Chrysler engineers who called themselves "The Ramchargers." It's interesting to note that besides the trophy, the Stock Eliminator received a set of four new whitewall street tires, four Moon disc hubcaps, a case of oil, and an oil pressure/amp gauge set. There was no money in super stock drag racing — YET!

## 1960

Several events happened in 1960 that would shape the lives of Americans for decades. It began innocently enough when Elvis was discharged from the Army in March, and Coca Cola was marketed in a can for the first time. On May 1, a U.S. U-2 spy plane was shot down flying over the Soviet Union, effectively ending any arms negotiations between the U.S. and the U.S.S.R. Before the end of the month, the U.S. launched the Midas II, the first spy satellite. The Cold War was just a blink away.

Another war was taking shape, too: the stocker war. It all started to come together — the horsepower race was on and all the major manufacturers were taking part. The major sanctioning bodies, NHRA, AHRA, and NASCAR, started to promote the stock classes. For the first time, the print media started to take notice. Suddenly, stockers were featured in the newspapers, magazines, and movies, and people everywhere were talking about the fast cars. For car dealers, all of these events meant more people in the showrooms.

The rules and regulations for 1960 were basically the same as they had been before. NHRA had seven basic stock classes from S/S through F/S, but for the first time, there were provisions made for special automatic transmission classes. NHRA recommended that automatic classes be added "wherever competition warrants." In other words, if you had a 10-car field, and only one car had an automatic transmission, then he was forced to race "heads up" with the standard transmission cars. However, if you had three automatics, the strip operators could make a special automatic class.

It's interesting to note some of the Stock Class rules for 1960, since many of them would be drastically changed within a matter of months. Some of those first rules that would later be changed included:

- Clutches must be the specific type, year, and make as the car.
- Distributors must be the correct year, make, and model as the car, but "non-visible modifications are permissible."
- Exhaust headers are permissible, but must be routed through the mufflers and tailpipes. No open by-passes permitted.
- Floor shift transmissions permitted when listed as optional equipment.
- Floor shift conversion kits will not be permitted.

Many of these rules changed as early as 1961; some were simply ignored by both the teams and the associations.

In the horsepower race, Pontiac took the lead with the 348 horsepower, 389ci Trophy 425-A engine. Jim Wangers of Royal Pontiac recalls: "Bunkie Knudsen had started the Super Duty program in late 1956. The original program had used a lot of aftermarket equipment, such as Iskendarian cams and Hedman Headers, in a program to see how much punishment a motor could take without breaking. It was 'super duty' for the engine.

*Jerry Maycuck goes off against a '60 Pontiac at Erie Dragway in 1960. Even though he was giving up some 48 horsepower to the '60 Pontiac, his car was properly set up and he knew how to get the most horsepower to the ground. Thus Maycuck was consistently the winner of S/S at Erie.* (Jack Bleil)

"In 1960, Knudsen created the Super Duty Group, which was led by Malcolm 'Mac' McKellar. It was from this Super Duty Group that all the high-performance parts were created and used, first at Daytona on the high-bank track, then with the drag racing teams that were springing up around the country. All the parts were designed and developed through the Super Duty Group, but many were actually manufactured by aftermarket companies like Isky.

"The only way a dealer got the new Super Duty equipment was to apply to the Super Duty Group and get on a list of known racing background people. Then you got the parts to go racing. Except for Mickey Thompson, the West Coast dealers were not interested in racing per se — the people who bought Pontiacs in California wanted comfort and prestige. Bunkie Knudsen and Mickey Thompson were business partners. Thus Mickey Thompson got all the newest Super Duty equipment, and was the only Pontiac threat out there. Chicago was actually first as far as Pontiac hot rod dealers were con-

cerned. Detroit, with Royal, Packer, and Red Holman Pontiac dealerships, was second."

For the first time, the Borg-Warner T-10 4-speed transmission, factory available in the Chevy since 1958, was now available throughout the Pontiac line. Pontiac introduced 8-lug aluminum wheels which saved about 80 lbs. (20 pounds on each wheel) over the standard steel wheels. The big Pontiacs weighed in excess of 4200 lbs., but the Trophy 425-A with the correct set of rear gears and a good driver, could turn the quarter mile in the low 14-second bracket.

Chevrolet stood pat with the 335 horsepower Turbo-thrust V-8 until both Ford and Pontiac upped the ante. In the late Spring of 1960, Chevrolet released a new, hotter camshaft that brought the horsepower of the 348 up to 350. In the lightweight Biscayne sedan, a 350 hp S/S Chevy, equipped with the T-10 close ratio 4 speed and one of the many Corvette axle ratios that were available (ratios between 3.08:1 and 5.38:1 were available, with 4.56:1 being the best combination) kept the Chevys very competitive.

Ford finally woke up and saw the handwriting on the wall, and made the greatest number of changes of all the Big Three to increase horsepower. Since the supercharged '57 Fords, Ford's entry into S/S racing hadn't been very competitive. Both the '58 and '59 Fords were slower due to weight problems. In the vernacular of the time, "suddenly, it was 1960!" and Ford had a hot item. The stocker war took life.

Ford used the same basic 352ci block assembly but outfitted it with new high-compression heads. The Daytona Heads had a 10.6:1

*Harold Ramsey won the '59 Nationals, and competed at the '60 Nationals, with a fuel-injected '57 Chevy. In 1961, Ramsey graduated to a 348 horsepower '60 Pontiac A/Stocker sponsored by Union Park Pontiac in Wilmington, Delaware. Ramsey became one of the biggest names in Pontiac drag racing with his Union Park S/S and A/FX cars.* (Drag Race Memories)

compression ratio with larger intake (2.03") and exhaust (1.56") valves. The bigger valves benefited from a new camshaft that used solid lifters in place of the hydraulic units used in both '58 and '59.

With a single, large four-barrel carb mounted atop a new redesigned aluminum intake manifold, and using special cast-iron exhaust manifolds designed for performance, the Ford S/S combination put out an honest 360 horsepower. Combined with the standard Ford 3-speed transmission and with a 4.57:1 rear gear and EquaLok limited-slip differential, the '60 Fords were consistently in the low 14-second bracket, right beside the big Pontiacs and Chevys. The 360 hp V-8 was not available with an automatic transmission (neither was any solid-lifter, high-performance Chevrolet V-8), and Ford didn't have a 4-speed transmission — YET.

Dodge and Plymouth shared the same engine and performance options in 1960. One of those options was a radical new intake manifold design — the Sonoramic ram induction with two four-barrel carbs. The idea behind the ram induction intake was that most engines have a certain amount of overlap in cam timing, when both intake and exhaust valves are open at the same time. At high RPMs, the overlap caused by a partially open exhaust valve actually pulled more fuel/air mixture into the cylinder. At low RPM under full throttle, the opposite actually occurred. The open exhaust valve had more pressure than the intake side, and caused the fuel/air mixture to be polluted or lean out, resulting in less horsepower and torque.

Most four-barrel carburetors had special vacuum-controlled secondaries that wouldn't allow full-throttle operations at the lower RPM scale. The Chrysler engineers, many of whom were involved in the Detroit car club known as The Ramchargers, knew that if you increased the distance between the open exhaust valve and the air inlet, i.e. the carburetor, the overlap problems were diminished and low RPM horsepower and torque were increased. With hot rods like the club's C Altered '49 Plymouth, *The High And The Mighty*, the answer was relatively simple. Just extend the intake manifold straight up and away from the valve assembly. You could cut a hole in the hood and mount the carbs on top. It wasn't pretty but it definitely worked, except you just can't cut a hole in the hood of Dad's stock automobile and have carburetors blocking the driver's view.

The Chrysler engineers designed a pair of long intake manifold extension tubes that went over the top of the rocker arm covers, ending above the inner fenderwell on each side. On top of the outer end of each of these extension tubes was mounted a Carter Aluminum Four-Barrel (AFB) carburetor. Each tube was 30 inches in length, with individual intake runners that were tuned to offer maximum torque at 2800 rpm. The result was an increase of about 25 lbs. of torque, to a total of 460 lbs., over the standard low-profile two four-barrel intake on the high-performance '59 Dodge D-500 engine. Horsepower was only marginally increased from 305 to 310 when the Sonoramic induction setup was added to the 361ci engine; and up to 330 horsepower with the 383ci engine, but it was available over a broader RPM range.

Throughout the late Spring and early Summer of 1960, the drivers tested and refined their combinations. Dealer-sponsored teams began to spring up all over the nation. Pontiac was a major force based on its success at the '59 Nationals. Pontiac teams from Royal Pontiac, Woudenberg Pontiac, and Union Grove Pontiac were some of the big names. By this time, Arnie "The Farmer" Beswick had sold his '54 Olds trophy-winner and joined the Pontiac camp. The Royal Pontiac team had three cars competing: a 4-speed car in S/S, a Hydra-Matic car in S/SA, and the '59 car.

On the West Coast, a mechanic at Service Chevrolet in Pasadena, California was making a name for himself. Using a Clayton Dynamometer to bring the cars to their absolute maximum horsepower rating, the Don Nicholson-tuned Chevys were more than holding their own. Led by Don's own green Biscayne "business coupe," and Elwin Westbrook and Terry Prince, also driving 320 hp, 348ci 4-speed Biscayne coupes, the Los Angeles Chevys won Top Stock more often than not. Les Ritchey in Covina, California was the guy who could really make the Fords run. Most of the Top Stock runs in Southern California were usually between a Ritchey Ford and a Nicholson Chevy.

*Now this is the epitome of racing the family sedan. Clyde Coleman and Dave Juersivich campaigned this '62 Rambler American hardtop in M/SA, complete with all the goodies — home-built "TW Headers," Rader Wheels, and Casler super stock tires. With 125 horsepower, the Rambler was a consistent winner at Dragway 42 in 1965. (Author's Collection)*

Terry Prince, a young man from Gardena, California, recalls those early days. "It's 1960, and you know what? There's a lot of cars here in a new class called Super Stock; a lot of Chevys with a motor called a 348. I see Mike McClusky, a high school buddy. He has a '58 Chevy with a 315 horse 348 and a 4 speed. It has open headers and he's running about 100 mph. He's there with a friend who has a green '60 Chevy Biscayne that's running pretty good. Guy's name is something like Don Nicholson.

"There's also Lloyd Porter with a brand new '60 El Camino, single four barrel, 320 horse 348. He's racing and the car has less than 200 miles on it. Is he crazy or what? There are about 25 cars in Super Stock and my buddy goes down after two rounds. I walk away that night with some good 16mm movies of dragsters and roadsters. What? Take pictures of stock cars? I might as well shoot the San Bernadino Freeway!

"Lloyd Porter is the sales manager at Porter Chevrolet. And he's talking about putting up money for Super Stock competition. Possibly up to $200. I don't believe the money talk for a stock class. But he's trying to sell me one of these new Chevrolets. Something about 'win on Sunday and sell on Monday.' I figure he's gonna sell his car tomorrow, but he didn't win today. He must be crazy.

"March 10th, 1960, Porter Chevrolet. OK, $600.00 down and $89.00/month, and I'm sitting in a 1960 Chevrolet Bel Air, Royal Blue, with a 320 horse, 348, 4-speed transmission, and 4.56 Positraction. I'm now a certified Mom's car owner. 'Quick, let's get the car home and get a set of chrome reverse wheels on it before anyone from the car club sees it!' Later I add the necessary items: Sun tach, scatter shield, Hedman Headers, and some minor tuning by a shop whose claim to fame is that they work on Porsches and they're expensive.

"The car is turning about 14 flat and about 100 mph. After about six months of getting beat every Sunday at Pomona, one thing becomes painfully obvious. This guy Don Nicholson kind of knows

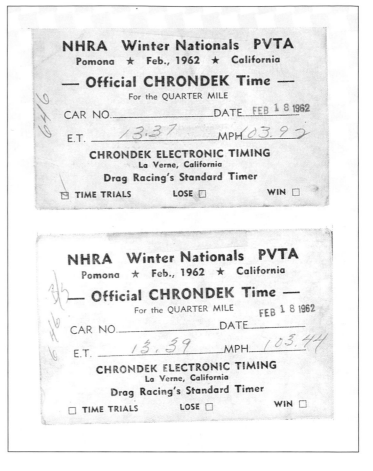

1962 Winternationals time slips for Terry Prince's B/Stock '60 Chevy. (Author's Collection)

*The semi-final run for B/Stock at the '62 Winternationals pitted Del Blades against Terry Prince, with Prince winning handily. Blades' '60 Chevy would advance all the way to the finals of Top Stock Eliminator at the '65 AHRA Winternationals, before bowing to the Ramchargers AWB Hemi-Dodge. (Terry Prince)*

what he's doing. I'm getting tired of seeing the back end of that damn green Biscayne. Not only does he run real good, but everyone with his sticker, 'Dyno-Tuned by Don Nicholson', is also kicking ass.

"Earl Wade works at Service Chevrolet with Don Nicholson. A few words with Earl and I think: Gotta have him work on my car. He really loves what he's doing. Earl says, 'Bring the car to Service Chevrolet, we'll dyno tune it, and see if we can't help you run a little bit better.' Before long, Jardine Headers are on the car, the heads are off and they're doing a valve job, the chassis has seen a bit of work to get things working a bit better. A little bit of carburetor work and some driving tips and the car is turning 13.80s at over 102 mph! I'm still not winning S/S yet, but the racing is sure a lot closer. And I'm going a lot further before that damn green Biscayne beats me!

"The next year of racing is great. I didn't win everywhere, but that lousy green Biscayne is owned by someone else. Nicholson has teamed up with Mike McClusky on Mike's '61 409 car. We're starting to travel all over California to race — Half Moon Bay, Fremont, and Vaca Valley, racing guys like Gas Ronda and the Northern California boys. There is actually some money to be made. Super Stock is paying $200 - 300 bucks, and A/S is $100. I remember thinking, 'Let's get out of here quick with the money before they realize they've made a mistake.'

"By now we're flat towing the cars with a tow bar. The car is now ready to race as soon as we get to the strip. Just take off the tow bar and go race. I learned a lesson one night up at Half Moon Bay: Never let anyone else drive your car. That night, Nicholson had already beaten Ronda in the S/S final. I was down to the final against Ed Terry and his A/S Ford. Well, since there's money on the line, I decided to let The Man, Don Nicholson, drive my car. Wrong! Don missed a shift, 2nd to 3rd. Damn! And I knew I could have won.

"My '60 is now running 13.60s consistently, at 103+ mph. By the end of 1961, my car could win anywhere and we hadn't had the short block apart yet. An NHRA rule change put the car into B/S. It now made sense to go into the short block and make it .060-inch overbore. More cubic inches mean more horsepower! The '62 NHRA Winternationals are coming up soon."

Four D/Stock Chevys coming off the line together at Dragway 42 in 1961. It was quite common at Dragway 42 to run four lower class stockers at the same time, if the class was heavy with cars, just to get through the many large stock classes every Sunday. However, there could be a problem in determining a winner if the cars ran close at the finish, since the win light would only show which "lane" was the winner, not which car in that lane. (Jack Bleil)

The B/Stock trophy run at the 1962 Winternationals had Terry Prince's '60 Chevy against Joe Oliphant's '62 Ford set up by Les Ritchey and Performance Associates. The Don Nicholson-prepared Chevy took home the trophy with a time of 13.52 at 103.09 mph. Les Ritchey was as legendary to Ford fans as Don Nicholson was to Chevy. (Terry Prince)

The popularity of the super stock cars finally began to make an impact on the print media of the time. (ABC Sports still hadn't discovered drag racing.) The June 1960 issue of *Motor Trend Magazine* devoted a major article to the subject of "Stock Car Drag Racing." This was the first extensive article about the head-to-head competition being waged at drag strips all over the nation between the top high-performance vehicles that were available at a local dealer. The consensus was that Ford's 360 hp engine was tops in the stick categories, with Pontiac handily winning the automatic transmission nod. Speeds ranged between 97 and 105 mph, with elapsed times in the high 13-second bracket for all types.

NHRA went into the print media for the first time when it published the first issue of its own newspaper devoted strictly to drag racing. *National Dragster* was first published on February 12th, 1960, just in time to spread the first word about the results of the first Winternationals, which was co-sanctioned by NASCAR and NHRA at Daytona Beach on February 7th, 1960. NHRA also launched its new points system, where drivers could win points for class wins, eliminator wins, and national records that they set. This all counted toward the crowning of an overall National Points Champ, which would be awarded after the Nationals in September. Stockers would be at somewhat of a disadvantage since national records for Stock class were not kept until 1962.

Some interesting names appeared in those first issues of *National Dragster*, names that would appear regularly over the next decade or more. Race results from strips around the nation included these winners: Hubert Platt in D/Gas, Al Eckstrand won S/SA, The Ramchargers won C/Altered, Hayden Proffitt drove a B/Dragster to victory at 9.84 seconds, and a Corvette won in Southern California from the team of Lloyd Porter and Don Nicholson out of Service Chevrolet in Pasadena.

Another new excitement was added to the NHRA schedule of events with the NHRA stamp of approval on the first Regional Records Meet, held at Inyokern Drag Strip in the California desert during May 1960. It was the first time that NHRA recognized elapsed-time records. Yet once again, the Stock classes were left out as no Stock records were recorded. Record Runs were held at strips all over the nation, including such famous strips as Detroit Dragway; Atco Dragway in New Jersey; Dragway 42 in West Salem, Ohio; Amarillo, Texas; and on and on — but not for Stock classes. In fact, at several Record Runs, no Stock classes were even run. The guys in the Hot classes didn't like the fact that the Stockers were stealing some of their thunder.

## 1960 NATIONALS

When Labor Day 1960 arrived, everyone was ready. At the 1960 Nationals, which were again held at Detroit Dragway, NHRA ran all the Stock classes at night after all the Hot Car categories were finished. Class winners included Jim Wangers driving the Royal Pontiac entry in Super Stock stick class. *Hot Chief No. 1* won the class with an elapsed time of 14.14 at 102.04 mph. George Chaltin's supercharged '57 Ford took A/Stock in 15.24 seconds at 92.30 mph.

Super/Stock Automatic class went to a name that would soon be synonymous with automatic class wins — Al Eckstrand. The Detroit lawyer drove a '60 Plymouth equipped with a Sonoramic ram-inducted 383ci Golden Commando engine. His times of 14.51 seconds at 97.82 mph were good enough to hold off the big Hydra-Matic-equipped Pontiacs, including *Hot Chief No. 2*. A/Stock Automatic went to Frank Burnett in another '60 Pontiac at 15.53 and 92.97 mph.

On Monday afternoon, the top fifty cars from the entire stock field lined up for the Stock Eliminator run-off. It was Ford against Chevy, Pontiac against Plymouth, Chevy against Chevy. The final pairing went pretty much as everyone expected, a pair of Pontiacs. The Pontiacs had been running consistently all weekend, but no one had expected the final race to be between a pair of cars from the same team.

The final two eliminator runs were between Wangers in the Royal *Hot Chief No. 1* S/S car and a Chevy; and Jack Kay in the S/SA Royal car, *Hot Chief No. 2*, that beat a Ford to gain the finals. The times were 14.31 for Wangers and 14.27 for Kay. When the starter dropped the flag for Stock Eliminator, Wangers came out of the chute first, pulling a half-car length lead. Wangers held his gate shot all the way to the end, winning the Stock Eliminator title with a time of 14.13 at 100.44 mph.

The Top Stock Eliminator *Hot Chief No. 1* was a '60 Catalina 2-door hardtop, equipped

with the Trophy 425-A engine rated at 348 hp. The engine had been given the "Royal Treatment" by mechanics Pete Seaton and Dick Jesse. Dick Jesse would later become famous as the builder-driver of one of a handful of Pontiac funny cars — the '65 GTO named *Mr. Unswitchable*. Pete Seaton would later drive a '63 FX Pontiac, and then build a number of Chevy-powered funny cars named *Seaton's Shaker*.

The Royal Treatment included the addition of the new Daytona cylinder heads developed for NASCAR racing. The new heads had bigger valves and heavier valve springs, offering a 10.75:1 compression ratio. Using a #7 McKellar camshaft, Wangers shifted the T-10 4 speed at over 6000 rpm. Both Royal cars used Goodyear tires that had been recapped with soft Butyl rubber. The car weighed almost 4200 lbs., but had recorded best elapsed times of 13.81 at 104.40 mph prior to the Nationals.

The Stock Eliminator title at the '60 Nationals was the first big drag win for Pontiac, and for Wangers and the Royal team. It was the first time that major attention was given to the stockers at any event. Sales of the '61 Pontiac were very brisk right from the start, mostly achieved because of both the Top Stock victory and by NASCAR wins by other Pontiac drivers. The saying "Win on Sunday, Sell on Monday!" was true, and the other manufacturers took notice. However, it's interesting to note that the *National Dragster* coverage of the '60 Nationals gives only a small paragraph to the Stock Eliminator competition, and doesn't even list the winners of the Stock classes.

Buddy Garner was the first NHRA Worlds Point Champ driving a C Altered. In second place was Earl Rowe with a Super Stock Automatic '60 Pontiac Catalina sedan. I wonder how many points Rowe would have had if he had been able to set any National Records.

*Winner of Top Stock at the '60 Nationals was Jim Wangers driving the Royal Pontiac entry* Hot Chief No. 1. *The Royal Oak, Michigan S/S Pontiac was powered by one of the 363 hp Trophy 425-A engines, that were built with over-the-counter parts and then given the "Royal Treatment." Wangers turned a 14.14 at 102 mph on the run for Top Stock. In the other lane is Pete Seaton, driving another Royal Pontiac. (NHRA via Leslie Lovett)*

# CHAPTER THREE

# 1961 — SUPER STOCK COMES OF AGE

Events occurring all around the world in 1961 changed the attitudes and lives of Americans. John F. Kennedy was inaugurated on January 20th and he found his new job was not an easy one. The Soviet Union, led by Nikita Kruschev, was clearly out for world domination, and Cuba was building a communist power right in America's back yard. On April 17th, the CIA-backed invasion of Cuba was launched at the Bay of Pigs. It failed miserably and marked history forever. In South Vietnam, U.S. personnel began using helicopters and an internal Pentagon report advised President Kennedy to increase troop strength in that conflict. In August, the Soviet Union created a major crisis by erecting electrified barb wire fences across the center of Berlin — the beginning of the Berlin Wall.

The race into space continued as the U.S.S.R. launched Vostok I, putting the first man into outer space. One month later, Alan Shephard, one of the original Mercury 7 astronauts, was launched from Cape Canaveral, Florida. Shephard didn't go into orbit, but it was a first step for the United States.

In contrast to the world's troubles, super stock drag racing had a breakout year in 1961. Teams and personalities started to become known to the general public, and to automobile enthusiasts in particular. Teams like The Ramchargers, Bob Ford Inc., and Jim Wangers and the Royal Pontiacs, and individuals such as Don Nicholson and Arnie Beswick became the talk of local car hangouts. This was also the year when the media finally began to sit up and take notice of the top stocker categories at the strips. In fact, entire books started to surface dealing with how to race the family sedan at the strip.

With the increased interest by the fans and media, and the high-revving, big-horsepower engines becoming available, NHRA began to take a much longer look at the rules regarding stock classes, both for safety and to allow the drivers to use all the available horsepower the factories were building into the cars.

The first thing that NHRA did was to add additional stock classes, from top to bottom. In 1960, Super Stock was everything from 0-12.59 lbs. per advertised horsepower. In 1961, Super Stock only went to 10.59 lbs./hp. A/Stock was now 10.60-11.29, B/Stock was 11.30-11.88, and C/Stock was 11.89-12.49. Additional classes were added from D/Stock through K/Stock, for a total of 12 classes.

There were other significant changes that allowed the S/S driver/mechanic to pull the maximum horsepower out of the factory engines. For the first time NHRA allowed open exhausts on stockers, as long as they exited in front of the mufflers, and were permanently routed through the factory system when closed. Also, the open header dump tube could not be any larger in diameter than the original factory exhaust headpipe. This immediately opened a new industry, and companies like S&S Headers, Jardine Headers, and Belanger Bros. Headers sprang into existence to compete against Hedman Headers in equipping the nation's top stock cars.

Another change was allowance of any battery-operated ignition system, which led to use of aftermarket distributors like the Mallory Rev-Pol and Spaulding Flamethrower. Also, for the first time, floor shift conversion kits were permitted sparking still another new industry, with Hurst-Campbell and Drag Fast rapidly becoming the favorites. Of course, at least part of this was due to the fact that both Pontiac and Dodge released the Hurst 3-speed floor shift conversion as a regular production option, or RPO.

New safety regulations for stockers included mandatory use of a flywheel shield, commonly known as a scattershield, on all manual shift cars entered in classes between S/S and C/S. These cars were consistently revving well over 6000 rpm and a clutch assembly exploding at those RPMs could be deadly. Most were simple armor plates welded around the factory clutch housing. There would soon be new blow-proof cast clutch housings coming from Ansen Automotive and R.C. Industries. NHRA also allowed any factory heavy-duty clutch and pressure plate in the same top stock classes.

Another change was allowance of any gear ratio — providing the gears fit into the original rear axle housing. Now a super stock driver could get the maximum amount of horsepower available at the foot, down to the rear wheels. However, now there was the problem of getting that horsepower onto the pavement — i.e., traction.

NHRA allowed use of traction bars or any device that would help transmit torque to the frame and/or prevent violent rear spring windup under acceleration. The torque was now transmitted directly to the tires. NHRA allowed any tire as long as it was only one size larger than the original equipment tire. Soft rubber cheater slicks were allowed if they had passenger-car type tread and they weren't any wider than the original equipment tire width. Most of the hot stock drivers ran soft rubber tires made from butyl rubber, like the Atlas Buchron and Goodyear Butylaire.

The increased interest in Super Stock racing brought a greatly renewed horsepower race and advertising campaign. The object was to win and many dealer ads stated: "Win on Sunday, Sell on Monday!" Pontiac was again the leader, but it wouldn't last for long.

## THE MAJOR PLAYERS

### PONTIAC

Most of the Pontiac super stock cars that were sold at dealerships were originally equipped with the Trophy 425-A V-8 that displaced 389 cubic inches and was rated at 348 horsepower. Then the teams modified them with use of over-the-counter heavy-duty parts, known as Super Duty parts. Most of these had been developed in testing to make the car more reliable through racing, be it NASCAR or drag racing. Pontiac engineers developed cams and heads that greatly increased the horsepower just to see what it would take to break one of the new Trophy series engines. It was from these parts bins that the Super Stock race motors were built. The really serious teams pulled the old 425-A engine out and set it aside.

Into the empty engine compartment went one of the "available over-the-counter only" heavy-duty engine blocks. The block was completely different from the standard 425-A block. It had four-bolt main bearing caps to keep the high revving forged-steel crankshaft together. The 425-A crank was a cast unit. The top of each cylinder had a small chamfer cut into the wall that matched the new com-

pression chamber. Along with the new block went a heavy-duty oil pump and an 8-quart oil pan.

The pistons were forged rather than cast, and when combined with the new heads, they had an 11.2:1 compression ratio, up from 10.75:1 in the 425-A engine. The cylinder heads themselves, had larger intake and exhaust valves, hardened high-ratio rocker arms, heavier valve springs, retainers, and push rods. The machined combustion chamber was slightly shallower but elongated to allow clearance for the bigger valves. This was the reason for the chamfered cylinder bore.

Valve timing was controlled by a special McKellar #7 grind camshaft. The #7 cam was specifically designed for drag racing, with horsepower being developed in the 4200 rpm range and beyond. It used mechanical lifters instead of hydraulic types as in the 425-A, and easily revved to 6500 rpm. The intake manifold was an aluminum unit that mounted a trio of Rochester two-barrel carbs, basically the same system as used on the 425-A including vacuum-operated secondary operation. All the top teams removed the vacuum system and replaced it with a mechanical progressive linkage that opened the end carburetors at designated points so as not to flood the engine under hard acceleration.

There were many other heavy-duty parts in the package including a special centrifugal advance; dual point distributor; special tuned cast-iron exhaust manifolds; deep groove pulleys for the water pump and generator belts; a clutch fan that would float at high RPMs instead of absorbing horsepower; a heavy-duty clutch assembly with a lightened flywheel that allowed the engine to rev quicker; lightweight aluminum bumpers and radiator; a heavy-duty 3 speed with Hurst floor shift; the T-10 wide ratio 4-speed transmission; and rear axle ratios from 2.56:1 to 6.14:1, all available with the Saf-T-Track limited slip differential. The preferred drag racing gear was 4.55:1 with Saf-T-Track.

When all these heavy-duty parts were put together, it added up to an advertised rating of 363 horsepower, which actually was much closer to 400 horsepower when dyno-tuned. However, the NHRA rules at this time recognized only advertised horsepower. NHRA officials got smarter, later. It was the 363 horsepower version that found its way to the top drivers like Lloyd Cox of the Mickey Thompson team (tuned by Hayden Proffitt), Jim Wangers and the Royal Pontiacs, Arnie Beswick, Harold Ramsey driving the Union Park Pontiac, and Bob Harrop on the East Coast.

The same engine could be used with the 4-speed Hydra-Matic transmission for competition in Super Stock and A Stock Automatic classes, depending on which body style was used. In a sedan body, the combination ran S/S, but in a convertible, it could run as low as B/S. Lloyd Cox, with his wife Carol driving, campaigned this combination successfully in A/SA throughout 1961. However, the Hydra-Matic had to be beefed to be able to take the increased torque and to shift at the RPM that offered maximum horsepower. The pressure regulator valve was modified by shimming the regulator spring. The shift points themselves were modified to hold the transmission in a certain gear to higher RPM.

*Jim Wangers drove Ace Wilson's Royal Pontiac in S/S class at the '61 Nationals. Royal Pontiac was the biggest name in Pontiac racing east of California, and had several cars in various classes, including a pair of identical Catalina coupes at the '61 Nationals, one for S/S and the other for S/SA. (Jim Wangers)*

*Interior of the '61 street race car showing the Sun tachometer on top of the dash, a Hurst floor shift conversion, and the dual gauge panel under the dash with oil pressure and ammeter gauges. Other than those changes, the interior was completely factory stock, with full carpet and floor mats. (James Genat/Zone Five)*

*The typical 1961 Ford Super Stock entry was a Starliner hardtop equipped with the 375 or 401 hp version of the 390 Ford engine, a 3-speed transmission with a Hurst shifter, 4.10 limited slip rear axle, and Atlas Bucron tires. Ford didn't release the 4-speed transmission until mid-year. This street Ford was timed at 14.4 and slightly over 100 mph. (James Genat/Zone Five)*

Many dealers like Royal Pontiac, performed these modifications for anyone who wanted it — voiding the warranty of course. However, racing the car in any fashion, either on the street or on the track, also voided the warranty. The elapsed times for the modified automatic cars dropped at least 1/2 second over a factory stocker.

In late Summer of 1961, with the 409 Chevys and 401 Fords winning consistently at the strips, Pontiac made the following announcement: "Pontiac is now offering to qualified drivers a 421 cubic inch high-performance engine option. The engine is rated at 373 horsepower and features dual four-barrel carburetors, a solid-lifter camshaft, and high-capacity aluminum exhaust manifolds. The 421 engine is available only with related heavy-duty driveline components. It can be fitted to any Catalina or Ventura 2-door model." What this all meant was that a few drivers around the country, notably the Mickey Thompson team and Royal Pontiac in Detroit (who had *qualified* drivers) could install a 421 cubic inch racing engine in their drag car from parts available over-the-counter.

The 421 used a 1/4-inch longer stroke on the crankshaft, with a .30-inch overbore to obtain the 421 cubic inches. The cylinder heads were the same as those used on the 363 hp engine. Instead of the normal three two-barrel carburetion, the 421 had an aluminum two four-barrel intake, mounting a pair of the big Carter AFBs. The 421 came from the factory with those beautifully designed aluminum exhaust manifolds, that even had an open bypass to exit exhaust gas without restrictions. Of course, being available to only a few teams, the 421 Pontiacs were forced to run in the Optional Super/Stock (OS/S) class. Clearly, the 421 Pontiac had established itself right at the top of the class from the time it was announced.

## FORD

Ford continued to build on its successful 1960 Super Stock entry. Ford increased both the bore (to 4.05") and stroke (3.78") of the 352 engine, which now offered 390 cubic inches. However, the 390ci block used in the super stock car was totally different from the standard production 390. The block casting was internally heavier and had a special oiling system cast into it. Although the crank was a cast-iron unit rather than machined as on most of the other super stock engines, it was very strong. The camshaft was the same as used in the 360 hp engine from 1960, with mechanical lifters that would easily rev over 6500 rpm. Using the same aluminum intake manifold and Holley four-barrel carburetor as on the '60 engine, the '61 Ford entry into Super Stock was rated an honest 375 horsepower.

Ford didn't stop there. With the introduction of the Chevy 409 and the 363 hp Pontiac, Ford released two additional pieces that would keep its entry competitive in the top stock classes. First was a neat cast-aluminum intake manifold that mounted three Holley two-barrel carburetors. Called a "6V Package," and available only over the Ford parts counter at a cost of $206.71 complete with air cleaner, linkage, and fuel lines, the 6V Package brought the horsepower rating up to 401 and was released just prior to the '61 Pomona Winternationals.

Two significant pieces of the 6V Package were developed using hot rod technology. The linkage was a mechanical, progressive type rather than the vacuum-operated styles used on other factory multiple carburetor installations. The mechanical linkage opened the end carburetors at different throttle points to avoid flooding the engine under acceleration. The 6V Package used a fuel block with rubber fuel lines, rather than the standard metal fuel lines used on GM and Chrysler multiple-carb units. With a low-restriction air cleaner, the 6V Package had an air flow capacity of 840 cubic feet per minute, compared to 600 cfm on the single four-barrel 375 hp engine.

Ford still suffered from having to use a 3-speed manual transmission. Both Chevy and Pontiac had the Borg Warner T-10 4 speed. In May 1961, Ford released a 4-speed transmission that had been under development for some time. The problem was trying to find the right gear ratio for Ford's engine and car weight. Ford used the same basic Borg Warner T-10 4 speed as Chevy and Pontiac, with a longer tailshaft housing to mate the new 4 speed to a standard heavy-duty driveshaft. However, the gear ratios were different from both Pontiac and Chevy.

Pontiac used a 2.54:1 1st Gear, 1.92:1 2nd Gear, 1.51:1 3rd, and 1.1 4th; while Chevrolet used the close ratio 4 speed with a 2.20:1 1st, 1.66:1 2nd, 1.31:1 3rd, and 1.1 in 4th. Ford split the difference with a 2.37:1 1st Gear, 1.78:1 2nd, 1.37:1 3rd, and 1.1 4th. (Bill Jenkins adapted the same gears in Dave Strickler's *Old Reliable* cars.) With the new 4 speed, the 401 hp Fords were right in the thick of the Super/Stock competition, both in speed and the all-important elapsed time or ET. Ford ETs were in the mid-13 second area, with speeds of around 104 mph.

## DODGE AND PLYMOUTH

Dodge and Plymouth began the year with the same basic combinations as they had in 1960, a 383ci wedge V-8 equipped with the Sonoramic ram induction and two Carter AFBs, rated at 330 hp; or a standard inline two four-barrel engine rated at 325 hp. Most of the slightly heavier Dodge and Plymouth entries fell into the new A Stock class. In A Stock, both stick and automatic, the Dodge and Plymouth entries were very competitive. Yet, it was a slap in the face that they didn't have an entry for the top stock class. However, by the late Summer of 1961, Chrysler had released several new items that put both Dodge and Plymouth squarely into the thick of Super Stock competition.

First was the redesign of the ram induction manifold. The old long ram had internal passages that were about 24 inches long, and offered peak horsepower at around 2800 rpm. These long ram tubes actually cost horsepower above 4000 rpm, which is where you want your peak horsepower for racing. The Chrysler engineers shortened the internal passages from 24 inches to about 16 inches in length. This changed the horsepower curve drastically and peaked horsepower between 4,500 and 5,000 rpm. The new short-ram intake looked almost identical to the long-ram version externally.

To take advantage of the new short-ram intake's ability to raise the peak horsepower RPM, Chrysler released a new high-lift camshaft that used adjustable mechanical lifters. Other high-performance options included a transistor ignition with a hotter coil that increased available spark, and a Hurst floor shift conversion for the 3-speed manual transmission. Chrysler recommended use of Hedman Header Co. tube exhaust manifolds. The mechanical cam, transistor ignition, and Hedman Headers were sold over-the-counter only.

In late Summer of 1961, both Dodge and Plymouth released the 413ci version of the Chrysler wedge motor, known as the B Block, in a Maximum Special Police Package option. The 413 used the same wedge heads and short-ram manifolds as the 383, and of course, all the over-the-counter options also fit the 413. The factory rated the 413 Maximum Special Police Package option at 375 horsepower with either the short-ram intakes or the inline two four barrels.

However, Chrysler withdrew the 413 from both Dodge and Plymouth production before enough were built to qualify as a stock option. At the time, NHRA required a minimum of 500 units to be factory built or available, to qualify for Stock class, so only the 383ci was available for the 1961 National Drags. The reason would be readily known when the '62 high-performance models were released.

## CHEVROLET

When the 1961 Chevrolets were introduced, the top performance option was again the 350 hp Super Turbo-thrust 348ci V-8. It would soon be evident that this would not be enough to compete in Super Stock. In early 1961, just prior to the NASCAR Daytona Speed Weeks race, Chevrolet released a new engine — RPO 580. To the rest of the world it would be known forever as the "409."

*Art Martin was one of the lucky few to get a factory-built '61 Chevy with the 409 engine. Ordered from Moses Chevrolet in Esko, MN, Martin ordered a Biscayne sedan, with heater, whitewall tires, 2 speed wipers, tinted windshield, heavy-duty brakes and springs, hub caps, and anti-freeze. The 409 engine was an additional $376.60, 4-speed transmission cost $188.30, and $48.45 for the Sun tachometer, bringing the total to $3,289.70 delivered! (Art Martin)*

Many people think the 409 was simply a bored and stroked 348 engine. While it may appear to be true from external observation, the 409 was actually an entirely new engine. Because of the 3/16-inch increase in the bore for the 409, most of the available 348 engines would have been too close to the water jacket for safe operation. Chevrolet designed and cast an entirely new engine block for the 409, with new water and oil passages in the casting. Along with the increase in the bore, the 409 stroke was lengthened 1/4-inch and the revised block used a forged crankshaft. The piston rods were much beefier, along with being longer. The 409 pistons were Thompson-forged pistons with a high dome and produced a 11.25:1 compression ratio. The '61 409 also came with a six-quart oil pan as found on the NASCAR racers.

The cylinder heads for the '61 409 were the same as used on the 350 horsepower 348 engine, with 2.07" intake valves and 1.72" exhaust valves. The camshaft for the '61 409 was quite different from any 348 camshaft, with extra long ramps and timing. The entire valvetrain was beefed on the 409 with larger, tubular push rods and heavy-duty single spool valve springs with dampers. The intake manifold was aluminum and looked almost exactly like the 340 horsepower 348 intake. However, parts from the 348, such as the intake manifolds, would not interchange with the 409 engine due to the taller block. Thus the intake from the 348/340 hp engine would not mate up with the head surfaces and bolt pattern of the 409.

*Don Nicholson, known as Dyno Don because he was one of the first to use a Clayton Dynamometer to set up engines and chassis, campaigned this 409 '61 Impala hardtop throughout 1961. Nicholson is seen here at the '61 Nationals where the car classed as Optional Super/Stock (the predecessor to Factory Experimental). Don won Stock Eliminator at both the '61 Winternationals and National Drags. (Drag Race Memories)*

*Art Martin's blue Biscayne in early 1962 at Minnesota Drag Strip, Anoka, MN. Martin's 409 Chevy had Jardine Headers, which cost $158.00 post-paid from California, 4.56:1 Positraction rear end, and recap cheater slicks. The '61 409, RPO 580, had only a single Carter four-barrel carburetor and was rated at 360 hp. The shoe-polish lettering cost a couple of pennies. (Art Martin)*

On top of the new intake was a single Carter AFB four barrel. Again, it looked like the same carburetor as found on the 340 hp 348 but it was much larger in the amount of air it was capable of flowing. Chevrolet rated the new 409 Turbo-fire V-8 at a very conservative 360 horsepower. Dynamometer tests revealed that the '61 409 was actually putting out between 380 and 390 horsepower when properly tuned. With the available 4-speed close ratio transmission and many rear axle ratios with Positraction, the 409 put Chevrolet right into the top of the Super Stock class.

The stage was now set for a very memorable drag season. It began with the first "Big Go West," which was actually the second annual NHRA Winternationals Drags. In February 1961, the meet was changed from Daytona Beach, Florida to the Los Angeles County Fairgrounds in Pomona, California. The dates were February 17, 18, and 19, 1961. Throughout late 1960 and early 1961, the various teams were tuning and testing in anticipation of their first big challenge meet; everyone except the Chevrolet teams. They were still waiting for the arrival of the new 409 engine, which wasn't even put into production until January 1961.

Conveniently, right after the finish of the NASCAR Daytona 500 race, several 409 engines became available. Marvin Panch's Ford won the Daytona race, with 409 Chevys finishing 8th and 9th despite having many problems; problems the drag teams would not encounter. Some of the now-available 409s went north, some went west, some stayed in the south. Their destinations were Chevrolet drag teams at places like Service Chevrolet in Pasadena, California; Ammon R. Smith Chevrolet in York, Pennsylvania; and Rudolph Chevrolet in Phoenix, Arizona.

In York, a 409 found its way into a maroon '61 Biscayne 2-door sedan that was named *Old Reliable*. In Pomona, three of the engines found their way into competing Chevrolets — the red Biscayne sedan from Rudolph Chevrolet, the white Impala 2-door hardtop from Don Steves' Chevrolet, and the green Biscayne of Mike McCluskey. All three cars were built and set up by Don Nicholson. Known as "Dyno Don," Nicholson already had a reputation in Southern California as "the man" with Chevrolets. Both Sanders' and McCluskey's Biscaynes, and Don Nicholson's Impala were assembled and tuned on the Clayton Dynamometer at Nicholson's shop in Service Chevrolet.

## 1961 WINTERNATIONALS

When the gates at Pomona opened for technical inspections, the biggest names in Stock Class drag racing were all in line: Les Ritchey's big 401 hp Ford; Dyno Don and Frank Sanders in 409s; Jim Wangers had one of the new 421 Royal Pontiacs; Dave Strickler brought *Old Reliable*; Arnie Beswick's *Passionate Poncho* out of Morrison, Illinois; Hayden Proffitt tuning and driving the Mickey Thompson Pontiacs; Dick Harrell's 409 Chevy out of Carlsbad, New Mexico; the Bob Ford Galaxie out of Detroit; and Pete McCarroll's 375 hp Ford that was set up by Traco Engineering. They were all there. You might ask where the Dodge and Plymouth entries were. They were also there, just not in Super Stock. They were still limited to use of the 383ci Sonoramic engine, which put them squarely in the top of A Stock.

On Saturday afternoon, the cars lined up for class eliminations. It was apparent right from the start that the Fords and Chevys were the quickest in Super Stock. The Pontiacs were all gone by the end of the first round. The final pairing for Super Stock class winner was somewhat unique — two cars tuned and prepared by the same man. The Super Stock class eliminator run paired Frank Sanders in the Rudolph Chevrolet 409 against Don Nicholson's 409 Impala sponsored by Don Steves' Chevrolet.

When the flag was dropped, Sanders charged out of the gate first and held on to win Super Stock class in 13.63 seconds at 105.26 mph. It was a classic gate job, today known as "reaction timing." However, at the Pomona Winternationals there was no light system to measure it; just a guy with a starter flag. It was one of the few times in his career that Nicholson was ever left at the gate. The A Stock trophy went to another Dyno Don-tuned car, the '60 Chevrolet of Bill Patterson. Little notice was paid to the B Stock win by Bruce Morgan's '57 Chevy. It would become very important later in the year.

On Sunday afternoon, the stockers lined up for the Mr. Stock Eliminator runoff. NHRA announced that the 50 fastest stockers would vie for the Mr. Stock Eliminator title. This would include cars in Super Stock, both stick and automatic, A Stock and B Stock. The

*Old Reliable sits in front of Ammon R. Smith Chevrolet in York, Pennsylvania in the Summer of 1961. Driven by Dave Strickler, and tuned by Bill "Jiggs" Jenkins, this was the first of a long line of Old Reliable Chevrolet race cars. The maroon Biscayne sedan originally had a 350 hp, 348ci Chevy engine, but one of the new 409s was added after their release in January 1961. (Author's Collection)*

*There were a great many Corvettes that competed in stock sports classes during the early 1960s. George Vagotis campaigned this '61 Vette with a 290 hp, 283ci Chevy engine in C/Sports class at Quaker City Drag Strip in 1963. Note homemade exhaust header caps in the fenderwell, and the tow bar bracket on the front. Vagotis' 'Vette ran in the mid-13-second bracket at Quaker City Drag Strip. (Author's Collection)*

*In the semi-final race for Top Stock eliminator at the '61 Nationals, Dyno Don shut down Arnie Beswick's Passionate Poncho '61 Pontiac S/S class winner. Don's white '61 Impala was equipped with the optional 2 four-barrel intake and camshaft, which would be a production option in 1962. NHRA classified all such '61 409s as Optional Super Stock. (Drag Racing Memories)*

end result was a repeat of the Saturday class eliminations. Dyno Don eliminated Les Ritchey and the last of the Fords in the last semi-final run. The final two cars? Both 409 Chevys, driven by Frank Sanders and Dyno Don Nicholson. This time when the flag was dropped, it was Nicholson who pulled the gate job. The white Impala led all the way, winning with an ET of 13.59 seconds at 105.88 mph.

Dyno Don's winning Impala was set up typically of all the professional Super Stockers at that time, although Don's engine was tuned for maximum performance on the Clayton Dynamometer. The car was a standard '61 Impala coupe without the Super Sport trim package. The S/S package was not available until early Spring. Don's Impala had originally been equipped with a 350 horsepower 348 V-8, close ratio 4-speed transmission, and a Positraction rear end. The Dyno Don treatment included reworking the distributor, rejetting the big Carter AFB to increase the fuel-air mixture, and adjusting the cam timing and valve settings for maximum horsepower.

The Impala had the Police Option suspension and heavy-duty brakes. Don then further modified the suspension by raising the front slightly for better weight transfer under acceleration. Nicholson had a local muffler shop (owned by Jerry Jardine) design a set of tube headers to replace the factory manifolds. The Jardine headers were of the Tri-Y design, meaning that the four exhaust tubes joined into two which then joined into a single large collector that exited the exhaust gases into the front fenderwells. The 4 into 2 into 1 minimized problems with exhaust valve overlap, and they were considerably lighter in weight.

Although the front tires were standard 8.50x14 whitewall tires, the rear tires were two of the soft butyl rubber Firestone Butylaires in the NHRA-allowable size of 9.50x14. The soft butyl rubber gave

maximum traction for a street tire design. However, while the later super stock cheater slicks were run at very low pressures, Dyno Don's Impala had the Butylaire's pumped up to almost 50 lbs.! Frank Sanders' Rudolph Chevrolet car was equipped and set up virtually identical to the Nicholson Impala, although marginally lighter as it was a Biscayne sedan. Both Sanders and Nicholson ran ETs in the mid-13-second range throughout both the Super Stock class and Stock Eliminator competitions.

Between the Winternationals and the first National Drags held at Indianapolis Raceway Park, NHRA conducted a large number of Record Runs and Divisional/Regional Championship races. Of course, the Record Runs meant very little to those in Stock Class since NHRA still did not list official Stock Class records at that time. This hampered many of the stocker drivers, like Bruce Morgan, who were involved in the Worlds Points chase. It was in 1961 that NHRA decided to break the Worlds Points Championships into two categories, one for the Hot cars like rails, gassers, and altereds; and a second one for the stockers. By the time that the Indy Nationals rolled around, the top five Stock points leaders were Harold Ramsey and his S/S Pontiac, Bruce Morgan with his B/S '57 Chevy, Lennie Kennedy in D/SA, Jim Price in S/S, and Joe Burney's F/S.

## 1961 NATIONALS

The 1961 NHRA Nationals were held over Labor Day weekend at a new site — Indianapolis Raceway Park, located about 5 miles from the legendary Indy 500 Brickyard. Top stockers from all over the nation attended the first Indy Nationals. For the '61 Nationals,

*Art Martin's '61 Biscayne 409 Chevy, now professionally lettered, competed in B/S at Minnesota Drag Strip in 1962 turning a best time of 13.14 at 112 mph. At the '62 Nationals, Martin's 409 made it to the final four before falling to Arnie Beswick's Pontiac. Almost all the strips at this time, used a flag man to start the races. The "Christmas Tree" starting system was still a year away. (Art Martin)*

NHRA added still another new class at the top of the Stock Classes — O/SS or Optional Super Stock. It was a class for cars that were using recently released factory parts that were not readily available to the general public, or vehicles that did not meet the minimum production standards, such as the 413 Sonoramic '61 Dodges and Plymouths. This class evolved into the Factory Experimental class.

Entered in O/SS this first year was a '61 Pontiac from the Mickey Thompson stable with one of the new 421 engines. It was tuned and driven by Hayden Proffitt. "Dyno Don" Nicholson brought his Winter National's Champion '61 Impala, which was now equipped with a new pair of heads, a bigger camshaft, and a two four-barrel intake mounting a pair of the big Carter AFBs. Dave Strickler's *Old Reliable* Biscayne had the same equipment. Don Turner had one of the new 6V multiple carburetor systems on his '61 Ford from Ed Martin Ford in Indianapolis running in O/SSA. The winner of Top Stock Eliminator was expected to come from one of these cars.

Saturday's class eliminations saw several familiar names in the winners' circle. S/S was won by Arnie "The Farmer" Beswick in a '61 Pontiac. Carol Cox won S/SA in another '61 Pontiac. Both cars were equipped with the 363 hp engine. Frank Dade got the first victory for the Dodge camp, winning A/S in a '61 Dodge with the 383 motor in 14.51 seconds at 101.25 mph. B/S came down to a pair of '57 Chevys, driven by Richard Hilt and Bruce Morgan, with Hilt taking the win. However, it was discovered that Hilt's 283ci Chevy engine had non-stock valve spring retainers and he was disqualified. As they said, "Stock is stock!" In the King of the Hill class, Hayden Proffitt defeated all comers in his O/SS '61 421 Pontiac Catalina sedan. He turned an amazing 12.55 seconds on the trophy run, at 110.29 mph. Proffitt's Pontiac was easily the fastest and quickest stocker at Indy.

The story was much different during the Stock Eliminator runoffs on Monday. Again, the fastest 50 stockers, including the O/SS cars, lined the staging lanes. All the name drivers were there: Nicholson, Strickler, Sanders, and Harrell, in Chevy 409s; Wangers, Ramsey, Beswick, Cox, and Proffitt, in Pontiacs; Ritchey, Turner, and Ronda, in Fords; Bud Faubel and Ray Christian in Plymouths; and Al Eckstrand driving the Ramchargers '61 Dodge S/S entry.

*Bruce Morgan at speed at San Gabriel Drag Strip in 1961. Morgan won B Stock at the 1961 NHRA Winternationals with a time of 14.06 at 101.12 mph. The Don Nicholson-tuned '57 Bel Air went on to sweep the honors for NHRA World Stock Champion in 1961, winning a new 1961 Royal-prepared Pontiac S/S car at the '61 NHRA National Drags for his efforts. (Mike Morgan)*

*Thumper was the NHRA National Record holder for B/S in 1964. Driven by Gene Carter, the '61 Impala had one of the 360 hp 409s for power. Carter's '61 409 was the B/S trophy winner at the '64 Nationals with a time of 13.22 and 107.78 mph. (Drag Racing Memories)*

*A poor photo of Dave Strickler grabbing a gear in* Old Reliable *at York US 30 Dragway in 1961. With 409 power, and equipped with the optional 2 four-barrel intake, the car set the national record for O/SS at 13.24 in the Fall of 1961. (Drag Racing Memories)*

The racing was the best anyone had seen so far in any of the stock classes, with all the top stock entries running between high 12 and low 14 seconds in elapsed time. Eckstrand defeated the awesome Pontiac from the Mickey Thompson team, with an ET of 13.48 seconds at 108.56 mph. You ask how the slower car could beat the faster car? The NHRA had devised a starting system where the slower car got a head start, usually a measure of car lengths out in front of the quicker car. Thus the slower car had a shorter track to complete. Later, when the Christmas Tree starting system was installed, the slower car would leave a few tenths of a second before the quicker car.

During the final elimination runs, Dyno Don shut down Arnie Beswick's *Passionate Poncho*, then defeated Eckstrand in the Ramchargers Dodge when Eckstrand missed a shift. That should have made Dyno Don's white Impala a two-time national winner. However, Don's 409 engine was discovered to have illegal valve springs and possibly illegal carburetors (NHRA hadn't gotten the word yet from Chevrolet about the new carbs), thus disqualifying him. There would be no Mr. Stock Eliminator at the 1961 National Drags.

Bruce Morgan's run to the title in B/S, even though he lost in the finals, was enough to garner him the amount of points he needed to become the NHRA Worlds Points Champ in Stock Class. His prize — a new 1961 Pontiac Catalina, equipped with the Trophy 425-A engine rated at 368 horsepower with the Royal Pontiac Treatment. Within weeks, Morgan was racing the new Pontiac in S/S class and setting records.

Speaking of records, it was October 1961 when NHRA established the first Stock Class records. The first stock records were set at York, Pennsylvania, home strip to one of the quickest Chevys in the nation — *Old Reliable*, driven by Dave Strickler and tuned by Bill

"Jiggs" Jenkins. (He wouldn't become "Grumpy" until later.) At the end of the meet, a new record was set in Optional Super Stock by the *Old Reliable* team. By the end of the day, *Old Reliable* owned the elapsed time end of the record at 13.24 seconds. On the West Coast, the Mickey Thompson Pontiac which had set everyone back on their heels at the Nationals, set the new speed record at 109.22 mph at the

*By 1964, the 375 horsepower '61 Ford Galaxies were competing in C/Stock. Champion Speed Shop out of South San Francisco sponsored this '61 Ford in C/Stock Automatic when it competed at Half Moon Bay Drag Strip. (Mike Garcia)*

Inyokern Drag Strip in the California desert. Both ends of the Super Stock record were set at Inyokern by Bruce Morgan, using the '61 Pontiac that he won in the Worlds Points competition.

Jim Wangers, the driving force behind the Royal Pontiac program, recalls an interesting story. "Royal Pontiac had built a blueprinted NHRA S/S car to be delivered to the winner of the '61 NHRA Stock Points Championship. Bruce Morgan wins the Championship and the Pontiac S/S Catalina. George Hurst presented Bruce with the keys, but Morgan isn't real elated about winning the Pontiac. You see, he's a die-hard Chevrolet man. I presented him the documentation for the Catalina, including the 'no warranty sheet.' If he encounters any problems with the car, I told him to call the people at Royal Pontiac, and we'd take care of it.

"Morgan returned to California and almost immediately starts to race the car. The car is really well set up and tuned, we called it the 'Royal Treatment,' and he even sets the record for S/S in the Fall of 1961. Soon, problems started to surface. Problems that Morgan couldn't handle. Morgan forgot about the 'no warranty' paper, and calmly takes the car to his local dealer for warranty work. But the dealer knows the car was built for racing and therefore has no warranty of any type. Morgan is really upset, and began to bad mouth both Pontiac and the car. Finally, after almost destroying the engine, he pulls the Super Duty drivetrain, and replaces it with a standard 389 engine and sells the car. With that, George Hurst vows never again to offer a race car as the prize. It would be a standard production automobile from then on."

With the end of the '61 drag season, and the introduction of the new 1962 automobile lineup, all the teams started to get ready for the

*The Trophy run for Stock Eliminator at the '61 Nationals pitted Al Eckstrand in the Ramchargers A/Stock '61 Dodge, against "Dyno Don" Nicholson's O/SS Impala. Nicholson easily won the race when Eckstrand missed a shift in the 3-speed stick Dodge. Don was disqualified for having illegal valve springs and carburetors. Thus there was no Stock Eliminator at the '61 Nationals, as disqualification of the winner also disqualified everyone else. (Drag Racing Memories)*

new season. This time there was a pair of new and very serious and awesome challengers — the Dodge and Plymouth 413 Ramcharger entries. Time would prove 1962 as the year of the 409, both for Chevrolet and the Beach Boys.

*Dyno Don sold his '61 Impala after the '61 Nationals to make room for his new '62 Bel Air 409 SS/S car. The car was campaigned for the next couple of years as the Kentucky Colonel, driven by David Heath of Owensboro, Kentucky, seen here making a pass at Erie Dragway in 1962. Heath ran the match race circuit and in B/FX over the next year. (Jack Bleil)*

*Royal Pontiac sponsored a '61 Pontiac S/S race car to be given away to the winner of NHRA's Stock Car Points Championship. The car, a 368 hp Catalina hardtop, was won by Bruce Morgan, who campaigned a '57 Chevy to victory in the NHRA points race. Morgan then campaigned the Pontiac for a short time in late 1961. (NHRA courtesy Leslie Lovett)*

*Bruce Morgan makes a pass in the '61 Pontiac that he won as NHRA World Champ. Morgan set a new NHRA record for Super Stock class at the Dust Devils Drag Strip in Inyokern, California in November 1961 with a time of 14.04 and 104.40 mph. The Pontiac was equipped with the 363 hp Trophy 425A engine and was tuned by Dyno Don Nicholson, whose name was synonymous with anything that ran good in Southern California at the time. (Mike Morgan)*

# CHAPTER FOUR

# *1962 — SUPER SUPER/STOCK*

The year dawned bright and full of hope. John H. Glenn, Jr. rocketed into space on February 20th, becoming the first American to circle the globe. Five months later, the U.S. launched the first telecommunications satellite, *Telstar*.

In the world of music, new dances were the rage throughout America, led by the Twist, Locomotion, Limbo Rock, Mashed Potato, and the Monster Mash. On the West Coast, a new group called The Beach Boys began singing songs about surfing. While in England, a small rock group replaced its drummer with someone named Ringo Starr.

Around the world, events continued to darken American attitudes. The conflict in South Vietnam escalated and Agent Orange was first used. This chemical would be classified many years later as a major carcinogen, after affecting hundreds of thousands of people who were exposed to it. Conflict also occurred within the borders of the United States when the Supreme Court ordered a black student be admitted to the University of Mississippi. Riots ensued when the student tried to register and U.S. Marshals were called to restore order.

The darkest moments came in October when the world stopped and watched as events unfolded in Cuba. It was there that U.S. spy-planes discovered Soviet missiles, ostensibly with nuclear warheads, just 90 miles off Florida's beaches. President Kennedy forced a showdown with Kruschev and the Soviets by blockading Cuba and putting U.S. armed forces on alert. The missiles were withdrawn and the world took a collective sigh of relief. It was the closest to all-out nuclear war the world has ever seen.

To many, the excitement brewing on race tracks and in car dealer showrooms was a welcome distraction to world events. There was only one year when literally <u>anyone</u> in America could go to a local dealer and buy the same vehicle that was being raced in both the top NASCAR and drag racing classes: 1962. If you saw Don Nicholson run the Ramchargers on Sunday afternoon at the local strip, you could walk into the showroom the next day and buy one. If the dealer didn't already have what you wanted on the lot, then you could place your order and six weeks later you'd have the same car that Dyno Don started with. Then it was a matter of tuning, purchasing the necessary extras like headers and safety equipment, and setting up the chassis, then you were ready to run. If you knew anything at all about engines, your car would run within about 3/4 of a second

of the top dogs. If you bought one of the Dodges or Plymouths, all you needed were some tires!

The rules for 1962 were basically the same as they had been for 1961, with two exceptions: the definition of a "stocker" and the new Factory Experimental class (FX). The new definition for "stocker" was that the car had to be available as is, off the assembly line. No more over-the-counter parts being added and still remaining in Stock class. Those "built" cars were now in FX. NHRA allowed for up to 23 Stock Classes. At the top was a new class: Super Super/Stock Class, for the top-of-the-line showroom-available stockers. NHRA had classes from SS/S through L/S, with automatic transmission classes from SS/SA through G/SA only.

In the SS/S classes, both stick and automatic, the breakdown was 0 – 9.59 lbs./advertised horsepower. In 1961, the top class was S/S at 0 – 10.59 lbs./hp. The cars that ran S/S in 1961 still ran S/S, but the breakdown was now between 9.60 and 10.59 lbs./hp. SS/S Class was set aside for only the new model year vehicles with the top horsepower options, and the manufacturers took note of this right from the start. All the other class breaks remained the same except at the bottom where K/S stopped at 27.99 lbs./hp. L Stock would now be the class for cars like stock Model A Fords with the original 4-cylinder engines.

There were several minor additions to the actual class rules to compensate for adjustments that some of the teams had made at the close of the 1961 season. For instance, under "Air Cleaners," ram tubes or other-than-stock ducting to either the air cleaner or carburetor was prohibited. Several of the drivers in 1961 had scoops on the hood or flex tubing ramming air to the carbs. There was no rule for this in 1961, but it would be illegal in 1962. Additionally, hood openings and/or hood scoops not of original equipment manufacture were not permitted.

For the first time, NHRA allowed use of any heavy-duty or "explosion-proof" pressure plate and flywheel for stockers, allowing the use of such after-market units from Schieffer and Weber. Flywheel shields, i.e. scattershields, were required in all the Factory Experimental classes, and from SS/S through A/S. Interestingly, NHRA also required scattershields on *all* Chevrolets having the 283ci engine in B/S and C/S. A stock 283 with solid lifters could easily rev way over 7000 rpm, and several cars suffered a clutch failure during the 1961 season, resulting in minor injuries to both drivers and spectators from clutch shrapnel.

Also for the first time, beginning on June 1, 1962, all cars competing in Stock Classes were required to have safety belts installed. It was the last thing the tech guys checked before you went up to the line to run — seat belt installed and you were wearing it! NHRA also allowed progressive throttle linkage to be installed on stockers in lieu of the vacuum-operated multiple carb set-ups from the factory.

Under "Tires," the only change was that NHRA specified how wide a tread could be, based on the width of the casing used, i.e. a 7.50 casing could have a 6 1/2 inch tread width. The rule really didn't mean a whole lot since they also stated that any wheel/tire that will fit in the original wheel well could be used. Thus everyone went to the 9.00 size casing which allowed a 7" tread width, the maximum allowed. The tires still had to have some type of tread pattern, however. Magnesium wheels were not permitted.

The new Factory Experimental (FX) Classes came as a result of what had happened near the end of the 1961 season. In the late Summer of '61, many of the factories had released various parts to selected teams and drivers. Parts that would be standard production items in '62, but were not available to the general public. Indeed, several manufacturers released entirely new engine combinations, like the 421 Pontiac and 413 Dodge and Plymouth. Chevrolet introduced a new set of cylinder heads and a dual four-barrel intake that were slated for production in 1962. NHRA created a class at mid-season for these cars: Optional/Super Stock.

The OS/S class in 1961 became three FX classes for 1962 — A, B, and C/FX. The rules were simple: Optional equipment not necessarily factory assembly-line installed and/or showroom available would

run in one of the FX classes. The same rule applied to all equipment announced on/or after June 1, 1961. You could run any engine or option listed by the manufacturer for the engine model used if it was approved by the NHRA tech people. That left a very large gray area for drivers to build a car using many different factory parts and compete in one of the FX classes.

NHRA compensated a little for this by breaking the class down by cubic inches rather than advertised horsepower as in Stock Class. The class breaks were 0 – 8.99 lbs. per cubic inch for A/FX, 9.00 – 12.99 lbs./ci for B/FX, and 13.0 or more for C/FX. There were some very interesting combinations built for the FX classes such as Tom Sturm's C/FX '62 Chevy Bel Air hardtop, the same basic vehicle used by most of the top drivers in SS/S.

Sturm's Bel Air coupe was equipped with a 283 Chevy block and a 327 crankshaft for a total of 302 cubic inches. (Did Sturm know about the Z-28 of later years?) Sturm used the heads, camshaft, and Rochester fuel injection from the '62 Corvette. Thus he had all factory-stock pieces, although nowhere else was this combination listed as available. Evidently Chevrolet authorized this combination to NHRA at some point, as Sturm was allowed to compete in C/FX throughout the 1962 season.

The top class in FX was reserved for those teams that could gain access to the manufacturers' engineers for parts when needed. *When needed* was the key phrase. If the Chevys started to run away with SS/S class, then Pontiac (or Dodge, Plymouth, and Ford) would release something to bring the class competition back in line. For a short time until the item was assembly-line available, these cars would compete in one of the FX classes.

Of course, there were the true factory experimental cars, that were actually hot rods that had been built with the knowledge and cooperation of the factory. These included vehicles like the '62 Pontiac Tempests built by Royal Pontiac and Mickey Thompson, equipped with the 421 engine; or the '62 Dodge Dart that had a 413 Ramcharger engine installed; or the Chevy IIs with fuel-injected 327 Corvette engines.

## THE CARS

### CHEVROLET

For the 1962 model year, Chevrolet introduced parts that had been made available to several of the teams in late Summer: new heads and camshaft, plus the two four-barrel intake. Cars that were equipped with these new parts were forced to run in OS/S class, the forerunner of the FX classes. It was this combination that Chevrolet would have available for anyone in 1962.

The new 409 engine had different pistons, not only to those used in the '61 engine, but to each other. The new pistons had a large valve relief milled in the top that required different pistons for different cylinders to match up with the valve position in the head. Thus pistons nos. 1, 4, 5, and 8 were the same; while 2, 3, 6, and 7 were

*The Old Reliable Drag Team hooked up and ready to tow at the dealership in late 1961. The Strickler-Jenkins team broke in an engine on the streets of York, Pennsylvania. This is the reason for the hastily hooked up street exhaust system. (Susie Strickler)*

matched. The crankshaft and rods remained the same as they had been in '61. The oil pump was modified to provide almost double the oil pressure over '61, from 40 psi to 75 psi.

The new cylinder heads had larger valves for both intake and exhaust ports. The intake valves were increased from 2.066" to 2.203", while exhaust valve size went from 1.72" to 1.734". One of the biggest changes made increased the actual port size almost 1/4 inch. Chevrolet also increased the valve spring tension on the '62 heads, and made the rocker arm studs a little longer, then pinned each stud to eliminate the possibility of the stud pulling loose during high-RPM operations.

Cars delivered from the factory had an actual compression ratio of about 10.2:1, even though they were advertised as having an 11.25:1 ratio. The reason — Chevrolet delivered the vehicles to the normal driver with two head gaskets for each head, thus lowering the ratio to minimize piston burning and engine knock during street use. The first thing that every Chevy SS/S team did was to tear down the

*The legendary 409 Turbo-Fire engine as installed in* Old Reliable II. *With two Carter AFB 4-barrel carburetors and the early 1962 solid lifter camshaft, the engine was rated at 409 horsepower.* (Author's Collection)

engine and replace the two head gaskets with a single copper gasket to get all the advertised horsepower.

Mated to the new heads and redesigned to take advantage of the larger ports, were two new intake manifolds, a new single Carter AFB four-barrel unit for NASCAR operation, and a new two four-barrel design that accepted a pair of 525 cfm Carter AFBs. With the single four-barrel carburetor, the '62 409 was rated at 380 horsepower compared with 360 in the '61 package. The dual four-barrel engine was rated at 409 horsepower, thus keeping up with the Chevrolet legacy, of being able to put out one horsepower for every cubic inch.

In the Spring of 1962, Chevrolet introduced a service package of new parts for the 409. If you got the whole package, it included a new cam, valve springs, exhaust pushrods, a new single four-barrel intake manifold, and a new pair of free-flowing exhaust manifolds. The package installation did not raise the *advertised* horsepower at all. It did however, raise the *actual* horsepower a great deal. However, most of the serious drag teams did not use the entire service package, as most of the parts were aimed at the serious street-driven 409.

The drag teams were only interested in the new valve train, i.e. the new cam and valve springs. The new camshaft had more lift, from .440" in the '61/early '62 cam, to .480 with the service package cam. The new cam was much wilder in timing with 322° duration on the intake side (317° on the early cam), and 320° on the exhaust (301° on

the early cam). Coupled with the new cam were all new valve springs, that offered increased spring rates and reliability due to a new method of manufacture.

Although the new exhaust manifold design was a vast improvement over the original design, adding up to a 10% increase in actual horsepower on the street, almost all of the drag teams discarded the manifold for the new design lightweight tubing headers coming from many different aftermarket companies. Some teams and drivers designed their own such as Frank Sanders with the Rudolph Chevrolet team in Phoenix. His headers were so successful that many other drivers had him make a set for their cars, and he founded the S&S Header Company. Dave Strickler's *Old Reliable II* initially used S&S Headers, as did Hayden Proffitt on his car.

Two other changes were included after the beginning of production — one for increased performance and reliability, the other for safety. For performance, a new single-point distributor with vacuum advance was added that increased available spark from the coil as well as improving overall economy on the street. Finally, Chevrolet began installing a new pressure plate made of pearlitic, malleable iron that could withstand RPM ranges up to 10,000 without coming apart. Of course, the '62 Chevrolets could be equipped with seat belts, which were required if you wanted to race.

## PONTIAC

As with Chevrolet, the new '62 Pontiac entry for SS/S used the same engine options that had been made available to certain teams in late Summer 1961, i.e. the 421ci, 373 horsepower engine. Except, it was available right off the assembly line.

The cylinder block assembly was the Super Duty (SD) block with the four-bolt main bearing caps as found on the 363 hp racing engine. The 421 engine was bored .30" over to 4.093", with the stroke being increased a whopping 1/4", from 3.75" to 4.0". Interestingly, the 421 blocks were already overbored .30 from the factory, bringing the displacement to an actual 428 cubic inches, which was legal under NHRA rules. The Mickey Thompson forged-aluminum pistons offered a compression ratio of 11.0:1. The pistons had a .030–.035 clearance between the wall and the piston skirt, which is very loose tolerances for a street engine.

The first 421s used the same basic head assemblies as the '61 363 hp engine, with 1.92" intake valves, and 1.66" exhausts. By the time of the Winternationals in February 1962, the valve size had been increased to 2.02" intakes and 1.76" exhausts. Combined with the redesigned combustion chamber, the 421 really breathed well. Actuating the valves was a McKellar #10 grind camshaft with mechanical lifters. On the top was an aluminum dual plane, two four-barrel intake manifold mounting a pair of Carter AFBs.

The Pontiac engineers went to a lot of trouble to design and cast a beautiful pair of aluminum exhaust manifolds for the 421, with tuned passages that paired up cylinders to eliminate exhaust overlap that could rob horsepower. These cast beauties were then bolted to a 3"

*Dave Strickler is interviewed on the "Sunday Report" for WTHI-TV after winning the Easter Pennsylvania Stock Car Championship in the Summer of 1962. Tuned by Bill Jenkins, (he was known as "Jiggs" then), The* Old Reliable II *won over 90% of the races it was entered in, including match races against 1963 model cars with much greater horsepower. (Susie Strickler)*

outlet flange that mated the manifold to the exhaust pipe. However, there was a 3" opening on the bottom of the flange that had a bolt-on cap for open exhaust operation. When capped, the exhaust was directed through a second 2 1/4" opening in the side of the flange, that routed the exhaust to the mufflers. However, no matter how efficient these manifolds were, the tubing headers that were being marketed, were much better, being lighter in weight and tuned to a better horsepower range. So much for the ideas of the brilliant engineers.

Conservatively rated at 405 horsepower, the '62 421 was a true racing engine. Everything about it was heavy duty or performance oriented. The 421 had special high-capacity oil and fuel pumps, heavy-duty clutch assembly with a lighter-weight flywheel, heavy-duty driveshaft, wide ratio 4-speed transmission with a Hurst shifter from the factory. The rear axle assembly was the normal Pontiac Saf-T-Track limited slip differential with a 4.30 rear axle ratio. The factory recommended the engine be shifted at 5500 rpm and the 4.30 gear

was a good one for that RPM range. As with the exhaust manifolds, most of the drag teams used gear ratios of 4.55 and 4.88, shifting the big engine at over 6000 rpm.

Pontiac didn't stop with a new engine combination. Pontiac engineers realized that it would take a lot of horsepower to overtake the lighter Fords and Chevys, not to mention the unibody Dodges and Plymouths. A factory-built Catalina hardtop with the 421 engine and various heavy-duty parts, including the aluminum wheel package, weighed 4070 lbs. A 409 Impala weighed only 3750 lbs., and most of the Chevy teams were running the even lighter Bel Air hardtops and Biscayne sedans.

With that in mind, Pontiac began building a number of Catalina coupes and sedans with aluminum body components. The front fenders, hood, bumpers, bumper brackets, radiator support panel, and radiator were aluminum. Some '62 Super Duty cars also had aluminum doors and trunk lid. With the aluminum wheels, tubing head-

*One of the Pontiac drivers who didn't switch was Jim Wangers and the Royal Pontiac Catalina sedan. Sporting a colorful red and gold paint job, the Royal Pontiac would run in the mid-12s in legal super stock trim. Wangers and the* Royal Pontiac *rarely competed on the match race circuit because of commitments to Pontiac research. (Jim Wangers)*

*Car names were not the sole property of a certain team, although some became registered trademarks later. Ralph Fisher drove the Crivelli Chevrolet Old Reliable B/S 409 Impala at the 1965 NASCAR National Drags held at Dragway 42. Every sticker could mean additional prize money if you won the class. (Author's Collection)*

ers, the aluminum cased T-10 transmission, and the usual weight-saving by deleting radio, heater, and sound deadener, the really serious Pontiac teams could shave almost 300 lbs. off the curb weight of the car and still be legal.

## FORD

For the 1962 model year, Ford saw that the 390ci, 401 hp engine just wouldn't be able to do the job, either on the high bank track or at the strip. Nothing beats cubic inches and Chevy, Pontiac, and Chrysler were all releasing engines with over 400 cubic inches. With plenty of meat in the block, Ford opted to bore each cylinder an additional .80", bringing the bore to 4.13". Using the same stroke as the '61 390 engine, that brought total cubic inches to 406.

Although the 406 had the same stroke as the 390, Ford engineers made changes to the counter-weights due to the fact that they were making changes to the pistons and rods. The rods were heavier in every way than comparative ones in the 390 engines, and the pistons were a totally new design. Slightly shorter in height, the 406 piston had a flat-topped dome (390 pistons were dished out), which, when combined with a new combustion chamber design, brought the compression ratio to 10.9:1. That was advertised compression. When brought to specified tolerances, the compression ratio could go as high as 11.4:1 and still be NHRA legal.

The valvetrain used the same camshaft as the 401 hp engine, but had bigger exhaust valves. The exhaust valve was enlarged to 1.625", while the intake valves remained at 2.03". The carburetion system and ignition source remained the same as it was with the 401 hp '61 engine. With a single large Holley four barrel on an aluminum intake, the 406ci engine was rated at 385 horsepower. When

equipped with the triple two barrel 6-V Option, it brought advertised horsepower to 405 hp at 5800 rpm.

With the available Borg-Warner T-10 4-speed transmission and one of the optional rear axle ratios (down to 5.83:1), the 406 Ford, **when properly set up**, was a real stormer and right in the thick of the Super/Super Stock competition. That was the clue — when properly set up. It was harder for the average shade-tree mechanic to make a Ford run than any of the other types. However, in the hands of a good Ford mechanic like Les Ritchey of Performance Associates, or John Healy of Tasca Ford, the 406 Fords won their share of races.

## DODGE AND PLYMOUTH

It was at the Chrysler camps where the most changes were made, and the results were astounding. Everything about the '62 Dodge and Plymouth resulted in increased performance, even if it wasn't designed that way.

First off, the '62 Dodge and Plymouth introduced the unibody construction, which revolutionized the car industry. With unibody construction, there was no actual frame under the car. The car had a subframe, which held the engine and front suspension units. The main body and floor pan were assembled with stiffeners at various points to make the units as strong as the other makes which had a standard frame underneath. In fact, the '62 unibody was some 30% stronger longitudinally over the '61 model.

The designers didn't stop there. The dash was aluminum with a printed circuit instead of wiring. The steering gear housing was aluminum. Even the starter motor was aluminum instead of steel. The Torqueflite automatic transmission was reduced in size and weight.

*The* Glenn E. Thomas *Dodge was driven by Marvin Ford (strange name for a Dodge driver!), and was powered by one of the long-ram 413 Dodge super stock engines with a 3-speed standard transmission. Seen here at Pacific Raceways, Seattle, WA, in March 1962, Ford's Dodge would eventually fall to Proffitt's 421 Tempest for A/FX honors at the '62 Winternationals. (Raj Reddi Collection)*

All of this could be had with the six-cylinder engine. This added up to a weight savings of well over 200 lbs. over the '61 models, while increasing the handling of the car at speed.

Then the engineers built an engine. At the beginning of the '62 model year, the biggest engine that was available for Dodge and Plymouth was the 305 hp, 361ci engine. No longer was the 383 available with the Sonoramic ram induction system. Had the engineers given up on super stock racing? Not on your life! In early Spring of 1962, the Chrysler engineers unleashed the new short-ram version of the 413ci engine that they had teased the car enthusiasts with in the late Summer of 1961.

Based on the "B" block assembly that had been introduced in 1959, the 413 had a longer stroke than either the 361 or 383, which resulted in higher cylinder banks, thus the "B" block was often referred to as the "raised block" engine. The 413 had a special forged steel crankshaft with extra clearances built in. The "new" 413 engine was made to rev. Two sets of forged-aluminum pistons were available. One set had a high dome and an 11:1 compression ratio. The second set of pistons had a much higher dome and a 13.5:1 compression ratio.

A totally new head was used on the 413 drag engines with both intake and exhaust ports a full 25% larger in area than the standard 413 head. Intake valves were 2.08" in diameter, with a redesigned valve having a tuliped face. The tuliped valve allowed greater flow into the combustion chamber, as well as saving a small amount of weight throughout the valvetrain, a very desirable effect at high RPM.

The exhaust valves were a full 1/4" larger in diameter over the '61 Sonoramic engine. Both intake and exhaust valves had dual springs with dampeners. The 413 drag engines had a new, fully adjustable rocker arm assembly originally designed for Chrysler marine engines. The camshaft used in the drag engine had .495" lift, with mechanical lifters. The 413 drag engine was designed to rev at least 6500 rpm, which would be normal on the drag strip.

On top of the new engine block sat a completely redesigned short-ram intake system mounting a pair of Carter AFBs. Using the '61 short-ram intake system as a start, the Chrysler engineers shortened up the intake runners even more, from 16" to 15", which effectively raised the maximum horsepower/RPM level in the engine. Instead of having the carburetors mounted directly opposite each other across the top of the rocker arm covers, the engineers staggered them, i.e. the driver side carb sat on the left front corner of the engine, while the passenger side carb was at the right rear. This increased the serviceability of the engine without sacrificing anything in the horsepower range.

Chrysler engineers also designed a superb set of exhaust manifolds to go with the rest of the high-performance package. Each manifold was designed to separate different exhaust pulses that might cause a restriction. The manifolds swept up and back in a smooth arc from the exhaust ports down to a 3" head pipe. Each manifold passage was almost 2" in diameter. Compare this with the 409 Chevrolets that were 2.5" where all the passages came together! The 3" headpipe then went down under the car, ending in a 3" col-

lector pipe with a cap. The street exhaust was connected to the collector with 2" pipes that joined with the mufflers.

The entire exhaust system used 2" pipes from collector to tailpipe. Of course, the professional teams discarded these wild looking exhaust systems in favor of lightweight tubing headers, many of which were even more exotic looking than the factory manifolds. Anyone who has ever heard one of these factory hot rods make an all-out pass with open headers, will tell you what a distinctive sound they made. Every spectator knew the sound.

The engine was rated at 410 horsepower with the 11:1 compression ratio, and 420 horsepower with the 13.5:1 pistons. Dodge called the combination the "Ramcharger 413," while Plymouth called it simply the "Super Stock 413." However, both Dodge and Plymouth would still be hindered in Super Super/Stock class by the fact that they had only a heavy-duty 3-speed manual transmission. Of course, equipped with the legendary 727 Torqueflite automatic, the cars were virtually unbeatable in Super Super/Stock Automatic class. More than once, the SS/SA Dodges and Plymouths won Top Stock honors at meets around the country. Everyone soon joked that a Dodge or Plymouth win was automatic.

## FACTORY EXPERIMENTAL

All the major manufacturers sponsored certain one-of-a-kind vehicles that were built just to run in the new Factory Experimental (FX) class. Some built very limited production options to make their models more competitive not only at sanctioned meets, but in the newly created match racing circuit. It didn't matter to the public or the advertising men, that you couldn't buy the V-8 powered Chevy IIs that Dyno Don was running in FX, or the Mickey Thompson Tempest with a 421 engine, or (Holy Cow!) a Dodge pickup truck with a 413 short-ram package installed. They cheered mightily on Sunday and bought on Monday.

### CHEVROLET

Chevrolet had two packages that fell into the FX categories in 1962: the V-8 Chevy II and the RPO Z-11 lightweight 409. The 409 Z-11 option was a change to the new 730 cylinder heads with bigger valves, installation of the new 735 camshaft with dampered valve springs, and the new all-aluminum, two-piece intake manifold that sported a pair of the big Carter AFBs. The '62 Z-11 cars did not have an outside air induction system as would be found on the '63 Z-11 cars. Also, the front fenders and hood were stamped from aluminum instead of sheet steel.

There were a total of seven initial sets of parts that were put into service in August 1962. Chevrolet began issuing the Z-11 parts to the bigger name drivers around the country, including Dave Strickler, Don Nicholson, Hayden Proffitt, Frank Sanders, and Ronnie Sox. However, Chevrolet stamped many more sets of the aluminum front-end pieces and many other drivers and teams installed these parts on their cars.

NHRA classified all these Z-11 equipped cars as FX, with the lighter Bel Air coupes falling into A/FX class, where they were not competitive with the 421 Tempests. Most of the drivers and teams opted to bolt the Z-11 parts on Impala hardtops, where the added weight took them down into the very top of B/FX class. In fact, the final run for B/FX at the Nationals was between Dave Strickler's Z-11 Impala and Don Nicholson's Z-11 Impala. Following the end of the official drag season at the Indy Nationals, most of the teams again installed the Z-11 options on the lightweight Bel Air coupes and began the match race circuit. However, these cars bore little resemblance to those that competed in SS/S at the Nationals.

Several of the teams built Chevy II coupes and station wagons equipped with 327ci Corvette V-8s for competition in the FX classes. The V-8 coupes and sedans fell into A/FX, while the V-8 station wagons were in B/FX. Chevrolet already was rumored to have the V-8 Chevy II as an option, and indeed, the V-8 Chevy II came off the assembly line in 1964. Yet in 1962, the only way you could have a V-8 in your Chevy II was to build it and Chevrolet made that as easy as possible by supplying a kit over the parts counter.

The kits were available to install either the 283ci or 327ci V-8 into any model of the Chevy II series. The difference being in exhaust manifolds between the two V-8s. Each kit included everything you needed to do the conversion: complete wiring harnesses, bigger radiator and hoses, new motor mounts, clutch rods, and front sump oil pan to clear the Chevy II steering rods. A larger set of dual exhaust pipes and mufflers completed the engine accessories. The brakes were replaced with heavy-duty, sintered metallic units. A heavy duty front stabilizer bar and rear traction bars were also part of the kit. Chevrolet also included a special floor pan hump to fit over the 4-speed transmission. All of these parts would later be used on the factory-built V-8 Chevy IIs.

Bill Thomas Race Cars had a heavy hand in a lot of Chevrolet racing enterprises, including preparation of Hayden Proffitt's 409 Chevy Bel Air coupe, and was one of the primary leaders in building the Chevy II V-8 cars. He would later be a primary innovator in installing the 409/427 W engine and 396/427 engines in Chevy IIs. Many of the dealers and drivers built their own Chevy IIs to compete with the 421 Tempests. Don Nicholson, sponsored by Don Steves Chevrolet, had both a Chevy II coupe and station wagon at the 1962 Winternationals. The B/FX wagon won the class.

## PONTIAC

Whereas the V-8 Chevy II had complete factory backing going as far as offering a kit to install the small-block Chevy into a Chevy II, the 1962 Pontiac 421 Tempests were strictly home-built, with factory backing. This all changed in 1963 when factory-built 421 Tempests made their appearance on the nation's drag strips. Still, in 1962, there were few of these wild Tempests in existence.

Two that set the pace were the Royal Pontiac Tempest and the Mickey Thompson Tempest. Both were built almost identically,

although several hundred miles apart. Thus, it must be assumed that Pontiac Motor Division had a big hand in their construction, much like the V-8 Chevy IIs.

One of the things that made the installation simple was the fact that the Pontiac 4-cylinder engine, the normal engine found in the Tempest, was actually half of a V-8. Thus the engine mounts were the same and steering box clearance was already in place. A standard passenger car V-8 oil pan was used. With that in mind, the engine could be dropped into place and bolted up. Of course, the floor pan had to be cut to make room for the big clutch housing and 3-speed or 4-speed transmission.

The entire rear transaxle assembly was discarded and replaced with a narrowed Catalina rear end housing. Tubing headers were used to route the exhaust back to dual glass-pack mufflers and tailpipes. A standard radiator was installed. The engine itself was the 405 hp Super Duty engine that was powering all the Catalina coupes in S/S, except for using a McKellar #11 grind camshaft, which wouldn't be factory available until 1963.

How potent were these 421 Tempests? Ask the competition. At the 1962 Winternationals, the Tempests (weighing almost the same as the Chevrolet 409 Bel Air coupes) were running in the low 12-second bracket, which was at least 1/2 of a second quicker than the regular SS/S cars.

*One of the wildest cars at the '62 Nationals was the Dragmaster Golden Lancer, a '62 Dart powered by one of the 413 Ramcharger super stock engines. The legendary Dragmaster team of Jim Nelson and Dode Martin, built the car to compete against the 421 Tempests in A/Factory Experimental, and held the A/FX national record at 12.26. (Tom Schiltz)*

## DODGE AND PLYMOUTH

The Dodge answer to the 421 Tempest was the 413 Lancer. The only known example that was allowed to compete in a stock class, although it was FX, was the Dragmaster *Golden Lancer*, a standard 1962 Lancer 2-door sedan that had a 413 Dodge Ramcharger engine installed. The *Golden Lancer* was the creation of the legendary Dragmaster team of Dode Martin and Jim Nelson.

Starting with a standard Lancer sedan, the Dragmaster team removed the old 6 cylinder and dropped in the Ramcharger V-8, one of the 420 hp versions with the 13.5:1 compression ratio. The only modifications necessary under the hood, were reshaping a portion of the firewall and heater opening to clear the intake; and cutting a hole in each inner fenderwell so that the exhaust headers could exit down into the rear of the front fender.

Everything else mated right up to the original Lancer items — motor mounts, steering, oil pan, etc. The transmission crossmember had to be modified slightly, and the lower radiator outlet was moved to the extreme right to clear the oil filter. The only major change was dropping the steering drag link to clear the oil pan. Behind the heavy-duty clutch assembly was the T-85 3-speed manual transmission, with a Hurst shifter. The 727 Torqueflite could have been used had the Dragmaster team desired.

At the rear was a big Dodge Dart "police option" rear axle assembly, with Sure-Grip limited slip differential. A police option driveshaft was also used. The big car rear axle assembly was mounted to standard Lancer rear springs. Dragmaster fabricated a very unique set of traction bars from 1" steel tubing. The little red Lancer coupe had a complete interior, although both radio and heater were deleted. The first time out, the Dragmaster *Golden Lancer* turned a 12.68 and 113+ mph, making it quite competitive with the 421 Tempests in A/FX.

The Dragmaster team also built another unique machine for B/FX class, the Dragmaster *Ram Truck*. It wasn't very pretty, but the yellow pickup ran very well. The Dragmaster team started out with a standard Dodge D-100 half-ton pickup truck, equipped with a slant 6 engine and Loadmaster automatic transmission. Again, out went the 6 and in went a standard 413 Ramcharger engine and 727 Torqueflite automatic transmission. The engine was one of the 13.5:1 compression drag engines, the same as used in the *Golden Lancer*. A Dragmaster engine setup and tune, a Mallory Rev-Pol distributor, and a set of Horsepower Engineering Headers were the only changes needed to make the truck run.

The chassis was adjusted as per the standard of the era, raising the front end two inches and lowering the rear the same amount. The thought was that a raised front accelerated the weight transfer to the rear. With the 413 engine and the weight of the pickup truck, the vehicle dropped into the very top of B/Factory Experimental Class. With these modifications, the *Ram Truck*, driven by San Diego radio disc jockey Dick Boynton, ran consistent times in the very low 13s and high 12-second bracket.

*One of the more unusual entries in FX class was the* Ram Truck, *built by the Dragmaster team that had also done the Golden Lancer A/FX entry. Starting with a Dodge D 100 half ton pickup, Jim Nelson and Dode Martin installed one of the 413 Ramcharger engines and a Torqueflite automatic. Driven by Dick Boynton, a radio DJ in San Diego, the Ram Truck competed in B/FX and was competitive with times in the low 13s.* (Tom Schiltz)

## FORD

There was a single Ford product built for A/FX competition to go against the Pontiac 421 Tempests and Corvette-powered Chevy IIs. It was called the *Challenger* and was the original prototype for the Ford Fairlane Thunderbolts which were to be produced in 1964. The 1962 406 Fairlane was the brainchild of Andy Hotten at Detroit Steel and Tubing, a company that will appear more and more throughout the story of Ford progress in the super stock drag field. Andy and his people at DS & T were the first to engineer the big Ford engine into the little Fairlane.

The installation wasn't the simplest as the Fairlane engine compartment has a pair of shock/spring towers that protrude into the area where the big 406 was going to rest. The tower walls were completely removed and the top was reinforced with a set of arms that tied them to the cowl. Big Ford Galaxie springs and shocks were used on the front. The motor mounts were fabricated in the shop, both for the engine and the 4-speed transmission. Portions of the firewall and floor pan had to be cut and rewelded to make room for the clutch housing/scattershield and 4 speed. Cooling was accomplished by using a Galaxie radiator system.

The biggest problem was exhaust. The factory exhausts would clear the shock towers, but they were completely inadequate for high performance use. A modified set of Hedman Hedders was used to run the exhaust down and out through a large set of oval collector pipes. Other problems called for cutting down the length of the generator, which in turn forced a rewind, and moving it around to clear the exhaust headers. The battery was moved to the trunk area, but that was a weight transfer item.

Surprisingly, the rear drivetrain components were basically Fairlane items that were modified by the Detroit fabricating company. Using a Fairlane rear axle assembly, they installed a Galaxie limited slip differential that had turned down bearings to fit the smaller housing. The stock rear springs were de-arched to remove some of the stiffness. This allowed the car to squat on the suspension. A set of Traction Master bars were added to prevent rear wheel hop. M&H Racemaster Super Stock tires were used for traction.

The finishing touch was to cut the hood center out and a Thunderbird hood with a scoop was welded in its place. Additional cooling under the hood was accomplished when 24 louvers were punched along each side of the Thunderbird scoop. Inside, the car was totally stock with front bucket seats and a full rear seat, and even included a radio! Following the modifications, the little red Fairlane was sent to Tasca Ford in East Providence, Rhode Island, for testing.

Bob Tasca, owner of Tasca Ford, then turned the car over to his race car crew, John Healey and Dean Gregson. Tasca Ford had a lot of experience running an S/S Ford Galaxie that was driven by Healey. Healey and Gregson made a lot of little changes in refining the FX competitor, redesigning the exhaust header system for better flow characteristics, and installing an electric fuel pump and larger fuel lines.

An interesting side note is that, although NHRA rules state you must have a stock type fuel pump in stock classes, they don't say that

*In the Fall of 1961, Dave Strickler and Bill Jenkins completed the preparation of* Old Reliable II, *the SS/S Chevy they would campaign in 1962. Strickler related that they had a car on order from Chevrolet that didn't arrive in time to complete it for the '62 Winternationals. So they pulled a 409 Bel Air hardtop from the Ammon R. Smith inventory, and set it up for racing.* (Susie Strickler)

*Another successful car in A/Stock was the ex-SS/S Catalina of Skip Stegenda, here coming off the line at US 131 Dragway in Spring 1965. The* Hairy Canary Too *was sponsored by Goodwin Pontiac, and had the 405 horsepower 421 engine package complete with aluminum front end and Ford truck hood scoop.* (John Lacko)

it has to work. By running a much higher fuel pressure with the electric pump, the stock pump can be over-ridden and forced to remain open all the time. Healy then cut off the actuating lever for the stock pump and spaced the pump away from the engine block, allowing the pump, thus the fuel, to remain cooler during competition. An old coffee can with a coil of copper tubing inside and filled with ice, kept the fuel mixture as cool as possible.

One last item that the Tasca Ford team changed was the transmission. They discovered that the big C-4 Cruise-O-Matic transmission allowed more power to actually get to the ground, much the same as the Chrysler teams had found with the 727 Torqueflite. With Healey and Gregson alternating as driver, the little red Fairlane started to make a name for itself, turning ETs in the 12.70 range, and speeds around 115 mph. This put the Fairlane right in the thick of the A/FX competition. However, NHRA didn't see it that way. Even though the Fairlane *Challenger* was a one-off project with factory backing, the same as the Dodge *Golden Lancer* in A/FX, NHRA classed the Tasca Fairlane in A/Gas.

### 1962 WINTERNATIONALS

The annual NASCAR Winternationals Drags were held in Daytona in 1962, right on the big Daytona oval track backstretch. There were over 900 entrants in 47 different classes. NASCAR paid some $9,000.00 in prize money, plus two 327 fuel-injection Corvette engines, and a 406 Ford S/S engine. A couple of names that would later become famous in the annals of super stock racing were among the 900: Tom Crutchfield, later of Button Motors fame, with a 409 Impala, and Bob Harrop. Harrop was driving a '61 Ford and won Stock Eliminator with a time of 13.02. Harrop was normally associated with Pontiacs for Union Park Pontiac, and later the famous *Flying Carpet* Dodges.

The Winternationals in Pomona, California would be the first test of the new super stock cars that Detroit was marketing. For most of the nation, it would also mark the first time anyone had ever seen the new Super Super/Stock (SS/S) front runners. On top of that, it was the introduction of another new stock class: Factory Experimental. Only the GM camps participated in this at the NHRA Winternationals meet; however, that would change by late Summer.

Every make was well represented at the Winternationals. Chevrolet had a large number of entries with familiar names: Ronnie Sox, Don Nicholson, Dave Strickler, Butch Leal, Frank Sanders, and Tommy Grove — all driving 409 Chevys. At Ford were the Galaxies of Gas Ronda driving the Bill Waters Ford; John Healey in the Tasca Ford entry; Les Ritchey with the Performance Associates Galaxie; Dick Brannan with the Romy-Hames Ford out of South Bend, Indiana; Len Richter driving the Bob Ford entry from Detroit; and Mike Lieber's Ellico Ford Galaxie. There were many others.

Pontiac was loaded for bear with the likes of Hayden Proffitt's Mickey Thompson-prepared three cars which included one of the new 421 Tempest coupes, the Royal Pontiac team had the other Tempest, plus the SS/S Catalina sedan. Lloyd and Carol Cox were

also driving S/S Pontiacs, and of course so was "The Farmer" Arnie Beswick. The big Dodge and Plymouth 413 cars with the short-ram intake manifold had just been released and NHRA put them into FX class with the 421 Tempests and V-8 Chevy IIs.

*Sponsored by Frank Vego Ford in Atlanta, GA, Phil Bonner quickly garnered a name for himself and his screaming SS/S Ford Galaxies. Big Ma Mau, No. 2 had one of the 405 horsepower, 406 Ford super stock engines, with a 4-speed transmission. The holes in the grill ducted air to the three 2-barrel Holley carburetors when the car was set up for match racing. (Drag Racing Memories)*

Class runoffs began on Saturday morning for S/S and SS/S, both stick and automatic, as well as the FX eliminations. Although the new short-ram Dodges and Plymouths ran well, they were no match for the 421 Tempests of Wangers and Proffitt. When the rubber smoke had cleared, the final for A/FX matched the Glenn E. Thomas 413 Dodge, driven by Marvin Ford, against the Mickey Thompson-prepared 421 Tempest driven by Proffitt. Proffitt took the A/FX class win with a run of 12.37 seconds at 117.27 mph.

Don Nicholson drove a '62 Chevy II station wagon to victory in B/FX with a run of 12.55 and a speed of 108.96 mph. The little white wagon was certainly not the prettiest car at the track (they called it the *Ugly Duckling*), but it got exceptional bite with the station wagon weight on the rear wheels. Under the hood was a +.060 327 Corvette motor with Rochester fuel injection and 4-speed transmission. It was something that would be very familiar on the strips in 1966, when V-8 Chevy IIs would dominate Stock Eliminator. C/FX was won by Wayne Weihe, in a '62 Dodge Lancer with a four-barrel equipped slant six motor. His winning time of 15.67 seconds was enough to outlast the onslaught of the hot Corvairs and Falcons.

*One of the 409 drivers that defected to the Plymouth camp was Tommy Grove. Grove raced a SS/S 409 Impala at the '62 Winternationals, but had signed with Melrose Motors in March, to tune and drive the first of many Melrose Missile Plymouths. The 409 Chevy was relegated to the role of tow car for the SS/S Plymouth, seen here in March 1962 at Pacific Raceways. (Raj Reddi Collection)*

*Another car from the Nalley-Nicholson stable of SS/S Chevys, was Hubert Platt's yellow Biscayne sedan, seen here at the 500 Shopping Center waiting in line for tech inspection at the '62 Nationals. Platt's 409 Biscayne ran in the high 12s in legal form, and in the low 12s in match race condition. (Tom Schiltz)*

Super Super/Stock Automatic was loaded with big Fords and Pontiacs, with a few of the long short-ram Chrysler products thrown in, including a Chrysler 300 sponsored by *Hot Rod Magazine*. (Within a month, the SS/SA class would be dominated by the new short-ram Mopars.) The trophy run matched the *Hot Rod Magazine* Special, driven by Gary Nichols, against another Mickey Thompson Pontiac, the SS/SA Catalina sedan driven by Lloyd Cox. Nichols was caught sleeping when the flag went up and Cox jumped out to a car-length lead, holding on to win SS/SA with a time of 13.00 and a speed of 107.78 mph.

Super Super/Stock was a battle between a bunch of 409 Chevys and 406 Fords, and one 421 Pontiac. The Pontiac was another of the M/T cars, tuned and driven by Hayden Proffitt. As the Fords and Chevys eliminated each other, Proffitt just kept advancing. Dave Strickler eliminated Mike Lieber's and Les Ritchey's Galaxies to get to the finals. Strickler left Ritchey on the line badly, then Ritchey missed 2nd gear, and Dave cruised to the win to set up the match with Nicholson's 409. The race against Nicholson was so close that no one at the starting line or in the stands could tell who had won until the electronic timers lit up the win light in Strickler's lane. The final round matched two of the nations best drivers: Proffitt and Strickler.

When the final round of SS/S was called to the line, Hayden Proffitt's blue Pontiac drew the spectator side; with *Old Reliable* and Strickler in the pit lane. As the flag went up, Proffitt pulled a classic gate job on Strickler and had an instant one car-length lead. Both drivers were flawless from that point on, shifting the 4 speeds so quickly that it sounded like a pair of automatic transmissions. At the

end of the quarter mile, the one car-length lead had stretched into three and Proffitt was the winner with a time of 12.75 and 111.94 mph. Proffitt even rubbed it in as he waved good-bye to Strickler at the 1000 foot mark.

Super Stock was won by still another Pontiac, when Jess Tyree turned a 13.11, and S/SA was won by Lloyd Cox's wife, Carol, in another Proffitt-tuned Pontiac, turning 13.06 and 107.65. That meant that Pontiacs had won all four of the top stock classes. A/S went to the Chevy of Terry Azevedo, while Terry Prince drove a Nicholson-prepared '60 Chevy to victory in B/S.

A/SA went to still another Pontiac driven by Don Bennett, who drove his '62 Pontiac all the way from Clinton, Iowa to win the class in 14.21 seconds. B/SA was the first Ford victory when Bill van Vliet took home the class trophy with a time of 14.11 seconds and 96.87 mph. There were now just 24 hours before the Stock Eliminator runoffs.

Sunday dawned with the typical Southern California sunshine and temperatures in the mid-50s; a great day for racing! At noon, the fastest 50 stockers began lining up for the Mr. Stock Eliminator

*The Nalley-Nicholson Dyno Shop was the most respected super stock preparation facility in the nation in 1962, being behind not only Don Nicholson's 409s, but also Hubert Platt and his brother Huston Platt. (Marv Smith)*

runoff. Proffitt let everyone know that he was ready with a blast of 12.52 during time trials. There were some interesting results and many upsets during the day. Carol Cox, winner of S/SA, beat Hayden Proffitt's S/S '61 Pontiac to advance. Lloyd Cox's SS/SA '62 Pontiac put Mike Lieber's 406 Ford on the trailer.

In a very big upset, Dave Strickler got out of the gate ahead of Hayden Proffitt, leading the big blue Pontiac all the way to eliminate Proffitt in the very first round. Don Nicholson shut down the Fords of both Les Ritchie and Gas Ronda, as well as Carol Cox's S/SA Pontiac to advance to the finals. It would be an all Chevy final. It was about 4 p.m. when the two white Chevrolet Bel Air coupes pulled to the line together.

On the spectator side was the local favorite, Dyno Don Nicholson driving the Service Chevrolet white 409, tuned, set up, and driven by Nicholson. Again in the pit lane was *Old Reliable II*, the Ammon R. Smith 409 driven by Dave Strickler and tuned by Bill Jenkins. The flagman put the tip of the flag on the red light buttons and held it tightly. If either car jumped the start, a big red bulb would glow in his lane.

Both engines revved to about 3000 rpm and the drivers waited. When the flag went up, it was a clean start. Nicholson jumped out to a car-length lead with Strickler in hot pursuit. The shifts were flawless all the way through with *Old Reliable* making a very strong charge at the end. The winner? Spectator side!

Strickler and *Old Reliable* had run the quickest they had ever run, and the quickest any stocker had run in eliminations — 12.55 seconds. However, the lead that Dyno Don had grabbed right off the line was enough. Don's 409 turned 12.84 at 109.22 to win the Winternationals Mr. Stock Eliminator trophy for the second straight

*The Hoffman Ford '62 Galaxie SS/S was tuned and driven by "Mr. Ford" Bruce Larson! Larson would remain with Ford until 1966, driving an incredible Shelby Cobra to victory in AA/Sports at the '65 Winternationals, before changing to Chevrolet in 1966 with the famous USA-1 Chevelle and Camaro funny cars. (Charley Morris)*

year. In addition to the huge trophy, the winner received a new color television. It would be one of the last races that Nicholson would run as a Southern Californian.

He recognized that the big money was in match racing at the drag strips in the south and east, not in NHRA competition. He moved to Atlanta that Spring, setting up his dynamometer at Nalley Chevrolet, taking his trophy-winning 409 Bel Air with him. (At this time, drivers actually owned the cars they raced. The dealers who sponsored most of the cars, simply helped with parts.) The Nalley-Nicholson team would be a Chevrolet scourge on the East Coast super stock teams for the next two years.

Between the end of the Winternationals and Labor Day weekend, the super stock teams had their hands full with record runs, points meets, and match racing. Right after the winter meets, the Dodge and Plymouth short-ram 413 cars began making their entrance. So many were built that all the sanctioning bodies classified them as legal Super Super/Stock cars, both sticks and automatics, whether they were the 11:1 engine rated at 410 hp or the 13:1 engine rated at 420 hp. Dodge and Plymouth teams sprang up everywhere.

Some drivers switched car makes and dealerships to take advantage of sponsorships or simply a much quicker or more consistent vehicle. Tommy Grove had a 409 Chevrolet at the NHRA Winternationals, but switched to Plymouth in the Spring of 1962. Thus was created the famous *Melrose Missile* team sponsored by Charlie DiBari's Melrose Motors in Oakland, California. Hayden Proffitt, THE Pontiac man with the Mickey Thompson team, switched to a 409 Chevy in the Spring of '62, eventually teaming up with Bill Thomas Race Cars and Cone Chevrolet in Fullerton, California.

*Certainly one of the biggest names in drag racing, especially on the West Coast, was Bill "Maverick" Golden. Long before he drove the* Little Red Wagon *wheelstander, Maverick drove for Bob Smith Dodge in Glendale, CA. Maverick won the AHRA '62 Winternationals Top Stock crown. Golden's cars were always a step ahead of the competition, with exotic traction systems and modified transmissions, much to the chagrin of the NHRA tech inspectors. (Bill Golden)*

The southern match race circuit started drawing huge crowds. When the word went out that Nicholson was racing Bonner nearby, or Strickler was going to be at the same strip as Healey and the Tasca team, or the Ramchargers were going to be at the NHRA meet at Dragway 42 against Arlen Vanke, the crowds would fill the stands. Strip promoters saw full stands, which meant money, lots of money; enough money that the strips could afford to pay a team or driver to come and set up a match between two drivers or teams or just car makes. It was a very interesting Spring in 1962.

Don Nicholson, of course, switched from Service Chevrolet in Pasedena, California, to Nalley Chevrolet in Atlanta, Georgia. Once he was with Nalley, they added several other names to their team of 409 SS/S cars, including Hubert and Huston Platt, and later in the season, Eddie Schartman, one of the quickest handlers in the Midwest. John Healey and Tasca Ford emerged as one of the top names in Ford racing. Phil Bonner was the top Ford guy in the south.

Not all the teams got into match racing. Jim Wangers recalls: "In 1962, we (Royal Pontiac) actually had very little to do with the match

*With green wheels and whitewall cheater slicks, a shirtless Dave Strickler (safety regulations were a little lax in 1962) launches the* Old Reliable II *from the line at York US 30 Dragway in early Summer 1962. Tuned by Bill Jenkins, the Old Reliable team laid claim to being the "Nations' Quickest and Fastest" with recording times in the middle 12s consistently. (Matchracemadness)*

*The Ramchargers were a car club made up of Chrysler engineers. They probably had the most successful racing team ever put together. Their 1962 Dodge, while certainly not pretty, was powered by the new 413ci Ramcharger engine rated at 420 horsepower. With a Torqueflite automatic transmission, driver Al Eckstrand was easily the quickest of the Dodge-Plymouth super stock contingent in 1962. (Jack Bleil)*

race circuit, even though we were the most requested Pontiac team in the country. There were a number of reasons for that. Pontiac was interested in 'sanctioned events' only, and we were pretty restricted to just that. Besides, we were heavily involved in the development of the Super Duty program and the testing of the new parts.

"We did venture down to Dragway 42 for a match with our biggest rival in Ohio — Arlen Vanke. But that was about the extent of it. However, we were more than slightly involved in some of the racing on Woodward Ave." When asked about the outcome of the match with Vanke, Mr. Wangers couldn't recall.

When the '62 racing season began, the NHRA records for O/SS (i.e. A/FX) were jointly held by Dave Strickler at 13.24, and Hayden Proffitt at 109.22 mph. Interestingly, the S/S record was held by Bruce Morgan in the '61 Pontiac that he won in the NHRA Points Championship at 14.04 and 104.40 mph. By Nationals time in '62, the records had taken a dramatic drop. The A/FX record was 12.26 held by the Dragmaster *Golden Lancer*.

Dave Strickler had used the Chevrolet aluminum parts and the new Z-11 intake and heads on his SS/S *Old Reliable II* Bel Air and set the record for B/FX at 112.80 mph. He put the car back to SS/S for the Nationals and used the FX parts on an Impala, *Old Reliable III*, which ran B/FX at the '62 Nationals. The C/FX record was held by Tom Sturm and his wild '62 Chevy Bel Air with a fuel-injected small block. Tom set the record at 14.15 and 100.24 mph at Pomona in August.

The records for factory stockers also took a beating. In SS/S, the speed record was held by Dick Harrell's 409 Impala at 111.47 mph, while the ET record was down to 12.71 in the '62 Dodge driven by

Dick Lateen out of Portland. Bob Harrop's '61 Pontiac upped the S/S speed record to 109.54 mph.

The big news was of course, in SS/SA, where the big 413 Dodges and Plymouths were having a heyday. Bill "Maverick" Golden, driving the Bob Smith '62 Dodge, set both ends of the record at the Pomona NHRA Division Meet in August with a run of 12.50 and 112.40 mph. No less than 29 stock class records were set at the Pomona meet. Those records would stand through the end of the year.

The Stock Class Points Champ was the C/FX record holder, Tom Sturm out of Garden Grove, California. Tom's red '62 Chevrolet Bel Air was an unusual combination, but a legal one for FX class which allowed cross-breeding of different engine parts, as long as they were all of the same year as the car. The 4 speed-equipped Bel Air hardtop held both ends of the national record for C/FX. Throughout the Spring and Summer of 1962, Sturm was hitting every NHRA record run and regional and divisional meet he could get to, putting 23,000 miles on himself and the car in the process. It paid off as Tom ended the year with 320 total points to win easily. In addition to the big trophy, Royal Pontiac and Hurst, again, donated a new Pontiac to the Stock Points Champ — a stock Grand Prix hardtop.

## 1962 NATIONALS

Labor Day Weekend 1962 saw the biggest gathering of super stocks in the history of the National Hot Rod Association. Fords, Chevys, Dodges, Plymouths, and Pontiacs came from every corner of the nation. All were vying for the title of Mr. Stock Eliminator. The coming of age of the Chrysler short-ram 413 engine, with the superb Torqueflite automatic transmission, brought with it a mass exodus of drivers into SS/SA class. Where the other makes had to tune and really work to get their cars to run competitively, anyone could walk into a local Dodge or Plymouth dealer, plunk down the cash, push the "D" button on the dash and literally run right with the best drivers and cars in the country. If you knew how to really set up the car and make it go, it was usually an automatic Top Stock Eliminator victory wherever you raced.

Yet, at the Nationals, you were up against the best of the best. Don Nicholson, Butch Leal, Dave Strickler, and now, Hayden Proffitt were all driving 409 Chevys. Jim Wangers, Arlen Vanke, Harold Ramsey, and Howard Maseles brought 421 Pontiacs. The Ford camp was well represented by Dick Brannan, Bill Lawton, Len Richter, Les Ritchey, and Gas Ronda. Against these stalwarts were the Dodge and Plymouth automatic winners: Tommy Grove, The Ramchargers, Al Eckstrand, Bill "Maverick" Golden, Bud Faubel. Even two of the top dragster drivers, Don Garlits and Art Malone, had SS/SA entries. So popular was the class and the 413/Torqueflite combination, that both *Hot Rod* and *Motor Trend* magazines fielded entries.

On Sunday, the class runoffs were held. Over 70 cars were entered in SS/S alone. Although the Dodges and Plymouths had more than enough horsepower, the lack of a 4-speed transmission put them at a decided disadvantage. Round after round went to the

4 speed-equipped Chevys and Pontiacs. Strickler eliminated the final 413 Plymouth to reach the semi-finals.

The last four cars were Dave Strickler's *Old Reliable II* 409, Jim Wangers' Royal Pontiac, Arlen Vanke's Pontiac, and Hayden Proffitt with the Cone Chevrolet 409. Both Chevy drivers were up to the task and defeated the big Pontiacs to set up an all-Chevy final.

Between the rounds, Proffitt, who tuned and drove his red 409, and Bill Jenkins, the wrench behind Dave Strickler's consistent white 409, could be found under the hood frantically attempting to cool down the big Chevy engines. Engine blocks were drained and filled with cold water. Ice was packed around the intake manifolds. Clutches were adjusted and tire pressures were checked and rechecked.

When Buster Couch called the final two cars to the starting line, spectators in the stands were on their feet. On the tower side was the white Chevrolet with the green lettering that said *Old Reliable II*. In the pit lane was the red Cone Chevrolet entry. When starter Leo Errara brought the green flag up off the foul button, the white car jumped. Strickler had about a car-length lead right out of the hole, and held onto that lead through the entire quarter mile. The red Chevy was catching him and made it very, very close at the end but the hole shot had been enough. Strickler won SS/S class with a time of 12.97. Proffitt lost with a quicker time of 12.83. They would meet again the next day.

In SS/SA class, there were over 25 entries, almost entirely 413s with Torqueflites. The Fords and Pontiacs were eliminated by the

*Hayden Proffitt warms up the Casler cheater slicks in the staging lanes at Lions Drag Strip in Los Angeles during the late Summer of 1962. Proffitt had already received the new Z-11 intake, camshaft, and aluminum fenders, and was running A/Factory Experimental at the time. By September, he would remove all the Z-11 equipment and qualify in Super Super Stock at the NHRA Nationals, winning Top Stock Eliminator. (Matchracemadness)*

*After winning Stock Eliminator at the '62 Winternationals, his third straight Stock Eliminator title, Dyno Don Nicholson moved from Southern California to the land of match racing — Atlanta, Georgia — sponsored by Nalley Chevrolet. Here is Dyno Don's 409 Bel Air in the parking lot of the 500 Shopping Center following NHRA tech inspection for the '63 Nationals. The car is classed B/Factory Experimental, indicating it has the aluminum front end and Z-11 engine parts released in late Summer 1962. (Jack Bleil)*

end of the first round. Ray Brock drove the *Hot Rod Magazine* car past Bill "Maverick" Golden's Dodge, before losing to the Ramchargers in the next round. Bill Campbell shut down Art Malone. The Ramchargers Dodge, with Jim Thornton driving, had been running the fastest and most consistent ETs all day. They met their match against Al Eckstrand, a Detroit lawyer and another member of the Ramcharger team.

The final run for SS/SA matched a pair of 413 Dodges: Bud Faubel in the *Tip Toe* Dodge, and Al Eckstrand driving the Stanford Dodge. Both cars had been running in the 12.60s all day. When Errara brought the green flag up, Eckstrand exploded out of the chute and continued pulling away throughout the entire quarter mile. Eckstrand won with a time of 12.72 at 113.35 mph. Faubel had

his worst time of the meet with a 13.11. The cars and drivers now retired to begin preparations for the Mr. Stock Eliminator runoff, that would match the top 50 cars based on elapsed time.

All was not lost for the Pontiac faithful however, as Bill Sasse drove another Vanke-tuned Pontiac, to victory in S/S class over Bob Harrop, both driving '61 Pontiacs; and Carol Cox took the S/SA trophy in one of the Mickey Thompson-prepared '61 Pontiacs, with a time of 13.69 and a speed of 106.25 mph. The A/SA trophy also went to Pontiac when Ralph Hardt drove to victory with a time of 14.43 in his candy blue '61 Pontiac.

In the Factory Experimental classes, it was a mish-mash of little cars with big engines and big cars with lightweight body components. In A/FX, the favorites were the 421 Tempests of Mickey

Thompson, driven by Lloyd Cox, and Royal Pontiac, driven by Dick Jesse; plus the Dragmaster *Golden Lancer*, a '62 Dodge compact powered by a 413 short-ram engine. Ford had a handful of Galaxies with lightweight fiberglass fenders and hoods including Dick Brannan and John Healy. The one-off Tasca Ford Fairlane powered by a 406ci, 405 hp Ford was forced into A/Gas class by NHRA inspectors.

Jesse drove the Royal Tempest around the Tasca Galaxie, and Cox put the Dragmaster *Golden Lancer* on the trailer. The final run matched the two Tempests with the 421 powerplants. As the flag went up, the metallic blue Tempest from the Mickey Thompson stables pulled away for the victory, winning with a time of 12.66 and a speed of 115.68 mph.

In B/FX, two of the top names in SS/S racing were again matched against each other. Both Don Nicholson and Dave Strickler had identical '62 Impalas equipped with the optional Z-11 pieces, including the aluminum front fenders and hood. Strickler's car was completed just prior to the Nationals and used the same equipment that he had removed from his Bel Air coupe which held the B/FX national record. Both drivers left the line at the same time. Both crashed 2nd gear at the same time, and 3rd, and 4th. At the end of the quarter, Nicholson's yellow Impala pulled a slight lead over the *Old Reliable III*. Nicholson won with a time of 12.93 as compared to Strickler's 12.96. Tom Sturm added more to his World Points numbers with the win in C/FX at 14.71.

On Labor Day Monday, at precisely 12 noon, the fastest 50 stockers paraded down the quarter mile before matching up for the first round of Mr. Stock Eliminator. Every name was in the parade: *Tip Toe*, *Old Reliable*, *The Lively One*, *Hot Chief*, *Suddenly II*, *Res Ipsa Loquitur*, *Maverick*, *Rebel*, and on and on. Then they all returned to the starting line and began the long elimination process.

Jim Wangers pushed the Royal Pontiac past the Ed Martin Ford Galaxy. Howard Maseles' Packer Pontiac eliminated Bader. Maverick put Ray Brock and the *Hot Rod Magazine* Plymouth out of the run-

*Al Eckstrand leaves the line at Detroit Dragway in the late summer of 1962. Running several engine pieces that would not be available until 1963, the car was entered in A/FX class. (The Ramchargers team designed and tested many of their own pieces, then put a Dodge part number on it!) Note the traffic light starting system, predecessor to the "Christmas tree." (Drag Racing Memories)*

ning, then turned around and lost to Jim Thornton and the Ramchargers Dodge in the next round. In a surprise during the semi-final round, Hayden Proffitt shut down Dave Strickler, who had beaten him the previous day for the SS/S title. In the second reversal in a row, Jim Thornton's white Ramcharger beat Al Eckstrand's Dodge, the winner of SS/SA on Sunday to advance to the semi-final against Dick Brannan's *Lively One* Ford. Brannan's Ford was out of the gate first but the big Dodge went right around him to win going away.

That left two cars: the red 409 Bel Air of Hayden Proffitt and the

*Two of the biggest names in Chrysler racing history prepare to go at each other at the '62 Nationals. In the far lane is Bud Faubel and his* Tip Toe *Dodge; while Al Eckstrand brings the Stanford Dodge* Res Ipsa Loquitur *to the line in the run for SS/SA. Eckstrand won with a time of 12.72. (Jack O'Dea)*

The entire Old Reliable Drag Team poses for the camera after winning SS/S class at the '62 Nationals. Dave Strickler is 2nd from the left, while Bill Jenkins is in the middle with white pants and a smile. Note the Nationals number on the car, painted on white paper to cover up the original '201' painted on the car. The gentleman 3rd from the right is Beamer "Pop" Strickler, Dave Strickler's father. (Susie Strickler)

At the '62 Nationals, the Old Reliable Drag Team brought a pair of 409 Chevys: the SS/S Bel Air hardtop, and a brand new B/FX Impala that had the aluminum front fenders and hood, with Z-11 engine components. A big crowd was always around when Bill Jenkins, under the hood of the B/FX Old Reliable III, began working his magic on the 409 engines. (Susie Strickler)

*Bob Youtz, one of the East Canton "Chevy Boys," ran this '62 Corvette for so long that even he cannot recall how many years. The 340 horsepower Corvette competed in D/Sports at the 1966 Nationals, turning ETs in the low 13s. Youtz later modified the 327ci engine and ran B/Modified. Youtx still owns the car today.* (Author's Collection)

*The typical handicap start system at drag strips not equipped with the new Christmas Tree starting system, was to give the lower class car a head start in feet based on the class record. This is an early round of Top Stock at Erie Dragway, matching a S/SA '63 Dodge, an A/S 409 Impala (right lane) and a B/S 409 Impala, which got the handicap start. Jack Bleil states that "three at a time was only tried once at Erie due to the narrow strip."* (Jack Bleil)

white Ramcharger Dodge driven by Thornton. Both cars had been running consistently in the 12.60s throughout the competition. Both drivers staged very carefully, Ramcharger in the pit lane, and Proffitt's Chevy in the tower lane.

When Errara's flag came off the foul button and started its upward swing, Proffitt slipped his foot off the clutch. The big red 409 leaped off the line with half a car-length lead. Thornton's big Dodge was in hot pursuit. When Proffitt grabbed 2nd gear, the Chevy jumped another half-car length ahead over the Dodge. Proffitt shifted flawlessly to hold off the hard-charging Thornton, winning Mr. Stock Eliminator with a time of 12.83 seconds at 113.92 mph. Thornton had a losing time of 13.12.

What were Proffitt's winnings for capturing the title of Top Stock in the nation? How about a set of new tires from Moon Equipment Co. (and they weren't even racing tires!), $200.00 from Sun Electric Corp., and a big trophy. Compare that to winning a single match race at one of the southern strips where they paid upwards of $500.00 to the winner and one quickly realizes why the top drivers would rather run the southern match race circuit than the prestige of winning at an NHRA national event.

The 1962 racing season was over for all intent and purpose. There were still match races to run throughout the south, but the official competition had ended. It was time for the big names to get with the manufacturers and find out what was coming in 1963.

*One of the better running 409s was the blue Impala of Jerry Gribbons from Painesville, OH. Gribbons named the car* The Original Stovebolt, *then changed it to the* Jerry G, *which was both his name and the name of a popular Cleveland DJ. Gribbons (left) and Dick Advey stand with the car outside the House of Speed. Note the "C" decal in the rear window indicating a Dragway 42 season Class Champion. (Barb Hamilton Advey)*

*409s were everywhere in the '62 – '63 drag season. Unlike Ford entries, it was very easy to pull maximum horsepower from the 409. Les Surridge campaigned this A/S Biscayne sedan at Pacific Raceway in 1965. Note the extra long, heavy traction bars, which were typical of the era. Surridge's 409 ran in the mid-12 second bracket. (Russ Griffith)*

*The Goldenrod, built and driven by Ron Nemeth, was the main competition for Jerry Gribbons' Jerry G in A/Stock at Dragway 42. Seen here at the NHRA Regional Meet in May 1965, the car has more match race look than stocker, with hood scoop and open headlight buckets to duct air to the engine. Gribbons and Nemeth were a constant threat in A/S, as well as for Top Stock on any given Sunday. (Author's Collection)*

*Although the big Fords didn't win a lot of national events in SS/S in 1962 due to their weight, they were very strong in later years in some of the lower classes. Harry and Bobby Fermier campaigned this '62 Galaxie with the single four-barrel, 380 hp 406 Ford engine, in B/S through the 1965 season. Note the wrinkled sidewall to the big M&H super stock tires. Running pressures down below 10#, the tires had to be fastened to the rim by sheet metal screws to keep them from slipping. (Joel Naprstek)*

# CHAPTER FIVE

# 1963 — THE YEAR OF FACTORY EXPERIMENTAL

This was a year of personal loss to people throughout the world. Pope John XXIII died on June 3 after a long and agonizing illness, tugging on the sympathies of people worldwide. A few months later, on November 22, President Kennedy was assassinated in Dallas. It was a day no American would ever forget, no matter how young or old.

The entire year was not totally without some high points. Martin Luther King led a civil rights march in Washington, D.C. where he gave his famous "I Have a Dream" speech. Also in the news was Rock and Roll as a group of five friends formed under the name of The Rolling Stones, and another new group, The Beatles, released the song "Please, Please Me." The air waves were filled with the music of the Miracles, Temptations, Four Tops, Jan and Dean, and the Beach Boys, while on theater screens people were treated to Frankie Avalon and Annette Funicello in the first of many beach party movies.

The world of stock car racing had become so popular that all the major manufacturers were taking part in the great horsepower race for top stock honors. However, it was beginning to come to an end. Officials at General Motors felt racing wasn't worth the time and money invested in development. All the years of hard work had progressed to one-off, special programs to develop parts for racing. However, normal passenger car programs benefited little from the racing programs. General Motors cars were already the best sellers in spite of the big advances made in racing by Ford and Chrysler. So in 1963, General Motors dropped out of racing, except for a few drivers. That left only two manufacturers actively sponsoring the major drag teams.

Another reason 1963 was the beginning of the end for racing was because of a new rule change. NASCAR and NHRA followed AHRA with a limit on maximum cubic inch displacement in Stock Classes. For the next six years, no stockers could have more than 427.2 cubic inches from the factory in NHRA, 430ci in AHRA.

Besides the limit on cubic inches, the rules for 1963 remained essentially the same. The class designations were changed as SS/S was deleted at the top and replaced by S/S. All the other classes moved down one notch, i.e. last year's S/S became A/S, A/S became B/S, and so forth. Under the class requirements, NHRA now limited the amount a car could be raised or lowered, either front or rear, to 2 1/2 inches. Many of the teams were raising the front and/or lowering the

rear to gain a weight shift advantage (which actually hindered weight transfer, but it looked like it worked).

Other rules changes of note included overboring of engines. In '62 you could bore an engine a maximum of .60" for clearances and to allow for wear. Beginning in 1963, the limit was .30" for '63 model engines, as long as the overbore did not break the 427.2ci limit. Replacement pistons now had to retain the same basic design pattern as factory pistons. Also, for the first time, the size of the opening on exhaust headers was not limited to the same size as the original equipment exhaust pipes. The new limit was 3 1/2 inches in diameter.

For safety reasons, flywheel shields were now required on all standard shift cars down through E/S, and mandatory on any vehicle with a solid lifter, small-block Chevrolet. Also, safety helmets were now required in all the FX classes, and highly recommended in all the other classes. Seat belts were mandatory and each driver was checked to see if his belt was on and buckled immediately prior to pulling to

The trophy run for A/Stock class at the '63 NHRA Nationals matched Don Gay's '62 Pontiac against Northwind, a '62 409 Bel Air set up by Bill Jenkins, and driven by other members of the Jenkins Competition team. Gay defeated the Chevy entry with an ET of 12.81 and 111.52 mph. (Jack Bleil)

*Jack Chlebowski leaves the line at Erie Dragway in his AHRA A/Stock record holder in 1963. Proving that his 409 was competitive with the best of them, Chlebowski's Impala shows 11 win stickers from Dragway 42, and 4 more from Erie Dragway in the rear window. Chlebowski's best time with the Impala was 12.68 at 110.97 mph. (Jack Bleil)*

the starting line. The FX class requirements were unchanged with the exception that aftermarket mag wheels were now allowed.

Under AHRA rules, the lowest class was eliminated and all other Stock Classes were moved up one notch, with classes running from A/S through K/S. One difference between NHRA and AHRA rules was in the requirement for scattershields. Where NHRA required them in all the upper classes, AHRA did not, requiring them only on all small-block Chevy-powered cars having solid lifters. Beyond these changes, the other Stock Class rules were similar for both associations, except for AHRA's Formula Stock classes.

## THE PARTICIPANTS

### Chevrolet and Pontiac

The hand writing was on the wall almost as soon as the new model year option lists were introduced. Both Chevrolet and Pontiac had virtually nothing new to offer the high-performance enthusiasts because of GM's withdrawal from racing. Chevrolet did upgrade the 409 by introducing the new cylinder heads with bigger exhaust valves that were introduced in the late summer of '62 as part of the RPO Z-11 package. Also new for '63 production was the Mk. VI camshaft with extra-long duration, another part of the Z-11 package. Although the new '63 409 package had 16 more advertised horsepower than the '62 model at 425 horsepower, it was still basically the same combination.

Pontiac made even fewer changes in the production line high-performance packages. Pontiac made only one major change for '63 — a new set of high dome pistons that gave the S/D 421 engine a compression ratio of 12.5:1. The big 421 retained the S/D heads and McKellar #10 camshaft as the '62 engine. With dual four barrels, the new engine was rated at 405 horsepower. Along with the aluminum body panels from the '62 S/D package that was introduced at mid-year, the Pontiac and the Chevrolet would have been competitive if it hadn't been for new combinations introduced by other manufacturers. However, both Chevrolet and Pontiac would make mid-year changes that would bring headlines and win races in the FX classes.

### Ford

Ford introduced the '63 model year with the same engine options as were available the year before, the top option being the 406 rated at 405 hp with three two-barrel carbs. Like Chevy and Pontiac, Ford had a regular production option in the works that would put it at the top of the standard shift S/S class: the 427. Not only did Ford introduce the 427ci engine, it was built three ways — one for the street, another for NASCAR, and a third total package for all-out drag racing. We will concern ourselves only with the drag race version.

The new Ford engine was not simply a .10" overbore of the existing 406 block. The 427 cylinder block was an all-new design that incorporated several new innovations involving the bearing caps,

*Top Stock at Erie Dragway in the summer of 1963 usually involved the Dick Glenn Motors '63 S/SA Dodge, Knight Train, which had a 426 Stage II Ramcharger package. Things of note include the home-built tubing headers in the front fenderwell, American Mag wheels (illegal in NHRA S/SA), and white sidewall Casler cheater slicks on Rader Wheels (which were NHRA legal in S/SA). (Jack Bleil)*

rods, pistons, head design, intake and exhaust, and even body design. The main bearing caps, a familiar area of failure in previous Ford engines, were reinforced and then the bearing cap was cross-bolted, i.e. each cap had four bolts, two through the bottom of the block and two more through the sides.

Since the 427 didn't require an increase in the stroke of the engine, the crankshaft from the 406 was carried over and the rods were strengthened. Pistons were cast aluminum, with a high dome producing a compression ratio of up to 12:1. Even though the 427 pistons were larger in size than those of the 406, the 427 pistons were lighter. They also had little innovations for reliability, such as snap rings holding the piston pins in place.

Yet, it was in the head design where all the power was produced in the 427. Ford engineers enlarged both intake and exhaust ports on the 427, while smoothing out the passages. They then installed bigger intake and exhaust valves. The new intakes were increased .060 to 2.06", while exhaust valves were 1.625". The combustion chamber itself was redesigned to allow better fuel/air mixture to flow around the valves. A mid-year change offered even bigger valves for the 427, with intakes being 2.097" and exhaust valves at 1.66". A new mechanical lifter camshaft was used in the 427 with over 324$^\circ$ duration and .500" lift. The new valves had dual springs installed which allowed the driver to go through the gears at well over 6500 rpm. Topping off the package was a new aluminum dual four-barrel intake manifold that mounted a pair of the big Holley four throat 600 cfm carburetors. The combination was rated at 425 horsepower at 6,000 rpm.

As with the other factory drag engines, the Ford engineers went to considerable length to design the best set of cast-iron exhaust

*Karnig Karadizian makes a pass at Lions Drag Strip in the summer of 1963 with the Blair's Speed Shop '62 Plymouth. With a pair of blower scoops mounted on the hood over the Carter AFBs, the Plymouth was forced to run in AHRA Super Optional Stock at Lions, an AHRA strip. Karadizian also drove for the Milne Brothers super stock team on occasion. (Matchracemadness)*

manifolds in the industry. Long sweeping internal passages that ended with a long pipe extension that could be opened for drag strip operation were standard on the 427. A transistorized ignition was again offered for the top stock enthusiast. Ford retained use of the optional Borg-Warner T-10 4-speed transmission, and various rear axle ratios which could be ordered with an EquaLok limited slip differential.

*The 426 Plymouth Stage II Super Stock engine as installed in Tommy Grove's* Melrose Missile III. *The Stage II engine, which was rated at 425 horsepower, had a 13.5:1 compression ratio, with a pair of 725 cfm Carter AFB four barrels on top of the short ram intake. The Dodge equivalent was called a Ramcharger Stage II. (Zone Five)*

However, Ford didn't stop with increasing available horsepower. The body was also redesigned to gain aerodynamic horsepower, and to lighten the car. At the mid-year break Ford introduced an entirely new design, the '63 1/2 Galaxie 500 2-door hardtop. It had an angular fastback roof design that had been tested in the wind tunnel and found to be as much as 10% more aerodynamic over the notch-back coupe. On the NASCAR circuit the new roof was worth as much as 25 horsepower. Drag strip speeds would also be increased, although not by very much, maybe 1-2 mph tops; but that might be enough.

Later in the year, Ford introduced a lightweight body package for the drag strip competitors, including fiberglass front fenders, hood, doors, and trunk lid. Both front and rear bumpers and all brackets, were stamped aluminum. Ford even changed the actual frame to the lighter weight unit used under the 6-cylinder equipped 300 series sedans.

Inside the passenger compartment, there was no radio, heater, clock, or any convenience items. The original very comfortable front bucket seats were exchanged for a pair of lightweight bucket seats. A thin rubber floor mat replaced both the carpet and padding. All sound deadener was deleted, as well as underbody rust preventative. The Borg-Warner 4-speed transmission had an all-aluminum case and the bell housing was a special cast-aluminum unit made by RC Industries that doubled as a scattershield. All of these weight-saving changes shaved a phenomenal 700+ pounds off the delivered weight of the car, down from 4150 lbs. to 3480 lbs. ready to race. Initially, the lightweight Fords had to run in FX until the minimum number of units were produced.

## DODGE AND PLYMOUTH

The Dodge Ramcharger and Plymouth Super Stock cars that had been setting all kinds of records ever since their introduction in 1962, certainly didn't stand on their laurels. Taking advantage of the new displacement limits, the Chrysler engineers bored the 413 engine an additional 1/16" to bring the displacement to 426 cubic inches. Although the crankshaft remained the same as in the 413, the connecting rods were strengthened. Bearing surfaces had much larger oil grooves for better lubrication at high RPM.

The 426 also had redesigned cylinder heads with enlarged and smoothed ports on both the intake and exhaust side. Valve sizes were 2.08" for the intake and 1.88" on the exhausts. The combustion chambers retained the basic design of the improved 413 heads used in '62. Once again, two types of pistons were used depending upon the use of the vehicle. For normal street driving, the high dome pistons had an 11:1 compression ratio. For the all-out professional team, the pistons had an even higher dome producing 13.5:1 compression. These cars were definitely not intended for use on the street. It even said so on a special tag under the hood: "Caution — This car equipped with a maximum performance engine."

The 426 had a special high-lift camshaft with over 300° duration and a .509" lift, using mechanical lifters. Fully adjustable rocker arms

*Jim Wangers comes off the line at Detroit Dragway in the Royal Pontiac 421 Tempest wagon in the Spring of 1963. With the all-aluminum front end assembly, the wagons weighed in at 3,450 lbs. in legal A/FX trim and could run in the high 11-second bracket. (Jim Wangers)*

of lightweight aluminum body panels. Included were aluminum front fenders and hood, with integral air intake scoop, aluminum lower front body and splash pan. Front bumper for the Dodge was aluminum, while the Plymouth used a lightweight steel unit. Included with the lightweight package was deletion of all sound deadener throughout the body, no heater or hoses were installed, no undercoat was applied as a rust preventative (who drove these cars in winter anyway), and of course, they came without a radio. In the passenger compartment, a standard seat was installed, but all carpet and padding was deleted and replaced with a thin rubber floor mat. The battery was removed from under the hood and installed in the right rear of the trunk.

Installation of the lightweight package shaved over 160 pounds, almost all of it removed from the front end of the car. A Dodge or Plymouth sedan with the lightweight package weighed in at slightly over 3,200 lbs. While both Dodge and Plymouth met the minimum number of cars that were factory-built with the new Stage II package installed, i.e. 50 each, NHRA promptly upped the number without warning to 100. Both Dodge and Plymouth then went ahead and stamped a number of the lightweight packages and made them available to anyone who wanted them. Thus by the time of the Nationals, the Stage II Dodges and Plymouths were not only available for S/S and S/SA, they were top-heavy candidates to win the class and Top Stock Eliminator. They didn't disappoint anyone.

## FACTORY EXPERIMENTAL

In 1963 there were three basic types of factory experimental vehicles. First were those vehicles initially classified as FX simply because there weren't enough of them assembled before a particular race. Initially, NHRA set the standard at 50 vehicles, but then modified that (as mentioned previously) at mid-year to 100 vehicles in an attempt to keep the fiberglass and aluminum-equipped vehicles out of Stock classes. However, these vehicles were eventually built in numbers easily exceeding the 100 car limit, resulting in the Dodge, Plymouth, and Ford lightweights being eligible for Super Stock classes.

Second were the vehicles made in a certain quantity, but just not enough to qualify as a readily available car for S/S Class, such as the Z-11 Chevrolets and lightweight Pontiacs. Last were the one-off vehicles, or those that were built in such small numbers that they couldn't even come close to being accepted as a factory-assembled, readily-available vehicle, even though they were built with factory authorization. Examples of these would be the Pontiac Tempests with the 421 engines.

### DODGE AND PLYMOUTH

Other than the brief periods in which various Stage II and Stage III combinations were forced into FX class prior to being declared as legal Super Stock cars, neither Dodge nor Plymouth had a competitor for A/FX that was built just for that class. However, many of the

were used with the 426 engines. Each valve had dual springs and special retainers for high RPM use. Of course, on top was the now proven short-ram intake system mounting a pair of Carter AFBs. The only two transmission options were a heavy-duty 3 speed manual transmission with a Hurst Shifter and the venerable 727 Torqueflite automatic. Interestingly, both Dodge and Plymouth had the Borg-Warner T-10 available as optional equipment, but not with the 426 engines. Their reason — it was originally designed for a much smaller engine (the Chevy 283) and <u>would</u> <u>not</u> <u>take</u> <u>the</u> <u>abuse</u> offered by the big 426. Tell that to the guys who were running that same transmission behind their 409 Chevys, 421 Pontiacs, and 427 Fords.

All that was just Stage I in the '63 426 program. At the mid-year point both Dodge and Plymouth released Stage II in their drag race programs. With the Stage II 426, the combustion chamber was slightly modified to improve flow. A new camshaft was used, with more duration and lift, 308° and .520". The end result was more useable horsepower with the ram induction setup. So to take advantage of the increased flow available, Chrysler added a pair of even bigger Carter AFB carburetors to the short-ram manifold. The new Carters had 1/4" larger primary ventures, making both primary and secondary ventures at 1 11/16" bores, which increased the airflow from 525 cfm in the Stage I, to 725 in Stage II.

Just prior to the factory shutdown to begin retooling for the 1964 model year, both Dodge and Plymouth stamped out a number of sets

426 Mopar teams were competitive in A/FX, even though they weren't developed for the class. By simply switching to slicks instead of cheater slicks, the Dodges and Plymouths could run in A/FX.

## FORD

As with Dodge and Plymouth, most of the Ford cars running in FX classes were regular production vehicles that had not <u>yet</u> met the minimum production standards (100 vehicles) as required by NHRA. However, Ford did authorize one special vehicle that would run in A/Factory Experimental in 1963, and would ultimately lead to the production of the '64 Ford Thunderbolt.

The car was actually the second Fairlane conversion built for the Tasca Ford team, the first being the '62 Fairlane *Challenger*, with the 406 engine that turned 12.70s in the late Summer of 1962. The '63 car, named the *Zimmy I*, was powered by the latest 427 Ford as used in the Tasca Super Stock car. This time the Tasca crew

went all the way in making the Fairlane the ultimate in Stock competition. As with the '62 Fairlane, the *Zimmy I* was originally built by Detroit Steel Tubing. The '63 version took everything to the next level, and many of the ideas tested on the *Zimmy I* would be found on the 1964 version, which was built in quantity to meet NHRA's standards for Super Stock. That car was of course, the renowned Fairlane Thunderbolt.

The engine in the *Zimmy I* was the latest high-riser 427 built for use on the NASCAR tracks, but equipped with two four-barrels for drag racing. The entire front end of the car was a fiberglass reproduction, including the front bumper assembly. The fiberglass hood had to be bulged to clear the dual quads. Air was inducted to the dual four barrels from two holes cut in the radiator support panel, through a pair of flexible tubes to an air box over the carbs. Both of these would be standard on the Thunderbolt. Power was transferred to the rear through a standard Ford Borg-Warner T-10 4-speed transmission, and then to a Detroit Locker rear axle assembly that was narrowed to

*Jim Wangers and the Royal Pontiac charge off the line at Detroit Dragway in the Spring of 1963. Pontiac had two separate programs in 1963: the A/FX Tempest with 421 power and the B/FX 421 Catalina with the swiss-cheese frame. The B/FX Catalinas had aluminum front fenders, hood, and bumpers; and the frame had the entire bottom cut out and holes cut every few inches in the side rails. (Jim Wangers)*

fit the Fairlane. The battery, a big 95-lb. truck unit, was mounted in the right side of the trunk. Front seats were lightweight Econoline van units, while the rear seat was removed completely.

The exhaust system was the most exotic seen up to that time. Each exhaust pipe was 31" long and wrapped down under the engine before joining in a 14" long collector that exited beside the transmission. The chassis was refined many times before the right combination was chosen. The rear leaf springs were different for each side, 3 leaves on the left and 2 on the right. Large steel traction bars ran from the axle housing to a special cross member to keep the rear axle from hopping, thus losing traction off the line. The front suspension was modified exactly opposite that of the rear, with a soft spring and shock on the left front to allow the car to torque easier, and a stock spring and heavy-duty shock on the right side to absorb and transfer the torque to the rear.

Being that Ford authorized the conversion, and NHRA put its stamp of approval on the entire conversion, the Tasca Fairlane was allowed to run in A/Factory Experimental. It was the only one in existence and it consistently turned times in the low 12-second bracket, setting the A/FX record at 12.21 in late 1963.

Which leaves us with the GM teams from Chevrolet and Pontiac. Both had announced that 1963 was the last year in which they would be sponsoring racing teams in any sport, be it NASCAR, Indy car, or in drag racing. Both manufacturers would go out with a bang — Chevrolet in A/FX, and Pontiac in both A/FX and B/FX.

## PONTIAC

Pontiac had two separate ventures in the Factory Experimental classes — one with the Catalina full-size car, and the other with the Tempest economy car. First we'll analyze the '63 Catalina with the so-called "Swiss Cheese" option.

The '63 Catalina that Pontiac built to run in Factory Experimental was a standard Catalina hardtop coupe with a lot of aluminum body panels. As with the '62 drag package, the '63 car had aluminum front fenders, hood, inner fenders, radiator support panel, bumpers, and brackets. The gauge of the aluminum was thinner (26 gauge) than that used in the '62 package, reducing the weight a few more pounds. All the insulation was left out at the factory. No radio or heater parts were installed. Even the glass was replaced with Plexiglas. On top of the hood was a scoop that was very familiar to Ford mechanics and truck drivers. It had originally been designed for a Ford dump truck, but this design was reversed. Pontiac bought a bunch of these and gave them all Pontiac part numbers, turning them around to face into the air stream. It was ingenuity in action!

The greatest change occurred in the frame. The standard Pontiac frame was a box tube affair that ran around the outer edge of the body. It was both rugged and very heavy. Pontiac designers first removed the entire bottom rail, making the frame a u-shape section. Then they cut large holes every few inches in the side rails. Thus the nickname became the "Swiss Cheese" frame. Pontiac designers saved

*All factory-built Z-11s were installed in standard Impala hardtops, and all were identically equipped in every way except for color. On the right side of the firewall is the plenum that ducted fresh air from the base of the windshield, through the cowl slots, to a specially designed air cleaner originally designed for NASCAR racers. (James Genat/Zone Five)*

another few pounds by equipping the car with a single small tail pipe and muffler. With an aluminum-cast scattershield and 4-speed case, the package was complete. In race ready trim, i.e. with a few gallons of gas and coolant in the radiator, the Swiss Cheese Pontiac weighed in at a very comfortable 3300 lbs.!

Pontiac added a little more punch to the very potent 421 Super Duty engine that would power the lightweight Catalina. The heads were redesigned with larger ports having slightly altered internal contours. The combustion chamber was also altered for better breathing. With a new set of over-the-counter high-dome pistons, the compression ratio was 13.0:1. Improved dual valve springs and lightened valves, allowed the 421 to rev well over 7000 rpm using the McKellar #10 camshaft. Interestingly, all the Swiss Cheese Catalina coupes were delivered from the factory in the same color scheme, silver with a blue interior.

Initially classified as A/FX by NHRA, the Swiss Cheese Catalinas were built to run in B/Factory Experimental. For A/FX, Pontiac unleashed the 421 Tempests. Two varieties were built, 421 Tempest 2-door coupes and 421 Tempest station wagons. All were identical in every respect save the body style; all except one built by Arlen Vanke. Most of the factory-built Tempest A/FX cars were subsequently modified to Vanke's equipment later in the year.

The factory built thirteen cars: seven coupes and six wagons. Each had the same 421 engine as found in the B/FX Catalinas, except a McKellar #11 camshaft was used. That was where the similarities with the Catalinas ended. Although the factory cars retained the

*The mighty Chevrolet 427 Z-11 engine, conservatively rated at 430 horsepower. Although it looks like a late version of the 409 motor, inside the Z-11 was totally different, from the additional .15-inch added to the stroke, to the two-piece high-rise aluminum intake mounting a pair of huge Carter AFBs. Even the fuel pump rod was different from the 409. (Zone Five)*

original drive-line and transaxle from the 326 V-8 Tempests, the Pontiac engineers designed a radical new transmission for use behind the 421 engine. They combined the two-speed planetary gearsets from two Tempest automatic transmissions, replacing the normal torque converter with a manual clutch assembly. One of the two-speed gear setups was mounted in front of the rear axle differential, while the second set was behind it.

However, the clutch was only used to start or stop the Tempest. All upshifts were done without using the clutch. In a few years, this same type of setup (an automatic with a clutch) was known as a "Clutch-Flite." All the factory-built Tempests had aluminum front fenders, hood, and bumpers, with the same modified Ford dump truck scoop on the hood as the B/FX Catalinas. As with the factory-built B/FX Catalinas, the Tempests all shared the same basic paint scheme. The coupes were silver with blue interiors, while the wagons were white with a blue interior. With the aluminum package and the 421 engine, the 421 Tempest coupes weighed in at slightly over 3200 pounds, while the wagons weighed 3450 pounds. How quick were these cars? Several accounts mention Tempest coupes routinely running in the mid to low 11-second bracket.

The car built by Arlen Vanke was totally different from the factory cars. Arlen had purchased a 1963 Tempest coupe for his wife to drive, but within a few weeks of delivery Mrs. Vanke had to find a new way to get around town. Her Tempest had been transformed into a genuine A/FX beast. The Vanke team had pulled the 4-cylinder engine and transaxle assembly out of the car. Into the engine compartment went one of the latest S/D 421 engine packages, the same as found in the factory 421 Tempests.

Instead of running one of the beefed up transaxle assemblies as in the factory Tempests, Vanke used a standard Borg-Warner 4-speed transmission behind the 421. He also replaced the transaxle assembly with a narrowed standard Catalina rear axle assembly. In 1964, this same combination would be known to the world as the Pontiac GTO, but with a 389 engine of course. Pontiac supplied many of the lightweight parts that were being used on the factory Tempests, and it was more than equal to any of the factory-built 421 Tempests.

An interesting note to the '63 Pontiac story comes from Jim Wangers. "In 1963, we had only the two cars to race: the Swiss Cheese Catalina for B/FX which we were very successful with, and the Tempest station wagon for A/FX. After 1963, Royal Pontiac never fielded another true competition car with the Royal banner. We built NHRA legal cars for other people. Not until 1966 and the Royal GTO driven by Milt Schornack, was another Royal car in competition.

"By the way, the two '66 GTO Tiger cars were public relations' vehicles that kept Pontiac and the GTO in the eye of the buying public. We did campaign the one car in C/S at all three NHRA nationals in 1966, Winter, Spring, and Summer. But for the most part, the two GTOs attended the meets with the idea of passing out tickets to the spectators. The winning ticket holder got to drive the one GTO Tiger against a mystery driver from Royal. The 'Mystery Tiger' was all dressed up in a tiger outfit and raced against the holder of the winning ticket. It was a very successful ad campaign, and NHRA went along with it."

## CHEVROLET Z-11

The best of the FX entries had to be the Chevrolet entry, known to the world as the Z-11. RPO Z-11 was an entire package set up just for drag racing. A standard Impala 2-door hardtop was the basis for the Z-11, but, like its Pontiac cousin, the similarities ended there. The entire nose was stamped from 26-gauge aluminum, including hood, front fenders and inner fenders, radiator support panel and fan shroud, and the bumpers were aluminum. No radio, heater, or insulation were installed at the factory. The battery, a commercial heavy-duty unit normally used in buses, was installed in the right rear of the trunk.

Under the hood was an entirely new engine. Although it looked for all the world like a 409, the Z-11 engine was 427 cubic inches. This was achieved by increasing the stroke .15" to 3.615". The bore remained the same as in the 409 at 4 5/16". The pistons were a new design of forged aluminum that featured a taller dome and lightened, but longer, rod. Compression ratio with the Z-11 427 was an aston-

ishing 13.8:1! The camshaft used in the Z-11 was the new Mk. VI with .511" lift.

The dual quad intake manifold was a high port two-piece unit. Both of these items were retained from the '62 Z-11 engine. Unlike the other manufacturers, Chevrolet designed an air intake system that took air in off the base of the windshield, directed it through an opening in the right side of the firewall, and ducted it directly into the specially designed air cleaner assembly into the dual Carter AFBs.

Chevrolet built a total of 57 Z-11 Impala coupes in the 1963 model year. The first batch of 25 Z-11s were released to specific drivers on December 1, 1962, with the first car going to Dave Strickler at Ammon R. Smith Chevrolet in York, Pennsylvania. The second batch of 25 were released to the dealers on January 1, 1963. The final 7 cars were released to dealers sometime in late winter 1963.

It was in January 1963 that I saw my first Z-11 Impala. Actually I saw six of them all at the same dealer. I had purchased a new '63 Corvette from Dutch Folk Chevrolet in Akron, Ohio. I visited this dealership quite often as it was known to be a hot rod dealer. Dutch Folk Chevrolet had built and campaigned one of the rare B/FX Chevy II station wagons. This particular day, my salesman came up to me and asked me to step outside the back of the parts department. Behind the parts building was an area called "the bull pen," a barbed wire enclosure where all the hot rod cars were kept to keep them

*Pontiac built a total of 13 Tempests powered by the 421 super-duty engine: 7 coupes and 6 station wagons. The factory-built Tempests used the regular production transaxle, but had two 2-speed automatic transmissions modified to give a 4-speed automatic with a clutch that was used only to start the car. The Al Hodges Pontiac wagon was driven by Red Snell out of Cocoa, Florida. (Tom Schiltz)*

from being stripped at night. I went outside the back door and saw six white Impala coupes. The flags on the fenders told me they were equipped with the 327 engine (409 cars said "409" above the small crossed flag emblem). I looked inside and saw that they were all 4-speed cars. Looking at the salesman I said, "So what?" assuming they were 327 cars. He said, "Look at the window sticker."

As I read it, it looked like something straight out of the magazines: aluminum fenders, 4-speed transmission, 427 V-8. A 427 V-8?! Chevrolet didn't have a 427 V-8? They did now! The salesman opened one of the hoods, a very flimsy hood that twisted and buckled as it went up. It looked like a 409: W-shaped valve covers, dual quads, and a strange air cleaner that was fastened to the right side of the firewall. Hmmm, very interesting. The Impala sticker price was high for the time, something over $4,100.00.

He also informed me that you had to have some type of special license, either NASCAR or SCCA, to get one of these cars. I never pursued it any further than that. I couldn't buy it so why look at it. Such was my first experience with the legendary Z-11. Later on, we found out that Folk Chevrolet was evidently some type of distribution point for the cars as it was rare for any dealer to even see *one*, much less six. The next time I saw a Z-11, there were again six of them but this time they were at Dragway 42 for the *Drag News* Stock Car Invitational. Each one was driven by a famous Chevrolet driver: Strickler, Nicholson, Sanders, Platt, et al. (More about that meet later in this chapter.)

Terry Prince recalls a similar tale about his first look at a Z-11 Impala. "About three weeks before the '63 Winternationals, I get a

*At the '63 Winternationals, NHRA classified three of the Z-11 Impalas as A/FX because they were running slicks, which were legal in FX class. The other five Z-11s had cheater slicks and NHRA put them into a special class — LP. Here is Tom Sturm's white Z-11 against Mike Lenke and the Bourgeois & Wade Z-11 in an A/FX class match. Sturm won the race with an ET of 11.87, but the class was won by Bill Shrewsberry in the Mickey Thompson 421 Tempest. (NHRA via Leslie Lovett)*

call from Jerry Chastain, the General manager at Service Chevrolet. I was running the dyno in the shop now that Don Nicholson had gone to Atlanta. Chastain said to come up to the showroom. 'I have something to show you.'

"Holy Smoke, this car is awesome! The car in the showroom is a maroon '63 Impala. No big deal you say. Except this one has a few goodies. A 427 engine, all redesigned with good valves, ignition, heads, carburetors, new rumpety-rump cam, and a redesigned valley cover manifold to keep the fuel charge cold.

"But the killer piece was the aluminum front end: fenders, hood, front and rear bumpers. This was commitment. In front of your eyes was the evidence that Chevrolet was serious about racing. And here it was, the '63 Impala Z-11 race car. There aren't very many of them, and if you're going to race a Chevrolet in S/S, you better get one or you can take your car and give it to Grandma for groceries.

"Well after a lot of talking with Chastain, I can't talk *him* into buying it. So I pull out the newspaper ads about the Winternationals and he commits to spending about $1,500.00 on the car, if *I* buy it! Okay, I can't pass this up. So, with some help from Dad ('Another race car! What do you want with another race car?'), it's mine. A down payment of $600.00 and $105.00/month.

"On the way home I stopped at NHRA to have the car checked out by Mr. Desmuke. He said 'Yep, no problem, S/S at the Winternationals.' We then drive the car on the street overnight to Bakersfield just to get some miles on the drivetrain. Then returned to

*The West Coast's number one Ford driver was named Gas Ronda. Ronda's beautiful dark candy red 427 Galaxie was sponsored by Downtown Ford in Los Angeles, and prepared by Les Ritchey's Performance Associates, the Ford specialists in Southern California. He ran A/FX at the '63 Winternationals losing to the M/T 421 Tempest. (Drag Racing Memories)*

the shop at Service Chevrolet, closed down the dyno area, and slept on benches in the garage for the next two weeks. We had 13 days to get the car ready for Pomona.

"The engine comes out and the block is sent for machining. The body comes off and everything that doesn't absolutely have to be there, is taken off. The rear suspension is reinforced. The front end gets set up for extra travel and uplift shocks are installed. A bare 409 motor is installed with the 427 heads and the body is reinstalled. Now the car goes to Horsepower Engineering for a set of tubing headers. Back to the shop with a day to spare. The car is back together and being run-in and tested on the dyno. We're ready to race!"

Is NHRA ready for the Z-11?

## 1963 WINTERNATIONALS

The first test of the new S/S combinations was the 1963 NHRA Winternational Drags, held over the weekend of February 15, 16, 17, 1963. The third "Big Go West" was again held at the Los Angeles County Fairgrounds in Pomona, California. All the big names were there: Don Nicholson, Hayden Proffitt, and Dave Strickler headed the Chevrolet list. The Ramchargers, Bill "Maverick" Golden, and Al van der Woude driving the Dragmaster entry, headed the Dodge contingent.

Plymouth was well represented by the Golden Commandos, Tommy Grove and the *Melrose Missile*, plus a pair of Southern

*The best-known West Coast Plymouth was the* Melrose Missile, *driven by Tommy Grove. This is the restored No. 3 Missile with which Grove won the '63 Winternationals S/S class, having a time of 12.37 and 114.94 mph. Grove was one of the few Dodge/Plymouth drivers to race a 4-speed transmission in S/S, as most of the Mopar contingent opted for the Torqueflite automatic transmission. (Zone Five)*

California favorites, the Milne Brothers' '62 and '63 Plymouths and Darrell Ritchey driving a '63 Plymouth sponsored by Ritchey & Ritchey Flying A Gas Station. Ford entries included Les Ritchey, Bill Lawton and the Tasca Ford, and a local favorite named Gas Ronda. (Ronda's real name was Gasparelli Ronda, but from an early age he went by the nickname of Gas. What a great name for a race driver!) Pontiac was represented by the Mickey Thompson team entry driven by Bill Shrewsberry, 16-year-old Don Gay driving the Gay Pontiac A/Stocker, and of course, the Royal Pontiac team.

The Winternationals would be strange in that some of the Factory Experimental cars were put into an entirely new class created just for the Winternationals: Limited Production, or L/P. The week prior to the Winternationals, Terry Prince and Butch Leal drove their Z-11s to the NHRA tech people for inspection and classification. Bill Desmuke, the head of NHRA tech inspectors, passed

both cars and gave each driver a letter stating the cars were qualified to run in Super Stock class. However, upon arrival at the strip, both Prince and Leal were informed that they would have to compete in a new class called Limited Production. There were not enough of the Z-11s in production to qualify them for either S/S or FX. Yet, three other Z-11s were classed as A/FX. The reason stated was that those Z-11s were running regular slicks, which were legal in FX. The other five Z-11s were said to be running cheater slicks and thus not qualified for FX. It was rumored that Ford was the force behind the Z-11s being thrown together in L/P class. The lightweight Fords were also thrown into L/P, leaving only Dodge and Plymouth entries for both S/S and S/SA classes.

Terry Prince continues the story. "The shocker comes when we get to Pomona. 'Sorry guys, not enough of these cars have been made so we're going to make a special class for you. And you can watch

*Jim Wright makes a pass during the '63 Winternationals in the* Motor Trend Magazine *Super/Stock automatic Dodge. Both* Motor Trend *and* Hot Rod *magazines fielded super stock Mopars in the '62 – '63 seasons. John Geraughty, who also shared the driver chores, kept the big 426 in tune, while Jim Wright set up the chassis. Neither magazine won a major title.* (Matchracemadness)

everyone else race in Super Stock!' After going through the expense of buying the car, and the money and effort to prepare the car for this race, now we're told to watch everyone else race for all the marbles. I can't say I didn't have fun with the car. Running in L/P, A/FX, and A/MP was a ball. But, we bought these cars to run in S/S. To this day, I can't tell you who was the perpetrator of the entire thing. But I can tell you it left a real sour taste in my mouth that remains even today."

When the meet was over, several interesting trends were observed. First, the Dodges and Plymouths literally ruled both stick and automatic Super Stock classes. Al Eckstrand drove the Ramchargers '63 Dodge to both low ET and top speed for a stocker at 12.12 seconds and 117.03 mph. The ET mark was tied with Bill "Maverick" Golden's '63 Dodge, who also turned 12.12. Both cars were running in S/SA class. Tommy Grove was the quickest car in S/S stick class.

There were only twelve cars in S/S class, which was normally filled with Fords, Chevys, and Pontiacs. The rules changes regarding factory availability left only Dodge and Plymouth entries. In the end it was an all-California shoot-out for the trophy between Tommy Grove in the '63 Plymouth *Melrose Missile III* and Al van der Woude driving the '63 Dodge from Dragmaster. Both cars were similarly equipped with 425 hp 426 engines, ram induction, and three-speed manual transmissions. Grove's *Missile* won going away with an ET of 12.37 at 114.94 mph.

Even more interesting was Super Stock automatic class, which had every big name entered. The Ramchargers, Golden Commandos, Maverick, another *Melrose Missile*, and several lesser-known cars from in and around Southern California. The final run was between a pair of these Southern California unknowns: Darrell Ritchey driving the beautiful tan '63 Plymouth, sponsored by Ritchey & Ritchey

*Bill Shrewsberry comes off the line during time trials at the '63 Winternationals. The little blue LeMans coupe was equipped with one of the 405 hp, 421 Super Duty engines, with two 2-speed automatics and the transaxle assembly arranged to offer four forward speeds around. Shrewsberry and K.S. "Tiger" Pittman shared driver duties in the A/FX Lemans, with Shrewsberry taking the A/FX crown with a time of 12.04 at 116.27 mph. (Matchracemadness)*

*Easily the biggest name in Dodge race cars on the West Coast was Bill "Maverick" Golden. His "yellow cab" S/SA Dodge was always in the running for Top Stock wherever he appeared. "Maverick" introduced many innovations, including dual traction bars facing both front and rear, and modified shift points in the Torqueflite transmission. NHRA banned the traction bar set-up.* (Tom Schiltz)

Flying A Gas Station, having 415 hp; and Bill Hanyon driving the Milne Brothers '62 Plymouth. Hanyon's 420 hp '62 Plymouth won the class with a time of 12.30 seconds at 115.38 mph.

A/Stock class was made up of many of the same cars that had competed for Top Stock Eliminator at the previous Winternationals and Nationals. The 409 Chevys, 406 Fords, and 421 Pontiacs were all veterans of the Indy Nationals. The final run for A/Stock honors was between a real veteran — Dave Strickler driving the *Old Reliable II* 409 Chevy that had won SS/S class at the Indy Nationals — and a new kid who would become a familiar name from this date on — 16-year-old Don Gay driving the '62 421 Pontiac out of Gay Pontiac stables in Dickenson, Texas. At the green light the old veteran hole-shotted the young kid and won going away, posting an ET of 12.38 seconds and scoring top speed of any true stocker at 115.68 mph. Young Don Gay was close on his heels and would reverse the tables at the Nationals later that year.

The Limited Production class was made up of five Z-11 Chevys and a number of 427 Ford Galaxie fastback hardtops with the light-weight fiberglass front-end pieces. The Z-11s were clearly dominant in the class. Bill Lawton's Tasca Ford L/P car beat Les Ritchey's Bob Ford entry, which in turn went down in defeat to Butch Leal's Z-11 in the next round. Hayden Proffitt's Cone Chevrolet entry, was the favorite to win the class based on his performance in SS/S at the '62 Nationals. In Round 1 he fell to Terry Prince, the new kid out of Service Chevrolet.

The final run came down to Frank Sanders in the Rudolph Chevrolet Z-11, against Terry Prince and his Z-11. Sanders took control on the top end, beating Prince with an ET of 12.01. Prince was right beside Sanders going through the traps, and turned a losing time of 12.03. Sanders' Z-11 was found to have an illegal camshaft and thus disqualified, and NHRA did not award the trophy to the second place finisher. The entire class was disqualified leaving Terry Prince with another bitter taste in his mouth for NHRA competition. On top of that, Sanders was banned from NHRA racing for the 1964 season.

The FX classes were a real hodgepodge of entries with the big Ford and Chevy entries being forced in L/P. Aluminum-nosed '63 Pontiacs such as Jim Wangers' Royal Pontiac entry, fell into A/FX, even though the car was built for B/FX. As did the sole Ramcharger car with the new aluminum front end. The class win went to Bill Shrewsberry driving the Mickey Thompson 421 Tempest at 12.04 seconds and 116.27 mph. The few Chevrolet Z-11s that qualified for A/FX fell to the little Tempest, including Hayden Proffitt, who drove Tom Sturm's Z-11 after he had lost in L/P to Terry Prince.

Some of the new 427 Fords with fiberglass front ends dropped into B/FX, as did 409 Chevy Impalas equipped with the Z-11 intake manifold. Dick Harrell won the B/FX class with his black '62 Impala Z-11, but was disqualified for illegal cylinder heads.

*Another long distance racer was Bill Lawton and the Tasca Ford S/S Galaxie, The Go-Getter II, who towed all the way from Providence, Rhode Island for the '63 Winternationals. The car had the recently released lightweight front end package and NHRA put it into L/P against the Z-11 Chevys. Lawton lost to Butch Leal's Z-11 in Round Two of L/P.* (Drag Racing Memories)

C/FX class was the most interesting in makeup as many teams took advantage of the rules that allowed cross-breeding of engine parts from the same year. There were a couple of '62 Chevys that were equipped with 283ci engines and 327 crankshafts giving a final size of 302 cubic inches. These cars were equipped with the special high-performance Corvette heads, and at least one had the 62 fuel-injection system installed. In C/FX, a '62 Chevy driven by Joe Ritter won the class at 14.72 seconds ET. One of the Chrysler entries was the '62 Dodge Dart driven by Ron Root, a Los Angeles policeman, equipped with a slant-6 engine that had a Carter AFB four barrel on a modified ram manifold.

On Sunday the first round of Top Stock Eliminator was run. The fastest 50 stockers lined the staging lanes when the call went out for Top Stock. This included all 34 S/S and S/SA cars, and the fastest of the A/S and A/SA cars. Using a staggered start with the new Christmas Tree start system (wherein the slower class got a few tenths of a second head start based on the class national record), the cars were paired off. Another new wrinkle in the NHRA rules for Top Stock was that all hoods would remain closed once the first race had started. There would be no tinkering of any kind, no icing of radiators and manifolds, and no addition of water or oil. It would play an important part in the final rounds of Top Stock.

Dave Strickler's *Old Reliable II* A/Stocker drew Darrell Ritchey's *Hawaiian Punch* '63 Plymouth and came out on the short end. The winning cars in both S/S and S/SA were matched up and Bill Hanyon beat Tommy Grove's *Melrose Missile III* by .07 seconds! The Ford and Pontiac entries were eliminated about the end of the third round. Ritchey's tan Plymouth S/SA shut down Don Gay's big A/S Pontiac in the quarter-final rounds. The last six cars in Top Stock were five Plymouths and the Ramchargers' Dodge. Al Eckstrand drove the Ramchargers' *Candymatic* Dodge past Ritchey's Plymouth to set up the final round of three cars, which rapidly became two.

The final three were Eckstrand and the Ramchargers' car, Doug Lovegrove and the Mashak Plymouth, and the Golden Commandos' '63 Plymouth driven by Bill Shirey. When the call came for the final two rounds, the Golden Commandos' Plymouth drew Lovegrove, with the Ramchargers' car making a bye or single run. The fierce competition finally started taking a toll. Lovegrove noticed a vibration in his '63 Plymouth that got worse the closer to the starting line that he got. He finally had to turn off the engine and open the hood, thus he was eliminated. Some bolts had vibrated loose in the torque converter which could have been disastrous had Lovegrove not shut it down at the starting line.

That left only two cars in the running for Top Stock. Instead of a bye for both cars, it was decided to run them heads-up for the Top Stock trophy. Both of these cars were also having problems. The Plymouth had a loose throttle linkage that was causing some very erratic runs. One time the throttle would open all the way, the next time it would bind and not allow full throttle. The Ramchargers' Dodge had even bigger problems. A new transmission had been

installed just prior to the Top Stock eliminations and someone had left a filler plug out allowing transmission fluid to run out on every run. After five runs the transmission was starting to slip from the low fluid pressure.

The two cars pulled to the line and staged — Eckstrand and the Ramchargers' Dodge in the left lane and Shirey in the Golden Commandos' Plymouth in the right. Eckstrand staged a couple of feet behind the starting light beam. This allowed the car to creep forward a bit when the power was brought up to launch RPM. When the green light came on both cars leaped out of the chute. The Plymouth throttle worked perfectly and the Ramchargers transmis-

*Frank Sanders makes a pass at the '63 Winternationals in the Rudolph Chevrolet Z-11 Impala. For some reason, NHRA classified the Z-11 Chevrolets into two different categories: A/Factory Experimental if the car arrived with racing slicks on the rear; and Limited Production if the car came to Pomona wearing super stock cheater slicks. Sanders' mint green Z-11 won L/P class with a time of 12.01 at 119.01 mph. (NHRA via Leslie Lovett)*

sion didn't slip a bit. About the halfway point, the Dodge started to pull away and Eckstrand held on to win by about a car length over Shirey at 12.44 seconds and 115.08 mph.

Eckstrand's Top Stock Eliminator was a standard 1963 Dodge 330 2-door sedan, equipped with a 426ci Ramcharger. Other than a super tuning job performed by Eckstrand and his crew, the big Dodge had only three modifications: a set of tubing headers designed by the Ramchargers team themselves, a floor-mounted Hurst shifter that worked the 727 Torqueflite to perfection, and a set of the new M&H Racemaster Super Stock tires. The Golden Commandos' Plymouth was equipped almost the same.

At the AHRA Winternationals Drags held at Phoenix Dragway, the results were interesting to say the least. Under AHRA rules, the Ford and Chevy lightweights were allowed to run in S/S classes. Virtually the same field of cars that had competed at the NHRA meet were at Phoenix, and many of the times were dipping into the 11-second bracket. Al Eckstrand drove the aluminum-nose Ramchargers' Dodge to low ET at 11.78 seconds during time trials, with the Z-11 Chevys right on his heels.

One of the more interesting tales of the AHRA meet involved the team of Dick Harrell and Grady Bryant. Harrell had one of the new Z-11 Chevrolets running in S/S, while Bryant had a B/S 409 Chevy.

Their partnership was a low-budget operation and they used to tow each other to the strips using log chains instead of a tow bar! They couldn't afford a tow vehicle. Changing the rear axle ratio from 4.88:1 to a standard 3.36:1 ratio in the big Z-11, Harrell log-chained Bryant's B/S Chevy all the way from Carlsbad, New Mexico, to the drags at Phoenix and then back home again, a trip of some 400 miles each way! Once at the strip, they changed the rear axle ratio back to 4.56 and went racing — at least, that's the story going around.

With all the big names in attendance, the run for Top Stock was expected to really be a show. During the day, the AHRA technical people got wind of some shenanigans going on in the stocker pits with

*Bill "Maverick" Golden against Don Gay during time trials at the '63 Winternationals. Maverick's Dragmaster-prepared Dodge was a favorite in Southern California but he would suffer with mechanical ills throughout the meet. Young Don Gay, 15 years old at the '63 Winternationals, would lose to Dave Strickler in A Stock competition, but he gained his revenge at the '63 Nationals. (Matchracemadness)*

regards to fuel. When Top Stock was called to the staging lanes all cars were directed to drain all the fuel from their gas tanks, then refill from the tanker truck that offered ultra high test gas to all the racers. A funny thing happened to all those cars that were running in the high 11-second bracket. They ran rough, missing and coughing during the eliminations. Strickler's big Z-11 wouldn't run at all! The only one that did run was Harrell's. He had been using strip gas all along.

Most of the 11-second hot shoes were put down in the first rounds. The final run was between two unknowns: Darrell Ritchey driving the tan Ritchey & Ritchey Flying A '63 Plymouth, and Dick Harrell's white '63 Z-11 Chevrolet that had just log-chained another race car some 400 miles to the strip. The Plymouth had been running about .30 quicker than the Chevy throughout the meet. The first race was disqualified with a red light start. Under NHRA rules, a red light start was instant elimination for the guy that jumped the starter. However, under AHRA rules, the race was simply rerun. This time both lights went green and Harrell charged out of the gate. His hole shot was enough and Harrell won a close race at 12.91 seconds.

At the end of the two winter meets, the score was Dodge — 1, Chevy — 1. Between the winter meets and the Nationals there were records to be set, points to accumulate in the Points Championships, and something new that was added — match races. Match racing had been around for many years although most of it was done by the

*The* Drag News *"Mr. Stock Eliminator" Top Ten, with Terry Prince in at #5. (Terry Prince)*

*The run for the #5 spot on the* Drag News *"Mr. Stock Eliminator" list was between Terry Prince, holder of the #5 spot, and challenger Mike Lenke with the black Bourgeois & Wade Z-11. The match race was held at San Gabriel Drag Strip in the Summer of 1963. Anyone could challenge for positions 6 through 10, but only a member of the top ten could challenge for the top five spots. (Terry Prince)*

biggest names in racing, the top fuel guys. The big supercharged gas cars had gotten into match racing the year before, but again, only between the biggest names. Now it was time for match racing the big super stockers.

Terry Prince recalls. "All right, so we can't run S/S. Let's go see where we can race. The March Meet at Bakersfield. I'm not sure what the class was called, but there was more than just Z-11s in it. Both Ford and Chrysler had some L/P cars at Bakersfield. Slicks were allowed and most of the cars had them. I stayed with my 7" Caslers for two reasons. One, I couldn't afford new slicks. And two, I couldn't afford new slicks. I ran at Bakersfield, but lost to Butch Leal in the early rounds.

"One of the real icons for drag racing was *Drag News.* Even though it's been out of print for many years, it's still the model for getting the news to the racers quickly, and for building interest and promoting races. *Drag News* wasn't fancy, but it had more news

*Naturally, the first to receive the new 1963 Dodge super stock package was the team that, for all intent and purpose, created it — The Ramchargers. The Ramchargers Candymatics, both of them, were standard Dodge 330 sedans with the Stage II engine and aluminum front end package. Somewhere along the line, both cars became Dodge 500 sedans, of which Dodge built exactly none. NHRA allowed minor customizing, so the Ramchargers team added fancy taillight trim and bumpers to the rear, a legal way to change the weight distribution of the car. (Jack Bleil)*

*On the other side of Detroit was the Plymouth equivalent to the Ramchargers team. They were called "The Golden Commandos," and were sponsored by Hamilton Motors. The Commandos campaigned three cars in 1963 — this Stage II sedan in S/SA (incorrectly marked in this early photo), a station wagon also in S/SA, and later in the year another sedan in A/FX. Bill Shirey lost to Doug Lovegrove with the S/SA car at the '63 Winternationals.(Drag Racing Memories)*

*Ad for the match race between Bourgeois & Wade and Terry Prince for the Drag News #5 spot. (Terry Prince)*

than advertising. And you had it in your hand by Tuesday after the weekend's races. There were all kinds of 'wars' — camshaft wars, header wars, tire wars; and of course the driver or team wars. Those days are long gone, and I don't think we had a clue as to what we had at the time.

"Match race! Fontana, 'Drag City' to Californians and Jan & Dean fans, always had a good program. Top fuel, supercharged gassers, stockers, even jet cars. Jet cars, what a sight! One Saturday night, I'm approached by a track official. It seems some people thought it would be a good idea to see a jet car run against a stocker!

"'OK Mr. Prince, for $50.00, you will start at the 1/8th mile spot. Mr. Romeo Palamides and his jet car will start at the starting line.

Since he doesn't have complete control of the exact moment his afterburner will kick in, we will put a flagman in front of you. When he sees the jet car move, he will flag you off.' Sure, $50.00. If I can do this four times, I can afford that new set of slicks for the car.

"Let me tell you what a jet car that's going 200+ mph is like when it passes within a few feet of you. Have you ever had a truck pass you on the highway when you're just standing on the shoulder? The windstream at 60-70 mph is enough to blow you over. But I don't know that at this point. I figure that from the 1/8 mile point, I'm doing about 100 in the traps. The image in the mirror is that of a giant

black hole chasing you. And it's getting bigger by the second. And along with that awesome image chasing you down, is this ungodly sound — WHOOOOOOOOOOOOOOOOO. BAM!

"While Palamides is threading the needle at 200 mph, between me and the side of the strip, he goes by and immediately blows my car about eight to ten feet sideways. And I'm doing over 100! I fight to keep the car upright and in one piece for the next eight to ten seconds. The rest of the night I spend trying to figure out what sanitarium the guy escaped from. And who talked ME into this?!

"The *Drag News* Mr. Stock Eliminator List; what a great concept.

*Bill Hanyon makes a pass at the '63 Winternationals with the Milne Bros. '62 Plymouth. The Milne Bros. Fury was equipped with the 420 hp version of the 413 Super Stock engine. Hanyon swept aside all the competition in Super Stock Automatic at the '63 Winternationals with the '62 car, turning a time of 12.30 at 115.38 mph on the trophy run. (Matchracemadness)*

You start with the top ten stock drag cars in the nation, establish a format where anyone on the list can challenge any other member of the list for his spot, including the No. 1 spot. But if you aren't in the Top Ten, you can only challenge for spots 6-10 on the list. The spot holder gets the advantage of setting up the match race at the strip of his choice, usually his home strip, and he calls the strip owner and cuts a deal for both appearance and prize money.

"The holder of the spot wins. The strip operator wins. The challenger wins. And the fans win. Everyone wins. This concept opened the door for the stock classes to start making some big money just to appear at a particular strip. In 1963, I had five match races on the West Coast and reached the #5 spot on the *Drag News* list. I remember running Jack Bayer's Z-11, Earl Wade driving the Mike Lenke Z-11, Dave's Chevron, etc. We also traveled to Madera, Fresno, and Vaca Valley for other races. All in all, it was a great year. But when it was over I had to sell the car while it still had some value."

In the southern part of the U.S., the stocker was king. Southern drag strips had begun matching up Super/Stock cars from all over

*The city of Atlanta not only had the biggest name in Chevrolet racing, Don Nicholson, it also had "Flyin' Phil" Bonner, salesman for Al Means Ford. Bonner fielded two cars in 1963. The Al Means Ford car was a legal S/S car (most of the time), with the lightweight front end package and 427 Hi-Riser engine. The other car was the LaFayette Ford match race car, that Bonner built but didn't drive. It was driven by various Ford NASCAR racers at headline-drawing match races with other NASCAR teams and drivers. (Drag Racing Memories)*

the nation with big money prizes (top money prize for a class winner in stock classes was $50.00 at NHRA meets). The strip promoters knew that a match race between the fastest Ford and fastest Chevy would pack the stands. It was just such an environment that lured Don Nicholson away from his home and friends in Southern California for Atlanta, Georgia in the Spring of 1962. Drag strip owners were now paying super stock drivers money just to make an appearance at their raceways. Of course, there was always someone waiting to take on the factory guys.

These match races were run under southern rules, i.e. "Run what you brung." Anything went as long as the car had the appearance of a stocker and weighed in at a set standard. Many of the match race cars bore little resemblance to the same vehicle when it competed in a sanctioned stock class. Interiors were gutted down to having a single bucket seat. Lightweight body components were allowed. Any size engine was allowed. Also, any gasoline was allowed, including some that emitted a very strange odor.

There were some ingenious methods of making these cars much lighter than normal. At least two drivers moved the entire body of their cars 1" to the rear on the frame mounts, thus creating, for all intent and purpose, the first altered wheelbase cars. Dick Brannan's Ford is reported to have had no springs in the rear seat at all. The only thing holding the upholstery off the floor was string. Dave Strickler's *Old Reliable II* had large sections of metal removed from the ends of the firewall and replaced with mylar tape, which was painted white to match the rest of the body.

The Ramchargers weighed in right on the money at one match race and then towed to their parking spot in the pits, where it took three men to remove <u>each</u> rear slick! The reason — each tire was filled with water and weighed over 200 pounds each! With the regular tires used for racing, the big Dodge was now about 400 pounds under the weight limit set for southern-style racing.

It's interesting to note that both Dave Strickler and Don Nicholson opted to match race their '62 Chevrolet Bel Air hardtops rather than modify the big '63 Z-11 cars that were actively competing in A/FX around the nation. Neither car was anything like the A/S car from which they evolved. The Strickler car had an engine that was about 460 cubic inches, and used the aluminum front end pieces. At times, the interior was removed. The results? A car that ran 12.3-second ETs in A/S class when it was legal, was now capable of very low 11-second times under match race rules! All the major players in super stock racing took part in match racing to one degree or another.

Record runs and points meets were a different story. They could be called Regional or Divisional Drags, or Points Meets, or simply Record Runs. At these races, the cars had to meet all the necessary rules that governed the class they were entered in, be they NHRA or AHRA rules. Points were awarded for national records that were set, and for class and eliminator victories in the chase for Points Championships.

Several national records were set and reset throughout 1963. At the end of 1962, the record for SS/S was held jointly by Dick

*One of the more famous names in the southern match race circuit was that of Ronnie Sox. Teamed with Buddy Martin, "Mr. 427" received one of the second batch of 25 Z-11s produced by Chevrolet, because of his success with his SS/S '62 409 Bel Air, Carolina Thunder. The Sox & Martin team, along with the Don Nicholson team, and Dave Strickler's* Old Reliable, *were virtually unbeatable in 1963. (Drag Racing Memories)*

Ladeen's 1962 Dodge, with an ET record of 12.71 seconds; and Dick Harrell's '62 Chevrolet with a recorded top speed of 111.47 mph. The S/S record was held by Bob Harrop's '61 Pontiac at 109.54 seconds. Bill "Maverick" Golden held down both ends of the SS/SA record at 12.50 and 112.40 mph. In FX class, the Dragmaster *Golden Lancer* set the A/FX record at 12.26 seconds at an August 1962 meet at Pomona. Dave Strickler's *Old Reliable III* held the B/FX speed record at 112.60 mph. Tom Sturm set the C/FX record at 14.15 seconds and 100.24 mph in his '62 Chevrolet.

None of those records would stand for long. Several class records were changed because of the new 1963 rules that eliminated such classes as SS/S and SS/SA. Ladeen's record now stood for S/S, Harrell's was now a A/S record, Bob Harrop was now in B/S, Maverick's SS/SA record was now the S/SA time to beat, and so on throughout the various classes. It could get confusing.

The Winternationals at Pomona saw several of those marks fall. Tommy Grove's *Melrose Missile III* set a new standard in S/S at 12.50 seconds. Dave Strickler's *Old Reliable II* took the A/S record away from Dick Harrell with a time of 12.66 at 114.58 mph. Darrell Ritchey's '63 Plymouth set the S/SA record at 12.33 and 115.03 mph. The records in FX stood.

By the Fall of 1963, several records had been broken again and again, often by the same people who had set the original standard. The Potter Brothers' '63 Plymouth out of Spokane, Washington, set the S/S national ET mark at 12.45 seconds and 117.84 mph, which lasted for about a week before Dick Brannan broke it again with his

'63 427 Galaxy at York, Pennsylvania. York was the home strip for Dave Strickler and the *Old Reliable* team. Dave took the opportunity to reset his own B/FX record to 12.32 seconds and 117.49 mph.

The A/FX record took a beating in December 1963 when first the Tasca Ford '63 427 Fairlane pushed the speed record to 121.29 mph. However, it was the Grand Finale Drags held at Half Moon Bay, California when everything broke loose. No less than 21 national records were set, including 17 stock and stock sports records. Plymouths reigned supreme in the top stock classes as Tommy Grove drove the *Melrose Missile III* to a new S/S record at 12.00 seconds and 118.26 mph; and Hayden Proffitt, now driving a new Plymouth A/FX car out of Yeakel Plymouth in Downey, California, set the ET record for A/FX at 11.97 seconds. It was the first official 11-second stocker record, although Grove's 12.00 S/S record was as close behind as you could get. Even that record didn't last as "Akron Arlen" Vanke took the new A/FX 421 Tempest to Alton, Illinois and set both ends of the A/FX record at 11.89 and 123.11 mph.

## CHANGES IN RANKS

In the Spring of 1963, there were some changes within the ranks of Super Stock. One of the biggest was Al Eckstrand splitting away from the Ramchargers' team, in a dispute over who was going to

Tom "Smoker" Smith drove the Smoker #2 S/SA Plymouth for the Rickar & Davis Plymouth dealer in Washington, DC. The gold Plymouth was one of the early Stage I Super Stock Plymouths without the aluminum front end and hood scoop. With home-built tubing headers in the front fenderwell, Smith's Plymouth would usually run in the mid-12-second bracket at Aquasco, Dragway. (Drag Racing Memories)

drive and how many drivers the team actually had. Eckstrand had been the driver at the Winternationals, winning Stock Eliminator with the Ramchargers' Dodge. However, Jim Thornton and Herman Mozer both had begun driving the car. Eckstrand decided that three drivers were two too many, and left the team.

Eckstrand bought his own Dodge and began campaigning the car without any sponsorship at all. Of course, with his connections at Chrysler (he was an attorney for the corporation), he didn't have too much trouble getting the necessary parts to make his car competitive with anyone, including the vaunted Ramchargers. His new '63 Dodge was appropriately named *Lawman*. In addition, Hayden Proffitt left Chevrolet for Plymouth, becoming the driver for Lou Baney's Yeakel Plymouth dealership.

There were three big meets prior to the Nationals: the first Annual AHRA Summer Championship Drags, the *Drag News* Invitational, and the Detroit Nationals. The AHRA Summer Championships were held at Aquasco, Maryland over the first weekend in June. Many of the top East Coast stockers were in attendance including Malcolm Durham's Z-11 Chevrolet, Tasca Ford's *Go Getter* Galaxie, Harold Ramsey's Union Park Pontiac, and Jim Wangers with the big Royal Pontiac Swiss Cheese Catalina that ran A/S under AHRA rules.

Durham captured the trophy for S/S with a time of 12.53 seconds. The Royal car shut down everyone in A/S with a slower than normal ET of 13.16 seconds. In S/SA, Dick Lawrence swept by the compe-

The #2 Z-11 went to "Dyno Don" Nicholson running out of Nalley Chevrolet in Atlanta, Georgia. The first 25 Z-11s had front end sheet metal stamped from 26-gauge aluminum, making them very prone to dents and tears. Note the tear on the bottom of the front fender. Another interesting point in this photo is the outer headlight being taped in place, as "Dyno Don" normally had fresh air ducts coming through the outer headlight buckets. (Drag Racing Memories)

tition with the Sites Brothers' '63 Plymouth out of Kansas City, Missouri, turning ETs in the 12.30s. Top Stock Eliminator came down to those three cars with the final being the Royal Pontiac Catalina against Lawrence in the big Plymouth. Lawrence cut his fastest ET to down the big Pontiac, and won going away at 12.30 seconds and 115.40 mph.

Over the 7th of July weekend, *Drag News* held its first annual Invitationals at Dragway 42, West Salem, Ohio. The highlight was of course, the super stocks that were in attendance. Six Z-11 Chevys were driven by Nicholson, Strickler, Platt, Lenke, Schartman, and Sanders. The Ramchargers brought two cars, the Golden Commandos brought three. From California came Maverick Golden and Bill Hanyon with the Milne Brothers' Plymouth. Pontiac was more than well represented with the likes of Arlen Vanke and Arnie Beswick, who brought no less than three cars.

Throughout the day, the eliminations were run. The Z-11 Chevys were all a bit off of their usual pace and fell one by one to the big Pontiacs. The Ramchargers turned back two of the three Golden Commando entries, then lost to Beswick. Maverick beat local favorite Wes Koogle's Dodge, then turned around and lost to Vanke. The Chevys seemed to delight in beating each other, as that was the way they were paired up. Nicholson first beat Sanders, then turned around and lost to Strickler, who then got beat by the new A/FX Tempest from Vanke.

*When the 1963 model year was introduced, Ford's entry for Top Stock remained the 405 horsepower, 406ci engine in a standard "notchback" hardtop body. Before the '63 Winternationals, Ford switched to the 427 engine rated at 425 horsepower. Dal Bargman's '63 Galaxie has one of the rare 406 motors, and ran C/Stock at Rocky Mountain Dragway in 1966, setting the national record in 1965. (Pete Garramone)*

*Malcolm Durham built and drove the Hicks Chevrolet Strip Blazer Z-11 out of Washington, DC. Durham, known as the "DC Lip," was one of the very few black super stock drivers at that time. This photo was taken at Aquasco, Maryland drag strip during the AHRA Summernationals where the "DC Lip" won S/S class in June 1963. Durham's Z-11 also set the NHRA record for A/MP in 1964 with an ET of 11.73. (Drag Racing Memories)*

*Ford answered the challenge of the Z-11 Chevys with the lightweight Galaxie hardtops, powered by the 427 Hi-Riser Ford engine. Even with fiberglass front fenders, doors, and hood, the Galaxies were still too heavy to be competitive in A/FX. However, by the time of the Nationals, the big Galaxies had been built in sufficient numbers to be classed Super Stock. This is Dick Brannan's Lively One S/S national record holder. (Drag Racing Memories)*

When it was all over, Top Eliminator was the Ramchargers' AA/Fuel Dragster. In the winner's circle as Top Stock Eliminator was a little white Tempest station wagon. Beswick's *Mrs. B's Grocery Getter*, won the *Drag News* meet with a time of 12.10. However, the racing wasn't over yet. Platt challenged Vanke for his spot on the *Drag News* Top Ten, but was turned back in three straight. He then turned around and made a single blast in an attempt on the A/FX record. This he accomplished with a run of 11.93.

The weekend immediately prior to the big Labor Day meets saw a gathering of the biggest names in stock drag racing at Detroit Dragway. Gil Kohn, owner of Detroit Dragway, put up a $4,000.00 purse to the overall winner of Top Stock at "his" Nationals. The Detroit Stock Car Nationals were different from other national meets anywhere else. All the cars competed against each other, in "run what 'ya brung" southern-style racing. The Z-11s competed against the big Dodges and Plymouths; the 421 Tempest coupes and wagons were running against the big Ford entries. At this meet, anything went. If it was available in any manner, it could be used on any of the entries.

The big Fords had the new high riser dual-quad intake and latest heads, along with the fiberglass front fenders and hood. Pontiac introduced the new Iskendarian 505 camshaft and offered a Ford dump truck hood scoop as optional equipment — both with Pontiac

*Even Mr. Top Eliminator himself, "Big Daddy" Don Garlits, had a super stock car in the early 1960s. However, the Garlits Dodge was usually driven by close friend Jim Kaylor, who also had piloted the Garlits '62 Dodge to many match race victories, including a big win over Don Nicholson at Covington, Georgia in late 1962. Note the high front/low rear attitude, the prevailing chassis set up of literally all super stockers of the era. (Matchracemadness)*

part numbers! A few of the Tempests were converted from transaxles to standard Pontiac rear axle assemblies. The Ramchargers entered a car that was so new that it had no lettering yet. Stan Antlocer had top speed in the Stan Long Tempest wagon, running 119.36 mph.

Kohn had two separate races set up: a Saturday night Class Elimination and a Sunday afternoon Top Stock crown. Most of the cars were en route to the NHRA National Championships at Indy and stopped off at Detroit to tune the cars and make a little money. Hayden Proffitt towed in all the way from Los Angeles, as did Gas Ronda and the Downtown Ford entry, and Bill "Maverick" Golden and his taxi yellow Dodge. Don Nicholson, one of the best Chevy

handlers in the country had a pair of cars at Detroit, his own and the Jackshaw Chevrolet car driven by protégé Ed Schartman. Neither Chevy was up to the task of handling the big Mopars on this weekend.

Right off the tow bar Proffitt cranked a 12.10 second ET. Hayden, one of the best drivers in the country, started wading through the lineup of super stockers, beating Bob Harrop's *Flying Carpet* Dodge and the new Ramcharger car to make the finals. In the other lane from Proffitt was Dick Dyke and the Wilson Motors Plymouth. He had gotten to the finals by beating the Ramchargers "A" car, Bill Shirey in the Golden Commando Plymouth, and Roger Lindamood in the *Color Me Gone* Plymouth. The two Plymouths

*Bakersfield, March 1963. Doug Robinson makes a pass during the '63 Bakersfield Fuel & Gas Championships in the Horsepower Engineering Super Stock Automatic Dodge. Robinson's Horsepower Engineering shop built custom tube headers for stockers and super stockers throughout Southern California, including Bill "Maverick" Golden's Dodge. (Matchracemadness)*

*At the AHRA Summernationals, both Don Nicholson and his protégé, Eddie Schartman, were in attendance. Schartman's Jackshaw Chevrolet Z-11, which was built from extra parts in the Nicholson shop, was teamed with "Dyno Don" at several meets in the Summer of 1963. In a heads-up race, the partnership set aside temporarily. Nicholson's car is just to the right of Schartman's. (Drag Racing Memories)*

## 1963 NATIONALS

The 1963 NHRA Nationals promised to be the biggest "Big Go" yet, and it delivered on that promise in every aspect — especially in the stocker camps. Every major name in the sport was there, and every manufacturer. It was already well known that both GM entries in the super stock wars, Chevrolet and Pontiac, would be withdrawn from factory-backed competition following the end of the 1963 drag season. Yet for one last time, they were all in attendance and competing against each other. Well at least they were competing, albeit not necessarily against each other.

The Nationals were almost a repeat of the '63 Winternationals, with Dodges and Plymouths completely dominating S/S and S/SA classes. Chevrolet and Pontiac with basically the same combinations that competed at the '62 Nationals, were no competition. The lightweight Ford Galaxies, although allowed to compete in S/S, simply didn't have the horsepower to beat the big Dodge and Plymouth entries. Both Chevrolet and Pontiac did make an appearance though, in the Factory Experimental classes, which they dominated.

In S/S and S/SA were the Ramchargers with two *Candymatics*, Bud Faubel's *Honker* Dodge, Tommy Grove and a couple of *Melrose Missiles*, John Barker's Cavalier Dodge, the Golden Commandos brought no less than three entries (two sedans and a station wagon), and '63 Winternationals Top Stock driver Al Eckstrand brought his

left the line together, with the black Yeakel car pulling away about half way down, then holding on for the win at 12.36.

The runoff on Sunday for Top Stock was a totally different story, however. The Ramchargers "A" car, the *Candymatic*, was once again running as it should, turning ETs in the 12.10 range. Against Proffitt, Jim Thornton pushed the *Candymatic* to low elapsed time of the meet at 12 seconds flat. Proffitt went 12.19 in a losing cause. It was a sign of things to come the following weekend when the Ramchargers' team took charge of the entire NHRA show at Indy.

The Ramchargers' cars took advantage of every little loophole in the rules to gain an advantage. An example of this was the fact that both Ramchargers Dodges were 330 2-door sedans with 500 series chrome and emblems; but Dodge didn't make a 500 sedan! The 500 series cars were hardtop and convertible models, with extra chrome and bumper guards; dress-up items mostly. The cars retained the 330 interiors, and they had Hurst floor shifts to control the Torqueflite — the only car so-equipped at the Winternationals.

One of the areas that was open to interpretation was "minor customizing." NHRA rules allowed minor customizing in any class. The Ramchargers took advantage of this by adding the 500 chrome around the taillights, the 500 rear bumper and bumper guards, and some other 500 items — always on the rear of the car. This made the cars weigh about the same as a stock 330 Ramcharger car, which made up for the fact that the Ramchargers had acid-dipped certain parts like the doors, to lighten the front end.

*The Sites Bros. Stage II Plymouth,* Suction II, *was driven by Dick Lawrence out of Kansas City, Missouri. At the AHRA Summernationals, held at Aquasco, Maryland in the first weekend of June 1963, Lawrence not only won S/SA class over a field that included the Ramchargers and Golden Commandos, he also took Top Stock Eliminator when he beat Jim Wangers and the Royal Pontiac swiss-cheese Catalina, turning a 12.30 and 115.40 mph. (Drag Racing Memories)*

new *Lawman* Dodge. One driver that would rather switch than fight was Hayden Proffitt. Proffitt, the '62 Top Stock Eliminator in a 409 Chevy, who had one of the potent Z-11 Chevys earlier in the year, was now piloting a new '63 Plymouth from Yeakel Plymouth. Ford was well represented with entries from Tasca Ford, Gas Ronda, Len Richter's Bob Ford entry, and of course, Mr. Ford himself, Dick Brannan brought *The Lively One* out of Romy-Hames Ford.

*The Aquasco Dragway flagman gives the go signal for trophy run in A/S at the AHRA Summernationals. Jim Wangers defeated the Ford for the A/S victory but lost Top Stock Eliminator to Dick Lawrence and the Sites Bros. '63 Plymouth. Under NHRA rules, the Royal 421 Catalina would run in B/FX class.* (Author's Collection)

In A/S and A/SA, the entry list had all the flavor of the '62 Nationals with Don Nicholson and Dave Strickler driving the same cars they had competed with the previous year. Bill Abraham brought the *Golden Arrow II* A/SA, but he had major headaches from a new name that would become legend in the years to come: Ron Mandella. Another 409 Chevy from the Jenkins Competition shop was the red '62 Bel Air coupe named *Northwind*, that was handled by three of the Strickler-Jenkins team members: Joe Tryson, Arnie Waldman, and Joe Gardner.

Another Chevy driver that defected was Tom Sturm. Sturm had been the '62 Worlds Points Champ in stock class driving a C/FX '62 Bel Air coupe. He also had piloted a new Z-11 Impala at the '63 Winternationals. For this year's Nationals, Sturm was in a new '63 Mercury powered by a 427ci engine that was all set up for A/Stock. His main competition in A/S was the youngster from Dickinson, Texas, Don Gay, driving the Gay Pontiac '62 Catalina sedan.

In A/FX, the majority of the entrants were driving Z-11

Chevrolets. Dave Strickler brought the fourth version of *Old Reliable*. Don Nicholson was there with two cars, one driven by himself and the other by "Fast Eddie" Schartman. Ronnie Sox and Buddy Martin brought the Friendly Chevrolet Z-11 out of Burlington, North Carolina. Frank Sanders towed in all the way from Phoenix, Arizona, only slightly less distant than Mike Lenke with the Bourgeois & Wade Z-11. Several Dodge and Plymouth entries using new over-the-counter parts were also forced into A/FX class.

The big news in A/FX was the introduction of the intermediate cars powered by the biggest engines available. There were several of the 421 Tempests including Arnie Beswick, Arlen Vanke, and Jim Wangers and the Royal Pontiac. Both Tempest coupes and wagons were entered in A/FX. The excitement centered around the Tasca Ford entry, a '63 Fairlane jammed with the latest 427 Ford super stock engine. This was the forerunner to the legendary Thunderbolt '64 Fairlane.

In B/FX were the lightweight Pontiac Catalinas with the Swiss Cheese frames. Arlen Vanke was there with the *Tin Indian III*. Harold Ramsey, George DeLorean, and a number of other Pontiacs made up the majority of the field. Several lightweight Fords were in B/FX with the Pontiacs. There were also the unusual entries like the Dragmaster RamTruck and the Ford F-100XL pickup out of Stu Wilson Ford in Dearborn, Michigan. Built along the lines of the Ram Truck in 62, the F-100XL had a 427 Ford under the hood.

*One of the big names in Southern California super stock racing was Bill Hanyon driving the Milne Bros. Plymouth out of Pasadena. Hanyon had two cars entered at the '63 Winternationals, a '62 and '63 Plymouth, both S/SA cars. Hanyon won S/SA over the likes of the Ramchargers, Golden Commandos, and "Maverick" Golden, using the '62 car, turning a 12.30 ET.* (Tom Schiltz)

*One of the most prolific dealerships was also one of the smallest. Bridenthal Ford, in tiny Greensburg, Ohio had this '63 lightweight Galaxie in S/S at Dragway 42 in August 1963. Bridenthal's team campaigned two Thunderbolts and a D/S Fairlane in 1964. Note underside of the hood without bracing or springs. (Ken Andruss)*

When the call for class eliminations came on Saturday, it was all Dodge and Plymouth after the first round of S/S and S/SA. Dick Brannan fell to the Golden Commandos in S/S, who in turn were beaten by Tommy Grove and the *Melrose Missile*. The eventual S/S Class Winner was an unknown outside of Ohio as John Barker drove the '62 Cavalier Dodge to victory. However, Barker's big 426 Dodge was declared illegal when it was discovered to have the latest camshaft installed — legal in A/FX but not in S/S.

S/SA was hotly contested between no less than 40 Dodges and Plymouths. Both remaining Golden Commando cars, a 426 sedan and station wagon, and the two Ramchargers cars began a slow process of elimination. The Ramchargers eliminated the Golden Commandos sedan. The *Candymatic Too* knocked Billy Kidder out of the race, then turned around and shut down Eckstrand in the *Lawman* Dodge. The final was something rare in drag racing — two entries from the same team running for the trophy. Jim Thornton drove the original Ramchargers *Candymatic*, while teammate Herman Mozer was at the wheel of the *Candymatic Too*. Thornton cut a quicker light and took an early lead over Mozer, holding on to the finish at 12.23 seconds and 116.42 mph.

A/Stock was every bit as good a race as S/S. Dyno Don eliminated himself by cutting the light a little close and seeing the big red bulb. Tom Sturm's big Mercury had problems throughout the week with blown engines and broken transmissions and just couldn't cut the ETs that were necessary to compete. The final came down to the Jenkins-tuned *Northwind* 409 Chevy against the kid from Texas, Don Gay, and his very potent 421 Pontiac sedan. The kid won, cutting a very quick 12.81-second ET. Bill Abraham made it an all-Pontiac sweep in A/S when he shut everyone down in the automatic end of the class at 13.28 seconds.

*Another of the aluminum, swiss-cheese Catalinas was the Wynn Engineering Special, driven by George Delorean. Initially, NHRA had the Catalinas classified as A/FX, although they were correct weight and legal for B/FX. Pontiac 8-lug aluminum wheels were rarely used on the lightweight Catalinas. All the B/FX Catalina coupes were identical, with silver exteriors and blue interior trim. (Drag Racing Memories)*

*During the early summer of 1963 Hayden Proffitt made another switch, this time from Chevrolet Z-11 to 426 Stage II Plymouth, driving the Yeakel Plymouth SS/A. At the Detroit Nationals, Proffitt indicated that he would be a very formidable contender, by coming off the trailer at 12.10. Proffitt beat Roger Lindamood's* Color Me Gone *Plymouth for the S/SA class win. (Drag Racing Memories)*

The two cars to beat in A/FX were Dave Strickler's *Old Reliable IV* and the Tasca Ford *Zimmy I* Fairlane. Most of the Z-11 Chevys were cutting ETs in the low 12-second bracket, but the York, Pennsylvania Chevy and big Fairlane were clearly ahead of the pack. However, the big Ford developed a transmission problem during a run against Don Kimball's Z-11, and went back on the trailer. The big Tempests were running in the 12.20s to 12.40s, as were the A/FX Dodge and Plymouth entries. The Ramchargers S/SA entry was cutting ETs quicker than the FX entries.

Strickler shut down both Nicholson and Ronnie Sox en route to winning the A/FX trophy at 12.17 seconds and 118.11 mph. Jim Wangers in the Royal Pontiac entry in B/FX easily beat out the other Pontiac and Ford entries to win the class at a great 12.59 seconds. Ron Root, the Pomona, California policeman with the wild little 6-cylinder Dart, won C/FX at 15.12 seconds.

On Monday the staging lanes were filled with the top entries for Top Stock Eliminator. There were 28 entries in all: 11 Plymouths, 9 Dodges, 5 Fords, 2 Chevys, and Don Gay's Pontiac. One by one

*Several points of interest may be noted in this photo of Don Nicholson coming down the return road at Detroit Dragway in June 1963, including the open headlight buckets used to draw fresh air into the engine compartment, the aluminum hood scoop, which was another Ford truck item with a GM Part number, and the very wrinkled condition of the lightweight aluminum bumpers and 26-gauge aluminum fenders. (James Genat/Zone Five)*

Detroit National Stock Invitational decal and bumper sticker. (Author's Collection)

Detroit Dragway Flyer for the Detroit Dragway National Stock Car Championship, showing every big name in S/S racing, including six Z-11 Impalas. (Zone Five)

Don Nicholson at Detroit Dragway on June 22, 1963. Don's Chevys were always set up the same, with the front end raised, either by using a donut on top of the spring mount or by using Chevy truck spindles, and lowered rear, either by heating the rear coils or by cutting a coil out. Don's cars with the distinctive crossed Chevrolet flags were always the most colorful too. (James Genat/Zone Five)

The Little Wed Wat was a '63 Ford Galaxie, with a 390ci, 330 horsepower engine and 4-speed. Running in NHRA D/Stock, the functional hood scoop added for AHRA competition had to be taped shut to be NHRA legal. Note all the win stickers on the windshield. (Author's Collection)

*Bill and Helen Golden were a working husband-and-wife team through-out his long racing career. Bill is measuring the tread on his Casler cheater slicks to make sure they do not exceed the 7-inch limit. Bill "Maverick" Golden toured the East Coast in the Summer of 1963, one of the first drivers to make a profession of drag racing. (Bill Golden)*

the cars were eliminated. Strickler's '62 car went down to the Ramchargers, the Golden Commandos put down Tommy Grove's *Missile* and set low ET of the meet at 11.97 seconds, the first legal super stock car to break into the 11s. The final rounds came down to both Golden Commandos cars, both Ramcharger entries, and Al Eckstrand's *Lawman* Dodge.

The Commandos, by virtue of their 11-second run, were favored to win. However, one Commando car lost to Eckstrand, while the other went down to defeat at the hands of Mozer in the *Candymatic Too*. The final run was between two old friends, now running against each other for the top stocker prize of the year. Mozer lined up in the tower lane, Eckstrand took the pit side. At the Green, both cars came out side by side. It remained that way until the halfway mark when

Mozer edged ahead of Eckstrand by a fender length, holding that lead through the traps. His winning time was 12.22 seconds at 116.73 mph, against Eckstrand's losing time of 12.23 seconds and 114.94 mph. The 1963 Nationals had been an all-Dodge show with the exception of Strickler's A/FX and Little Eliminator victories.

Since the FX cars were not eligible to run in Stock Eliminator, NHRA put them into Little Eliminator against a number of gas class entries. Both Strickler and Wangers shut down all the gassers to make it an all-Detroit final in Little Eliminator. Using the handicap starting system, the big red, silver, and blue Pontiac left first, with the big white Chevy in hot pursuit. Wangers had left a little too early and a big red light glowed in his lane. Foul start! However, it really didn't matter if he fouled or not as Strickler's big 427 went around the Pontiac at the 1000' mark to win at 12.10 seconds and a phenomenal 126.16 mph. Wangers 12.61 seconds was consistent with his ETs all day long.

A very interesting side note to the '63 Nationals was the fact that NHRA had disqualified Hayden Proffitt and the Yeakel Plymouth SS/A because the fuel check revealed he was using something other than pump gasoline. It turned out that Hayden had mixed some left-over Sunoco 270 from Detroit Dragway, with some Texaco Supreme bought at an Indianapolis gas station. When his fuel was checked (the only one out of some 60 S/S entrants), the result revealed something that was different from the strip gasoline. NHRA disqualified him.

Proffitt immediately flew to Detroit to inquire about the Sunoco used at the strip. It was 100% pure, he was assured. He also had his crew take a sample from his tank and take it to a local lab for testing.

*Another Pontiac at the Drag News Invitational was the Packer Pontiac out of Detroit, Michigan and driven by Howard Maseles. As with all the swiss-cheese Catalinas, they had silver exteriors with blue interiors. The term "swiss cheese" came from the fact that the frames had large holes cut in them every few inches for lighter weight. (Tom Schiltz)*

*'63 Nationals decal and pit pass.* (Author's Collection)

*Mayflower*, and another driver who switched from Chevy to Plymouth: Bruce Morgan. Morgan had won the 1961 NHRA Worlds Stock Points Championship using a '57 Chevy B Stocker. He then campaigned the '61 Pontiac S/S car that he had won for the Points Championship. However, in early 1963, both he and Hayden Proffitt were lured away from GM by Lou Baney at Yeakel Plymouth.

Don Grotheer won U/S in a Z-11 Chevrolet at 12.88 seconds ET. Dyke took the U/SA trophy in 12.36 seconds with the Wilson Motors Plymouth. Top Stock Eliminator brought together all the top cars from U/S, U/SA, S/S, S/SA, A/S, A/SA, and B/S and B/SA — a field of about 50 cars. The final pair of cars were Dickie Harrell's Z-11 Chevrolet, and Dick Dyke's 426 Plymouth. Dyke's Plymouth took the lead right off the starting line and held on turning an identical ET to that posted when he won U/SA — 12.36 seconds at over 117 mph.

*Pit action at the '63 Nationals showing both the* Old Reliable II *A/S Bel Air, and the* Old Reliable IV *Z-11 Impala. Strickler would win both A/FX and Little Eliminator with the no. 4 car, but lose A/S to Don Gay's Pontiac. Smoke is from the loose clearances built into the 427 Z-11 engine.* (Susie Strickler)

They reported it was 100% pure gasoline with no additives. NHRA ignored all the tests and reports. Proffitt was out at the '63 Nationals. He sued NHRA following the end of the '63 season. He served papers to everyone involved with the decision at the '64 Winternationals. Guess who represented him — Al "The Lawman" Eckstrand.

The AHRA National Championship Drags were held at Green Valley Raceway outside of Fort Worth, Texas over Labor Day weekend. As with previous AHRA events, many of the classes had entries that were completely different from those found at NHRA meets. For instance, the big Z-11 Chevys that were forced into LP class at the NHRA Winternationals and A/FX at the NHRA Nationals, ran in Ultra Stock class (U/S) under AHRA rules. This pitted them against other Ford and Mopar vehicles of the same weight and engine size.

AHRA had always been a stepchild as far as the media were concerned. The biggest names usually went to the NHRA events, despite big money prizes at the AHRA meets. The factories saw the prestige of NHRA competition as better for sales and ordered most of the biggest names to Indy over Labor Day. This in spite of the fact that AHRA actively promoted the stockers much more than NHRA. At Green Valley were the cars that would have been competitive at the NHRA meet, but which probably would have lost, especially in light of the times being turned at Indy that same weekend.

Chevrolet was well represented by Frank Sanders' Rudolph Chevrolet and Dickie Harrell, both driving aluminum Z-11 Chevys. A few of the top Plymouth entries included Dick Dyke's Wilson Motors entry out of Sioux City, Iowa, the Garland Motors

When the 1963 season ended, it closed a big chapter in the history of super stock racing — the GM chapter. No longer would GM sponsor any type of racing, which left only Ford and Chrysler to battle it out for Top Stock. Yes, there were many Chevrolet and Pontiac super stocks in '64, but all would use the previous year's engines in the current year's body styles. All would be home-built, thus qualifying for either Gas or Modified Production classes.

In match racing, where anything went, the GM products could hold their own — at least until the introduction of the 426 Hemi. It would be 1966 before GM returned to racing, and then it was not an all-out factory effort, at least not to the public. However, GM did pour support to the many drivers and teams that had Chevelles, 4-4-2s, and Chevy IIs in the upper stock classes.

*The winner of Stock Eliminator at the* Drag News *Invitational, Arnie Beswick's* Mrs. B's Grocery Getter *Tempest wagon, wasn't quite as quick at the '63 Nationals. Although he beat the* Frederick Motors Big Bad Dodge *in this round of A/FX, the 421 wagon fell to Strickler's Z-11 Impala in the final rounds.* (Drag Racing Memories)

*The best running Ford was the A/FX 427 Fairlane from Tasca Ford. However, Bill Humphries missed a shift on this run against Don Kimball and the Salina Chevrolet Z-11. Tasca's Zimmy I would set the national record for A/FX in October. It lasted about a week before Arlen Vanke smashed it with the* Running Bear *Tempest.* (Drag Racing Memories)

Running Bear, *the 421 Tempest built by Arlen Vanke then authorized by Pontiac, was completely different from any of the other '63 421 Tempests in A/FX. Arlen used a standard Borg-Warner 4-speed transmission and Catalina rear axle assembly. It worked and Vanke set the National Record for A/FX at Alton, Illinois in the fall of 1963 with a time of 11.89. The white hood was a new replacement aluminum part.* (Drag Racing Memories)

*Dave Strickler makes the turn out of the staging lanes at the '63 Nationals in the (now) A/S* Old Reliable II. *He lost to Don Gay's Pontiac for A/S honors. The crumpled fenders are a result of driving off the trailer ramps.* (Susie Strickler)

The flagman waves off Jim Thornton in the Original Ramchargers Candymatic car, #980, against Herman Mozer in the Candymatic Too, #979, at Detroit Dragway in late September. It was a repeat of the run for S/SA class at the '63 Nationals. Mozer was also Stock Eliminator in the Candymatic Too, defeating Al Eckstrand's Lawman Dodge, 12.22 to 12.23. "T" on the windshield meant the car was in a trophy run — yellow disc for class, orange disc for Stock Eliminator. (Drag Racing Memories)

"The Farmer" at speed at Beeline Drag Strip in Phoenix, Arizona, in early 1965. Arnie Beswick's 421 Tempest coupe, now equipped with a standard 4 speed and Catalina rear axle assembly and sponsored by Gay Pontiac, took the A Modified Production trophy at Bakersfield with an ET of 11.60 and a speed of 126.80 mph, with no factory support. The 421 Tempest had originally been one of the two Tempests built and campaigned by Mickey Thompson. (Matchracemadness)

*Arnie "The Farmer" Beswick makes a pass at Bakersfield with the famous* Mrs. B's Grocery Getter *A/FX Tempest station wagon. The '63 421 Tempest wagon took Beswick to Stock Eliminator honors at both the '63 Nascar Winternationals and the* Drag News *Invitational held at Dragway 42 in July 1963. Under 1964 NHRA rules, the little station wagon was forced to run in A Modified Production class. (Matchracemadness)*

*Bud Faubel continued to race his Honker Dodge well into the 1964 season, even after his '64 version of the Honker was finished. Here he is at 75-80 Dragway, Frederick, Maryland waiting for the flag against Herb Freels and the Hurricane S/SA Dodge in late 1963, with the Stage III Ramcharger package.*
*(Drag Racing Memories)*

*The Milne Bros. Plymouth team brought two cars to the '63 NHRA Nationals: the light blue S/SA sedan and a dark blue A/SA station wagon, co-sponsored by Reynolds Auto Supply. With the stock all-steel front end, and using the Stage II 426 Super Stock engine, the station wagon fell into A/Stock Automatic class. Bill Abraham won the class.*
*(Tom Schiltz)*

*Another Z-11 that continued to hit the match race circuit in 1965 was Malcolm Durham's Strip Blazer. Now campaigned by Jerry Hotchkiss, the Z-11 was still plenty strong when it came to Piedmont Drag Raceway for the Lee Malkeme's Benefit Race in early 1965, with times in the high 11s. The competition this day was the fabulous Falcon of Hubert Platt.*
*(Author's Collection)*

The big S/S and B/FX Pontiacs were heavy enough to fall into B/Modified Production class even with the 421ci engine. This is the Edwards Pontiac Catalina sedan, tuned and driven by Chuck Wright, at Magnolia Drag Strip in 1965. The Edwards sedan was all-steel, but was capable of times in the 12.70 seconds. (Bruce Baker)

Gene Shindle comes off the line at Pacific Raceways in the Grassi Motors S/SA '63 Plymouth. Although Shindle owned the Stage III Plymouth, he and Dave Grassi shared the driving. The S/SA Plymouth was capable of times in the very low 12-second range in legal form. (Russ Griffith)

The end of the '63 season did not necessarily mean the end of racing for the Z-11 Impalas. Many were sold and competed on the match race circuit into 1965. Wally Bell bought Hubert Platt's Georgia Shaker Z-11, repainted the rear fenders and called it the New York Shaker. (Author's Collection)

# CHAPTER SIX

# 1964 — THE TIMES, THEY ARE A'CHANGING

**T**hings were very different in the United States with a new President, Lyndon Johnson. On August 4th, several North Vietnamese gunboats attacked U.S. Navy destroyers. It was all the action that President Johnson needed to begin full involvement of U.S. forces in the ongoing conflict in South Vietnam.

In the Middle East, ominous clouds loomed with the formation of the Palestine Liberation Organization (PLO). It was another hot spot for the world to watch.

A welcome distraction came from the music world as the Beatles conquered the unsuspecting American youth. On April 4, the *Billboard Hot 100* listed five Beatles songs all tied for the Number 1 spot. It was an era of the British Invasion as The Rolling Stones, The Animals, and the Dave Clark Five dominated the music charts.

For super stock drag racing, 1964 was a strange year. There were great changes that evolved into the Ford Thunderbolt-type cars and the development of the Chrysler Hemi. Those changes, following on the heels of GM's racing ban, brought about the total demise of General Motors as far as racing was concerned; and not just super stock drag racing. There would be almost no competition from GM automobiles in NASCAR either. General Motors would remain on the outside of the competition, happy to sell GTOs and Chevelles to the public. However, Ford and Chrysler unleashed some very potent competition, and the resulting races were incredible. The match race circuit also saw its share of great races from Chevrolet and Pontiac teams.

The rules for Stock classes in 1964 remained virtually the same as they had been in '63. One minor change was that lower class sports cars would now compete with regular production full-size cars. Only the top two classes, A and B Sports, remained outside the rules of Stock Class.

Two changes that involved Factory Experimental cars from previous years were put in place for '64. Prior to 1964, any one-off vehicles from the previous year were allowed to compete with the present year's vehicles in FX classes. In 1964, ONLY the current year experimental vehicles could compete in any of the three FX classes. All previous year FX competitors now fell into a totally new class called "Modified Production."

In Modified Production (MP), the rules were a combination of stocker rules, with a little of the Gas class thrown in — very little. All the rules for Stock class regarding street equipment were incorporated in the MP Class, i.e. lights, horn, body modifications, etc. All of these items not only had to be in place, but also in working order. Any engine could be used in any body as long as it didn't involve any type of modification to the firewall. Lightweight body parts, i.e. fiberglass and/or aluminum, were taboo unless the car had them when delivered from the factory. Tires allowed were of the cheater slick variety, in that they had to have a tread design of some type, and a maximum width of 7 inches. Carburetion was limited to up to two four-barrel carbs or three two-barrels, on any type of intake manifold. Thus the lightweight aluminum Chevys, Pontiacs, Fords, and Mopars that had been running in FX in 1963, could now legally run only in MP class in '64.

*At the beginning of the 1964 season, Mercury released the 427 Comet. Built to compete in A/Factory Experimental class, there were eleven Comets built: ten 2-door coupes and one station wagon. The wagon was campaigned by Don Nicholson, who switched from Chevrolet after the '63 season. Seen here at Detroit Dragway in Spring 1964, the wagon had already been handed over to Eddie Schartman when Nicholson's coupe was finished. (James Genat/Zone Five)*

*There were times when different year cars were forced to run "heads up" against other cars with much greater horsepower. A race at Erie Dragway in 1964 matched the Hine Motors '62 413 Dodge against the Hartley Motors '64 Dodge Hemi-Charger, without benefit of a handicap start. The '64 Dodge was later modified with the 2% wheelbase alteration as well as having a beam axle. (Jack Bleil)*

## Dodge and Plymouth

At the beginning of the 1964 drag season, the Dodge and Plymouth drag racing packages were virtually identical to that of late 1963. When the 1964 cars were introduced, the drag package for Dodge and Plymouth included the new Stage III engine modifications. Although still rated at 425 horsepower at 5600 rpm, the Stage III engine was easily the most powerful wedge engine ever built to date. It had a completely new set of heads that featured 2.08" intake valves and 1.88" exhausts. The ports were opened up so big that previous intake manifolds wouldn't bolt up. The combustion chambers had undervalve intake bowls. Combustion for the Stage III was 12.5:1.

The camshaft used on the Stage III was also new and radically different from any previous design, with .520" lift and over 300° duration. With mechanical lifters and stiffer valve springs, the Stage III could easily rev to over 6500 rpm. Carburetion remained as before, a pair of 725 cfm Carter AFBs on the short-ram manifold, which had to be redesigned to fit the Stage III heads. The Stage III could be had with either the proven 727 Torqueflite or the new Chrysler 4-speed manual transmission. Included with the Stage III drag package was the lightweight front end package of aluminum hood and scoop, aluminum bumpers and supports, and aluminum fenders. That was the drag package at the beginning of the '64 model year.

## Ford

Ford had two programs in 1964, one for the full-sized Galaxie and Mercury, and another for the Fairlane and Comet. Both packages were developed around the basic 427 Hi-Riser drag race engine that had been used in Ford drag cars since early 1963. With the 4,100 lb. Mercury Marauder hardtop, the standard 427 Hi-Riser with 11.5:1 compression, mechanical lifter camshaft, and high-rise, dual-quad intake system, was rated at 425 horsepower. It was offered with a 4-speed transmission only. With the heavy weight of the Mercury, the car was a natural for A/Stock class.

The 427 Galaxies were another breed of cat entirely. These cars were all-out drag racing machines in every way. Although they used the same basic 427 Hi-Riser engine, the '64 Mk.II 427 included a new camshaft, redesigned heads with larger ports and 2.19" intake valves, with 1.73" exhausts. High dome pistons and a redesigned combustion chamber added up to a phenomenal 14:1 compression ratio! It definitely was not a street engine. The new high-rise, dual-quad intake was used with a pair of 780 cfm Holley four barrels. To get air to the carburetors, a large flexible duct system drew in fresh, cool air through the inner headlight openings and radiator support panel.

Where previous Ford Galaxies had used lightweight fiberglass front fenders, hoods, and bumpers to bring the weight down, the '64 Galaxie drag package was even more exotic. The entire body was acid-dipped to make the overall metal skin as thin as possible; and Ford used the 300 series sedan frame, which was much lighter

*Doug Lovegrove's Mashak Plymouth goes against Tommy Grove and the* Melrose Missile V *during Top Stock Eliminator runoffs at the '64 Winternationals. Grove won the race at the starting line as Lovegrove left before the Green. Grove won with a time of 11.63 and a speed of 124.13 mph. (Author's Collection)*

than the Galaxie frame. The only exception was the hood, which remained fiberglass and had a distinctive teardrop-shaped bubble over the high-rise, dual four-barrel setup. Even the front bucket seat mounts were "swiss-cheesed" to save weight. Yet, with all this weight-saving, the car was still too heavy to get into S/S class, much less be competitive. However, the lightweight Galaxies fell right into the extreme top of AA/Stock, where they not only were competitive, they dominated.

The other side of the Ford drag racing program was the renowned Ford Thunderbolt and Mercury 427 Comet programs. The 427 Comets were all by themselves in development. Originally only eleven A/FX cars were built, ten hardtop coupes and one station wagon, all originally painted white. The package started with a standard Comet Cyclone hardtop that had the usual lightweight

fiberglass front fenders, hood, bumpers, and doors. To lower the weight even further in front, a 6-cylinder radiator was used, and the side windows and rear glass were replaced with Lexan. The cars were even delivered with American magnesium wheels on the front. The racing weight was 3240 lbs.

Under the hood was the now-standard 427 Ford Hi-Riser Mk.II drag engine, with the new head design and 14:1 compression ratio, except that it said "Mercury Super Marauder" on the valve covers. Although rated at 425 horsepower, the new engine was putting out well over 500 horses on the Ford dyno. Detroit Steel and Tubing shoe-horned the 427 Hi-Riser into the engine compartment of the Comet with minimal changes. One major change was a reduction in the height of the shock towers to clear the heads and exhaust manifolds. The dual Holley four-barrel carburetors drew fresh air

*Doug Lovegrove's Mashak Plymouth puts it to Herman Mozer in the '64 Ramchargers car in the semi-final of Top Stock Eliminator at the '64 Winternationals, turning an 11.69 ET at 121.78 mph. Mozer lost with a better ET of 11.57, and better speed of 125.52, but was caught napping at the start. Lovegrove would lose Top Stock Eliminator to Tommy Grove's* Melrose Missile *on a red light. (Matchracemadness)*

*One of the answers to the Dodge Chargers and Chrisman's supercharged Comet, was Arnie Beswick's* Mystery Tornado, *a '64 GTO with a supercharged 421 Pontiac engine. Seen here in a '65 match race with the Ramchargers altered wheelbase '65 Dodge funny car at US 131 Dragway, Beswick's GTO could get down into the 10-second range, and in the 9s running nitro. (John Lacko)*

through a pair of scoops on the leading edge of the hood, rather than through the flexible hose intakes found on both the lightweight Galaxie and the Thunderbolt Fairlanes.

Behind the big 427 Super Marauder engine was a standard Ford T-10 4-speed transmission that used a Galaxie heavy-duty drive shaft and standard big Ford rear-axle housing with large traction bars to eliminate wheel hop. The first three hardtop coupes were delivered to Bill Shrewsberry, Tom Sturm, and Jack Chrisman. Chrisman's car was never a super stock or FX vehicle however, being powered by a fuel-burning, supercharged 427 Ford engine and running in B/Fuel Dragster class. The lone Comet station wagon was campaigned by Don Nicholson, who later got into a hardtop coupe. Nicholson then offered the station wagon to "Fast Eddie" Schartman and they campaigned together throughout 1964. All the 427 Comet drag cars were classified A/FX by NHRA due to the limited number of cars built. DS&T also built at least ten B/FX Comet coupes, powered with the 289ci small-block Ford. Other than the motor, they were exactly the same as their 427 big brothers.

In 1963, when NHRA had issued its 7.5 pounds-per-cubic-inch and 427 cubic inch limits, all the major drag programs were able to meet those limits using regular production family sedans. The 426 Stage III Dodges and Plymouths came in right on the money using aluminum components. So did Chevrolet with the Z-11 427 '63 Chevrolet Impala. Ford was always just too heavy to come close to the limits, a little too heavy to be competitive, and Ford didn't like losing.

The answer to Ford's woes was found with the development of the Tasca 406ci '62 Fairlane (that NHRA forced into B/Gas class in 1962) and the 427ci '63 Fairlane, which competed in A/FX and set a new national record for the class in the Fall of 1963. Ford would build an entire drag package around the Fairlane sedan, and power it with the new Mk.II 427 Hi-Riser engine. Enough of these new machines would be built to have them compete in Super Stock class (NHRA minimum was 100 vehicles built).

The Fairlane program was turned over to the Detroit Steel and Tubing Company that built other specialty vehicles for Ford. Beginning with a standard Fairlane 2-door sedan (one hardtop was built for Phil Bonner), DS&T removed the entire front end, doors and bumpers, and replaced them with fiberglass units. The interior was gutted and the front seat replaced by a pair of Econoline buckets seats, while the rear seat was removed entirely. All glass save for the windshield, was replaced with Lexan plastic, and the rear window mechanisms were removed.

Under the hood, the subframe was modified to accept the big 427 engine. Inner fenders, control arms, springs, and shock towers were modified to make room for the engine, the same as had been done with the Comet drag package. The DS&T people even designed a set of tubing exhaust headers to fit the 427 Fairlane installation. Behind the big 427, the buyer had a choice of either a standard Borg Warner T-10 4 speed — complete with R.C. Industries scattershield — or a beefed-up C-6 Ford Cruise-O-Matic.

The rear axle assembly was a Detroit Locker limited slip unit. The rear frame assembly was beefed with the addition of a heavy steel crossmember that connected the front mounts of the rear springs. The extra crossmember looped under the driveshaft, which conveniently provided the necessary driveshaft safety loop required by NHRA. To this reinforcement was bolted a set of heavy-duty torque arms, i.e. traction bars, which were welded to the rear axle housing. Heavy-duty rear springs and shock absorbers finished off the package.

Several of the new prototype Fairlane Thunderbolts were offered to the big names in Ford's super stock program. Dick Brannan got the #1 test vehicle. Others went to Bill Lawton at Tasca Ford, Butch Leal, Gas Ronda, and Mickey Thompson in California. These cars can easily be differentiated from the later Thunderbolts in that they had a distinctive clover-leaf hood bubble, rather than the normally accepted teardrop design. All were painted the same basic color — maroon. By the time the 1964 NHRA Winternationals began, the Thunderbolts, although classified A/FX at this early date, were ready for all comers.

*"Mr. 427" at Pomona in 1964. Ronnie Sox was beaten by Jack Chrisman in Bill Shrewsberry's Comet in A/FX, but came back to win Factory Stock Eliminator at the '64 Winternationals by beating Don Nicholson's Comet wagon. Sox's Comet was powered by the 427 Ford Hi-Riser engine rated at 425 horsepower. It just said "Mercury" on the valve covers. (Drag Racing Memories)*

## CHEVROLET AND PONTIAC

At General Motors camps, the mood was somber to say the least. The racing ban had caused irreparable damage. Chevrolet teams like Dick Harrell and Malcolm Durham, were busy bolting 427 Z-11 engines into Chevelle bodies. Pontiac teams did have the new '64 Tempest GTO, but these were equipped with 360 hp versions of the 389 Trophy engine and competed in B/Stock. Several Pontiac teams including Arnie Beswick and Jess Tyree, did campaign GTOs with 421 engines similar to the Z-11 Chevelles. However, all these ventures were classified as A/Modified Production under the new NHRA rules. Under AHRA rules, and in match racing, the GM teams were entered in A/XS for Experimental Stock.

## 1964 WINTERNATIONALS

NASCAR held its '64 Winternationals at Spruce Creek Airport, near the Daytona Speedway, with 1,163 entrants in some 70 different classes. Everything that NHRA had, NASCAR had at Spruce Creek and 67,000 spectators loved it. Any drivers who didn't wish to tow cars all the way to Arizona for the AHRA meet or on to Pomona for the NHRA meet, were in attendance at Spruce Creek.

They raced for eight straight nights at Spruce Creek. When it was over, there were several familiar names at the top of the stock winners list. FX was won by Joe Deaton and the Tom Coward A/FX Comet. Ultra Stock stick went to David Heath's '64 Dodge. Ultra Stock Automatic went to Bob Harrop's '63 Dodge. Billy Jacobs won both A and B Super Stock Automatic with '63 Dodges.

In B/Super Stock was "The Farmer" Arnie Beswick and his '63 Catalina coupe. He also brought both the *Grocery Getter* 421 Tempest wagon, and the *Run-About* 421 Tempest coupe. On the final night of the NASCAR meet, they ran the Super Stock Eliminators — one for stick and the other for automatic. Even though he had gotten beat in FX by Deaton's Comet, Beswick turned the tables on all the big Fords to win S/S, beating the Ed Martin Ford Thunderbolt with a time of 11.66 and 121.21 mph. S/S Automatic Eliminator went to Harrop and his big '63 Dodge Ramcharger.

NASCAR had a S/S race every night of the winter event. Other winners included Hubert Platt in U/S and Allen Hyder's Z-11 in A/SS. Jack Sharkey's '63 426 Dart won FX one night with a time of 12.37, and Ed Martin's Ford Thunderbolt won in U/S with a time of 12.45. The overall winner was Beswick and the 421 Tempest coupe, *Mr. B's Run-About.* Arnie was protested by one of the losers, but the subsequent teardown revealed nothing. Arnie's prize was a new Ford Falcon convertible.

The 1964 NHRA Winternationals were held at Pomona over the second weekend in February, 1964. It would be the best "Big Go West" ever. NHRA and the Pomona Valley Timing Association had made several improvements to the strip at the Los Angeles County Fairgrounds, including the addition of a safety net at the end of the strip to catch out-of-control dragsters.

*One of the first teams to arrive at the '64 Winternationals was the Ramchargers. They brought both the '63 Nationals winner, as well as a new '64 Dodge Candymatic (on the trailer). Jim Thornton took the '64 car to the finals in S/SA, before red-lighting against John Rogers and the Town & Country Plymouth. (Raj Reddi Collection)*

*Hayden Proffitt (#612) goes off against Yeakel Plymouth teammate Roger Warren (#615) at the AHRA Winternationals. Both cars are identical Stage III Super Stock Belvederes, except that Proffitt used a Torqueflite automatic, while Warren shifted the new Chrysler 4-speed manual transmission. (Author's Collection)*

As usual, the biggest names in stock car drag racing were in attendance, either racing for Top Stock or for the top rung in the Factory Experimental class. In A/FX there were Comets throttled by Don Nicholson, Tom Sturm, Bill Shrewsberry, Ronnie Sox, and Ed Rachanski. The previous year's A/FX cars were now placed in the A/Modified Production class.

The Fairlane Thunderbolts were in Super/Stock class: Gas Ronda, Dick Brannan, Bill Lawton, Phil Bonner, and Butch Leal. There were also a few Mopars in the class including the *Dodge Boys* Dodge of Dave Strickler, and Tommy Grove at the wheel of the *Melrose Missile V*. In Super Stock Automatic was Bill Hanyon in the Milne Brothers Plymouth, Bill Shirey driving the Golden Commandos Plymouth, Al Eckstrand driving his new *Lawman* '64 Plymouth hardtop, John Rogers driving the Town & Country Plymouth that was tuned by Frank Sanders, and of course, Jim Thornton and Herman Mozer wheeling the Ramchargers entries.

At the end of class eliminations, a Comet had won the A/FX crown (naturally). Bill Shrewsberry beat Don Nicholson in the early go, then beat Tom Sturm for the class trophy, winning with an ET of 11.78 seconds. This was reasonably slow considering that the FX Comets had been tuning up at the local strips with ETs down to 11.08 seconds. Don Nicholson's *Ugly Duckling* Comet wagon had established low ET for the class at 11.44. In the end, Shrewsberry's consistency brought him the trophy. In B/FX, Jerry Harvey drove one of the new lightweight 427 Galaxies to the trophy win.

The Thunderbolts literally owned S/S class, just in shear numbers alone. Gas Ronda dropped Dave Strickler's new Dodge hardtop in the first round, then beat Tommy Grove in the second round. The final six rounds saw six Thunderbolts and a lone

Plymouth (driven by Jerry Grosz). Grosz fell to Bill Humphrey leaving an all-Thunderbolt finals: Humphrey against Gas Ronda, and Dick Brannan against Butch Leal.

Ronda beat Humphrey and Leal bested Brannan to make the final go for Super Stock. At the Green, it was Ronda out of the hole first. Leal valiantly chased but couldn't catch the red Thunderbolt.

*Al Eckstrand brought the Lawman Plymouth to Pomona, only to lose to John Rogers in S/SA, and to Doug Lovegrove in Top Stock Eliminator. Just barely visible is the lettering on the new Goodyear Super Stock drag tires, introduced at the '64 Winternationals. (Raj Reddi Collection)*

Gas Ronda won the class turning an ET of 12.05 seconds at 120.16 mph. The Thunderbolts were quick but not nearly as quick as the automatic Mopars.

The automatic Dodges and Plymouths were clicking off ETs in the 11-second bracket throughout S/SA. The new Ramchargers '64 car was running in the mid to low 11-second bracket to set the standard, beating Roger Lindamood's *Color Me Gone* with an ET of 11.53 seconds. Out of the desert came a new name: John Rogers. Rogers was driving the Town & Country '64 Plymouth hardtop that was set up and tuned by Frank Sanders. Sanders had won the previous year's Big Go West in LP class with a Z-11 Chevy, but was disqualified for using an illegal cam.

Banned from driving at the '64 meet, Sanders had switched to Plymouth, got a new sponsor, and recruited Rogers for his driver. Along the way to the final in S/SA, Rogers shut down some of the best in the business: Al "Lawman" Eckstrand in the fourth round, then Bill Shirey in the Golden Commandos entry went down in the 5th. Rogers shut down Herman Mozer in the Ramchargers '63 car in the semi-final when Mozer red-lighted. Jim Thornton in the '64 Ramchargers car, made a bye run to meet Rogers in the final go.

Rogers jumped the much quicker candy-striped Dodge out of the gate and held on for the win at 11.83 seconds and 119.84 mph.

A familiar name was in the winners circle for A/Stock: Don Gay. Gay's veteran '62 Pontiac sedan blasted a 12.68 ET for the class win. His little brother Roy didn't fare as well in B/Stock as his new GTO lost the class to Bill Hoefer driving a '62 409 Impala that went 12.88 and 111.11 mph. A/Stock Automatic was won by a Ford driven by Don Brown in 13.14 seconds. In A/Modified Production, Pete Petri, driving one of Les Ritchey's '63 Ford A/FX entries, won over Dick Dempsey's old A/FX Plymouth with an ET of 11.75 seconds and 119.20 mph. That ET would have easily won both L/P and A/FX in 1963.

On Sunday, two separate stock eliminator titles were crowned: Factory Stock Eliminator and Top Stock Eliminator. Factory Stock Eliminator was open to the FX cars only. Ronnie Sox driving the Brinsfield Lincoln-Mercury Comet hardtop, beat Don Nicholson's Comet Wagon with an ET of 11.49 seconds. The time for the losing Nicholson: 11.47 seconds! Sox had gated Nicholson for the win.

Whereas Factory Stock was dominated by the Comets, Top Stock would be dominated again by the Mopars. When the call came for

*Showing how much attention that Chrysler Corporation devoted to the drag racing program, the winner of Top Stock Eliminator at the 1964 NHRA Winternationals received a new '64 Dodge presented by NHRA, the Hurst Corporation, and of course, Dodge. (Raj Reddi Collection)*

*Dick Brannen and the Romy-Hammes Thunderbolt goes against Herman Mozer in the '63 Ramchargers car during the Top Stock eliminations at the '64 Winternationals. Mozer's big Dodge, which had won Top Stock at both the '63 Winternationals and Nationals, dispatched Brannen's Thunderbolt to advance to the next round, losing to eventual Top Stock Eliminator Tommy Grove in the next round. (Matchracemadness)*

Top Stock Eliminator, the staging lanes looked like a Who's Who of drag racing. It promised to be a no holds barred, knock down, drag out battle. The Mopars were heavily favored due to their consistently better ETs, but the Thunderbolts promised to make it interesting. If any of the Mopars were caught napping, they would be chasing Fairlane taillights through the traps.

However, with each successive round, the Thunderbolts were slowly thinned out. Gas Ronda went down to Tommy Grove's *Melrose Missile V* in the first round. Dick Brannan put Hayden Proffitt's Plymouth on the trailer with an 11.70 ET. Phil Bonner also won in the first round with an impressive 11.68-second time. Brannan was the last Thunderbolt but fell to Mozer in the '63 *Candymatic* Dodge in the quarter finals.

Jim Thornton drove the Ramchargers '64 car to victory over the winner of S/SA — Jim Rogers and the Town & Country Plymouth. Al Eckstrand shut down Bonner's Thunderbolt in the third round. Doug Lovegrove drove the Mashak Plymouth to victory over Don Grotheer and Al Eckstrand to make the finals.

The last semi-final matched Tommy Grove's *Melrose Missile V*, one of the handful of manual transmission 426 Mopars in competition, against Thornton's '64 Ramcharger. Grove's masterful shifting brought victories over Roger Caster's Yeakel Plymouth, "Dandy" Dick Landy's Dodge, and Gas Ronda before drawing Thornton. It would take a real bit of driving or luck, if Grove was to win this round.

On the previous bye run, Thornton had shocked everyone with an 11.45-second ET! However, this round would be another story. The lights went green and Grove jumped out ahead of Thornton, taking a full half-car length lead out of the gate. With no mistakes in shifting the Chrysler 4 speed, Grove held on to win at 11.66 seconds. Thornton set low elapsed time for all stockers in a losing round at 11.36 seconds! Once again, the old drag racing adage prevailed: "If you snooze, you lose!"

The final for Top Stock Eliminator would be somewhat anti-climactic. The yellow Lovegrove car was in the pit lane, with the wild looking *Missile* on the spectator side. Lovegrove's automatic Plymouth had been running in the high 11-second bracket throughout the eliminations, about 3/10ths behind Grove's *Missile*. As the lights clicked down to green, Lovegrove leaped out of the hole a full 1 1/2 car lengths ahead of Grove, but only one side of the tree was showing green. Lovegrove's lane light glowed a bright red — a foul start for the Plymouth. Grove cruised to victory with a time of 11.63 at 124.13 mph. The Winternationals Top Stock Eliminator was the *Melrose Missile V* driven by Tommy Grove.

The Winternationals were over. Now it was time for record runs and match races. It was also just after the end of the winter meets that Chrysler unleashed the most powerful stock engine ever built. One that would write and rewrite the records over the next 10 years. It was called the 426 Hemi.

## CHRYSLER 426 HEMI

Immediately prior to the NHRA Winternationals, Chrysler Corporation unveiled a completely new engine at the Daytona Speed Weeks: a 426 engine with hemispherical heads. The hemi-head design had been around for a long time. Although the Chrysler hemi-head engines of the 1950s are the better known, the first hemi-head engine was almost a Chevrolet idea, since Zora Arkus-Duntov, Father of the Corvette, is credited with development of the Ardun overhead conversion for the Ford flathead V-8s. The Ardun (short for ARkus-DUNtov) head was a hemispherical head design that was produced in England during the 1940s, less than 10 years prior to development of the Chrysler hemi-head engine.

The 1964 version of the hemi-head engine was developed using the new Chrysler tall block or "B" block, the engine that was powering the super stockers which were already terrorizing the nation's drag strips. It, of course, had many changes that were needed to incorporate the new hemi-head design.

*A favorite of the West Coast Chevrolet fans, Larry "Butch" Leal switched to Ford following the GM racing ban. Leal drove one of the 4-speed Thunderbolts, which came from the factory complete with an RC Industries "blow-proof" bellhousing, commonly known as a scattershield. Leal lost to Gas Ronda in the S/S final, but was victorious at the Nationals. (Drag Racing Memories)*

*Dave Strickler (in white pants) talks with Bill Jenkins (behind man in black coat) about how to pull a few more horsepower from his S/S Dodge at the '64 Winternationals. Strickler, who had won SS/S, A/FX, and A/S at previous national meets, fell to Gas Ronda's Thunderbolt in the first round of S/S. (Raj Reddi Collection)*

Quite simply, the hemispherical head had a large pocket for the combustion chamber in the shape of a dome. This allowed a larger amount of fuel/air mixture to be ingested into the engine. This was also made easier by using a much larger valve than could be used with the wedge engine design, both intake and exhaust. Thus, more fuel/air mixture coming in and larger volumes of spent gasses exhausting created large amounts of available horsepower. The 426 Hemi certainly delivered on the formula.

Although based on the B block basic design, the new engine had several significant changes including new oil galley passages to mate up with the new head design, and cross-bolted main bearing caps on the crankshaft. High-domed pistons offered a compression ratio of either 11.0:1 or 12.5:1 in the drag engines.

The heads themselves bore a great resemblance to the earlier design, as one might expect. However, they were a totally new design. They did use a similar dual rocker arm shaft assembly to actuate the valves. The valves were huge — 2.25" for the intakes and 1.94" for the exhausts. Compare this to the Stage III 426 wedge engine with 2.08" intakes and 1.88" exhausts. Both intake and exhaust passages and ports were also huge to move the massive

*One of the more interesting cars at the Winternationals was the C/FX Dodge Dart, tuned and driven by Pomona Police Lt. Ron Root. The Dart was powered by the 225ci Dodge Slant-Six engine, modified with an Offenhauser aluminum intake mounting a Carter AFB four barrel. The Dart ran mid-14s, with speeds over 95 mph. (Author's Collection)*

*In addition to the Carter AFB and Offy intake, this 225ci Slant Six had an Iskendarian 505A cam and lifters (all with Dodge part numbers), and a transistorized ignition. The car was set up by Les Ritchey's Performance Associates for C/FX, but ran E/MP at Pomona. Root won both E/MP and Street Eliminator, turning an ET of 14.24 and 97.50 mph. (Author's Collection)*

amounts of gas. To save a little weight wherever possible, the valves had slightly smaller stems, and areas of the basic head casting itself that were not needed to pass coolant or oil, were removed during the casting stage.

On top of the hemi sat one of the tried and true aluminum short-ram intake manifolds, which was designed to fit the wider hemi-head design. A pair of Carter AFBs provided close to 1500 cfm of air. Camshaft for the 426 Hemi was based on the latest Stage III design offering maximum horsepower at greater than 5000 rpm. Horsepower ratings for the new engine were 415 hp for the 11:1 compression engine, and 425 hp on the all-out 12.5:1 engine — the same as both high-performance versions of the wedge motor. However, dyno tests indicated that the top hemi drag engine was actually putting out over 550 horsepower! The stage was now set for what would be one of the most memorable drag race seasons ever.

*Dick Landy charges out of the gate at Lions Drag Strip in March 1964 with his 426 Stage III Ramcharger-powered Dodge Polara hardtop. The silver Dodge competed in SS/A. Most of the very early 1964 Chrysler factory team cars used the sleek new 2-door hardtop body style rather than the lighter 2-door sedan body. (Author's Collection)*

Gas Ronda in the near lane, goes against Butch Leal for the trophy in Super Stock class at the '64 Winternationals. Ronda took the trophy with a time of 12.05 at 120.16 mph. Ronda would also win Top Stock Eliminator at the Hot Rod Magazine meet held at Riverside Raceway in June with a consistent 12.08 ET and 119.68 mph speed. Both Thunderbolts were maroon at this time, as were most of the early Thunderbolts. (Matchracemadness)

The final run for Factory Stock Eliminator matched the A/FX Comets of Ronnie Sox (near lane) and Don Nicholson. Nicholson's Comet wagon had beaten Bill Shrewsberry's A/FX class winner in an early round with a time of 11.60 and 121.13 mph. Dyno Don was second out of the gate to the Caliente hardtop of Sox, and lost the trophy turning a better ET of 11.47 to Sox's 11.49 seconds. (Matchracemadness)

## THE MATCH RACE SEASON AND NATIONALS

Immediately following the Winternationals, the match race season got underway with a vengeance. Select Dodge and Plymouth teams began re-equipping with the new Chrysler 426 Hemi engine. The Ford and Comet teams began the steady process of tuning for maximum performance, so as to be able to compete with the new Hemi cars once they were race-ready. There were still Chevy and Pontiac teams, even though they had no *apparent* factory sponsorship, nor any new engine developments that would keep them competitive; but competitive they were.

Using the lighter body styles of the Chevelle and Chevy II, but still powered by the old 427 Z-11 engine, several Chevy teams made a lot of noise on the *Drag News* Mr. Stock Eliminator list. In the Pontiac camps, the '63 Tempests with 421 engines, were still very competitive. Some had already converted to the new '64 Tempest GTO body style, and superchargers began making an appearance on stockers, at least on match race stockers.

At least three teams campaigned supercharged cars in 1964: two with full factory sponsorship, and the third was built in his own garage. First to complete a supercharged stocker, was the Dodge Chargers, a two-car Dodge public relations team fielded by the

*Tommy Grove and the* Melrose Missile V *comes out of the hole at Riverside Raceway during the* Hot Rod Magazine *1st Annual Meet, where he took the S/SA trophy. Grove had won Top Stock Eliminator at the '64 NHRA Winternationals, beating the Ramchargers in a semi-final heat with a tremendous hole shot: Grove 11.66, Ramchargers 11.36! If you snooze, you lose!* (Matchracemadness)

*Another defector from the GM camp was "Akron Arlen" Vanke, who switched from handling Pontiacs to driving an S/SA Plymouth sponsored by Arnett Chrysler-Plymouth. Seen here at Dragway 42 in April 1964, Vanke's Plymouth was one of the new Belvedere hardtops with the Stage III Super Stock package. (Ken Andruss)*

*Bud Faubel's '64 Honker set a new record in S/SA at 11.53 and 123.79 mph, during the NHRA Regional held at Cecil County, Maryland in May 1964. His red car was originally a Stage III wedge car, but was converted to Hemi power in early 1964, which explains the single headlights, a Hemi trademark, and double hump scoop, a wedge item. (Joel Naprstek)*

Dragmaster team. Driven by Jimmy Nix and Jim Johnson, the two Dodges were powered by 480-inch Dodge wedge engines, topped off with a big GMC 6-71 supercharger and Hilborn "Owl's Eye" fuel injection. Both cars used the standard 727 Torqueflite transmission to get the power to the big M&H slicks.

Both cars were lightened in every way possible. The two cars began life as a pair of S/S Dodge cars with the aluminum front fenders and hood. Then the bumpers, both front and rear, were removed entirely, and a custom-rolled pan was installed. Even the headlights were removed. The interior was completely gutted, with only a single front bucket seat installed. All glass was replaced with Plexiglas, and the window crank mechanisms were deleted entirely. The rear fenders were radiused to make an opening for the biggest pair of M&H slicks that would fit.

The supercharged Dodge Chargers were putting out well over 900 horsepower, and the cars were projected to run in the low 10-second area, with speeds approaching 150 mph. This was well within striking range of the fastest A/Gas Supercharged coupes in the country. Initial runs in the high 10s, with speeds of 133+, showed promise of things to come. Within the next year, Dodge and Plymouth Funny Cars, without superchargers, would be besting those times on every run.

The second supercharged stocker was the S/FX Comet Cyclone driven by Jack Chrisman. Using a supercharged, fuel-injected 427 Ford for power, the Sachs and Sons Comet went one step further than the Dodge Chargers. It ran on a nitro and alcohol mixture for fuel. With the nitro mix, the horsepower output was literally doubled and

estimates of 1500 horses wasn't far off. The Comet had so much horsepower that no transmission was used. The engine was connected directly to the rear axle. Looking inside the spartan red interior, one might be fooled by the Hurst shifter handle on the left side of the old transmission hump, but the Hurst operated the brake only.

Built to run exhibition shows only, the Comet quickly became a crowd favorite. Smoking the slicks the entire quarter mile, Chrisman's Comet was instantly famous. Drag Strip owners were

*Another record setter at the Cecil County Regional in May 1964, was the Tasca Thunderbolt, driven by Bill Lawton. The Zimmy II, now sporting a gold roof, cut an 11.69 at 122.22 for the S/S national record, and was regional Stock Eliminator. (Joel Naprstek)*

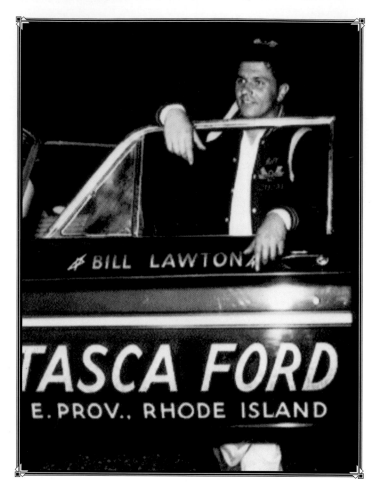

*The legendary Bill Lawton was the driver of the Tasca Ford Zimmy II Thunderbolt and a host of other Tasca Ford race cars in the 1960s. Lawton passed away in 1999. (Bill Carley via Tom Molyneaux)*

paying big money to have the blown Comet appear and make a single exhibition run in the low 10s at over 150 mph. By the time the '64 Nationals opened in Indianapolis, the car was consistent enough, and quick enough, to compete in B/Fuel Dragster class, and win!

The other car to compete in the new Super/Factory Experimental class (S/FX) was the *Mystery Tornado*, a 1964 GTO with a blown, injected 421 Pontiac engine, and driven by Mr. Pontiac himself, Arnie "The Farmer" Beswick. Without factory backing, the *Mystery Tornado* was built by Beswick to compete with the Dodge Chargers. Later, the drivetrain would be used to power Beswick's home-built, altered wheelbase '63 Tempest, and very successfully at that.

Most of the match race cars were reasonably within the limits of what was commonly thought to be stock, or at least A/Factory

Experimental. The Thunderbolts were at a distinct weight disadvantage against the big Mopars and their Comet brethren in A/FX, which is why they chose to stay in S/S at NHRA events. Under match race rules, it was typically "Run what you brung!" Cars came to race missing bumpers, sheet metal, interiors; and running huge motors far in excess of the 427 limit. As long as it looked stock, you were eligible to challenge the big name guys.

Of course, the *Drag News* "Mr. Stock Eliminator" match races had definite rules regarding minimum weight and maximum cubic inches. How you got down to minimum weight was your business. What you put into the match race motor was also your business, as long as you didn't exceed the maximum cubic inches called for in the rules. There were no limits on camshafts, compression ratio, nor carburetor type and size. No exotic fuels were allowed. The tires had to fit in the original fenderwells. No superchargers or fuel injection was allowed. In other words, the cars were reasonably close to the rules for a legal stocker.

*"Mr. 427" himself, the legendary Ronnie Sox with the newly painted red, white, and blue Brinsfield Lincoln-Mercury A/FX Comet. Note the colorful collectors on the Stahl Headers and fiberglass front bumper. (Drag Racing Memories)*

Every big name in the stocker business was involved and a lot of little names too. The little guys more than held their own against the big factory teams. Malcolm Durham, the "DC Lip," had a '64 Chevelle powered by a big-inch Z-11 motor. Dick Harrell's *Retribution* was a black Z-11-powered Chevy II, that he drove along with his black Z-11-powered '64 Chevelle. Beswick's '63 Tempests clearly were competitive as shown by the fact that he won Top Stock Eliminator at the NASCAR Winternationals over a field of some 64 cars, including a bunch of the factory-backed Comets,

*Although Pontiac wasn't officially in racing, the new 360 horsepower GTO was an instant winner in B/Stock class. Dan Ruzewski drove the Ed Reilly Pontiac GTO to victory at Presque Isle Drag Strip, an AHRA strip, which accounts for the unusual class designation of F2, B/S, for Formula 2 (multiple carburetors), B/Stock. (Jack Bleil)*

Thunderbolts, and Mopars. To prove that it wasn't a fluke, Beswick beat the best in the west, at the '64 Bakersfield Fuel and Gas Championships in March — again shutting down people like Ronda, Leal, Grove, and Proffitt along the way.

Chrysler countered the Ford Thunderbolt challenge with introduction of first, the 426 Super Stock hemi engine. That was followed by the building of four special Hemi-powered race cars that had the

*The Golden Commando #6, with John Dallafior at the wheel, comes off the line at Detroit Dragway in June 1964. In early 1964, Chrysler unveiled the 426ci Hemi engine for both NASCAR and drag racing. The production Hemi cars were all 2-door sedans, with the aluminum front end package. Hemi-powered cars, both Dodge and Plymouth, could easily be identified by the large, flat hood scoop, and single headlights with a full grill. (Drag Racing Memories)*

wheelbase altered for maximum traction, which then prompted Ford to develop and build the 427 Falcons. All of this was accomplished with one thought in mind — win the match race titles that were being touted by the various magazines.

*Drag News* had a field of Top Ten cars in the Mr. Stock Eliminator competition. This was strictly a challenge affair. Anyone within the Top Ten could challenge anyone else in the Top Ten for his position, including the No. 1 position. However, if you weren't already in the Top Ten, you had to challenge someone in the bottom five positions for his position, before challenging for a top spot, i.e. an unknown could not challenge for the No. 1 spot. The challenge matches were held at various strips around the nation, with big money prizes to the winner. There was also appearance money that was paid to the big name guys just to show at a strip. Hayden Proffitt was drawing up to $5,000.00 per appearance, whether it was a match race or not.

Of course, one of the ways to get a shot at the Top Ten, was to make yourself available the night of a scheduled match race. Then get into position in the staging lanes where you could be paired up with either of the two cars involved in the scheduled match race during time trials runs. If you beat one of the cars on a time run, then you had made a name for yourself and had bragging rights. "I beat Dyno Don the other night!", which could lead to a possible crack at challenging for a spot on the list.

Week after week, the challenge matches were run. At times there would be several challenge matches at the same strip on the same night. The newspapers and radio would scream it out, "Dyno Don against the Ramchargers. And Bud Faubel against Malcolm Durham! See it this Friday night at Cecil County Dragway!" Thousands of paying fans would be in the stands at every challenge match, cheering for their favorite driver or maybe just a car type.

Then of course, there were the Points Championships competitions held by both AHRA and NHRA, plus the Manufacturers Championships. Many of the same teams that were fighting it out for a spot on the *Drag News* list, were also in the points chase. The points cars were legal in every way, for whatever class they were set up for: Super Stock, FX, or even G/SA. Record runs were a big part of the points championships, and records were being broken at a feverish pace. The Manufacturers Championship was awarded to the car type that won the most races in that year.

There were several big races held prior to the Nationals. In March, there was the previously mentioned Bakersfield Fuel and Gas Championships, which had been almost exclusively a dragster event in the past, with a few of the big name gassers creeping in. The big stockers were so popular and in such an abundance, that the Bakersfield tech people made the decision to run the top stockers four at a time just to get through the classes in a reasonably short period of time.

The Thunderbolts were well represented in S/S; as were the 427 Comets in A/FX. Butch Leal took the S/S trophy in his Mickey Thompson-prepared Thunderbolt, with a fine run of 11.49 at 123.95 mph. Bill Hanyon, driving the Milne Brothers '64 Plymouth out of Pasadena, won S/SA with a run of 11.45 at 124.36 mph. The first

*Malcolm Durham burns through the resin powder at Cecil County in the Spring of 1964. Even though Chevrolet was not in racing in 1964, many of its cars were, and very competitive at that. Malcolm Durham's* Strip Blazer *Chevelle, was powered by one of the old '63 427 Z-11 engines. Built strictly for match racing, Durham's '64 Chevelle had fiberglass front fenders, hood, and bumper. (Drag Racing Memories)*

*Ad for a match race at York U.S. 30 Drag-O-Way (later the U.S. 30 Dragway) in the Spring of 1964. (Skip Norman)*

four-car eliminations were run in S/SA. Imagine seeing Dick Landy's Dodge, the Bourgeois & Wade Plymouth, Al "The Flying Dutchman" van der Woude, and Bill Hanyon, all facing off at the same time in the first round. WOW!

Over in A/FX, the few Dodges and Plymouths were completely over-matched against the 427 Comets. Jack Chrisman, making his first appearance in a legal Comet FX car, put Bill Shrewsberry's Comet through the quarter in a fantastic 11.34 seconds, to win the

A/FX crown over fellow Comet driver, Tom Sturm. This was the beginning of a long relationship between Chrisman and Comet as he would be the driver of the S/FX supercharged Cyclone from Sachs & Sons.

All the GM products that were built for match racing were forced into either Modified Production or Gas class as the Bakersfield rules were based on NHRA, which stated that only this year's, factory-built vehicles could compete in the FX classes. However, one name stood head and shoulders above everyone else — Arnie "The Farmer" Beswick. So much so that when the final run for A/MP was called to the line, it pitted one Beswick car against the other. None of the Dodges, Plymouths, or Fords could shut down the little Tempests. In one lane was the 421 coupe, *Mr. B's Runabout*. In the other was the 421 wagon, *Mrs. B's Grocery Getter*. Arnie drove the coupe to victory with a time of 11.66 at 126.80 mph.

In the early summer of 1964, several events were held that signaled what the national drags were going to be like. One was the AHRA Summernationals. Another was the *Hot Rod Magazine* Championships Drags. At the AHRA Summer Go, held at US 30 Dragway near Gary, Indiana on June 12, 13, and 14, all the big names in East Coast stockers were in attendance. AHRA rules seemed to have a class for whatever anyone pulled into the inspection lanes. It's been said that if you had a Radio Flyer wagon with a Hemi in it, AHRA would find a place for it.

The Dodge crowd welcomed the Ramchargers, Bud Faubel and his *Honker*, Dave Strickler, Roger Lindamood — all with new Hemi cars. The Golden Commandos, Arkie Spoon, Al Eckstrand, and Arlen Vanke represented Plymouth, again with new Hemi cars. Dick Brannan and Len Richter had Thunderbolts. Brannan also brought

*Len Richter drove the Bob Ford Thunderbolt out of Dearborn, Michigan at the AHRA Summernationals held at US 30 Dragway near Gary, Indiana. Richter's Thunderbolt surprised everyone by upsetting the mighty Ramchargers for the trophy in S/S. Richter put a big hole shot on Thornton's Ramcharger, winning with a time of 11.49 to Thornton's 11.10 seconds. (Drag Racing Memories)*

*One of the strongest running Chevys belonged to Dick Harrell. Harrell's '64 Chevelle was powered by one of the old 430 horsepower, 427 Chevy Z-11 engines. Here we have Harrell going against Butch Leal's Thunderbolt in a match race at Aquasco, Maryland. When it was running right, The Good Guys 427 Special could turn times in the low 11s. (Drag Racing Memories)*

his new 427 Falcon, that was built using the same technology as the Thunderbolt. He was entered in Super/Stock Experimental, against similar one-off creations like Dick Harrell's 427 Z-11 Chevelle.

Brannan's Falcon was one of two 427 Falcons built under authorization of the factory. The other went to Phil Bonner in Atlanta. Charlie Gray, head of Ford's Special Vehicles Division, sent two new '64 Falcon hardtops to DS&T, the same company that built the Thunderbolt Fairlanes, for the modifications.

DS&T stripped the Falcons of everything that was remotely connected with the original purpose of the car, leaving only the main body shell. Fiberglass fenders, hood, doors, and bumpers replaced the original steel parts. The rear fenders were bulged out to make room for the biggest set of slicks that would fit. All windows, except for the windshield, were replaced with thin Lucite. Both the front and rear seats were discarded, and lightweight bucket seats were installed. No rear seat was re-installed. Yet, the Falcons did have an original, full-factory dashboard and door panels. Thin carpet was installed without insulation.

Under the fiberglass hood, which had one of the famous Thunderbolt teardrop bulges, DS&T installed a 427 Hi-Riser Ford Super Stock engine identical to that being used in the Thunderbolts. The only modification needed for the installation was a shortening of the spring towers, and modification of the upper control arms for clearance with the 427 heads. Behind the 427 engine was an RC Industries scattershield, a Borg-Warner Ford 4-speed transmission, and a Detroit Locker 4.57:1 limited slip rear end. The rear suspension was a direct copy of that used under the Thunderbolt.

Built to run the match race circuit, the 3250-lb. Falcon hardtop was timed at 11.00 flat during trial runs. AHRA rules put both Brannan's maroon Romy-Hammes Ford Falcon and Bonners light blue Al Means Ford Falcon in the new S/SX class. NHRA classified both Falcons as A/FX. Would the Falcons have enough to beat the new 2% altered wheelbase Dodges and Plymouths? Time would tell.

The 2% altered wheelbase cars were a breed unto themselves. Only four were built in 1964 — two Dodges, one for the Ramchargers and the other for Dave Strickler; and two Plymouths, one each for Tommy Grove and Al Eckstrand. All began life as standard lightweight Super Stock 2-door sedans, powered by the 426 wedge engine. Grove and Strickler had 4-speed transmissions; while Eckstrand and The Ramchargers cars were Torqueflite automatics. All four subsequently had the 426 Hemi installed before the 2% modifications.

In the Summer of 1964, the four cars were shipped to Alexander Brothers Custom Shop in Detroit. The reason for the changes was relatively simple: If you alter the wheelbase slightly, the engine moves further to the rear, thus the weight distribution is drastically affected. The wheelbase was altered several ways. First the front K-member, was moved forward 3" from its original position. Then the upper control arm and torsion bar were replaced with items that reflected the necessary increase in length to match up with the new location of the front wheel.

*With Chevrolet out of racing, the top drivers were scooped up quickly. Hubert Platt, part of Don Nicholson's Nalley-Nicholson team in Atlanta, went with Phil Bonner and Vego Ford. His Georgia Shaker Thunderbolt was one of two campaigned by Vego Ford, the other belonging to Bonner. (Drag Racing Memories)*

*Al "Lawman" Eckstrand comes off the line at Indy Raceway Park in the 2% Hemi-Belvedere sedan. The car has a new aluminum front end, but still retains the old style wedge, double hump hood scoop. Chrysler authorized building four cars: 2 Dodges and 2 Plymouths. Eckstrand and Tommy Grove got the Plymouth entries. (Drag Racing Memories)*

In the rear, the axle assembly was moved forward 4" and the spring perches were reattached. The rear fenderwells were moved forward 5", but that was for tire clearance. The outer rear fender was cut and the entire fender opening was moved forward. Patch panels were then welded in place and the fender was primed and painted. At a quick glance, the cars appeared stock. However, if there was a stock vehicle next to it for comparison, it then became apparent that something was funny about these four cars. It was the first of what would

become known as the "Funny Car." The 2% cars would, however, look "stock" compared to the 1965 editions of the "Funny Car."

Other than the altered wheelbase, these four "funny" cars were similar to all the other A/FX Dodges and Plymouths, with stripped interiors, Plexiglas windows, and the aluminum front end package. Chrysler quickly notified the sanctioning bodies about the changes. All quickly gave the nod of approval, and classified the four cars as either A/FX in NHRA, or Experimental Stock in AHRA. The Hemi

*Forest Pitcock at the helm of the* Golden Commandos #5 *car, one of a handful of Hemi-Plymouth hardtops. Most of the new Hemi-equipped super stockers, both Plymouth and Dodge, were lightweight 2-door sedans. The Hemi-powered cars could be distinguished by the single headlight/full-span grille assembly. Most of the early Hemi cars had the older style twin bulge air intake scoop as found on the Stage III wedge cars. Pitcock won Top Stock at the Detroit World Championship Meet held in August 1964 at Detroit Dragway. (Matchracemadness)*

cars in S/S and S/SA retained the standard wheelbase, although many were modified with the 2% modification as soon as the sanctioning bodies gave approval to the original four cars.

How quick were the new 2% creations as compared with the standard S/S cars? Try 10.66 at over 131 mph for Strickler's Dodge. Normal times for a Hemi-equipped Dodge or Plymouth were 11.50s and 120+ mph. The other three cars were equally as quick and fast. Chrysler also notified all four drivers that the cars were built only for A/FX or the match race circuit. Other drivers soon converted their standard S/S cars to the 2% modifications, and some were modified even further. Bill "Maverick" Golden was one of the first to convert his standard S/SA Dodge to 2%. Dick Landy not only moved the front wheels forward the allotted 3", he also changed the torsion bar front suspension to a straight axle type used on the Dodge E-100 van.

At the AHRA Summernationals, Jim Thornton put the Ramchargers Dodge through the quarter in an amazing 11.06 seconds at 132.353 mph to set the standard for X/S class runoffs. It was the quickest and fastest times ever recorded by a stocker to that date. The Saturday night Mr. Stock Eliminator title saw a Dodge and a Ford wade through the competition.

The final round was between Len Richter and the Bob Ford Thunderbolt, and Jim Thornton and the Ramchargers Dodge. At first glance, it shouldn't have been much of a race. Thornton had been running very low 11s all night long; while Richter had really been cranking on the Thunderbolt to get down into the 11.30s. At the Green, the Thunderbolt leaped out ahead of the Dodge and never looked back. The winner: Richter's Thunderbolt at 11.49. The big Dodge had run an 11.10, but Thornton had been sleeping at the start. Thornton complained that the foul lights had malfunctioned, and that Richter had jumped the Green. The AHRA Tech crew refused to re-run the race, and Richter's win stood to the amazement of the crowd. Dick Brannan completed the Ford sweep by downing Dick Harrell's Chevelle with an 11.28 at 128.79 mph, to win the S/SX class with his 427ci Falcon.

Class winners included Dave Strickler's 2% Dodge in S/S Optional, with an ET of 11.18 and 128.40 mph; the Ramchargers 2% car won its class, S/S Optional Automatic, with an 11.04 and 130.05 mph; Richter's Thunderbolt won S/S at 11.18 and 123.29 mph; and Roger Lindamood's *Color Me Gone* Dodge took S/SA in 11.56 seconds at 126.76 mph.

*Hayden Proffitt puts the Yeakel Hemi-Plymouth through its paces at Lions Drag Strip in the summer of 1964. Proffitt's Hemi-Plymouth turned an 11.69, 121.00 mph on its first run; then brought the ET down to 11.28 within three weeks. Note new M&H "wrinkle-wall" slicks. Proffitt's Hemi-Plymouth was ejected at the '64 Nationals when NHRA claimed he was using an illegal fuel. Proffitt sued NHRA with Al "The Lawman" Eckstrand as his lawyer, and was victorious in court. (Matchracemadness)*

Gas Ronda's beautiful Poppy Red Thunderbolt was the winner of S/S at the first Hot Rod Magazine *Championship Drags held at Riverside International Raceway in June 1964. His Thunderbolt turned only 12.65, which was way off his normal pace, but it was enough as his opponent jumped the green light and fouled.* (Past Lane Auto)

There were several Chevy IIs built in 1964 with Z-11 engines, including the Tension II, *driven by Bud Richter. The red Chevy II sedan had a straight front axle and elliptical springs, similar to a Willys gasser suspension, and could pull the front wheels off the ground with every shift.* (John Lacko)

On Sunday, the runoff for Top Stock Eliminator went off. Again, Thornton was setting the pace with qualifying runs of 11.08 being common. Once again, the big candy-striped Dodge and gold Thunderbolt waded through the competition. The final three cars were Thornton, Richter, and Lindamood. In the semi-final round, Lindamood drew the bye run and made a solo pass. This left Richter and Thornton to repeat the previous night's action.

However, the upset Ford victory of Saturday night wasn't going to be repeated. Thornton watched the yellow lights click off one by one, then launched the big Hemi perfectly. Richter also came out of the gate about as quick as he had on Saturday night, and even stayed with the big Hemi-Dodge through 1st gear. Then Thornton's Torqueflite shifted into 2nd and destroyed all thoughts Richter had of a second upset win. The Dodge pulled away so rapidly that some fans thought the Thunderbolt had broken something. At the end, the candy-striped Dodge had almost a 5-car length victory, turning a fantastic 11.06, with a World Record Speed of 132.353 mph.

Top Stock Eliminator would be an all-Dodge final. In the left lane was the red and white candy-striped Ramchargers Dodge. In the right lane was the blue and white *Color Me Gone.* Both cars were literally identical 426 Dodge Hemi-Chargers, except one looked a little funny. Both were Torqueflite equipped, but one car was much quicker than the other. Indeed, the Ramchargers car was running almost half a second quicker than anyone else in the class.

As the yellow lights winked down on the tree, Lindamood took a chance and cut the last light very, very close. It was a green light start, and the blue and white Dodge charged out ahead of Thornton. Unlike the night before, Thornton made up the difference as soon as

he shifted into second. Again, the red and white Dodge went by the competition like he had stopped. Lindamood turned a very credible 11.41, but Thornton turned in another very low 11.08 to win going away. The 2% altered wheelbase cars were here to stay.

At the *Hot Rod Magazine* First Annual Drag Championships held at the new Riverside International Raceway facility in Southern

The Dragmaster Team unloads one of the Dodge Chargers at Dragway 42 on June 7, 1964. *The Chargers were the first supercharged team, using blown and injected 426 Max Wedge engines for power. NHRA created a class just for this type of car — S/FX for Supercharged Factory Experimental. Both Dodge Chargers were identical and usually had to run each other.* (Dave Edwards)

California, it looked like someone had turned back the clock to the previous Winternationals. Almost everyone who had attended the '64 Big Go West was in attendance. Some had newer cars like Don Nicholson, who brought both his new Cyclone hardtop and the old *Ugly Duckling* wagon, now driven by Eddie Schartman. Hayden Proffitt and Al Eckstrand both had hemi cars in A/FX, with Eckstrand's *Lawman* Plymouth having the new 2% modification. Again, the Thunderbolts dominated S/S.

The class runoffs saw very few surprises. Gas Ronda put his Poppy Red Russ Davis Thunderbolt through the quarter in 12.65 seconds to win the S/S trophy. Tommy Grove waded through the likes of Eckstrand, Proffitt, Landy, and Darrell Ritchey, to put the *Melrose Missile* into the winners circle for S/SA. In A/FX, Bill Shrewsberry put down the big Hemis of Proffitt, Grove, and Eckstrand; plus the 427 Comets of Tom Sturm and Don Nicholson. The Sachs & Sons Comet turned an 11.70 at 122.11 mph to Nicholson's 11.82 and 121.13.

Top Stock Eliminator would be between eleven cars: three Thunderbolts and eight Mopars. Tommy Grove red-lighted against Ronda's Thunderbolt, and Butch Leal put *Maverick* on the trailer, while the Ed Martin Thunderbolt broke, to highlight action in Round One. Now there were two Thunderbolts and four Plymouths. The two 'Bolts had to face each other in Round Two, with Ronda shutting down Leal at 12.04 and 119.84 mph. Leal's losing time was 12.10 and 120.00. There was less than a fender length between the two cars at the finish.

The final for Top Stock matched Al "Lawman" Eckstrand in the McCullough-Ricci wedge hardtop Plymouth, and Gas Ronda's Thunderbolt. At the Green, Ronda's Thunderbolt charged out of the gate and was gone. The candy orange and white Plymouth was in hot pursuit, but this was a Ford day and Ronda won by a full car length and a half, turning a 12.08 and 119.50, to Eckstrand's losing time of 12.21 and 114.21.

Between June 19th and the 21st, *Drag News* held its Second Annual Invitational, at Detroit Dragway. It would be a preview of the coming action at the Nationals. Class runoffs took place on Saturday night, and the top classes had familiar names in the winners' circles: Len Richter in S/S with the Bob Ford Thunderbolt and young Don Gay was the winner of A/S with his now-familiar '62 Pontiac Catalina sedan.

In A/FX, the big Comets and Hemis battled it out. Ronnie Sox and Don Nicholson were the favorites, but the Ramchargers and Roger Lindamood had Hemi-Dodges that were running as quick as any of the Comets. Sox put Phil Bonner's Thunderbolt on the trailer with an ET of 11.80. Jim Thornton shut down Bud Faubel's *Hemi-Honker* with an 11.85.

Sox drew a bye run in the semis, setting up a return match between Thornton and Lindamood. As the flag went up, it was Lindamood out of the gate first and holding on to win at 12.34. Thornton's Ramcharger Dodge was again quicker at 12.23, but had been caught napping at the start.

*Ford had Detroit Steel & Tubing build at least 100 Thunderbolts for the '64 season, so there were Thunderbolts everywhere you looked. Jim "Bull" Durham had one of the S/SA Thunderbolts sponsored by Wendle Ford Town in Spokane, Washington. He is seen here at the Cecil County Factory Showdown in the Summer of '64. (Drag Racing Memories)*

*The '64 AHRA Summernationals at Gary, Indiana saw the unveiling of a new car from Dick Brannan — a 427 Falcon hardtop. Using the shorter, lighter Falcon body, the car was all Thunderbolt underneath. Only two 427 Falcons were factory-built by Holman & Moody, one for Dick Brannan and a second for Phil Bonner. Here is Brannan pulling into Detroit Dragway in August 1965. The Falcon won SS/X at the AHRA Summernationals, turning 11.28 at 128.79 mph, beating Dick Harrell's Z-11 Chevelle. (Drag Racing Memories)*

In the Summer of 1964, Dodge and Jay Howell created what would become the most famous super stock vehicle ever built: the Little Red Wagon. It was initially built with thoughts of actually running some type of legal class, such as A/FX. The little pickup would easily run in the mid-10s at over 135 mph with a stock 426 Hemi engine. However, it was virtually uncontrollable and very prone to huge wheelstands, which became its hallmark. Here is Jay Howell making a straight, flat pass in the new Little Red Wagon, well before Bill "Maverick" Golden was in the picture. (Author's Collection)

The final run for A/FX was between the red, white, and blue Comet from Brinsfield Lincoln-Mercury, with Ronnie Sox in the drivers seat; and the blue and white Hemi-Dodge driven by Roger Lindamood. When the starter brought the flag up, Sox's Comet launched like a rocket, putting a two-car length lead on the big Dodge right out of the gate. As suddenly as things looked good for Sox, they went bad. He went for 2nd gear and missed the shift. While Sox is wildly trying to jam the 4 speed into 2nd gear, the big Dodge went by and Lindamood didn't look back, winning the A/FX trophy with a time of 12.29 and 120.00 mph.

A storm interrupted the eliminations on Sunday. When it finally dried up enough to race, Bill "The Professor" Shirey drove the Hamilton Motors '64 Plymouth to Top Stock Eliminator honors over a strong field. His Plymouth was one of the early 426 Stage III wedge cars with the aluminum front end and Torqueflite transmission. His final run for Top Stock was 12.79 at 118.73 mph. All these same names would be at Indy at the end of Summer.

Immediately prior to the Nationals came the (now) annual Detroit Nationals, hosted by Gil Kohn at Detroit Dragway. Kohn was paying big money to the winner, a dollar a foot: $1320.00, and the class rules were modified a bit to equalize the competition. There was a minimum weight requirement of 3200 lbs., and a minimum wheelbase of 114". Any size tire that would fit in the fenderwell was allowed, and they didn't need to have any tread on them either. Other than that, the cars had to be legal for whatever class they were built for. They all ran "heads up," meaning no handicap starts.

The big money drew many of the big names that were already en route to Indy for the Nationals: Nicholson, Ronda, Leal, Eckstrand,

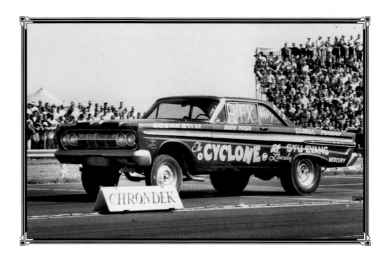

*Doug Nash handled the B/FX Comet* The Cyclone. *Built by Detroit Steel & Tubing, right beside the Thunderbolt Fairlanes, the B/FX Cyclones were identical to the A/FX 427 Comets, with fiberglass front ends and hood scoops. However, they used 289ci Ford small-block engines, with various Cobra parts like multiple Weber carburetors, dual 4 barrels, wild cams, etc. (Drag Racing Memories)*

Tasca, etc. Dyno Don set the stage when he came off the trailer with runs in the very low 11s, lifting the front wheels on every run. Another Kohn innovation was the multi-heat elimination that would

*Bill Lawton brings the* Zimmy II *off the line at the '64 Nationals. Although one of the most consistent Thunderbolts in the nation, Lawton was shut down in Round 1 of S/S at the Nationals, and didn't qualify for Top Stock Eliminator. The Thunderbolts were delivered from the factory with M/T Rader Wheels. (Drag Racing Memories)*

*Eddie Schartman charges off the line at the '64 Nationals in the* Ugly Duckling *427 Comet wagon. Both Schartman and Nicholson fell to the new 2% altered-wheelbase Mopars in A/FX. The fiberglass hood had two openings in the front to duct fresh air to the big Holley four-barrel carburetors that fed the 427 Marauder V-8. (Drag Racing Memories)*

eventually bring the fastest four cars to the line for Top Stock Eliminator. Kohn took the fastest sixteen qualifiers and ran them off in Heat #1. Nicholson won easily with four rounds between 11.22 and 11.13. In heat #2, Dyno Don couldn't compete, and Kohn ran off the next fifteen fastest cars. This continued until he had four heat eliminators: Don Nicholson's 427 Comet, Joe Smith and the Fenner-Tubbs Hemi-Plymouth, Len Richter and the Bob Ford Thunderbolt, and Forest Pitcock driving the Golden Commandos Hemi-Plymouth. Just right — two Fords and two Mopars.

With the three other qualifiers running in the 11.40 range, Dyno Don clearly had things under control. The two Plymouths were matched up first, with Pitcock and the Golden Commandos Hemi winning a close race. Next to the line was Dyno Don and the white Comet hardtop, against Len Richter's gold Thunderbolt. Nicholson had a big advantage and easily shut down the Bob Ford Thunderbolt to set up a final of Comet against Hemi-Plymouth.

When the Christmas tree started blinking down, both drivers brought the RPMs up. As the last yellow began to go off, Pitcock moved. The big white Plymouth charged out of the gate so far ahead of Nicholson that everyone, including Don, thought Pitcock had red-lighted, but the lights were all green. Dyno Don just put the big Comet in reverse and went back to the pits as the Plymouth went through the timing traps at 11.36 and 125.17 mph. The tree, which had malfunctioned immediately prior to the beginning of the Top Stock eliminations, had probably malfunctioned again. The $1320.00 was in Pitcock's pocket.

## 1964 NATIONALS

The '64 NHRA Nationals were, as usual, held over Labor Day weekend at Indianapolis Raceway Park. S/S was again loaded up with Ford Thunderbolts, and a few 4-speed Dodges and Plymouths. S/SA had the usual number of Dodges and Plymouths, many of which were powered by the new Hemi engine, with a handful of Cruise-O-Matic Thunderbolts thrown in. In FX, it was the 2% altered wheelbase Dodges and Plymouths, against the mighty 427 Comets, with at least one 427 Mustang thrown in.

The first three days of the Big Go were devoted to time trials and qualifying runs for various eliminators, including Top Stock. After the first few days of qualifying, twelve of the fifteen qualifying cars were Dodges and Plymouths. Only Bill Lawton, Gas Ronda, and Butch Leal's Thunderbolts broke up the Dodge and Plymouth parade. By the final day of qualifying, only Butch Leal was left. The sixteen car Top Stock field was made up of eight Dodges, seven Plymouths, and Leal's Thunderbolt.

On Sunday, the first class runoffs were held. Leal took the honors in S/S, beating Al Joniec's Thunderbolt with an ET of 11.76 and 122.78 mph. Both AA/S and A/S were disqualified, as Joe Orland's AA/S '64 lightweight Galaxie was discovered to have illegal valve lifters and push rods; while Don Gay's '63 National Champ Pontiac didn't have anything inside the mufflers.

In S/SA, the familiar Ramchargers candy striped Hemi-Dodge, with Jim Thornton driving, put down a strong field to take the win over John Dallafior and the Golden Commandos Plymouth, at 11.37 and 128.20 mph. Mike Schmidt's Desert Motors '64 lightweight Galaxie won AA/SA with a time of 12.18 at 111.80 mph. A new name took the honors in A/SA when Ron Mandella drove his '63 Plymouth station wagon, powered by a 426" Stage I Super Stock motor, winning the class with a time of 12.99 at 108.04 mph.

The A/FX class had everyone in the crowd standing and cheering. The field was made up of the four 2% Mopars, plus Bill Shrewsberry, Don Nicholson, and Ed Schartman's Comets, and Len Richter with the new *Hemi-Haunter* Mustang coupe with a 427" Ford under the hood. After the first round, it was all Mopar when Shrewsberry fouled, Nicholson missed a gear, and Richter got beat. Schartman had engine problems.

The A/FX final matched two of the best gear grabbers in the business: Dave Strickler and the "Dodge Boys'" 4-speed 2% Hemi-Dodge, against Tommy Grove and the 4-speed *Melrose Missile* 2% Hemi-Plymouth. The two cars came out of the gate side by side and it was all even until 3rd gear. That's when Grove missed a shift and Strickler pulled away for the win. Dave would've been hard to beat with a perfect run, as he turned an 11.04 ET. B/FX went to Fred Cutler with his one-of-a-kind '64 Hemi-Dodge station wagon, with an ET of 11.81 at 120.48 mph

In A/Modified production, the new home for last year's FX cars, this year's models with non-stock equipment, plus all the GM stuff that was built for the match race circuit, the winner was "Wild Bill"

*The final race for A/Factory Experimental was between Dave Strickler's* Dodge Boys *2% Dodge, and Tommy Grove and the* Melrose Missile VI *2% Plymouth. Grove had won Stock Eliminator at the '64 Winternationals, but missed a shift in the A/FX run against Strickler. Strickler would have been hard to beat with a perfect run by Grove, as he turned an 11.04 winning ET. The 2% wheelbase alteration is evident on both cars. (Drag Racing Memories)*

Flynn and his *Yankee Peddler* '64 Dodge. He beat Arnie Beswick for the title, although the win was controversial to say the least. Seems the win lights had been malfunctioning all day and NHRA officials had even reversed a couple of race results.

When the green light came on for the A/MP trophy run, the *Yankee Peddler* jumped out to a good half-car length lead. That soon evaporated and Beswick roared through the lights ahead of the Dodge with an ET of 11.68. Flynn's Dodge had run an 11.95. Lo and behold, the win light came on in Flynn's lane! A check to the starting line revealed that no foul had occurred on the part of Beswick, which would have resulted in a win for Flynn. Flynn was declared the winner since the Chrondek timers do not lie. Beswick protested vehemently but to no avail.

On Monday, the first rounds of Top Stock Eliminator were run. There were sixteen cars qualified, with Butch Leal's Thunderbolt being the lone non-Mopar entry. After the first round, it was again an all-Chrysler contest as Thornton shut down Leal 11.39 to 11.96. Round 2 began with Pitcock red-lighting against Thornton; Bud Faubel defeated Dallafior, thus eliminating both Golden Commando Plymouths; Dick Landy beat Bobby Harrop; and Jerry Austin fouled against Lindamood.

Somehow, Dallafior thought he had advanced to Round 3, probably due to another win light malfunction. However, he drew the unlucky straw and lined up against Thornton's Dodge in the first race. The NHRA tech crew caught the mistake and ordered Dallafior to return to the pits. Thornton then soloed at 11.49. Lindamood put Dandy Dick Landy on the trailer with an 11.36 and Faubel made a solo. That left three cars.

*The Ramchargers had two cars at the '63 Nationals, a 2% car in A/FX and this S/SA Hemi-Charger. Jim Thornton piloted the big Hemi-Dodge to victory in S/SA class, then advanced all the way to the trophy run in Stock Eliminator, only to lose to Roger Lindamood and the* Color Me Gone *Dodge, which turned an 11.31 on the trophy run. (Drag Racing Memories)*

Thornton was paired off with Faubel's *Hemi-Honker*, winning with the fastest time of the meet at 11.31. Faubel turned a losing 11.74. Lindamood cruised the *Color Me Gone* Dodge on a solo run at 11.49. Top Stock Eliminator was between the two stockers that had been the quickest throughout the meet.

In the left lane was the candy-striped Ramchargers, with Jim Thornton behind the wheel. In the right lane was the blue and white *Color Me Gone*, driven by Roger Lindamood. As the lights clicked down through the yellow, the crowd stood and held its collective breath. Green! Lindamood is gone, pulling away from Thornton all the way through the quarter mile. At the end, Lindamood had about a three-car length lead, winning with a time of 11.31, which tied Thornton's mark set just one race prior. Thornton ran 11.47 in a losing cause.

The '64 NHRA Nationals had truly been an all-Dodge event. Half of the Top Stock qualifiers were Dodges. Dodges won S/SA, A/FX, B/FX, and A/M, and all of the cars in the last three rounds of Top Stock were Dodges. Roger Lindamood and the *Color Me Gone* Dodge was crowned Top Stock Eliminator. On top of all that, "Big Daddy" Don Garlits won Top Eliminator in a Dodge-powered fuel dragster. It was a sweep that would never be matched again.

The AHRA Nationals were held over the same weekend as the NHRA Big Go in Indy, and the AHRA meet drew many of the drivers that NHRA thought would be at Indy. The reason: AHRA offered a big money purse for the winner of Top Stock. Phil Bonner, Hayden Proffitt, Bill "Maverick" Golden, Gene Snow, and Dick Harrell were among those who signed up for the AHRA races. It was the money, not the prestige of the NHRA event, that drew them.

*Bud Faubel and his second Hemi-Honker at speed during the AHRA Summernationals in June 1964. Faubel's Honker, now prepared by Bill Jenkins, was the NHRA S/SA record holder in the Spring of 1964, turning 11.53 at 123.79 mph. (Drag Racing Memories)*

Ford authorized several Falcons to be built with 427 engines, including this light blue coupe owned and driven by Phil Bonner. Competing in AHRA's Ultra Stock category, Bonner's 427 SOHC Falcon won both Top Stock and Mr. Eliminator titles at the AHRA Nationals in Green Valley, Texas over Labor Day 1964. (Matchracemadness)

Phil Bonner was the man to beat right off the trailer, when he put his new blue Falcon, one of only two built, through the quarter in 11.34 seconds. Lee Smith was close behind at 11.39 in the Learner Hemi-Plymouth. Top speed was Maverick Golden's Hemi-Dodge at 125 mph. In the final for Top Stock, Bonner faced Gene Snow's Hemi-Plymouth. When Snow red-lighted, Bonner cruised through the lights in 11.61. The next afternoon, Bonner repeated the trick, winning the Mr. Stock Eliminator title with a time of 11.45.

Immediately following the Nationals, an international event took place — the First British International Drag Festival. Drag racing had become a popular sport in England, and Wally Parks of NHRA worked with Sydney Allard, President of the British Drag Racing Association, to arrange a meet that would feature several of the prominent names in American drag racing, for a tour of British drag strips.

A couple of top names from the most popular NHRA classes went to England where they put on a show at six different drag strips between September 19th and October 4th. From Top Fuel went Don "Big Daddy" Garlits and "TV Tommy" Ivo. In Top Gas Dragster was Tony Nancy and Bob Keith. A/Gas Supercharged featured two of the fiercest competitors in the nation: K.S. "Tiger" Pittman and "Ohio George" Montgomery. From A/FX came Ronnie Sox and the red, white, and blue Brinsfield Lincoln-Mercury Comet, against Dave Strickler and the Dodge Boys 2% Hemi-Dodge.

The idea was for the American cars to race against each other, with points awarded to the winner of each round. This would determine the overall winner of the British Drag Fest. The racing was done on runways at airports and military bases throughout England. Strickler beat Sox in overall points, 337 to 309 to win the A/FX title. Best ET for the Comet was 11.72, while Strickler's big white Hemi-Dodge turned an 11.54. A good time was had by all who attended, and a second British Drag Fest was scheduled for 1965. However, for some reason, no stockers were included; just a field of eight Top Fuel cars were invited.

*At the NHRA Regional at Dragway 42 in May 1965, Kenny Vogt drove the Bob Ford Thunderbolt, the* Stinger I, *which competed in A/Modified Production because he was running slicks. Treaded tires like M & H Racemaster Super Stocks or Caslers, would have put the yellow Thunderbolt in S/S.* (Author's Collection)

*At the end of September 1964, NHRA sponsored a trip to England for an International Drag Fest that would showcase some of the best US drag racing machines and drivers. In stock class, there were two invitees: Dave Strickler's 2% Dodge, winner of A/FX at the Nationals; and Ronnie Sox and his Comet, winner of A/FX at the Winternationals. Points were awarded for each victory at the Drag Fest. Strickler won the competition by amassing a total of 337 points to Sox's 309. Strickler's best time on the British airports-turned-drag strips, was 11.54, to Sox's 11.72, far from Strickler's US national A/FX record of 11.05. (Nick Pettitt)*

One of the last meets for 1964 was the World Series of Drag Racing, held at Cordova, Illinois. This was another money meet, similar in concept to the Detroit Nationals. As such, they didn't have to abide by any association rules regarding classes. The World Series was governed by the National Association of Drag Strip Owners,

*In the far northwest, the man to beat was Bill Ireland and the Oregon Ford Dealers Thunderbolt. Ireland's car was one of the original 4-speed Thunderbolts. (Russ Griffith)*

which had class rules somewhat based on AHRA and NASCAR rules, i.e. the cars were all classified first by cubic inches to weight, then by carburetion type and number, then by cam type. The big money for Top Stock was $1,000.00. There was also money paid to the winner of each round in the Top Stock run-off.

Many of the big names from the Nationals were at Cordova for the World Series: Tommy Grove brought the *Melrose Missile* 2% Plymouth, Lee Smith had his Hemi-Plymouth, Joe Deaton had one of the 427 Comets, and a host of others. Grove's *Missile* was clearly the favorite, with ETs as low as 11.10. As quick as Grove was, he couldn't beat the starting system. The final run was between Grove and Lee Smith.

When the flag went up, Grove charged out of the gate and went on to victory. Or did he? There was a red light glowing in Grove's lane, giving the win and the $1,000.00 prize to Smith. However, many people said that Grove hadn't fouled. There was some mention of the starter having both flags on the foul button, but lifting only one, which made it appear that Grove fouled. Smith didn't care. He ran 11.26 against Grove, and took the check home with him. Oh yes, incidentally, Cordova was Smith's home track.

The NHRA Grand Finale meet was held at Amarillo, Texas and Joe Smith drove the beautiful dark purple Fenner-Tubbs Hemi-Plymouth to victory in Stock Eliminator. The '64 season was now over except for the never-ending match race circuit and new car testing. The next season was on its way, and it would bring the wildest bunch of super stockers the world had ever seen. So wild that they were funny. It was the beginning of the end of an era.

One of the final times that Ronnie Sox ran his '64 A/FX Comet was this December 1964 match race with the Hemi Hannah Plymouth at Fayetteville Drag Strip. Within weeks he would take delivery of his '65 AWB Plymouth. Note that the headers are now Tyree Headers, and the Comet wears the decal from the British Drag Fest: "United States Drag Racing Team". (Author's Collection)

Arnie "The Farmer" Beswick ran A/MP at the '64 Nationals with his Mrs. B's Runabout, the '63 421 Tempest coupe that he drove to victory at Bakersfield. By now the old 4-speed transaxle had been changed to a standard 4-speed and Catalina rear axle assembly. (Dave Edwards)

Hubert Platt backs through his own tracks in the gold dust, with the newest of his three Falcons, *The Georgia Shaker III*. Powered by an injected 427 Ford Hi-Riser wedge motor, the No. 3 Shaker also had the wheelbase shortened, and had a beam axle under the front, making the car very unstable at the speeds they were starting to reach — 130+ mph. (Brent Hajek)

In late 1965, the author ordered a Chevy II economy car. Yeah, right! It was powered by a 327ci Corvette engine putting out 350 horses. It had a 4-speed transmission and came with a 3.70 Positraction rear end. The little screamer also came with really big tires – 6.95x14 Goodyears, that simply exploded in smoke whenever you touched the gas pedal. With slicks, it was awesome! (Author's Collection)

E/Stock class was the home of the 283 horsepower, fuel-injected '57 Chevys. Bob Lambeck, later handling a SS-B Hemi-Dart, towed his '57 Chevrolet all the way from Sherman Oaks, California, to compete at the '66 NHRA Nationals. (Author's Collection)

The NASCAR Nationals M/SA trophy was just a plaque, but it was a Nationals win! (Author's Collection)

"Honest" Jerry Marteney drove this '59 Chevy L/Stock National Record holder at the '66 NHRA Nationals. The '59 Chevy was powered by a 220 horse 283 engine, with a 4-speed transmission. Although very few '59 Chevys were built with this particular combination, NHRA allowed that it was possible for it to exist, thus making it legal for L/S. Marteney's national record was 15.26 and 89.37 mph. (Author's Collection)

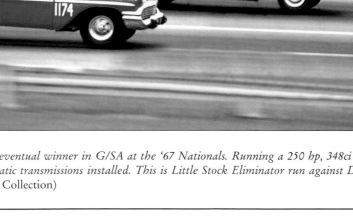

Gordon Kurtz's '58 Chevy sedan delivery was the eventual winner in G/SA at the '67 Nationals. Running a 250 hp, 348ci Chevy engine, the Sedan Delivery had one of the rarely available Hydra-Matic transmissions installed. This is Little Stock Eliminator run against Dave & Ben Wenzel's B/S Camaro, which was the eventual winner. (Author's Collection)

One of the most consistent winners at Dragway 42, Magnolia, and Quaker City, was the D/S '60 Biscayne of Geiger & Williams. The '60 was powered by a 320 horsepower, 348ci Chevy, with a 4 speed and Positraction. It ran in the mid-13s. (Author's Collection)

By the Summer of 1963, Bill "Maverick" Golden's "yellow cab" Dodge sported an all-new paint job, sponsored by the LA-Orange County Dodge Dealers. Maverick toured the south and east for match races with anyone who "wanted a piece of him." Seen here at the AHRA Summernationals at Aquasco, Maryland, Maverick's Dodge has the Stage II Ramcharger engine package including the aluminum front end with hood scoop. (Drag Racing Memories)

Another driver that turned to the 409 Chevrolet in 1962, was Hayden Proffitt, who switched from tuning and driving Pontiacs for Mickey Thompson. Seen here at Pacific Raceways in early Spring 1962, Proffitt's 409 Bel Air hardtop was prepared by Bill Thomas Race Cars, and equipped with Frank Sanders' S&S Headers. (Raj Reddi Collection)

Northwind, *the '62 409 Bel Air out of the Jenkins Comp shop was built and driven by team members Joe Gardner, Arnie Waldman, and Joe Tryson — with engine by the grumpy one, Bill Jenkins. The beautiful red and gold car was runner-up to Don Gay in A/S at the '62 Nationals. Note very long collector pipes on the Stahl Headers. (Drag Racing Memories)*

*Ben Smith drove the Ed Martin Ford A/SA '63 Galaxie, cutting ETs in the low 13-second bracket. He lost out to Bill Abraham and the* Golden Arrow *'62 Pontiac. Abraham's 13.28 was just enough to shut down the 427 Fords. Note the 12 class winner decals on the driver's window. (Drag Racing Memories)*

*Doug Kahl campaigned this '62 Plymouth for what seemed like decades, and was the 1965 NHRA World Points Champ with the D/SA Plymouth. Running the 383ci Plymouth engine, Kahl just kept re-adjusting the suspension, transmission, and carburetion until it was exactly right for the class. He then became virtually unbeatable. (Author's Collection)*

At the start of the 1964 season, both Dodge and Plymouth were willing to stay with the Stage III package for the 426 drag cars, which had actually been released at the end of the '63 season. Al Eckstrand had a beautiful Stage III '64 Plymouth Belvedere hardtop, resplendent in white and candy red paint, with the now familiar Lawman on the doors. Eckstrand's S/SA Plymouth went to the final in Stock Eliminator at the Hot Rod Magazine Drags in June before losing to Gas Ronda's Thunderbolt. (Al Eckstrand)

One look and everyone knew why they were called funny cars. This is the Sox & Martin AWB Plymouth at Piedmont Drag Raceway in March 1965. Not only was the wheelbase radically altered, but the bodies were acid-dipped to get the metal as thin as possible. Without paint, you could just about see light through the fender panels! (Author's Collection)

Following the end of the '64 drag season, Al Eckstrand sold his 2% Hemi-Plymouth to Joe Aed. Aed added a Hilborn fuel injection set-up and gutted the interior to make it a little lighter, and entered the car in NHRA C/Altered class. Aed's Plymouth won C/A at the '65 NHRA Nationals, then proceeded to set the national record for C/A. (Author's Collection)

*Don Nicholson arrives at Piedmont Drag Raceway in March 1965, still hauling his A/FX Comet on the same Chevrolet roll-back truck that he used when he campaigned the '63 Z-11 Impala. At least this year, he painted over the Chevrolet emblem on the flag. (Author's Collection)*

*One of the more unusual creations for the '65 season was Jerry Harvey's The Quiet One, a '65 Galaxie hardtop powered by one of the 427 SOHC Hemi Fords. Seen here at Dragway 42 for the NHRA Regional, Harvey's SOHC Galaxie competed in B/FX, winning the class at the '65 Winternationals with a time of 11.91, which is really hauling for a car that weighed 3855 lbs. (Author's Collection)*

*Dave Lyall's 427 Falcon had an all-fiberglass body; the only one ever built. The fiberglass Falcon had a wedge engine, but the light weight and short wheelbase made it a contender in A/FX. Lyall was a member of "The Lively Ones," a Ford team in Detroit. (Author's Collection)*

Dick Brannan's beautiful gold metalflake Goldfinger SOHC Mustang at Piedmont Drag Raceway for a match race with Dick Harrell's 427 Chevy II. The SOHC Mustangs were built to compete in A/Factory Experimental class. Thus they were at a decided disadvantage when going against the altered wheelbase Mopars. Running times in the mid-10s, Brannan handled Harrell's Z-11 Chevy II on this day. (Author's Collection)

In the Spring of 1965, Bill Thomas Race Cars put together three very unusual Chevy IIs with a fastback roof for the match race circuit. Seen here at Thompson Drag Raceway near Cleveland, Huston Platt's fastback Chevy II was still powered by a 427 Z-11 engine when a match race was scheduled with Eddie Schartman's 427 wedge Comet. (Author's Collection)

By the time of the '66 Nationals, Jerry Harvey's '65 Fairlane Thunderbolt, that had been powered by a 427 Hi-Riser wedge motor, now had one of the 427 SOHC Ford Hemis under the hood. Running in E/Experimental Stock, the candy-red Fairlane won the class with an ET of 10.97 at 127.47 mph. (Author's Collection)

Running in B/XS at the '66 Nationals, Bud Faubel roars off with his '65 AWB Plymouth, The Honker. Running the standard AWB chassis, the '65 cars would rapidly be outclassed by the newer tube-chassied funny cars. By 1968, they disappeared from the national scene. (Author's Collection)

It's 1966 and PeeWee Wallace campaigns his completely altered wheel-base '65 Virginian Plymouth at Dragway 42, running against Dave Koffell's Flintstone Flying Commando AWB Plymouth. Koffell's car was built from a wrecked hardtop. (Author's Collection)

Ronnie Broadhead's 4-4-2 Tiger Tamer was just that at most of the national meets in 1966. Running in C/Stock, Broadhead's 4-4-2 Olds was turning times in the high 12s. At the '66 Winternationals, he fell to another 4-4-2, driven by Pete Kost, who went on to win the class with a 13.17. (Author's Collection)

At least one '65 Fairlane Thunderbolt was built with 427 wedge Ford power, Darrel Droke's Downey Ford Thunderbolt, The Wonder Colt. Seen here at Dragway 42 for the '65 NASCAR Nationals, Droke's Thunderbolt won the B/FX at the '65 Nationals. In '66, it would get a new 427 SOHC motor. (Author's Collection)

Eddie Schartman came to Pomona with a pair of cars: his flip-top Comet funny car and this C/Stock Comet hardtop, powered by a 330 horsepower version of the Ford 390 wedge engine. With ETs in the high 12s, the Comets were an odds-on favorite to win the C/S at the '66 Winternationals, but Pete Kost's Olds 4-4-2 took the class. (Author's Collection)

Gus Zuidema's beautiful candy-apple red '66 427 Cobra held both ends of the A/Sports national record at 10.87 and 127.11 mph. The big Cobra was powered by a 427 Ford Hi-Riser SC engine, rated at 480 horsepower, and won A/Sports at the '66 Nationals. (Author's Collection)

The winner of Top Stock Eliminator was Jere Stahl and the Stiles Performance '66 Belvedere, with the 4 speed, 426 Street Hemi. Stahl beat Bill Jenkins' Chevy II in the final, 11.73 to 11.76. The race was actually won on the starting line as a big red light was glowing in Jenkins' lane. Foul start, you lose! (Author's Collection)

In 1967, Wally Booth returned to the NHRA Nationals with his '66 SS 396 Chevelle but the "plain Jane" white paint had been replaced by a gorgeous candy red and gold paint job. Booth was now running in the new Super Stock/D class, which he won with a time of 12.02 and 87.97 mph. In the new Super Stock division, you could run any cam and lifters, and any size wheel/tire that would fit in the original fender wells. (Author's Collection)

For 1967, Ronnie Sox had a veritable garage full of cars that he campaigned, including several Belvedere hardtops set up for various Super Stock class-es. This is the SS/B car called The Boss. It lived up to its name by winning class and Top Stock at the NIIRA Springnationals with a time of 11.02 against a national record of 11.63! Then Sox turned around and did it again at the Super Stock Nationals at Cecil County, Maryland. (Joel Naprstek)

Hubert Platt comes to the starting line at the '67 Nationals during the first round of Super Stock Eliminator. His SS/B Fairlane had been run-ning high 10s during time trials and class eliminations, but didn't have enough to beat Jenkins in the Top Stock run-off. Note that the car does not have the vinyl roof at this time. (Author's Collection)

Just before the Springnationals, Chrysler released the ultimate in factory-built drag racing machines: the Dodge Hemi-Dart and Plymouth Hemi-Barracuda. Both types were built at the Hurst Performance Research facility. "Dandy Dick" Landy received the first of the Hemi-Darts. The first runs saw Landy get into the 10.30s in the SS/B Dart. (Tom Schiltz)

Many of the top Mopar racers of the past three years lined up and got one of the new Hemi cars. Bill Stiles got a Barracuda, sponsored by the York, Pennsylvania Plymouth dealers, to run in SS/BA. He was runner-up at the Springnationals to both Dick Arons' Camaro and the clock, as he ran too quick. (Tom Schiltz)

Another unusual combination for A/Stock was Anthony Marino's '67 375 horse, 396 Chevelle El Camino. El Camino's weren't too popular due to the light weight of the truck bed. I'll bet Papa Joe's Pizza was much faster than any pizza delivery car today. (Author's Collection)

# CHAPTER SEVEN

# 1965 — IT WAS A VERY FUNNY YEAR

The new year dawned with a promise of another great drag race season, especially in the super stock and FX classes. The fans wouldn't be disappointed. However, something ominous was shaping up that would affect both the competition and the spectators.

In the Far East, the black clouds of war were hanging over Vietnam. On March 8, U.S. Marines landed on the beaches of Da Nang. At the same time, President Johnson unleashed Air Force and Navy bombers against North Vietnam.

In the United States, Malcolm X was gunned down in February. In March, Martin Luther King led the famous march from Selma to Montgomery, Alabama in an effort to get voting rights for all people. Unrest within the black community boiled over in August with riots in Watts, a suburb of Los Angeles.

Rock and Roll continued its stampede with hits like "Satisfaction", "You've Lost that Lovin' Feelin'", "My Girl", and "Turn, Turn, Turn". New singers came on the music scene and quickly gained popularity: Bob Dylan, Joan Baez, and Simon and Garfunkel. Folk rock brought a different sound that attracted the college crowd.

Different turns were also taking place in competition on the drag strip. The '65 race cars were rapidly becoming too great a challenge for the normal everyday race car driver and mechanic to be competitive. Even the big dealers couldn't afford a full sponsorship of one of the major teams. So it was, that districts began sponsoring a car or driver. The Atlanta Mercury Dealers sponsored Don Nicholson's Comet, while the Cleveland District Mercury Dealers sponsored Eddie Schartman's Comet. The Los Angeles Dodge Dealers had sponsored "Maverick" Golden's Dodge in '64. It was just becoming too expensive for an individual dealer, let alone a driver on his own, to pay all the expenses of a racing team to tour the country.

For the first time in the five years since super stock racing had really taken off, Ford would not have a true vehicle to compete in Super Stock. General Motors had already pulled out, so that left the Chrysler entries of Dodge and Plymouth, with their venerable Hemi engines, to fight it out for the title of Top Stock Eliminator at the major events.

With the lack of cars able to compete for Top Stock, NHRA decided to create a new eliminator — Factory Stock Eliminator. The Factory Stock Eliminator would be a heads-up competition between the new factory-built cars that would normally compete in A/Factory Experimental. That brought the Ford Mustangs, Mercury Comets, and altered wheelbase Dodge and Plymouth entries together in one class.

The GM home-built cars, i.e. the 427 Chevy IIs and 421 GTOs, were still forced out of the running for any stock eliminator, and forced into Modified Production classes in NHRA, even though most of those cars were built to run the match race circuit against the big factory guys. However, AHRA had classes set up for these cars — Super Stock Experimental (S/SX).

The rules for 1965 remained basically the same as they had been for 1964. However, there were a few big changes. One major change was an increase in the number of units produced to qualify for any stock class. In 1964, it had been established at 50 units. This was doubled in 1965 to 100 units produced. In the top stock classes, i.e. S/S,

*Ford had multiple programs for drag racing in 1965, some with Ford, some with Mercury, some powered by 289ci small block, and others with the awesome 427ci Single Overhead Cam Hemi-head Ford, or SOHC. This is the SOHC installed in Don Nicholson's '65 Comet Cyclone. Ford installed the SOHC engines in selected Comets, Mustangs, and at least one Galaxie and Fairlane. (Author's Collection)*

*To answer the challenge of the SOHC Comets and Mustangs, Chrysler developed the altered wheelbase super stocker. The rear axle assembly was moved forward a full 15 inches, and the front axle forward 10 inches, dropping the wheelbase to 110 inches. This is the Golden Commando Plymouth undergoing final preparation for paint. (NHRA via Brent Hajek)*

S/SA, AA/S, and AA/SA, NHRA approved using any flat-tappet camshaft — the first real change allowed in a stock engine. Tubular exhaust headers could now have 3 1/2" open outlets, known as collectors or dump tubes, and replacement mufflers could be any type as long as they met the minimum length of 18".

In the Factory Experimental classes, there was now a rule about altering the wheelbase, which could be relocated a maximum of 2% of the total wheelbase. The wheelbase standard itself, was established at 114" for any vehicle with a 427ci powerplant. Lightweight components, such as aluminum or fiberglass front end assemblies, were legal only in FX classes, unless a minimum of 100 parts or assemblies had been produced. Fenders could be altered for wheel/tire installation.

For tire requirements, FX cars could use anything that would fit in the wheelwell. Tires for Stock class cars were again limited to 7" maximum width and must have at least two 1/16" grooves or tread to qualify as an on-the-street tire. Custom wheels were allowed in Stock classes as long as they weighed more than the original equipment wheels. Magnesium wheels were allowed in FX classes. Modified Production rules remained the same as they had been in 1964. Because of the release of the new Ford Single Overhead Cam 427 Hemi-head engine, NHRA was forced to allow use of the roller lifter in FX classes.

One of the interesting sidelights in the 1965 NHRA rules was the beginning of factory horsepower "ratings." The car manufacturers, to get around safety and insurance problems, were under-rating the advertised horsepower in many of the cars built from 1963 on, especially those at the very top of the factory hot rod list. Chrysler rated the Dodge and Plymouth 426 super stock engines at 425 horsepower. They then rated the new Hemi engine at the same 425 hp, even though it was evident the Hemis were putting out at least 50-75 more horses than the old wedge combination. Competition results clearly indicated that the engine was putting out in the neighborhood of 500 horsepower.

NHRA decided to begin rating the horsepower on stockers based on their own calculations, which in turn were based on things like dynamometer readings and competitive performance, i.e. elapsed times and speeds that indicate how much horsepower a particular engine was really producing. They did however, pick and choose the engines they were going to re-rate. These included several Junior Stock class entries as well as the Top Stock guys. The little guys racing in Jr. Stock were really caught unawares. In early 1965, you really didn't know what class you were assigned to until you got to the track, even though you had built your car for a specific class based on existing rules.

The AHRA didn't have this type of problem in any class, as it rated all stock class vehicles by cubic inches-to-weight ratio first, then by carburetion type, then by camshaft. It made for a lot more classes, thus more guys were actually winners at the track, but it was a puzzler to the casual observer. AHRA officials said it had been getting too difficult to determine if a camshaft was stock or not, especially in light of the new legal replacement cams that many aftermarket manufacturers were selling, so they simply legalized all camshafts for use in stock classes.

*Shirley Shahan, the "Drag-On-Lady," comes out of the gate at Carlsbad Raceway in late 1964 with her new '65 legal S/SA Plymouth. Her Plymouth, prepared by Butch Leal and her husband H.L. Shahan, was a consistent winner on the West Coast in 1965. It would be 1966 before she won her first major title. (Glenn Miller)*

## DODGE AND PLYMOUTH

For 1965, the Chrysler engineers seemed content with the amount of horsepower that the big 426 Hemi was capable of producing. The S/S and FX cars were virtually identical to the late 1964 models that had been the scourge of the nation's drag strips. In fact, more than one competitor simply put new 1965 sheet metal on an old '64 racer and went to the strip. As the old saying goes, "If it looks like a duck and sounds like a duck, it must be a duck!" The 2% altered wheelbase cars were again forced into A/FX class, where they were competitive but not dominant. Stock wheelbased cars owned both S/S and S/SA classes, but then, they were the only cars that met class requirements.

Just prior to the 1965 NHRA Winternationals meet at Pomona, Chrysler released four new vehicles to compete in A/FX class: two Dodges and two Plymouths. The cars were standard S/SA hardtops, i.e. lightweight front end packages and Hemi engines, but with the allowed 2% wheelbase alteration. On the West Coast, Dick Landy

got a Dodge and Tommy Grove drove the *Melrose Missile* Plymouth; while back in Detroit, the Ramchargers Dodge and Golden Commandos Plymouth were finished just in time for the NHRA Big Go West. Grove's *Missile* made it all the way to the finals before losing to Bill Lawton and the Tasca Ford A/FX SOHC-motored Mustang. The Mustangs and Comets were clearly the class of the FX competition and Chrysler had to do something. The "something" had actually been underway for a couple of months, and would create a new term in drag racing — Funny Car.

Chrysler took twelve standard super stock race cars from the production line — eight new production S/S cars plus the four A/FX cars that had been at Pomona. The twelve cars were completely disassembled and gutted. The body panels were put in an acid dip tank and when they were removed, some were so thin that it seemed light could be seen through the metal. Then the real modifications began.

Just behind the front seat, 15" of the floor pan were removed and the entire rear floor back to the trunk area was cut and moved forward. This placed the rear spring mounts and axle housing 15" for-

*Don Nicholson's SOHC Comet Cyclone at Piedmont Drag Raceway in March 1965 for a match race with the Sox & Martin Plymouth. Bill Stroppe prepared three '65 Comet Cyclones for A/FX competition, with fiberglass front fenders, hood, and bumper. With a stock wheelbase and running pump gas, Nicholson's Comet would easily run mid-10s.* (Author's Collection)

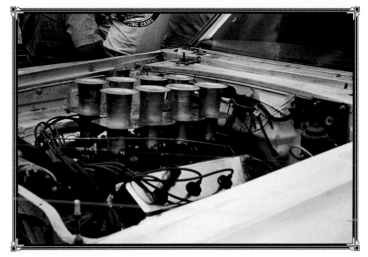

*Dave Strickler's AWB Dodge, charges off the line at Puyallup Dragway in early 1965. Strickler had one of the first AWB Dodges and was ready to race at the NHRA Winternationals. NHRA didn't know what to do with the new funny cars, and refused to classify them in any type of stock class, including A/FX. You can see the short injector stacks inside the hood scoop. (Russ Griffith)*

*By the end of February, Chrysler had authorized use of Hilborn fuel injection on the AWB Mopars. At first, the injection had short velocity stacks that mated up with the hood scoop opening. Later tests proved that much longer stacks increased horsepower over a broader range of RPM. The longer stacks made the cars look even funnier than normal. (Author's Collection)*

ward of their original position, bringing the rear wheels to a position just under the rear windows. Naturally, the rear fenders were also cut out and moved forward to bring them inline with the new rear wheel position. A steel patch panel was welded into place behind the altered rear wheel well, and the entire rear quarter area was then finished and primed.

The engineers didn't stop there, however. The front end assembly, i.e. cross-members, steering, and torsion bar assembly, was completely removed and discarded. A new lightweight cross member was installed 10" forward of its original position, and the steering and modified torsion bars were re-installed. Thus, the front wheels were now 10" forward of their original position. The wheelbase had been reduced from 117" on the S/S cars, to 115" on the 2% altered wheelbase A/FX cars, down to an astonishing 110" on these new radically altered wheelbase (AWB) cars.

The front fenders and hood had to be longer to match up with the altered front wheel position. This was done with fiberglass, which also replaced both front doors. All side windows were replaced with Lexan, while Plexiglas replaced both the front windshield and back glass. No interior trim was fitted and the cars had only a single bucket seat. Even the dashboard was fiberglass.

Everything was geared toward lighter weight on the front end. The 426 Hemi engine had aluminum heads and magnesium cross-ram intake manifolds. The battery was removed and replaced with a 75-lb. commercial battery mounted in the trunk. All the cars had steel skid

*Since NHRA wouldn't classify any of the new AWB Dodges and Plymouth as stock, Chrysler rushed four 2% cars into production for competition in A/FX: two Dodges — The Ramchargers and Roger Lindamood; and two Plymouths — the Golden Commandos and Tommy Grove's Melrose Missile. Grove lost to Bill Lawton's Tasca Ford SOHC Mustang in Factory Stock Eliminator, turning a 10.96 losing effort. (Skip Norman via Brent Hajek)*

plates over the gas tank that weighed in excess of 100 lbs. The cars were finished in December, just in time for the NHRA Winternationals.

In early January 1965, NHRA got its first look at these new stockers. Eight had already been built — four Dodges and four Plymouths. The drivers were handpicked by Chrysler and included Bud Faubel, Roger Lindamood, Bob Harrop, and Dave Strickler driving Dodges. Plymouths were driven by Lee Smith, Bill Flynn and a pair of Ford converts, Ronnie Sox and Butch Leal. The Ramchargers and Dick Landy in Dodges, and Tommy Grove and the Golden Commandos Plymouths would wait until after the Winternationals to take over one of the new AWB cars.

Everyone laughed at the new stockers except for NHRA's tech inspectors. Again, "if it looks like a duck …" These cars looked altered in every way, and NHRA promptly classified them as just that. It was at this time that Chrysler released the 2% cars to Landy, the Ramchargers, the Golden Commandos, and Tommy Grove, which were built specifically to compete in A/FX at the Big Go West. These four cars had the 2% wheelbase alteration that had been done on four '64 Dodges and Plymouths, which NHRA allowed in A/FX competition.

*On many of the Southern drag strips, the shut-down area was so short that the new A/FX cars needed a parachute to stop them before they ran out of strip. This is the Sox & Martin Paper Tiger AWB Plymouth at Piedmont Drag Raceway, near Greensboro, North Carolina. Note the wheelie wheel under the chute pack. (Author's Collection)*

*Butch Leal, "The California Flash," left Ford after his successful '64 season in Thunderbolts to handle one of the new AWB '65 Plymouths. Seen here charging off the line at Puyallup Dragway in Washington, Leal's Plymouth has the new taller injection stacks. He was runner-up to Ronnie Sox at the* Cars Magazine *Super Stock meet at Cecil County with a time of 9.85 on pump gas. (Russ Griffith)*

Following the end of the NHRA Winternationals, the four 2% A/FX cars were then returned to Detroit and modified to the 110" wheelbase models. Although several of the radically altered wheelbase cars were finished in time for the NHRA meet, none was

entered in competition. However, AHRA allowed the cars to run in one stock category and a few competed at the AHRA Winternationals a week after the NHRA meet.

**The A-990 Mopars.** The Dodge and Plymouth A-990 vehicles were the end result of rules changes dictated by NHRA, and the continuing special high-performance program at Chrysler to keep pace with both the rules and the competition (of which there would be none) in Super Stock. Following the end of the 1964 season NHRA banned the use of aluminum and/or fiberglass body components on stock and super stock cars, unless previously released at the minimum number. Thus the older aluminum and fiberglass-bodied Mopars and Fords would still be eligible to run in stock classes if they met the minimum production numbers.

The A-990 Mopar would meet these new rules head on and soundly defeat them. Chrysler took over 200 Dodge and Plymouth 2-door sedans from the assembly line and shipped them to the high-performance modification center. All new steel sheet metal was stamped for these vehicles from the thinnest possible sheet *steel*. This included front fenders, inner fenders, radiator support panels, doors, hood with scoop, trunk lid, front and rear bumpers, and supports.

The interior was also lightened as much as possible. The front bench seat was replaced with a pair of lightweight Bostrum bucket seats mounted on swiss-cheesed mounts. The rear seat was removed and replaced with cardboard. Lightweight glass was installed in the side windows which did roll up and down. Rear side windows made of the same lightweight glass were fixed in placed. Door hinges, handles, window regulators, and other trim were made of aluminum.

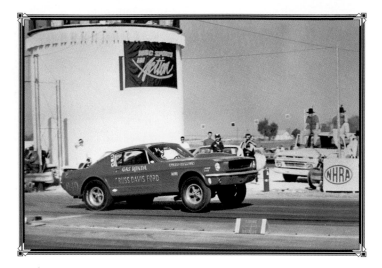

*Gas Ronda pulls the front wheels off the ground as he comes out of the gate in early 1965 with his SOHC Mustang. Holman & Moody built a total of eight SOHC Mustangs, counting the mule and the replacement car for the one Ronda wrecked. Ronda would win Top Stock at the AHRA Nationals with the Poppy Red Mustang, be runner-up at the NHRA Nationals, and would set a new national record for A/FX at 10.87 early in the year at Carlsbad, California. (Drag Racing Memories)*

Every item not needed to meet a rule or to make the car go, was deleted, including the sun visors, dome light, armrests, all carpet padding and sound deadener, and, of course, the heater and controls.

Under the hood, the big Hemi engine had the new aluminum heads that were cast with big lightening holes. The intake was either aluminum or magnesium. To meet Stock rules, the car needed a full exhaust, but not necessarily a *dual* exhaust. The A-990s had a single exhaust pipe and muffler that ran down the right side of the car to help pre-load the suspension. The new design super stock springs and shocks were installed. The battery was mounted in the trunk, again on the right side for weight distribution.

What did all this accomplish? Far more than the Chrysler engineers wanted. The initial batch of A-990s came out of the modification center weighing 500+ pounds less than a standard super stock car of 1964, and 250 pounds less than the NHRA requirement of 3,400 lbs. for a 426ci powered vehicle! Now they had to put weight *back into* the car to get it to weigh the correct amount for the class. The Chrysler engineers added a steel gas tank shield as if the car was going to race off-road, and a heavily-reinforced roll bar assembly. With standard steel bumpers and deck lids, the cars weighed in right on the money. An additional benefit — all of the additional weight was added in places that helped with weight distribution.

The A-990s would literally own Super Stock class for many years, being capable of running in the 10s at any time. Of course, for

the first two years they were the ONLY cars in the class at all. Very few manual shift A-990s were built, and all were equipped with the Chrysler 4 speed. Both Dave Strickler (Dodge) and Butch Leal (Plymouth) successfully campaigned 4-speed equipped A-990s. However, most of the cars were equipped with the venerable 727 Torqueflite automatics. Joe Smith and the Fenner-Tubbs Plymouth A-990 was virtually unbeatable over the next few years. His main competition came from the likes of Shirley Shahan and John Hagen, both in A-990 Plymouths.

## FORD

What prompted all this radical engineering at Chrysler was the introduction by Ford of the 427ci Single Overhead Camshaft Hemi-head Ford engine, and its installation in the new short-wheelbase, lightweight Mustang fastback and Comet coupes. Beginning with one of the new high-performance 427 Ford Hi-Riser engines that were terrorizing the S/S and FX ranks throughout the nation, Ford fitted it with a new oiling system, creating the "side-oiler" 427 Ford. The new block was of course, also fitted with new hemispherically-shaped pistons designed to go with the new head design.

On top of the engine block were new Ford-designed Hemi-heads offering (initially) a 12:1 compression ratio. The ports were quite different from Chrysler ports as Ford engineers had discovered an air flow problem within the intake side and corrected it. Beyond that, the main difference between the Chrysler Hemi and the Ford Hemi was in what lay inside the valve covers.

*One of the first SOHC Mustangs to make a big noise was Phil Bonner's* Warbucks. *Bonner came off the trailer at the AHRA Winternationals with a time of 10.83. Not bad for a break-in run! Seen here at York US 30 Dragway, Bonner's Mustang was capable of times in the low 10s. (Drag Racing Memories)*

*One of the first Mustangs to have 427 power was Dick Loehr's* Stampede, *powered by the 427 Hi-Riser wedge Ford. Seen here outside Rod Tyler Ford, Loehr's Mustang notchback coupe was built by Ron Pelligrini. The car ran in the high 10s with wedge power.* (John Lacko)

The Chrysler Hemi had pushrods actuating the valves with a cam/lifter/pushrod assembly buried in the top of the cylinder block. The Ford Hemi had a camshaft nestled in the head itself, which actuated the rocker arm/valve assembly, thus eliminating many of the moving parts in a standard overhead valve engine. The overhead cams were driven by a 6-foot length of timing chain that ran off a standard cam timing gear that ran off the crankshaft. The rocker arms opened huge valves within the hemispherically shaped combustion chamber — 2 1/4" intake valves and 1 61/64" exhausts.

Feeding these immense valves were a pair of 780 cfm Holley four-barrel carburetors atop an aluminum intake manifold. Spark plugs were located in the upper side of the combustion chamber, as opposed to Chrysler's Hemi having the spark plugs in the center of the combustion chamber. A special pair of cast exhaust manifolds were developed for the new engine, but these were discarded in favor of lightweight tubing headers, some of which were very exotic in design. The Ford overhead cam Hemi was quickly referred to as an SOHC Ford.

Testing began on the Ford SOHC engine in late 1964, with one actually installed in a 427 Galaxie hardtop and driven in and around Detroit by a Ford executive. Imagine being an unwary gas station attendant and opening the hood to find that monster motor underneath. (I had a similar experience with a strip tech guy that, upon opening the hood of my new 396ci Rat-motored Corvette, exclaimed to his buddy, "Hey Joe, come look. Some idiot put an Oldsmobile in a 'Vette!"). Ford's idea was never to put them into big, heavy Galaxies for lower class Stock victories. These new monster motors, dyno-tested at well over 600 horsepower on pump gasoline, were going to be installed in Bill Stroppe-prepared '65 Comet Cyclone hardtops and Holman & Moody-prepared '65 Mustang fastback coupes. All the cars were built to run in A/FX competition.

Four SOHC Comets were built initially, with handpicked drivers: "Dyno Don" Nicholson, the top Comet handler in 1964; Hayden Proffitt would give up his Yeakel Plymouth for the second Comet; and Arnie "The Farmer" Beswick would reluctantly change from his beloved 421 Pontiac Tempests to take over the driving chores of a Comet, and the "mule car" was turned over to George DeLorian. Eventually, both Proffitt and Beswick would relinquish their Comets for other types. Proffitt would build a '66 Corvair powered by a 427ci Chevy Semi-Hemi; and Beswick would return to his Pontiac Tempests. Several other '65 Comet A/FX cars were built and campaigned by other Mercury teams like Eddie Schartman, Billy Lagana, Ed Rachanski, and Chuck DiNino. However, these were powered by standard 427ci Ford wedge engines, at least initially, until production of the SOHC Ford motors was enough to re-engine some of these A/FX cars.

At least eight '65 Mustangs were built with 427ci SOHC motors, counting the mule car. Again, Ford handpicked the drivers that would receive them: Dick Brannan, Gas Ronda, Bill Lawton, Les Ritchey, Phil Bonner, Len Richter, and Paul Norris. As soon as the SOHC Mustangs began coming out of the Holman & Moody shop, there were other teams that ordered them, but with 427 Ford wedge motors under the hood. Holman & Moody built 427 Wedge Mustangs for Clester Andrews, Bob Hamilton, and Al Joniec. Bill Ireland got Phil Bonner's SOHC car after Holman & Moody finished Bonners' *Warbucks* Falcon. It was delivered without the SOHC powerplant, and Ireland installed a 427 wedge motor. Tommy Grove left Plymouth and the *Melrose Missile* team, and built his own, highly successful, 427 wedge-powered Mustang.

Where shoe-horning the old 427 wedge motor into a Comet was reasonably simple, jamming the 427 SOHC Hemi Ford into the Comet engine compartment was like trying to put 20 pounds of potatoes into a 10 pound sack! The biggest hurdle was where to find room for the massive Hemi heads. On the '64 A/FX Comet, the

*Don Nicholson checks the tire pressure in the huge M&H Racemaster slicks on his A/FX SOHC Comet Cyclone. With pressures below 10 lbs., the M&Hs were physically screwed to the wheels. Nicholson set a new record for A/FX at 10.56 and 131.96 mph. The Comet had three different induction systems: two Holley 4 barrels, four Weber two barrels, or Hilborn injection.* (Author's Collection)

*The match race circuit for 1965 had some of the best racing of all times. Chevrolet was well represented by Dick Harrell's* Retribution II *Chevy II, powered by still another old 427 Z-11 engine. Harrell yanks the front wheels at Piedmont Drag Raceway during this April 1965 match race with Dick Brannan's* Goldfinger *A/FX Mustang.* (Author's Collection)

front spring/shock towers were cut down for clearance. With the SOHC installation, they were completely removed and repositioned on the *outside* of the inner front fenderwell. Both upper and lower A-arms were moved outside the original subframe, and the front spindles were lengthened 2" to raise the front end of the vehicle for weight transfer. With the battery relocated to the trunk, there was now ample room to install the massive SOHC powerplant.

All four Comets were equipped with 4-speed manual transmissions and Ford big car 9" limited slip rear axle assemblies. To help put the horsepower down on the track, a pair of heavy-duty 2"x3" rectangular tube traction bars were installed to the additional bracing of the rear body pan that also doubled as a driveshaft loop. Inside the trunk was the 75-pound truck battery that doubled as both the electric power and additional weight over the rear axle. Plus a Lincoln suspension vibration dampener was installed over the right rear wheel. The vibration dampener just happened to weigh over 100 pounds.

While all this additional weight was added for weight transfer, a similar amount was removed from the front of the Comet. The entire front end, including fenders, hood, bumpers, and inner fender panels, was made of fiberglass. So were the doors and trunk lid. All glass except for the rear glass was replaced with Plexiglas. The back seat was removed and front bucket seats were replaced with ultra-light fiberglass seats. Even the dash was fiberglass. At 3215 pounds, the Comet was right in the top of the A/FX weight classification. Much of that weight was on the rear, where it was needed for traction.

The engine was the standard super stock version of the 427 SOHC powerplant. By the summer of 1965, Crane Engineering had developed a pair of new camshafts for the SOHC that really brought the big motor to life. There were several induction set-ups that any of the Comet (or Mustang) FX drivers could use. The cars were delivered with the standard dual Holley four-barrel carburetion.

In early Spring, Ford released both a Hilborn fuel injection set-up and a four two-barrel Weber carburetor setup for the SOHC engines. I witnessed a three-day race schedule with Don Nicholson in March 1965, that featured him running the two fours on Friday night, the Hilborn injection on Saturday, and the Weber carb setup on Sunday. There were removable plates on the underside of the red Comet hood that mated each of the three induction setups to the scoops that brought air in from the front of the hood. On Sunday night, Don shook up the troops with a 9.98 blast using pump gasoline and the Weber carbs.

## GENERAL MOTORS

The General Motors community was stuck out in left field since its withdrawal from racing that went into effect in 1963. Chevrolet did tease the enthusiasts a little bit with the introduction of the Corvette and Z-16 Chevelle powered by the 425 horsepower (375 hp in the Chevelle, although it was an identical engine) version of the 396ci Chevrolet "Porcupine Head" big block, also known as the "Semi-Hemi" and "Rat Motor". The 396ci Chevrolet engine was based on the Mark IV "Mystery Engine" that had terrorized the NASCAR circuit in 1963. When the engines held together, which wasn't very often, they were much faster than any of the competition.

One would think that the installation of this engine in the lighter-weight, shorter-wheelbase Chevelle would vault Chevrolet right back to the front of the competition, but the problems were many. Introduced in the late Spring of 1965, the cars simply weren't competitive with the bigger 427 SOHC Comets and Mustangs, nor with the Hemi Dodges and Plymouths; not enough inches, not enough cam, not enough carburetion, not enough horsepower. Plus the aftermarket people didn't have time to develop things like headers, intakes, and camshafts for the 1965 season. Add to that the many problems that the 396 engine had mechanically at the beginning of production and you'll wonder how any of them got into competition at all.

I had one of the 425 hp, 396ci Corvettes in 1965. Within the first week of running the engine hard, I broke all the rocker arm adjustment nuts — all of them — and there were no replacement parts. The car sat for three weeks. Then the big problems began to surface.

The engine would rev nicely to the 6000 rpm range, but as soon as you did, the engine would start making ugly noises. First was a broken valve spring on the left head, then a sucked valve on the left side. Both were replaced reasonably quick by the Chevrolet dealer. Then it sucked another valve on the left side, this time it damaged the piston. Two weeks later I'm back on the road.

I tried to race the car several times only to break it before I even got to the track. Finally, after five months of frustration, I traded it in. Of course, as soon as I traded in the Vette, Chevrolet recalled it. The engine blocks had a casting problem and not enough oil was getting to the left head assembly, causing the problems that I had encountered. However, within a few months all the problems were cured and Chevrolet was making noises at the strip, both in match racing and in Stock classes.

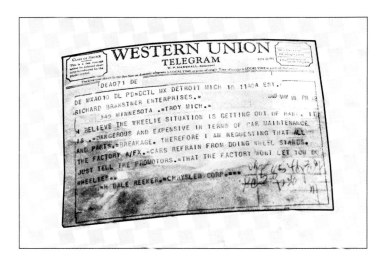

*"No wheelies" telegram from Chrysler. (Courtesy of Skip Norman)*

*Although NHRA frowned on the altered wheelbase funny cars, the match race circuit fans loved them. "Dandy Dick" Landy was always a favorite as he would pull a giant wheelie at least once during a show. Then he would make a little adjustment to the suspension and go straight as an arrow, with times in the high 9s at over 140 mph. (Drag Racing Memories)*

*The Oldsmobile 4-4-2 program was an instant hit with the street machine people. It stood for 400 cubic inches, 4 barrel, carb, and 2 exhausts. Available with either a 4-speed manual or 3-speed Hydra-Matic, the 4-4-2s ran in B/S and B/SA. The Clark Olds/Cadillac 4-4-2 competed in the NASCAR Nationals at Dragway 42 during August of '65, turning in low 13s. (Author's Collection)*

*"Dandy Dick" Landy charges off the line at Puyallup Dragway, Washington in the Spring of 1965. In late February, Chrysler released the Hilborn fuel-injection system for use on the AWB Dodges and Plymouths. The installation of the injection brought the ETs down into the low 10s. A healthy dose of nitromethane brought the ETs into the 9.70 range, phenomenal for a full-bodied passenger car. (Russ Griffith)*

Over at Pontiac, the dealers were delighted with the sales of the GTOs. The 360 hp version of the GTO was plenty for 99% of the street crowd. The same went for the Oldsmobile contingent. The sales of the GTO generated so much interest within GM that Oldsmobile came out with its own version — the '65 Cutlass 4-4-2, which stood for 4 barrel, 4 speed, dual exhaust. The 4-4-2 option was actually listed as B09 Police Apprehender Pursuit. Olds built 2,999 4-4-2s in 1965. There would be no *factory-backed* 421 GTOs or 4-4-2s this season.

There were, however, several GM competitors in the match race circuit. Dick Harrell still had his Chevelle powered by one of the still-strong running Z-11 427 Chevys; as did Malcolm Durham. Harrell would later put his motor into a Bill Thomas-prepared black Chevy II hardtop, then in a red Chevy II sedan body. Bill Thomas Race Cars also built three Chevy II fastback hardtops. They looked like a Chevy II with a Marlin roof, but under the hood was a 427 Z-11 motor. Huston Platt, Fritz Callier, and Dick Milner campaigned these wild beasts.

Later in the season, all the Chevrolet people replaced their Z-11 427 engines, with new 396 Semi-Hemis that were bored to 427 cubic inches. Of course, Pontiac still had Farmer Beswick and Jesse Tyree, driving GTOs with various size motors built for the match race circuit. Although GM was officially out of racing, their cars were still making noise at drag strips with southern-style match racers. However, none of these cars were able to legally race in S/S or even FX classes by NHRA rules. AHRA did have a class for them — S/SX or Super Stock Experimental. Although the GM cars weren't

able to compete heads-up with the others at the big NHRA meets, the match race season would be one of the best and wildest ever run.

*Looking down the side of the Dick Harrell Chevy II, the bulged rear fenders are evident. Harrell's Chevy II was also built by Bill Thomas Race Cars, and had a narrowed standard rear axle housing with big, heavy-duty traction bars. The bulged rear fenders could accommodate 10-inch slicks. (Author's Collection)*

## 1965 WINTERNATIONALS

The '65 Winternationals would be the first test of the new FX Fords, Comets, and AWB Mopars, but NHRA was not prepared to declare them as stock vehicles. Race officials told Chrysler representatives, upon viewing the first of the AWB cars, that none would be classified in any Stock or Factory Experimental classes. At NHRA, if your car was altered to extreme, it would immediately fall into one of the Altered classes with some of the wildest machinery in the automotive world. As it turned out, the new AWB Mopars were competitive in those classes after fuel injection and nitro were introduced.

However, a week before the NHRA Big Go West it was the AHRA's turn to set the drag racing world on fire. The AHRA Winternationals, held at the new Bee-Line Dragway near Scottsdale, Arizona, would see the introduction of those ridiculous looking Dodges and Plymouths with the rear wheels pushed forward. No less than 7 of the altered-wheelbase beasts were entered in the new Ultra Stock (U/S) class.

Ronnie Sox broke the U/S ice with a magnificent blast of 10.74 seconds, followed by Phil Bonner's *Warbucks* SOHC Mustang and Al Eckstrand in the Golden Commandos AWB car at 10.83. In Super Stock class, it was the usual all-Mopar show, with the Ramchargers, Golden Commandos, Dave Strickler, Tommy Grove, and Bill Jenkins battling it out. AHRA had another interesting class — Super Stock Experimental. This class was loaded with match race stockers such as Dick Harrell's 427 Chevy II and Chevelle, and Richard Petty's 426 Hemi-powered '65 Barracuda named *Outlawed*.

It seemed as if the AHRA had a class for whatever you brought to the track, or made one for it on the spot. AHRA also had two separate stock eliminator titles: Mr. Stock Eliminator and Top Stock Eliminator. Bud Faubel, Al Eckstrand, Mike Buckel in the Ramchargers Dodge, and Roger Lindamood waded through a field of 16 cars to make the semi-finals in the Mr. Stock Eliminator competition.

Eckstrand downed his crosstown rival Buckel, and Faubel eliminated Lindamood's *Color Me Gone* Dodge, to set up the final go of Dodge vs. Plymouth. Faubel's red and white *Honker* Dodge pulled

*Bill Jenkins left the Dave Strickler stable in 1965 and drove a new Hemi-Plymouth owned by "Doc" Burgess. At the NHRA Winter meet in Pomona, Jenkins swept aside the competition winning both Super Stock Automatic and Top Stock Eliminator, defeating Dick Housey's Plymouth with a time of 11.39. All the cars in Top Stock were running within thousandths of a second of each other and it was Jenkins' driving ability that brought him the trophy. (Matchracemadness)*

*One-off, home-built vehicles were allowed to compete at the AHRA Winternationals in 1965 in Super Stock Experimental class. Richard Petty, the King of Nascar, built a Plymouth Barracuda with a 426 Hemi engine; while Dickie Harrell had one of the venerable Z-11 427 Chevy engines in his black Chevy II. The "43 Jr" Barracuda was turning in the mid 10-second range on its first runs, with more than enough horsepower to overcome Harrell's "gate shot" for the win. (Matchracemadness)*

Eckstrand a bit out of the gate and held on to win at 10.96 and 129.31 mph, which was certainly not impressive considering the amount of engineering modifications that the car had. The old '64 A/FX cars had been running that quick.

On Sunday the call went out for the Top Stock Eliminator. Nine cars made up the field. After two rounds the field was narrowed down to three cars — two big Hemis and a '60 Chevy! The '60 Chevy was the D/S entry of Del Blades, and was powered by one of the old 348 W-motors that had gained fame in the early years of S/S racing. Against Blades and his D/S Chevy were none other than Dave Strickler's '64 Hemi-Dodge that had won the A/FX trophy at the '64 NHRA Nationals, and Mike Buckel driving the S/SA Ramchargers '65 Hemi-Dodge.

The task seemed insurmountable and was. Buckel eliminated Strickler in the semis, as Blades made a bye run. The final was the proverbial David and Goliath match, a 320 horsepower '60 Chevy against a 600 horsepower factory-sponsored Hemi-Dodge. Blades'

Chevy got the handicap spot and was off way ahead of the Dodge. Whatever the handicap was, it wasn't nearly enough, and the big Dodge blew by the Chevy as if it was standing still at about the 1000 foot mark. Ramchargers won Top Stock with 11.02 and 131.00 mph.

The week after the AHRA winter meet, the NHRA Big Go West was once again held at the LA County Fairgrounds in Pomona. "It never rains in Southern California" was certainly not the case in 1965. Heavy rain completely washed away all drag racing on the middle day of the three-day event. That meant that all the classes as well as the eliminator rounds had to be run on Sunday. When it was time for a class or eliminator to be run, drivers had to be ready. Anyone not in the staging lanes when their class was called was eliminated!

As with the last couple of national NHRA meets, both Super Stock classes were a one-vehicle class: Plymouth. Bill Jenkins drove Doc Burgess' *Black Arrow* to victory in S/SA class, while Bill Andress, out of Ann Arbor, Michigan had the only car entered in

S/S. That left the Top Stock competition. It was topped by a few familiar names, Dick Housey, Bill Shirey, and Bill Jenkins. Jenkins, of course, had been the guiding hand behind the Dave Strickler team for many years. He had now opened his own shop, Jenkins Competition, and was driving one of the cars he had set up, Doc Burgess' *Black Arrow* '65 Plymouth.

Jenkins had also tuned many of Bud Faubel's cars in the '63 – '64 era, even while Faubel was beating Strickler and the Z-11. He fell out of favor with Chrysler in mid-1965 when he wouldn't share information that he had developed or uncovered with the other Chrysler team members. In late 1965, Jenkins helped set up Jack Werst's *Mr. 5 & 50* Plymouth. Chrysler was so upset with him that the company sent Dick Housey to challenge the Werst/Jenkins team to a match race. The race came off, but not to Chrysler's liking, as Werst and Jenkins beat Housey three straight.

Of the 12 Plymouths entered in the Winternationals Top Stock, only one was a standard shift car — Bill Andress' Plymouth out of Ann Arbor, Michigan. He went out in the first round, losing to Paul Rossi. Jenkins put down the youngest driver in the field, Texan Hank Taylor. Dave Koffel shut down Bill Flynn and the Yankee Peddler Dodge. Dick Housey put Doug Lovegrove on the trailer. Bill Shirey and D.R. Spence rounded out the field after Round One.

Round Two saw Shirey best Rossi, Jenkins put down Spence, and Housey made a bye run when Koffel didn't make it back to staging in time. Remember, if you weren't in the staging lanes when your class or eliminator was called, you were gone. In Round Three,

*The ultimate crowd pleaser for match racing: Ford vs. Chevy. Dick Harrel's* Retribution II *'65 Chevy II against Dick Brannan's Goldfinger A/FX Mustang, Piedmont Drag Raceway, April 1965. Although Harrell was about as quick as any Chevy in the nation, the Z-11 Chevy II was no match for the mega-horsepower SOHC Mustang on this day. Brannan in three straight. (Author's Collection)*

Housey drew the bye run and set low ET in Top Stock at 11.32 seconds. Jenkins squeezed the *Black Arrow* a little tighter to beat Shirey, and cranked an 11.41 ET. Shirey had a better ET at 11.39, but again, the race was won at the starting line when Jenkins cut a quicker light.

When the call went out for the final in Top Stock, two cars came to the starting line: the red, white, and blue '65 Plymouth of Dick Housey; and the white '65 Plymouth *Black Arrow*, tuned and driven by Bill Jenkins. Housey owned low ET for stockers at 11.32. Jenkins had already won S/SA class. At the Green, the white Plymouth was out first by a few thousandths of a second. With the cars running very close in elapsed time, it was all that Jenkins needed. Top Stock Eliminator was Bill Jenkins and the *Black Arrow*, with an ET of 11.39 seconds, his quickest time of the meet. Again, Housey was quicker at 11.37, but Jenkins had won right at the starting line.

Now came the call for Factory Stock Eliminator. This brought all the A/FX cars to the staging lanes. Unlike Top Stock competition which was all Plymouth, the Factory Stock run-off was represented by four different makes. From Ford came five of the new A/FX Mustangs powered by 427 SOHC motors: Gas Ronda, Len Richter, Bill Lawton, Dick Brannan, and Phil Bonner. The Mercury camp was represented by all four of the new 427 SOHC-powered '65 Comets: Don Nicholson, Hayden Proffitt, Arnie Beswick, and George Delorian. There were two 2% lightweight A/FX Plymouths: Al Eckstrand driving the Golden Commandos entry, and Tommy Grove and the *Melrose Missile*. One of the two Dodges entered was the Ramchargers 2% car driven by Jim Thornton, and Roger Lindamood in *Color Me Gone*.

*Don Nicholson sprinkles the gold dust on the starting line prior to a match race with Ronnie Sox at Piedmont Drag Raceway. The gold dust was powdered resin. The drivers burned through the resin a couple of times, which turned it into a sticky, glue-like substance on the tires. All the drivers used it on the match race circuit. (Author's Collection)*

*Buster Couch watches the Christmas tree as Ronnie Sox gets the handicap start against Bill Lawton's Tasca Ford Mustang at the Springnationals. Sox's Plymouth at this time was a legal S/S Plymouth with unaltered wheelbase and a 426ci hemi with two four-barrel carburetors. That didn't last very long. (Drag Racing Memories)*

*Herb "Mr. 4 Speed" McCandless moves into the staging lights and lines up against Ed Knezivich at the '65 Springnationals during Top Stock eliminations. McCandless won S/S at the Winternationals, then changed the car to A/FX with the 2% wheelbase modification. (Drag Racing Memories)*

Round One indicated to the standing crowd that this is what they had all come to see. Gas Ronda opened the round by beating Eckstrand 11.06 to 11.21. In one of the most memorable races ever seen, Len Richter's SOHC Mustang put down Jim Thornton and the

*Al Eckstrand and John Dallafior shared the driving of the "Golden Commandos" AWB Plymouth throughout 1965. The Commandos car was the first of the AWB cars to receive the Chrysler-authorized Hilborn fuel injection, which cut the ETs from 10.70 down to 10.30. By the Springnationals, NHRA conceded a class to the AWB funny cars, appropriately named "Match Bash." (Drag Racing Memories)*

Ramchargers with one of the first stock runs to break into the 10-second bracket. Richter's Mustang came charging out of the gate at the Green and held on for the win at 10.99 seconds. Thornton's losing time was 10.95!

Bill Lawton cruised to victory over Don Nicholson's Comet, when the Comet got a little out of control and Dyno Don had to back off the throttle. Roger Lindamood put Dick Brannan's *Goldfinger* Mustang on the trailer, tying the Ramchargers for low ET at 10.95 seconds. Phil Bonner's *Warbucks* Mustang shut down Hayden Proffitt's Comet, and Tommy Grove's *Melrose Missile* beat Beswick's Comet. The only Comet to survive was George Delorian; he had a bye run to end Round One. Grove would be driving a Mustang the next time he met Proffitt.

Round Two saw five of the seven cars running in the 10-second bracket. Richter beat Ronda, 10.91 to 10.92! Lawton shut down the remaining Dodge of Roger Lindamood, 10.91 to 10.95. Delorian's Comet made it through the round when Bonner shut off and coasted to the finish line with a broken axle. Tommy Grove made a bye run, blasting a hot 10.96.

That left four cars in the running: Len Richter's *Quarter Horse* SOHC Mustang, George Delorian's Wynn Engineering SOHC Comet, Bill Lawton and the Tasca Ford SOHC Mustang, and Tommy Grove's *Melrose Missile* Hemi-Plymouth. Richter drew Delorian, and Lawton was matched up against Grove. When the Green came down, the white Comet leaped off the line; he had been too quick and the big red bulb was glowing in his lane. Richter didn't know it at the time and blasted off in hot pursuit. Bang, into second gear and the big Mustang slowed to a stop with a broken axle. Richter didn't have a spare axle and was out of the competition.

Next up came the maroon Tasca Mustang and the blue and white *Melrose Missile* Plymouth. Neither driver knew that Richter was out of the race and that for all intent and purpose, this was the final run for Factory Stock Eliminator. When the green light came on, the Mustang and Plymouth left the line together and stayed that way all the way through the quarter mile. No one at the starting line or in the stands, could tell who had won until the win light came on: Mustang! Lawton had turned a 10.93 to edge out Grove's 10.96.

The maroon Mustang returned to the starting line for the final against Richter. It was then that Lawton learned that Richter's Mustang was broke and unable to make the final. Lawton would make a bye run for the title. Just to prove that the win was not a fluke, Lawton really poured the coal to the big SOHC Mustang, blistering the quarter mile at 10.92 and 128.20 mph.

Ford made it almost a clean sweep of the top stocker classes by winning every major class with the exception of S/S and S/SA, where no Fords were entered. Jerry Harvey drove a '65 Galaxie that was SOHC-powered, to win the B/FX trophy. Bill Hoeffer turned back the class in C/FX with another '65 Ford Galaxie, powered by a 289ci Ford. Doug Butler won AA/S in a '64 Ford, and Bill Hanyon took home the trophy in AA/SA with another '64 Galaxie. Another big winner was the little 427 Cobra of Bruce Larson and Jim Castilou, that won the top Sports class. The only guy to break the Ford string was Dave Strickler, driving last year's A/FX winner to victory in A/Modified Production with a time of 11.47, and Junior Stock Eliminator, which was won by Dave Kempton in a C/SA '62 Plymouth.

*The #2 SOHC Comet went to Hayden Proffitt, who switched from Plymouth to drive the A/FX Cyclone. At the time of this photo, Proffitt's Comet has had a beam axle and elliptical spring front suspension added, as well as having Hilborn fuel injection on the big SOHC engine. Proffitt's Comet ran 9.95 and 139.53 mph at the AHRA World Championships in the Fall of 1965. (Russ Griffith)*

Following the end of the winter meets, the bulk of the racing was of the match-race "run what ya brung" style. There were a few matches that took place in California, and Texas was a hot bed of activity. However, it was in the South that match racing really took off. The strip promoters knew how to entice both the drivers and the crowds: money. Big purses would bring out the best cars and drivers, and the best drivers and cars matched against each other brought out big crowds, which meant more money was available for the big purses.

*A late Spring 1965 photo of the Ramchargers AWB Dodge, showing the final length of injector stacks used on the (now) nitro-burning, Hemi-Dodges. With injection and nitro, Mike Buckel put the Ramchargers Dodge into the high 8-second range at several match races. (Drag Racing Memories)*

There were also several big sanctioned meets before Nationals time. The March Meet, i.e. the Fuel and Gas Championships held at Bakersfield every year, was the first big meet after the Winternationals. By March, the Mopar teams had the kinks all worked out of the altered wheelbase cars and the times were phenomenal. Some of the cars had already switched to fuel injection.

The cars still didn't have a true stock class to run in, but that didn't matter. "Dandy" Dick Landy came off the trailer with his beautiful silver and black Dodge and calmly set the world on fire with a blast of 10.26 seconds and 138 mph! The crowd was stunned. Here was a full-size modern sedan, powered by a carbureted 426ci Hemi with an automatic transmission, that was turning within 3/10ths of a second of the fastest street machines in history — the A/Gas Supercharged Willys gassers of Stone, Woods, and Cook, and Big John Mazmanian. Where had these new fantastic elapsed times come from? Well, certainly most of it was in the fantastic weight transfer qualities of the altered wheelbase concept.

The other part of that equation was development of the new "wrinkle-wall slicks" that the big boys were using. M&H Tire Company had been the leader in stock class drag tire development from the beginning. Now the company unveiled its latest innovation, a lightweight, very thin sidewall slick, that was also very soft. It was made to be used at extremely low tire pressures — less than 10 lbs. was the normal pressure. The tires had to be physically attached to the wheel rim with sheet metal screws to avoid slippage, but the bite was tremendous. Landy's 10.26 was testament to that.

Next up was Butch Leal, "The California Flash", and his AWB '65 Plymouth. His time almost matched that of Landy. The SOHC Mustangs and Comets had no chance against these monsters, at least not at this time. The final for A/FX was between Landy and Leal. When the green light came on, Landy's silver Dodge jumped out to a half-car length lead and held it all the way through the quarter. It was an example of what the rest of 1965 was going to be like.

## 1965 Springnationals

In an effort to compete with the growing number of national events that AHRA and others were beginning to hold, NHRA decided to have a spring event — the NHRA Springnationals held during the first week of June at the newly constructed Bristol International Dragway in Bristol, Tennessee.

At the Springnationals, NHRA still didn't have a class that the AWB Mopars would fit into (the rules still stated a maximum of 2% wheelbase relocation allowed). However, the cars were so popular with the crowds throughout the South, that NHRA and the Bristol classification people created a class: Match Bash. The class was specifically designed to handle the new AWB Mopars. The Mustangs and Comets, and legal 2% Mopars, would still run A/FX class.

The run-off for A/FX class was something to behold. Most of the big name Chrysler guys had two cars at Bristol: a legal 2% A/FX car

*Action at US 131 Dragway in the Summer of 1965, with a match race between Pete Seaton's* Seaton's Shaker, *'65 396 Chevelle, and Butch Leal and the* California Flash *AWB '65 Plymouth. With the new 396/427 Chevy Semi-Hemi engine, the Chevrolet match racers started to become more competitive, especially on the match race circuit. However, the motor was so new that there was virtually no aftermarket equipment available, i.e. cams, intake manifolds, headers. Leal in three straight. (John Lacko)*

*The times for altered wheelbase stockers were becoming so quick that match races were scheduled with A/Gas Supercharged cars. Thompson Drag Raceway matched up the Stone, Woods, Cook A/GS Willys, against the Grand Spaulding Dodge. Doug Cook gets the Willys ready to burn through the resin as Gary Dyer waits. Cook had run as quick as 9.60, but turned 9.89 in defeating Dyer's Dodge. (Author's Collection)*

*Gary Dyer drove Mr. Norm's Grand Spaulding Dodge in 1965. The car had been a standard S/S Dodge, but had the rear axle moved forward 15 inches. The front axle position was stock. The Grand Spaulding car had a supercharged, fuel-injected Hemi for power, and many times was running healthy doses of nitro. ETs in the mid-9s were common. (Author's Collection)*

and one of the AWB cars for Match Bash. The field for A/FX was made up of 6 Mustangs, 3 Comets, 2 Dodges, and 2 Plymouths. Bill Lawton's Tasca Ford Mustang was the quickest of the bunch with an ET of 10.83, with Don Nicholson's Comet *Cyclone* close behind.

Round One saw Lawton shut down Herb McCandless' Plymouth; Melvin Yow's Dodge beat Al Joniec when the Mustang fouled; Bill Shirey's *The Professor* Plymouth knocked off Paul Norris' Mustang; Shirl Greer's Dodge put Phil Bonner's Mustang on the trailer; Don Nicholson downed Clester Andrews' Mustang; Dick Brannan's *Goldfinger* Mustang got past "Fast Eddie" Schartman; and Ed Rachanski's Comet made a bye run. That left 2 Mustangs, 2 Comets, 2 Dodges, and a Plymouth to fight it out.

Lawton's beautiful maroon Mustang once again was first through the quarter, putting Shirl Greer on the trailer. Next up was Nicholson's red Comet against Melvin Yow in the gold O.B. Hewett '65 Dodge. Yow's 4-speed transmission had been giving him fits all day and acted up again during the run with Nicholson. Not that he would have beat Dyno Don even with a good transmission. Nicholson coasted to victory when the big Dodge's 4 speed locked up.

Now it was Comet vs. Plymouth when Ed Rachanski matched up against Bill Shirey's blue and white Hemi-Plymouth. A close race into the lights — Plymouth! Shirey advanced to the next round as the only Chrysler product left. Brannan's gold Mustang made a solo run. Round Three matched the two Mustangs, Lawton and Brannan, with Shirey's Plymouth going off against the red Comet. Lawton was clearly the favorite in this race as he was turning about 3/10s of a second quicker times than Brannan.

Brannan had to gamble on his driving technique. He had to make up the difference at the start. Lawton knew this and tried to cut the tree a little closer than normal. He gambled on the starting system and lost. A big red bulb glowed in his lane as the two cars charged off the line, making Brannan's gold Mustang the automatic winner. That brought the big white Plymouth up against Nicholson. Again, the red Comet was a few tenths of a second quicker than the Plymouth. Shirey had to gamble on the tree. He cut the last light very close but it glowed green in his lane. The big Plymouth was out of the gate a full length in front of the red Comet. However, Nicholson had too much horsepower and caught the Plymouth at about the 1000 foot mark, blasting by for the win.

The final for A/FX class matched two of the biggest names in Ford drag racing: Dick Brannan and the Stark Hickey Ford *Goldfinger* SOHC Mustang, against Dyno Don Nicholson and the Atlanta District Mercury Dealers SOHC Comet Cyclone. Nicholson was a full 3/10s quicker than Brannan all day. Again, Brannan was forced to make up the difference at the starting line. Brannan cut the lights as close as humanly possible — Green! The gold Mustang takes a quick car length lead and the red Comet is in hot pursuit.

The red Comet caught the Mustang just as both drivers hit 4th gear and it looked like Brannan had stepped on the brake. The red Comet went by the Mustang to win going away. Nicholson's Comet, which had recently received a new pair of camshafts designed and developed for the SOHC Ford by Crane Cams, had at least 25 more horsepower on the big end than Brannan.

*Jess Belton had one of the rare, early 1965 Impalas that were still powered by the venerable 409 engine. With a single Carter AFB four barrel, Scavenger fell into B/S at the NHRA Regional meet held at Dragway 42. Prepared by Jenkins Competition, Belton's 409 was putting out a lot more horsepower than its advertised rating of 400 as it turned ETs in the 12.60 range. (Author's Collection)*

Next to the line were the cars for Match Bash: Bud Faubel's *Honker* Dodge, Lee Taylor's *Hauling Hemi II* Plymouth, Ronnie Sox's *Paper Tiger* Plymouth, Al Eckstrand driving the Golden Commandos Plymouth, Bob Harrop's *Flying Carpet* Dodge, and Dave Strickler's *Dodge Boys* Dodge. All six cars were radical-altered wheelbase Mopars, some equipped with the new Hilborn fuel injectors that Chrysler had recently released for the AWB Mopars. Ronnie Sox was the quickest of the field running in the 10.40s all day.

However, Ronnie tried to cut the tree a little too close against Harrop and left a big red bulb glowing in his lane. Harrop advanced to the final round against Strickler with a 10.47. Strickler's big white Dodge had been steadily dropping his ETs down to the level of Sox and Harrop, going 10.64 in the semi-final round. Harrop knew the race would be tight. He also knew that his ETs had remained constant, while Strickler's had been coming down all day. That meant that Strickler was finding more horsepower in the carbureted Hemi. Harrop took a chance.

When the green light came on, both white Dodges charged out of the chute. Dave thought he saw something out of the corner of his eye; there it was, a red light in Harrop's lane. Harrop charged through the traps ahead of Strickler, who simply cruised to victory, again turning 10.64 for the win. Later that month, Strickler did put the injectors on the big Hemi and went to the NHRA Regional at York, Pennsylvania. His 2500-lb. Dodge, radically altered with fuel injection, was put in B/Altered class by NHRA officials. Strickler proceeded to go out and set a new national record in B/A at 10.39 and 133.35 mph! A month after that, he set a new AHRA Ultra/Factory Experimental record at York, running a 10.44 at 133.53 mph.

It was now time for Top Stock Eliminator. The run-off for Top Stock called for the fastest 32 stockers from A/FX, S/S, and AA/S. With the new Christmas Tree starting system, it was possible to dial in the handicap start, rather than have both cars leave at the same time but at different spots on the drag strip. Now, the lower class vehicle would get tenths of a second advantages based on the difference between the class national records. If you ran on or below the national record consistently, you were usually in the running for the eliminator.

In the case of the '65 Top Stock Eliminator, the hands-down favorites were the A/FX cars, with the S/Sers close behind. At this meet, none of the FX or S/S cars were running close enough to the record to beat out the big Ford AA/SA of Mike Schmitt. Schmitt consistently ran on or below his own national record of 12.59. Schmitt's list of victories looked like a drag racing Who's Who: Don Nicholson, Phil Bonner, Ronnie Sox, Arlen Vanke, Ray Christian, the Ulrey Brothers, Herb McCandless. The final was between Schmitt and Bob Borkes, driving the Welsh Motors Dodge, with Schmitt winning 12.32 to 12.60 seconds. The $2,000 purse was reasonably big money for an NHRA stocker prize.

The next big meet for 1965 was the 2nd Annual *Hot Rod Magazine* Championships, once again held at Riverside Raceway in Southern California. Primarily a West Coast meet, the *Hot Rod Magazine* meet still featured a star-studded stocker field, including several of the best running of the new AWB Mopars like Dick Landy, Butch Leal, and Tommy Grove. In A/FX was the usual contingent of SOHC Mustangs and Comets like Gas Ronda, Hayden Proffitt, and Les Ritchey.

*Bill Thomas Race Cars built three of the fastback Chevy IIs in 1965: Huston Platt's* Dixie Twister, *Fritz Callier's CKC Racing Team, and Dick Milner's Alan Green Chevrolet in Seattle, Washington. All three were initially powered by Z-11 427 engines, but late in the season received 396 Chevy Semi-Hemis. In this '65 photo, Milner's Chevy II takes on Murray Mathews and the Pilgrims SS/A Plymouth at Puyallup Raceway. (Russ Griffith)*

The Top Stock run-off matched up the A/FX cars against the fastest of the S/Sers and AA/S cars. Included amongst these were the '65 Plymouth S/SA car of H.L. and Shirley Shahan. Shirley, known as the "Drag-On Lady", put down a pretty good field to win S/SA before putting away several of the top A/FX cars, including Gas Ronda's SOHC Mustang, to advance to the finals in Top Stock Eliminator.

Against her was the still phenomenal '63 Dodge of Ray Christian. Christian's Dodge was the old Ramchargers car that had won the 1963 National Top Stock Eliminator. Christian was making a run at the NHRA Points Championship and was in the middle of a tour of West Coast meets before returning to Columbus, Ohio later that summer. Christian's Dodge was as consistent as anyone could ask for, and held the national record for the class. Shirley had to spot the light blue Dodge about a half second. She made all of it up except for about two feet of fender, and the old Ramcharger was a winner again.

Late in August, just prior to the national meets held over Labor Day weekend, Gil Kohn again hosted the Detroit Nationals. As usual, almost anyone who was competitive, made it to the Detroit meet to both win a few bucks and tune up for the national championships. Kohn always had two separate stock titles: Exhibition and Stock Eliminator. Exhibition Eliminator matched up the wild and wooley AWB Mopars against "run-what-ya-brung" match race cars. Stock Eliminator matched up legal S/S and FX cars.

There were also two separate run-offs for each eliminator, one on Saturday and a second on Sunday. The winners of these two exhibition eliminators then faced each other for the overall winner. Mike Buckel drove the Ramchargers AWB Dodge to victory on Saturday when Ronnie Sox fouled, allowing Buckel to sit out the Sunday run-off and concentrate on tuning the car and chassis. He was turning ETs in the very low 10-second range to present a very formidable image.

On Sunday, they re-ran the entire class minus Buckel. Several upsets occurred, but none was more memorable than Bud Richter's victory over Butch Leal's AWB Plymouth. Richter's mount, the *Tension II*, was a '64 Chevy II powered by one of the old 427ci Z-11 W-motors. It was very quick for a Chevy, turning ETs in the mid 10.50s, but certainly not quick enough to beat any of the AWB Mopars.

In the Sunday races, Richter's Chevy II came up against *The California Flash* AWB Plymouth. At the Green, both cars charged out and the Plymouth took an immediate lead. As they neared the end of the quarter mile, Leal lost power. The little Chevy II charged by winning with an ET of 10.50 and 130 mph. It wouldn't last however, as his next foe would be Ronnie Sox. Sox's big red, white, and blue *Paper Tiger* AWB Plymouth was running the low 10s and easily dispatched the Chevy II to win the Sunday Top Stock title.

That set up a final race for overall Exhibition Eliminator between Mike Buckel, driving the Ramchargers Dodge, and Ronnie Sox's Plymouth — a rerun of the Saturday night Top Exhibition heat. When the call went out for the Ramchargers and Sox to come to the start line, only Sox showed. The Ramchargers car had fuel injector pump problems and couldn't get it fixed in time. Sox made a solo run

*By early Summer 1965, Koffel's purple Plymouth had a drastic change to compete against a winning Ford combination. Out came the 426 Hemi, and in went a wild 273ci small-block Plymouth engine with dual quads to compete in C/Factory Experimental against the Hoefer Bros. C/FX Galaxie. Everything else was still a Hemi car, including the aluminum front end and Hemi scoop. Note the sign in the front window, "Go-Fer Hoefer." (Author's Collection)*

for the title. In usual Ronnie Sox fashion, he didn't hold back anything even on the bye run. Sox turned a neat 10.19 on the title run.

In Top Stock Eliminator, Bill "The Professor" Shirey's '65 Plymouth A/FX car took victory on Saturday night, with an ET of

*Jack Werst, "Mr. 5 and 50," had been a Plymouth driver since the introduction of the short-ram 413 engine in '62. In 1965, he teamed up with Bill Jenkins on this A-990 sedan that held the national record in S/SA at 11.15 and 126.00 mph. Hurst lost to Bobby Harrop's A-990 Dodge at the '65 Nationals. (Drag Racing Memories)*

10.87, to earn the sit-out position for the next day. On Sunday, Dick Housey beat Dick Smith to set up an all-Plymouth final for overall Top Stock winner. Both cars were virtually identical 2% A/FX '65 Plymouth sedans. At the green light, Shirey's white and blue Plymouth was out of the gate about a half car length ahead of Housey, holding on for the victory with an ET of 10.83 and 127.75 mph. It was now time for The Nationals.

## 1965 NATIONAL DRAGS

Over the Labor Day weekend, the AHRA held its version of the Nationals. This year was quite different in many ways, not the least of which was the move from Green Valley, Texas to Lions Drag Strip in Long Beach, California. The second major change was a decision to divide the meet into two phases: Stockers and Hot Cars. The stockers would run on August 28th and 29th; the hot cars would compete the following weekend, September 4, 5, and 6. This change in scheduling allowed several of the big names to run both the AHRA and NHRA National Championships.

The AHRA meet would feature many of the match race stockers in open competition against one another. Dick Harrell was there with his wild Chevy II. Phil Bonner and Dick Brannan brought both their legal A/FX cars and their new match race cars. Hayden Proffitt had his SOHC Comet, now with an altered wheelbase, at Lions. In one of the biggest surprises of the year, Tommy Grove was at Lions but he wasn't driving the *Melrose Missile* Plymouth. In fact, he wasn't in any kind of Mopar. He was driving one of the new A/FX Mustangs, although his was powered by a 427 wedge motor. Taking over the reigns of the *Melrose Missiles* was Cecil Yother.

When the officials called for the first round of Top Stock, there were sixteen cars entered — 5 Mustangs, 4 Dodges, and 7 Plymouths — all legal A/FX or S/S entries. Gas Ronda's Mustang was clearly ahead of the pack with low ET at 10.43. Bob Stone's S/SA Plymouth was at the other end of the scale at 12.61. At the end of the first round, there were 4 Mustangs and 2 Plymouths left. At the end of Round Two, three of the Mustangs were matched against a sole Plymouth: Ronda, Ritchey, and Grove in Mustangs, against Bill Rieck's *Quarterbender* '64 Plymouth.

In Round Three, Ronda's red Mustang put Ritchey's silver Mustang on the trailer, while Rieck's Plymouth made an easy bye run when Grove couldn't make the call. That left the light green *Quarterbender* Plymouth to go against the red SOHC Mustang. Rieck had been running in the high 11s all day and shouldn't have been a match for Ronda's Mustang. He was up to the task, jumping

*Labor Day weekend 1965. Butch Leal's team members wait in line at the NHRA Inspection area set aside in the 500 Shopping Center in Indianapolis. Leal's* California Flash *Plymouth, one of the new A-990 Mopars in competition at the '65 Nationals, was a legal Super Stock car, beating Dave Strickler's similarly equipped '65 Dodge for the S/S trophy with a time of 11.56 and 124.82 mph. (Matchracemadness)*

the red Mustang out of the gate, and he was never headed. Rieck was the winner of Top Stock.

Or was he? Just prior to the mandatory teardown of Rieck's car, it was discovered that his car was built for match racing and had a 472ci Hemi in it instead of the required 426ci. It was the mistake of the technical crew as Rieck had filled out his entry card correctly, listing his engine size at 472ci, but they had put him into an S/S class. Rieck and the *Quarterbender* Plymouth were disqualified.

Under AHRA rules, Ronda would have to run any of the cars that Rieck had beaten en route to the final, including Bob Stone's Plymouth and Paul Norris' Mustang. Stone declined but Norris wanted a piece of the red SOHC Mustang. Back to the line went Ronda to face Norris' A/FX wedge Mustang. The two Mustangs left the line together but the red pony just kept pulling away. Ronda finished with 10.45, Norris with 10.56. Ronda won Top Stock Eliminator.

On Sunday, the 28th, AHRA ran the second stock eliminator title race, Mr. Stock Eliminator. Within this eliminator were the altered wheelbase cars that normally ran Experimental Stock. The field was made up of the A/FX Mustangs, plus Dick Brannan, Phil Bonner, Hayden Proffitt, and Dick Harrell — all driving match race stockers. The match race cars had to spot the legal FX cars a certain amount of strip, usually about 1 1/2 car lengths, about 30'.

After several wild rounds in which Brannan downed both Bonner and Yother, the final run-off matched two Mustangs: one legal A/FX car and the other a match race car. In the legal car was none other than Gas Ronda, driving the same car with which had just won Top Stock Eliminator. The match race Mustang was Dick Brannan's AWB *Bronco*.

However, Brannan's Mustang was something else. Not only did it have the altered wheelbase, stretched 5" in front and shortened 10" in the rear, the Mustang was lightened in every way possible. The interior was completely gutted, with only a single bucket seat and a roll cage. All side and rear glass was replaced with thin Lucite. The dash board was eliminated and replaced with a fiberglass panel, as were the door panels. There was no carpet or floor mat, and everything was painted light gray.

Under the hood was a tried and true 427 SOHC Ford powerplant, equipped with a Vertex magneto and a new pair of Crane Nitro 600 camshafts. A high-flow, aluminum radiator replaced the original FX unit, and a 5-gallon Moon fuel tank and electric fuel pump was mounted in front of the radiator. No inner fender panels were used. Even the oil pan was fiberglass. Where other FX vehicles had begun the switch to fuel injection, Brannan's Mustang retained the factory dual Holley four-barrel carburetor setup. Underneath, the Match Bash Mustang

*Joe Smith and the Fenner Tubbs Plymouth goes off against the Sites Bros.* Missouri Mule *during Stock Eliminator at the AHRA Winternationals held at BeeLine Raceway in Phoenix, Arizona. Joe Smith and the Fenner Tubbs car, one of the most consistent cars in competition, was NHRA World Stock Champ in 1965. Note the modified "traffic light" starting system above the Tubbs Plymouth.* (Matchracemadness)

*By July 1965, the A/FX Comets and Mustangs were being beaten on a regular basis by the AWB Mopars. Don Nicholson (and the other Comet drivers) had to go the AWB route to remain competitive. Don moved the rear axle forward 15 inches, then installed a beam axle and elliptical front springs, which moved the front wheels forward an additional 6 inches.* (John Lacko)

used a heavy-duty Ford 4 speed, that sent the 500+ horsepower to a modified FX rear axle assembly, which in turn sent the power to a pair of 11" slicks mounted on American Magnesium wheels.

When the two cars came to the starting line, Ronda was ushered across and took up his starting position 60' down the track. It should have been another win for Ronda. The *Bronco* had run as quick as 10.07 on Saturday when he had beaten Les Ritchey's A/FX Mustang. In an almost identical race to the Brannan-Ritchey race, when the green light came on it looked like Ronda had stalled, but he hadn't. Almost before Ronda's foot was off the clutch, the big gold *Bronco* was beside him and gone! Dick Brannan was Mr. Stock Eliminator with a time of 10.08 and a speed of 134.32 mph.

Between the rounds of both Top Stock and Mr. Stock, Lion's hosted several match races between cars vying for the *Drag News* overall Mr. Stock Eliminator title. Most of these were match race cars as there was no handicap start procedure in any of the match races that decided the outcome of the *Drag News* title. Dick Harrell was involved in two match races. On Saturday he challenged Hayden Proffitt's AWB Comet for his #4 spot on the list. Harrell was #7. The little Chevy II, powered by a 427ci Chevrolet Semi-Hemi, had the wheelbase drastically altered for match race competition.

On every run, Harrell would bring the wheels off the ground and carry them more than a hundred feet down the track. Impressive to the crowd, but not what you want in competition. Proffitt took the match in three straight, with a low ET of 9.95. Harrell's best run despite carrying the front wheels over 100' down the track, was 10.49. The Chevy II was a force to be reckoned with if Harrell could keep the wheels on the track.

On Sunday, Harrell and Tom McEwen had an impromptu match race just for the pleasure of the crowd. McEwen was handling the driving of the rear-engined Hemi-Cuda. Built similar to the wheel-standing Hurst Hemi-Cuda, McEwen's mount ran straight and true, no wheelies. The nitro-burning, supercharged Hemi-Cuda dispatched Harrell two of three races, with a best of 9.94. McEwen's top speeds were phenomenal — 160.71 mph in time trials!

As it had been since 1961, the NHRA Nationals were held over Labor Day weekend at Indianapolis Raceway Park. When eliminations began there were stockers everywhere — S/S and FX of course, and Gas class, Altereds, even in B/Fuel Dragster (B/FD)! NHRA still didn't have an official class for the new match race stockers, including the AWB Mopars and supercharged, fuel-injected stockers, so they placed them in the class that the rules said they fell into. It was going to be quite a show.

Some of the unusual entries were Steve Bovan's Chevy II, Jack Chrisman's Comet, Bob Sullivan's Barracuda, and Don Gay's blown, injected GTO, all in B/FD. There was even an American Motors Marlin powered by an injected 426 Chrysler Hemi. Altered class was full of the new AWB Funny Cars: Al van der Woude's *Flying Dutchman* Plymouth, Kenny Vogt's *Thunderbolt*, Phil Bonner's *Warbucks* Falcon, and Joe Aed driving the old *Lawman* '64 Plymouth. Even Don Nicholson had modified his wheelbase to be more competitive against the AWB Mopars, and found himself in the middle of B/Altered at the Nationals.

If they weren't in Altered, many found themselves in Gas classes, like Eddie Schartman's Comet in A/G, and Al Lynch's C/Gas Supercharged Mustang. However, most of the stockers weren't really competitive in these Competition classes. Dick Brannan's B/A Mustang made it to the trophy run only to break and hand the tro-

*Action at the May 1966 NHRA Regional at Dragway 42 matched Dave Koffel's* Flintstone Flying Commando *AWB Plymouth against Ken Holwick in the* Hemi-A-Go-Go *Dodge. Both cars ran in Super Ultra Stock-1, with Koffel taking the win at 10.18.* (Author's Collection)

*In the Summer of 1965, Ford built a pair of cars that were capable of handling anything the AWB Mopars could put out: Dick Brannan's match bash Mustang, and Phil Bonner's match bash Falcon. Bonner's Falcon was built by Holman & Moody, but Bonner bankrolled the car himself. Both Brannan's Mustang and Bonner's Falcon were built just to compete against the radically altered Mopars. (Drag Racing Memories)*

phy to the true B/A entry of Jack Ditmars, a Chevy-powered '34 Ford coupe. There were a couple of astonishing runs by a stocker in the B/FD ranks. Don Gay's beautiful red GTO, powered by a nitro-burning, supercharged, fuel-injected 421 Pontiac, turned an incredible 9.37 seconds to set the fans in the stands buzzing.

So with all the match race cars in Competition Class, what was left in the Stock Classes? Plenty! Super Stock stick and automatic classes were loaded with the new A-990 Dodges and Plymouths, led by Butch Leal and Dave Strickler in S/S, and Bob Harrop and Jack Werst in S/SA. The A/FX class run-off saw plenty of Mustang action, paired up against legal 2% Mopars such as Melvin Yow's O.B. Hewett Dodge. In B/FX class were a pair of new entries. Fred Cutler had a '65 Dodge A-990 sedan that was powered by a one-off 383ci Hemi engine. His main competition would be the '65 Fairlane Thunderbolt driven by Darrell Droke. Darrell's Thunderbolt was one of two built in '65, and was powered by a 427 wedge Ford.

AA Stock class was the most competitive, as it was filled with older 426 wedge Mopars, and '64 427 lightweight Galaxies. The older Pontiac cars found a home in A/S with Roy Gay, little brother of

Don, being the favorite with runs in the 12s all through time trials. Several older '63 Ford lightweight 427 Galaxies also were competitive in A/S. In the automatic end of the class, there were plenty of older generation Mopars and Pontiacs.

Class eliminations were held on Saturday, with some of the results being unexpected to say the least. In A/S, Leroy Stutzman was the winner over the much quicker Roy Gay when Roy left a bit early during the first round. Stutzman went on to defeat Dick Lorenze's '63 Galaxie for the class gold, with a 13.01. Bob Taylor's '63 Plymouth was the class of A/SA, winning at 12.72.

The AA/S stick and automatic classes were up next. The top sixteen cars in the field had ETs so close, the fans couldn't discern any of the winners without watching for the win light. Bob Coble's '64 Ford AA/SA was low at 11.96, with Bill Fish's '64 Ford AA/S being the slowest at 12.69. Most of the class was between 12.0 and 12.30.

The final run for AA/SA matched Ray Christian in the old Ramchargers '63 Dodge, against Dick Charboneau in a similarly-equipped '63 Plymouth. Christian was out of the gate first and led all the way, winning at 12.09 seconds to Charboneau's 12.10. However,

*Bill Lawton comes around the rear of his SOHC Mustang A/FX car at the '65 NASCAR Nationals held at Dragway 42, West Salem, Ohio. Lawton was the winner of Factory Stock Eliminator at the '65 Winternationals, beating Don Nicholson, Roger Lindamood, Tommy Grove, and Len Richter for the title. His winning time was 10.92 at 128.20 mph. (Author's Collection)*

the light blue Dodge was later disqualified, and the trophy went to Charboneau. This was the first year that NHRA awarded the class trophy to a second place car if the winner was declared illegal. In all previous years, the entire class was thrown out.

In AA/S stick class, it looked like a Ford dealership, with only a single Plymouth breaking up the line of '64 Ford Galaxies. That Plymouth was driven by Don Grotheer, a name that would be feared later in the decade for Pro Stock titles. Grotheer shifted the 4-speed '63 Plymouth through the seemingly endless line of Fords, meeting Bud Shellenberger for the class honors. Shellenberger had been running close to, but just a few thousandths behind Charboneau all day. He tried to cut the tree as close as possible, but he was a bit too quick and the big red bulb glowed as they left the line. Charboneau wins with an ET of 12.19.

Now it was time for the big boys to come to the line — the Super Stockers. In the stock class were four of the best gear-grabbers in the business: Arlen Vanke, Bill Andress, Dave Strickler, and Butch "The California Flash" Leal. Strickler and Leal were in new A-990 super stockers that were built just in time for the Nationals. As time trials progressed, Leal started fine-tuning the big Plymouth, and his ETs slowly started to drop. So it was no surprise when Leal and Strickler met for the S/S trophy run. At the Green, the orange and white Plymouth was out first, with Strickler's Dodge in hot pursuit. Strickler really poured the coal to the Dodge running an 11.57 and 126.93 mph, but the race had been won at the start as The California Flash had turned an 11.56 and 124.82 mph.

In S/SA were all the familiar names: Joe Smith and the Fenner Tubbs Plymouth, Bob Harrop in another hastily built A-990 car, Jack Werst's *Mr. 5 and 50* Plymouth, and Wes Koogle's *Original Dependable* Dodge. All were basically the same car, A-990 Dodges and Plymouths. Only 2/10ths of a second separated the entire class, with Smith low at 11.27 and Russell Funk high at 11.47. The final run

*Shirley "The Drag-On-Lady" Shahan, at the NASCAR Nationals at Dragway 42 in the Summer of 1965. Her '65 Plymouth, a legal S/SA car throughout 1965, was turned into a winning and injected 2% funny car in 1966, but not before she won the '66 Winternationals. (Author's Collection)*

*Another one-off vehicle built strictly for drag racing was the Golden Commandos Goldfish Barracuda. Sporting a copper metalflake paint job, and powered by a high-performance 273ci Plymouth, the Goldfish had an aluminum front end which was never detected by the officials. The car ran G/Stock at the NASCAR Nationals. (Author's Collection)*

Bill Shirey, "The Professor," drove this A/FX 2% Plymouth. At the '65 Detroit Nationals, Shirey won Top Stock and was overall Stock Eliminator when he defeated cross-town rival Dick Housey's A/FX Plymouth with a time of 10.83. (Author's Collection)

Another one-off car was Fred Cutler's The Roadrunner, a 2% '65 Dodge sedan powered by a 383ci Hemi engine. Cutler was a member of The Ramchargers team, and the 383ci Hemi-Dodge ran right on the B/FX record, but lost to Droke's '65 Thunderbolt. (Author's Collection)

for the gold matched Werst's Plymouth against Harrop's new Dodge. Both had been running in the 11.30s all day so it looked to be a really close race; and it was. Harrop's Dodge pulled away at the end to win with an ET of 11.39 to Werst's 11.44.

It was now time for A/FX class. The class had a few Plymouths and Dodges, including the 2% cars of Melvin Yow, Bill Shirey, and Herb McCandless, a couple of Comets including George Delorean and Paul Rossi, and a bunch of SOHC Mustangs. Most of the other nationally-known Comets and Mopars used altered wheelbase or fuel injection for the match race circuit.

The Mustangs were headed by Bill Lawton's Tasca Ford, Len Richter's Bob Ford car, and Les Ritchey and Gas Ronda from the West Coast. It was Melvin Yow who set the standard when he cranked a phenomenal 10.34 in Top Stock qualifying. Ronda was the quickest of the Mustangs at 10.51. When the final call came for A/FX, it matched a pair of drivers that raced each other all the time on the West Coast: Gas Ronda and Les Ritchey. Ritchey hole-shot Ronda at the Green, winning with an ET of 10.67 and 131.96 mph. Ronda was quicker at 10.63 but slower at the Green.

With the class run-offs complete, the drivers settled back and let their mechanics begin fine-tuning the cars for Top Stock Eliminator on Monday.

No less than 37 cars filed into the staging lanes when the call went out for Top Stock Eliminator on Monday. They were the fastest cars in the top classes: 8 from A/FX, 13 from S/S and S/SA, and 16 from AA/S and AA/SA. The ETs ranged from Melvin Yow's low at 10.34 to Bill Fish's 12.69, but that really didn't matter. The handicap start system would be in place in which each contestant was matched against an opponent and the national record in his class.

It took six rounds to decide a winner. Slowly but surely the AA/S Fords waded through the bigger and much quicker competition. The difference each time was the ability of the AA/S and AA/SA Fords to run right on their national record, or quicker. Many of the big FX entries were gone by the end of Round Two. Les Ritchey, the winner of A/FX class, lost to Harrop's S/SA Dodge in the first round. Dave Strickler's S/S Dodge put the A/FX runner-up, Gas Ronda, on the trailer.

The big Galaxies kept coming. Mike Schmitt shut down Jack Werst's Plymouth. Bob Coble sent Bill Lawton's Tasca Mustang back to the pits. The final brought a pair of the big '64 Galaxies to the line to fight it out, one 4-speed and the other an automatic. On the tower side was the white AA/S Ford of Bud Shellenburger, while the pit side saw another white '64 Ford, the AA/SA car of Bob Coble. At the Green, Shellenburger pulled about a half-car length hole shot, which Coble was unable to make up. Shellenburger won Top Stock with an ET of 12.16 against Coble's 12.32.

The Nationals were over, but there was still plenty of action at the World Finals in both AHRA and NHRA. First to come was the AHRA World Series, held annually at Cordova, Illinois. The four-day event held at Cordova Dragway, hosted many of the same cars that had recently run the NHRA Nationals. Many of the West Coast teams had remained behind for match races and the like, and took in the AHRA meet as a bonus. This included many top fuel rails, the match race stockers, and even Big John Mazmanian and his beautiful candy red '40 Willys A/GS car.

In the stock class action, the World Series had two Super Stock Bonanzas, one for match race stockers and the second for legal S/S entries. Lee Smith took home the $700.00 prize for Bonanza One

Proving how very dangerous the new match race stockers could be. (Top) Dick Brannan comes off the line at US 131 Dragway in May 1966 for a test run in the match bash Mustang, modified from the Bronco Mustang. With fuel injection, a stretched nose, and running on nitromethane fuel, the car turned 10.0 and 135 mph. (Left) Just before the timing traps, air got under the front end of the car and flipped it into the air, rolling it over several times. Dick Brannan stepped out of the mangled driver's compartment onto the engine. Only slightly hurt, Brannan was racing again within a couple of weeks. (Below) The remains of the Mustang. Although the car appears demolished, it was rebuilt and raced at the '66 Nationals with the "Bob Ford" banner on the gold and blue body, and continued to race into 1968 with Larry Coleman as the driver/owner. (John Lacko)

*Dick Jesse was one of four teams that never changed from Pontiac and remained competitive even though they seemingly were overmatched at every race. Jesse's Mr. Unswitchable '65 GTO with an acid-dipped body, Plexiglas windows, fiberglass front end, and an altered wheelbase, won its class at the '67 Nationals — BB/Fuel Dragster! Note the position of the injector stacks at the base of the windshield, indicating the injected 421 Pontiac was set back 10%. (Drag Racing Memories)*

with his AWB '65 Plymouth. Local favorite Jack Thomas drove the Chicagoland Dodge S/SA car to victory in Bonanza Two.

The real highlight was the match race between Gary Dyer and the Grand Spaulding Dodge, against Arnie Beswick. Both had supercharged, fuel-injected entries. Beswick's was a '64 Pontiac GTO with a big Pontiac motor. Dyer's '65 Dodge featured a just-as-big Chrysler Hemi, and both were running heavy doses from the nitro can. Interestingly, Beswick had not altered the wheelbase of his blown GTO, as almost every other match race car in the nation had done. Yet he was running consistently in the 9-second bracket!

As the cars came to the line for Round One, two crew members spread the gold dust (i.e. resin powder, which acts as a glue between the tire and track thus increasing traction) from 50' behind the start to about 50' in front of the line. Both cars fired up and the drivers rolled into the resin and brought up the RPMs, then launched! Both cars carried the front wheels well beyond the resin and stopped. Then they backed up into the resin again and launched. Again they stopped and backed up.

This time both drivers carefully lined up in exactly the same tracks they had made on the resin burnouts. At the Green, the big Dodge was gone with the white GTO in pursuit. The gap started to close. At the lights, it was Beswick! His time for the race was an absolutely amazing 8.92 seconds! It was the quickest a full-bodied stocker had ever run! Round Two was rather anti-climactic as the big Dodge lunched a rear end right on the starting line during the burnout. That gave the match to Beswick in two straight, but the fans would be talking about Beswick's 8.92 well into the 1966 season.

## WORLD FINALS

The NHRA inaugurated another first annual event in 1965 — The World Finals. (The Springnationals was the other inaugurated event.) This would be the final sanctioned national event of the year. To enter the Finals, you qualified by being the Points Champ or runner-up, for any division within NHRA in your class. The meet was held in October at the new Southwest Raceway outside of Tulsa, Oklahoma. It was truly a race of champions.

In the go for Top Stock Eliminator, there were 10 cars matched: 3 A/FX Mustangs, 2 AA/S '64 Fords, 2 S/S Plymouths, 1 SS/A Plymouth, and 2 AA/SA '63 Mopars: one Dodge and one Plymouth. The World Finals would use the new Christmas Tree handicap starting system, which dialed in the correct amount of time between the various national class records. Most of the names were familiar to any super stock fan in the nation, and included Gas Ronda, Bill Lawton, and Les Ritchey's Mustangs, Ray Christian and the old Ramcharger '63 car, and Mike Schmitt's '64 Galaxie, the World's Points winner from the previous year.

Round One was called to the line. Les Ritchey's mighty Mustang losing to Bob Spears' AA/S '64 Ford. Ray Christian advanced with a win over Gas Ronda. Local favorite Joe Smith and the Fenner-Tubbs '65 Plymouth automatically went to Round Two when Don Grotheer fouled. Arlen Vanke's Loehr Plymouth S/SA put last year's champ, Mike Schmitt, on the trailer. Bill Lawton cut a very quick 10.56 to defeat Dick Charboneau.

Spears' advanced in Round Two when Vanke fouled. Smith really got the Fenner-Tubbs entry moving, running 11.24 to down Ray

*"Wild Bill" Flynn drove the Yankee Peddler AWB '65 Dodge on the match race circuit in the '65–'66 season. Flynn's Dodge was one of the homemade AWB cars, which had only the rear wheels moved up. Flynn was runner-up to the Ramchargers in the 2,700-lb. class at the Cars Magazine meet. (John Lacko)*

Christian. Bill Lawton made a bye run to complete Round Two then drew Spears' big Ford Galaxie in Round Three. The white Ford was about as consistent as anyone could ask, but Lawton was up to the task. Lawton pushed the maroon Mustang to a 10.65. Joe Smith drew the bye and cruised to a 12.23.

That set up a final run between the Tasca A/FX Mustang and the Plymouth out of Lubbock, Texas. Both Lawton and Smith had been running right on or below their national records throughout the meet. As the yellow lights counted down, the big Plymouth left. Smith had the handicap lead and could leave several thousandths of a second before Lawton.

However, Lawton had enough horsepower and he had overcome the handicap throughout the Top Stock run-off. He knew he would have to run a perfect race to win, as Smith was as consistent as the

Ford was quick. He watched as the yellow lights continued to blink down in his lane, all the while watching Smith pull away. Last light — GO! Lawton was charging down the strip chasing the big Plymouth, but it didn't matter. He had calculated his start just a fraction too quick and the big red eye was lit up in his lane, a foul start. Joe Smith was the Top Stock Eliminator World Champ with an ET of 11.23.

With the exception of the on-going match race circuit to determine various magazine Mr. Stock Eliminator titles and several Record Runs to determine new national marks, the 1965 season had ended. Before it did, Dick Harrell put his mark in the record books when his new injected 396 Chevy II, the *Retribution II*, cut a 10.84 and 127.80 mph to set a new AHRA standard for S/SX. Already, 1966 had promise to be the wildest of all seasons; it would live up to that promise.

---

*Mike Schmitt's '64 Ford Galaxie, sponsored by Desert Motors, was the 1964 NHRA World Points Champion, and set the NHRA record for AA/SA with a time of 12.58. Seen here at the '65* Hot Rod Magazine *Championships in a time trial run against the EMPI H/Gas Volkswagen, Schmitt was Top Stock Eliminator at the '65 Springnationals and AA/SA winner at the Nationals. (Glenn Miller)*

# CHAPTER EIGHT

# *1966–1968 — THE ERA THAT TOP "STOCK" DIED*

One of the most violent years in the history of the United States was 1966. Mass killings and war news dominated the nightly news week after week. A man broke into the apartment of several young nurses in Chicago, killing eight. Another man took up a sniper's post atop the University of Texas and shot 44 people, killing 15. In the far off war in Southeast Asia, Air Force and Navy bombers hit oil depots in Haiphong and Hanoi, escalating the air war even further. Adding to the tremendous international pressure in the Far East, Red China launched its first nuclear-armed missile.

World events were influencing changes on the music scene. Different sounds and subjects were sung in hits such as "Ballad of the Green Berets", "Sounds of Silence", "Yellow Submarine", and "Wild Thing." Musicians made news in other ways, too. Jan Berry crashed his Corvette into a parked truck, effectively ending the string of hits for Jan & Dean.

The string of good fortune in super stock was also ending. Virtually all the manufacturers stayed away from new car entries into the Super Stock and F/X classes for the 1966 Winternationals. Changing body styles and ever-tightening competition rules were causing numerous problems for the auto makers.

Since Chrysler had released an entirely new body design for the Plymouth and Dodge, the company couldn't update an existing body to reflect the changes needed for legal A/FX competition. Chrysler wasn't willing to begin an entirely new program just for sanctioned A/FX class; especially not when the publicity and money was all in the new altered wheelbase Funny Cars. What had started in 1964 with the 2% altered wheelbase cars had escalated way beyond the term *stock*. By the end of the 1965 season, most of the Ford competition had also turned to the altered wheelbase to remain competitive. By that time the Dodge and Plymouth gang were using fuel injection instead of carburetors. Many were also running healthy doses of nitro instead of pump gasoline.

There still were a great many entrants in the classes of Super Stock and Super Stock Automatic, but these were cars originally built and campaigned in 1965. The A-990 Mopars, those that hadn't been converted into altered wheelbase cars, were still in competition. However, in Factory Experimental the rules were rigid. The entrant had to be of the current model year, i.e. a 1966 vehicle. Ford built or converted a few of the remaining legal A/FX '65 Mustangs to 1966 vehicles. Since they were virtually the same vehicle from '65 to '66, the teams simply exchanged necessary emblems and serial number plates. At least one actual 1966 Mustang was built by Holman & Moody for A/FX with 427 SOHC power — the Jerry Harvey Mustang.

In the summer of 1965, Ford unveiled two vehicles on the unsuspecting world of match racing: a Mustang and a Falcon that had shortened wheelbases and/or stretched front ends, gutted interiors, and were powered by very big versions of the Ford SOHC motor. Phil Bonner's *Warbucks* Falcon and Dick Brannan's *Bronco* Mustang quickly put Ford at the top of the match race circuit, although the Gary Dyers' 8.63 blast on almost 100% nitro exhibited just how much power could be generated with the Grand Spaulding Dodge Hemi. However, Don Nicholson's consistency with his '65 SOHC

*The beginning of the end for the meaning of stock. This is funny car row at the '66 Nationals. Two of the three flip-top Comets are seen: Nicholson's orange car and Kenz & Leslie's green car. NHRA created a special class for these exotic stockers: Experimental Stock. The cars looked stock with the body down, but the body was just a fiberglass shell over a full tubular chassis. The driver sat in the rear seat area. (Author's Collection)*

*There were three "new" 1966 Mustangs in A/FX, and two of those were '65 cars with '66 trim driven by Tommy Grove and Les Ritchey. Ritchey beat Grove for the AHRA Winternationals' Mr. Stock Eliminator crown, turning a 10.41. It's interesting to note that a year earlier, the time for Ritchey would have been unreal for A/FX. Grove lost with a 10.46 ET. (Pete Garramone)*

Comet, and his ability to change with the times (he altered the wheelbase and had injection by the end of the '65 season), kept him at the top of the *Drag News* Mr. Stock Eliminator list throughout 1965.

In 1966, everything went to the next level. Fuel injection and superchargers replaced the carburetion setups of 1965, and nitro was the fuel of choice. Altered wheelbases were the norm rather than the unusual. All of that was put into perspective with the display of Mercury's latest offering: the flip-top Comet of Don Nicholson. The casual glance didn't show too much — a nice orange Comet hardtop, stock wheelbase, no blower scoop, not even injector stacks through the hood.

The casual observer would remark, "What's so special about it?" Then a member of the crew would lift the front of the body shell and the observer would exclaim, "Why, this thing is more dragster than car!" Under the lift-up fiberglass replica Comet body shell, was a Logghe Stamping Company chrome moly tube frame. Front suspension was Autolite coil-over-shock on either end of the straight axle. No brakes were used on the front axle. The rear, also suspended on Autolite coil-shocks, was a heavy-duty Mercury unit, with a Detroit locker differential.

The interior amounted to a simple aluminum floor and wall around the driver's single bucket seat. "Dyno Don" sat in what would normally be the rear seat area, and almost in the center of the car. The engine sat well back of the standard position, and indeed, was actually inside the passenger compartment! Power was the 427ci

version of the Ford single-overhead cam engine with hemispherical heads. The valvetrain was actuated by a pair of Crane camshafts. Compression was a little low at 10:1, but that was due to the fact that all the flip-top Comets were built to run on big doses of nitro, which would be funneled into the huge pistons through a specially-designed Hilborn fuel-injection system.

The flip-top Comets astonished the unwary automotive world. Weighing in at a ridiculous 1680 pounds, trial runs set track records wherever they were performed. ETs ranged between 8.6 and 8.8. No one was tempting fate by pushing the car to its limits. Three of these beasts were built with injection and one was supercharged. The supercharged car was handed over to Jack Chrisman. The injected versions would be handled by Dyno Don, the Schartman-Steffey team, and the Kenz-Leslie team.

The unveiling of the Comets was the end of super stock as it was known. None of these cars could be classified in the loosest of terms as *stock*. They were exciting to watch but the factories wanted something to bring the people into the showrooms. Dodge and Plymouth were the only entries in S/S and S/SA classes, and those were 1965 models. Ford had 1964 Galaxies in AA/S. Dodge and Plymouth did have new models in A/S with the street hemi cars. Chevrolet had the Chevy II in A/S, Chevelle SS396 in B/S, and GTOs and 4-4-2s in C/S. Top Stock Eliminator was no longer won by the top stocker classes.

Chrysler answered with ultra-light Plymouth Barracudas and Dodge Darts. The Chevrolet gang met the challenge with tube-chas-

*The only true 1966 Mustang built for A/FX competition was Jerry Harvey's Mustang, which won the NHRA Winternationals A/FX crown by beating Les Ritchey's Mustang, with a time of 10.64. It isn't evident in this photo, but the Holman & Moody shop moved the rear wheels 2 inches forward on all the A/FX Mustangs. It was more than the allowed 2%, but NHRA officials closed their eyes; without the Mustangs there would have been no A/FX class in 1966. (Skip Norman via Brent Hajek)*

sied Corvairs and Corvettes, powered by injected and supercharged 427 Semi-Hemis. Mustangs abounded with stretched front subframes and shortened wheelbases. Older altered-wheelbase Dodges and Plymouths were further modified through the use of supercharged engines and completely gutted interiors.

So it was that the manufacturers released very potent drag race packages in their standard showroom-available sedans. Ford dropped the old 427 wedge motor, rated at 425 horsepower with dual quads, into the Fairlane. Finally, the Thunderbolt was going to hit the street. Of course, these new 427 Fairlanes were all steel, with complete interiors and other optional accessories.

Chrysler took the 426 Hemi-head drag engine, detuned it a bit, and put a pair of inline dual Carter AFBs on top. It was called the "Street Hemi" and was rated at 425 horsepower. (No matter how much horsepower an engine was capable of putting out, the factory always "rated" it at 425 hp, which is one of the reasons why NHRA began factoring many of the horsepower ratings.) The Street Hemi was available in any of the Dodge and Plymouth B bodies. Pontiac had the GTO and Oldsmobile still had the 4-4-2, although neither would run in the top Stock classes.

Chevrolet offered the 396 cubic inch Semi-Hemi in three horsepowers in the Chevelle: 325, 360, and 375 hp. The 375 hp also came with a solid lifter camshaft and a big Holley four barrel. This was the same engine that powered the '65 Corvette and was rated at 425 hp in the 'Vette. Somehow it lost 50 horses when it went under the Chevelle hood. The sleeper of the year was the Chevy II powered by a 327 cubic inch, 350 hp Corvette engine. These lightweight boulevard beasts weighed in about 800 lbs. less than the Street Hemis and 427 Fairlanes. It takes a lot of horsepower to make up an 800-lb. weight differential.

## WINTERNATIONALS 1966

The AHRA Winternationals were held over the weekend of February 11-13 at Irwindale Raceway just north of Los Angeles. Unlike the forthcoming NHRA Big Go West held the following weekend in Pomona, the AHRA winter meet had an open door to all the match race stockers who wanted to race. These drivers wouldn't have to race against real dragsters either; AHRA had a class for anything.

There were four Stock eliminator brackets: Unlimited Fuel Stock which had no weight limits, no wheelbase limits, and you could run either a supercharger or fuel injection, with nitro being the fuel of choice; Unlimited Gas Stock, which was actually limited to cars weighing 2500 lbs. or more, equipped with fuel injection, and running pump gasoline; Super Stock Eliminator, which matched cars weighing at least 3000 lbs., and running carburetors and pump gas; and Mr. Stock Eliminator that matched up the twelve class winners from FX to B/S, both sticks and automatics.

There were 20 cars entered in Unlimited Fuel Stock class, but most were just at Irwindale on shakedown missions. Dick Brannan,

*Bill "Grumpy" Jenkins came to the '66 Winternationals with a Chevy II powered by the 350 horsepower version of the 327ci 'Vette engine. The lightweight Chevy II was turning 12.0s in A/Stock, but it wasn't good enough to beat Don Grotheer's new Plymouth Street Hemi, which beat Jenkins in the A/S final with an 11.98. Jenkins won Mr. Stock Eliminator at the '65 Winternationals driving Doc Burgess' Black Arrow Plymouth. (Joel Naprstek)*

*In A/Stock there was one name that intimidated every other driver including "Grumpy" Jenkins – Jere Stahl. Stahl's '66 Belvedere sedan with a 4-speed, 426 Street Hemi under the hood, tied the national record of 11.66 with Bill Jenkins at the York, Pennsylvania Regional. Seen here at Island Dragway in 1966, Stahl's winning combination was the result of much work on making the new M&H "wrinkle wall slicks" work. (Joel Naprstek)*

Gas Ronda, Don Nicholson, Dickie Harrell's wild Chevy II, "Dandy Dick" Landy's new ultra-light '66 Dart, and Sox & Martin's new ultra-light Barracuda, were just some of the big names entered. When the class was called to the line, only six cars pulled into the staging lanes. When it was over, Dick Brannan's revamped '65 Mustang match race car, *Bronco*, was the winner at 9.19 seconds.

In Unlimited Gas Stock Eliminator were several altered wheelbase Mustangs, including Bill Lawton's Tasca Ford, Gas Ronda's new '66 stretched Mustang, Sox & Martin's Barracuda, and two older altered wheelbase Plymouths: Butch Leal's *California Flash* and Cecil Yother driving the *Melrose Missile*. (Tommy Grove, the original driver of the *Melrose Missile*, had switched to a new stretched Mustang.) Lawton was easily the quickest of the group at 9.57 during time trials.

The semi-final run matched Gas Ronda against Ronnie Sox, and Butch Leal against Lawton. Ronda easily beat Sox when Ronnie

*Les Ritchey's '65 Mustang (with '66 emblems) against Jerry Harvey's '66 Mustang for the trophy in A/FX at the NHRA Winternationals. The two Mustangs were the only two cars qualified to compete in A/FX in '66. Harvey's blue and gold 427 SOHC-powered Mustang pulled away from Ritchey to win the class trophy at 10.64. (Matchracemadness)*

*Bill "Grumpy" Jenkins' A/Stock Chevy II waits in line at Tech Inspection for the '66 Nationals. Even though you had been racing all year, and might have won one of the national meets, you still waited your turn in the line to the scales. Now called Grumpy's Toy, the Chevy II had set the national record for A/S with an 11.66 ET in July at York, Pennsylvania.* (Author's Collection)

*A meeting of the minds: Jere Stahl (standing facing car door) chats with Bill "Grumpy" Jenkins (leaning on door in Jenkins Comp shirt) in the '66 Tech Inspection line. Although they were heated rivals in A/Stock, Jenkins and Stahl were old friends and had worked together on many of the earlier Strickler-Jenkins Chevys and Dodges over the years.* (Author's Collection)

missed a shift and broke the transmission. Leal and Lawton came to the line together. At the Green they left almost side by side, Lawton pulling a slight lead and holding on for the win. Leal was actually quicker at 9.72 to Lawton's 9.73, but the race had been won on the starting line.

That left Ronda and Lawton. Ronda had uncorked an incredible 9.43 in the earlier rounds so it looked like this would be a heck of a race. At the green light, Lawton was gone and never looked back. He had a 2-car length lead going into 2nd gear, and cruised to victory at 9.78 seconds to Ronda's 9.85.

Super Stock Eliminator fell to the legendary Les Ritchey and his revamped '65 Mustang that was now a "legal" '66 Mustang A/FX car. He turned back the eight-car field with runs between 10.41 and 10.66, beating Tommy Grove's weber-carbureted Mustang on the final run.

Mr. Stock Eliminator was the final AHRA stock event. Basically, under AHRA rules, you could conceivably run in any or all three of the big gas stock eliminator races. Thus, many of the cars that competed in the Super Stock Eliminator, were also eligible for Mr. Stock Eliminator. Bill Lawton, winner of Unlimited Gas Stock Eliminator, was entered. So was Les Ritchey, fresh from winning the Super Stock Eliminator.

In the end there were two new names running for the Mr. Stock Eliminator title: Darrell Droke driving a '65 Fairlane Thunderbolt, now powered by a 427 SOHC motor; and Shirley "Drag-On-Lady" Shahan driving a '65 Plymouth S/SA. These of course, were

not the classes that Droke and Shahan competed in under AHRA rules. Under AHRA, Droke's Thunderbolt was FX-B/S, while Shirley was in FX-B/SA.

Since both cars ran on almost exactly the same AHRA national record, the run for Mr. Stock Eliminator would be heads up, meaning no one would get a handicap on the start. Shirley knew the Thunderbolt was quite a bit quicker than her Plymouth and gambled on the lights. She lost. The big red bulb glowed in her lane as she left the starting line. It didn't matter as Droke's SOHC Thunderbolt blasted an incredible 10.64 for the win. The "Drag-On-Lady" had an 11.14.

An interesting occurrence at the AHRA meet: Dyno Don was debuting his new flip-top Comet and the car actually flipped its top. Don had been running very gingerly, trying to get a feel for the new ride. During the first all-out blast in the wild new Comet Funny Car, air built up under the body, lifting the front wheels in the air at speed. Then the rear wheels also came off the ground! In an extreme nose-up attitude, the body suddenly ripped off the chassis and sailed off into the sky, clipping Don on the helmet as it flew by. The rest of the car, with Don still inside, settled back on the track. Don shut it down, pulled the chute, and walked away. It was the first of many, many wild rides that drivers of this new breed of funny car would take before the bugs got worked out.

When the gates opened at Pomona for the '66 NHRA Winternationals over the weekend of February 18-20, something was missing. For instance, in A/FX class, there were only a handful of entrants — all Mustangs with 427 power. B/FX class was similar, containing an even smaller amount of '66 Galaxies with 427 SOHC power. There simply wasn't anything else that the rules allowed to run in the classes. Jerry Harvey's Bob Ford '66 SOHC Mustang defeated Les Ritchey's updated '65 car for the title, with a winning time of 10.64. Mike Schmitt put down the rest of the class in B/FX with his Desert Motors 427 SOHC Galaxie. Ed Terry drove the Kleinman-Cole Ford '66 Galaxie to victory in C/FX, powered by a 289 Hi-Po Mustang engine with Cobra parts.

S/S and S/SA were again dominated by 426 Hemi Mopars in 1965 Dodges and Plymouths. In S/S, the winner was Butch Leal and his *California Flash* '65 Plymouth. Butch had the only car entered, and made an 11.50 bye run for the trophy. In S/SA there was more competition, with eight cars entered; but only two cars were competitive: Joe Smith and the Fenner-Tubbs Plymouth, and Shirley Shahan and the *Drag-On-Lady* Plymouth.

The trophy run pitted the pretty blonde Shahan from Tulare, California against the wily veteran Smith from Lubbock, Texas. Smith was fresh from winning the World Points Championships in 1965, and had been running about 2/10ths of a second quicker than Shirley all day — low 11.20s vs. mid-11.40s. Shirley's husband, H.L. Shahan, was frantically trying to coax just a couple more horses out of the big Hemi when the final run for S/SA class was called to the line.

The crew quickly jacked up the car and plastered a fresh coating of the new BX-10 liquid resin onto the Casler super stock tires. The yellow lights slowly clicked down to the green! Off went both Hemi-Plymouths. At the very start it appeared that Smith had a slight lead, maybe the width of the bumper, and it stayed that way

all the way through the timing traps. The winner: Smith! The purple Plymouth had turned an 11.32 winning time. Shirley's losing time was 11.33 seconds!

In A/S class, the first indication of the popularity of the new street machines began to show. Nine cars were entered, mostly older model S/S cars, including several 426 Max-Wedge Mopars, as well as one of the '64 Ford lightweight Galaxies with a 4-speed transmission. There were also four new '66s in the class: Bill Hoefer's 4-speed Hansen Dodge Street Hemi, Don Grotheer's 4-speed Edmund's Chrysler/Plymouth Street Hemi, and Bill "Grumpy" Jenkins and Frank Sanders in Chevy IIs. The Chevy IIs were equipped with the L79 option 350 hp, 327ci Corvette engines. Weighing in at slightly over 2800 lbs., the Chevy II was 800 lbs. lighter than the competition. NHRA rules required the 426ci Hemi cars to weigh a minimum of 3650 lbs.!

The quickest of the class was Hoefer, who recorded an 11.83 blast in time trials. Grotheer was right behind with a 12.01 run, and Jenkins recorded a 12.07 to stay with the pack. In Round Two, Grotheer and Hoefer hooked up in what was to be the race of the day. The two cars left the line together but Grotheer pulled a little on the top end; Grotheer at 12.01. Jenkins kept wading through the Mopars until there were only two cars left: Grotheer and the little red and white Chevy II.

At the Green, the little Chevy II, as it had been doing throughout eliminations, leaped out in front of the big red Plymouth. The much lighter Chevy II had almost two car lengths lead, but then the horsepower of the Street Hemi started to take hold. In second gear,

*One of the Ford guys who defected to GM in 1966, was Bruce Larson. Larson had run a successful S/S Ford and Cobra from 1961 through 1965, then built the USA-1 '66 Chevelle funny car, powered by an injected 427 Chevy. (Author's Collection)*

*The quickest car in B/Stock at the '66 Nationals was the 375 hp, SS 396 Chevelle of Wally Booth. Booth's Trumbull Chevrolet Chevelle held the NHRA national record for B/S. Booth's Chevelle was runner-up in B/S to Wiley Cossey's 427 Biscayne. (Author's Collection)*

*In the late Spring of 1966, Ford released the street version of the old Thunderbolt: the 427 Fairlane. Other than a complete stock interior, with carpet, and even a radio, the 427 Fairlanes were virtually identical to the '64 Thunderbolts. The Ulrey Bros. Lightning Bolt II competed at both the '66 and '67 Nationals, when they changed from A/Stock to Super Stock/C. (Author's Collection)*

Grotheer closed the gap to one length. In third gear he pulled even with Jenkins, and pulled away in fourth to win at 11.98. Jenkins ran a 12.10 in a losing effort. It was a race that would be repeated throughout all of 1966 at drag strips all over the nation: the little Chevy II doing battle with various Street-Hemi cars, sometimes winning, sometimes losing.

In A/SA, the situation was much the same as it was in the A/S stick class, with a few famous names thrown in for good measure. Eight cars were entered including past class winners Dick Charboneau's '63 Plymouth and Mike Schmitt's Record Holder '64 Ford from Desert Motors. Roger Lindamood of *Color Me Gone* fame, was driving the Snavely/Langford '66 Dodge Street Hemi. One other Street Hemi was entered, the *Brand X Eliminator* '66 Plymouth driven by Ken Heinemann.

When the call for A/SA eliminations went out, it was clear from the onset that Charboneau's aluminum-nosed '63 Plymouth was the car to beat. Charboneau had been running consistent 11.80s throughout the time trials. Heinemann's Street Hemi had qualified with a low ET of 11.81, but he wasn't consistent. Lindamood was running in the 12.00 bracket. Schmitt was in with 12.00s during the trial runs.

Charboneau's consistency told the tale as he marched to the trophy run. Lindamood drew Heinemann in the first round, with Roger hole-shotting the *Brand X* car for the win. Then Lindamood shut down Schmitt's big Ford, which just didn't have enough horsepower to compete against the Street Hemis. Next up for Lindamood was Charboneau, who promptly recorded an 11.87 to win going away. This set up a final between Charboneau and Fred Sanders, both driving veteran '63 Plymouths using Stage I Max-

*Action at the '66 Nationals starting line between Jenkins' Grumpy's Toy Chevy II and the Coble and Bolland '64 Ford in A/S. The little Chevy II screamed to victory turning a 12.09 ET. Jenkins' Chevy II weighed in at around 2,800 lbs., which was some 600 lbs. lighter than the Ford. (Author's Collection)*

*Here's something different, a 4-4-2 funny car. The Lutz & Lundberg 4-4-2* Much! *powered by a supercharged 425ci Olds. With a radical altered wheelbase, the 3,081 lb. Olds holds a national record, but for what class? It could run any number of different NHRA classes, plus about a dozen different AHRA and NASCAR classes. (Author's Collection)*

Wedge power and having aluminum front ends. Charboneau not only put a nice gate job on Sanders, but then he added to it on the big end to win going away, 11.81 to 12.18.

In the Junior Stock categories, many of the new '66 Pony and Muscle cars made up the classes. In B/Stock, the class was loaded with 375 hp Chevelles, a few old 409s and 421 Catalinas, and one black '66 Biscayne equipped with the 425 hp version of the Chevy 427 Semi-Hemi. That car was the *Casler Tire Special*, driven by Wiley Cossey, and was the test vehicle for Casler's racing tires. When the smoke had cleared, Cossey's black Chevrolet had won with a 12.49. He would be almost unbeatable in the class throughout 1966. In B/Stock Automatic, Tom Crutchfield drove the Button Motors '63 Dodge station wagon to victory at 12.59.

C Stock was another class loaded with new '66 car entrants. The 360 hp GTOs and Olds 4-4-2s fell into C/S, as did several older 409 Chevys and 427 Fords. The fastest of the class were the Comets with 335 hp versions of the 390ci Ford wedge engine. Several of the new GTOs, including the Royal Pontiac team, were disqualified for having a new Ram-Air intake system, which had not been declared legal in the class by NHRA as of the opening of the Winternationals. Still, there were 23 cars left in the class.

Low ET for the class was 12.86 by Milt Shornack in the Royal Pontiac GTO, but he was one of those disqualified for having a Ram-Air intake system. That meant that Ken Casteel's Comet was low at 12.95, followed by Ronnie Broadhead's 4-4-2 at 13.04, Les Shockey's and Roger Guston's Comets at 13.05. The class drew a couple of big names including Eddie Schartman and Billy Lagana, both of whom stepped out of their match race cars to race C/S

Comets. The Shockey Comet was tuned and set up by none other than Hayden Proffitt. It looked like an easy win for the Comets.

Someone forgot to tell the other entrants in the class that Comet was supposed to win. Many of the Comets fell by the wayside in Round One. By the semi-finals, all of the Comets were gone leaving a pair of '66 4-4-2s driven by Ronnie Broadhead and Pete Kost, and a big heavy '63 Ford driven by Dale Bargman. The big Ford had one of the 410 hp, 427ci Ford S/S engines and was very consistent in the 13.10 second range.

Broadhead met the big Ford in the semi-final, losing at the starting line. The big Ford cranked a slow 13.24 to Broadhead's 13.06 but the race had been won at the starting line. The final matched Kost's Holiday Motors 4-4-2 against Bargman's Ford. At the Green, both cars left together, with Kost pulling a slight lead in second gear. It was enough. Pete Kost won with a time of 13.15. Bargman lost with a time of 13.17. Paula Murphy, later a top Funny Car driver, drove a new 4-4-2 to the finals in C/Stock Automatic class. She lost the final to Wayne Torkleson's potent single four-barrel 427 '63 Ford, 13.40 to 13.55.

Top Stock Eliminator was run on Sunday afternoon. The 18-car field was made up of Butch Leal's S/S '65 Plymouth; Earl Jay in a '65 S/SA Dodge; Thomas Walls, Shirley Shahan, A.L. Simpson, Larry Apodaca, and Joe Smith in S/SA '65 Plymouths; Ken Heinemann, Roger Lindamood, Mike Schmitt, Tom Fox, Sy Mogel, Ed Doll, Jim White, Dick Charboneau, and Bob Spears from A/SA; Don Grotheer and Bill Jenkins from A/S. Low ET was Joe Smith and the Fenner-Tubbs '65 Plymouth at 11.33. High was Ed Doll's '63 Ford A/SA car at 12.55.

A couple of upsets occurred in the first round when Roger Lindamood shut down Butch Leal, and Dick Charboneau fouled against Larry Apodaca. Round Two saw Ken Heinemann's Street Hemi put Bill Jenkins on the trailer, Mike Schmitt beat Lindamood out of the hole, Shirley Shahan shut down Apodaca, and the upset of the meet when Grotheer put down Joe Smith. Round Three saw two of the remaining three Street Hemis face off against each other, with Heinemann taking the win when Grotheer fouled. The two remaining S/SA Plymouths then faced off with Shirley Shahan downing A.J. Simpson. Mike Schmitt made a bye run.

That left three cars: Mike Schmitt, Ken Heinemann, and Shirley Shahan. The two A/SA cars, Heinemann and Schmitt, would get the handicap start on the big blue and white S/SA Plymouth. Would it be enough? Heinemann drew the bye run, leaving Schmitt against the *Drag-On-Lady*. At the Green, the big white Ford was gone, almost a half second before the Plymouth. Shirley cut a good light at the start and caught the Ford just before the timing traps for the win.

That set up the final between Ken Heinemann's *Brand X Eliminator* A/SA Street-Hemi Plymouth, and Shirley Shahan's *Drag-On-Lady* S/SA Plymouth. The handicaps were dialed in: 11.64 for the A/SA Plymouth; 11.15 for Shahan, a difference of .49 seconds. The tree began counting down. The white Plymouth in the left lane, roared out of the gate at the green light in his lane. Shirley waited and waited as her side of the tree came down, all the while the white Plymouth was roaring towards the finish line.

Green! Shirley again cut a close light. She was out of the gate in hot pursuit. The big Hemi came alive in the upper RPM of first gear

*C/Stock class was always loaded with the new '66 intermediates: GTOs, SS 396 Chevelles, 4-4-2 Olds, and a handful of Comet GTs. Milt Shornack drove one of the Royal Pontiac GTOs at the Winternationals, turning low ET for C/S at 12.86. In the end, all the GTOs were disqualified for having the new "Ram-Air" hood scoop, which hadn't been in production long enough to suit the NHRA tech people. (Author's Collection)*

and the blue and white Plymouth started closing the gap. Ever so slowly, Shirley began making up the ground between her and the fleeing white car. When she shifted into third gear, it was as if someone lit a rocket under the *Drag-On-Lady* Plymouth. Just before entering the timing traps, Shirley caught and passed Heinemann for the win. Shirley Shahan became the first woman to win a major eliminator title at a sanctioned NHRA event, winning Top Stock Eliminator with a time of 11.26 seconds at 126.76 mph. Heinemann's losing time was 12.01 at 121.78 mph.

Junior Stock Eliminator was won by the big black '66 427 Biscayne from Casler Tires and driven by Wiley Cossey. The Street Eliminator title was up for grabs between a pair of factory stockers: Jerry Harvey's A/FX Mustang against Mike Schmitt's other Galaxie, the winner of B/FX. The Desert Motors '66 SOHC Galaxie got the handicap start and again it was almost a half second. Harvey's Mustang leaped out of the chute and caught the big red Ford at the 1100 foot mark, whizzing by for the victory in 10.68 seconds at 132.15 mph.

Between the Winternationals and the big Spring meets, the weekends were filled with match racing. To say it was Super Stock match racing would be an untruth. The match races were between the new all-out match race cars, running tubular chassis, supercharged and fuel-injected engines, and on fuel that didn't even resemble pump gasoline. The big money was in match racing Southern Style, meaning anything goes.

The "Run What Ya Brung" strip owners were paying huge amounts of money to bring a match between any two of these behemoths. The big draws were Sox & Martin, The Ramchargers, "Dandy Dick" Landy, Don Nicholson, Eddie Schartman, Hubert Platt, Phil Bonner, and a host of others. Even the GM troops were in the midst of the match race madness with Dickie Harrell, Arnie Beswick, Malcolm Durham, and Jesse Tyree representing Chevrolet and Pontiac well. Even the legal FX and S/S cars began converting to match racers during the Spring.

There was a large number of name stockers in the upper ranks of Stock Class. Names like Bill "Grumpy" Jenkins and his Chevy II, Mike Schmitt and his record-holding '64 Ford, and Roger Lindamood's Dodge Street Hemi. Out of the East came a name that was well known to all the stocker people: Jere Stahl. Stahl, popular for his exotic header designs specifically created to match certain engine/body combinations, had built a '66 Plymouth Street Hemi for A/S that would terrorize everyone in the class for the remainder of the season. However, fans wouldn't pay big money and pack the stands to watch a pair of high 11-second A/S cars go at it; not if the next closest strip had two of the 2000 horsepower, match race stockers going at it with runs in the low 9-second bracket.

## 1966 SPRINGNATIONALS

By the time of the NHRA Springnationals at Bristol, Tennessee, the handwriting was on the wall. When the call for class run-offs

*Wiley Cossey's Casler Racing Tires '66 427 Bel Air was the big winner of Junior Stock throughout 1966. Cossey not only won B/Stock over all the 409s and 375 hp Chevelles, he took home Junior Stock Eliminator at the Winternationals and B/S at the '66 Springnationals. His time for the Winternationals was 12.49 seconds. (Author's Collection)*

came, there were <u>no entries</u> at all in A/FX, and only one in C/FX. B/FX was won again by Mike Schmitt, who had become virtually unbeatable with his '66 Ford SOHC Galaxie. In S/S and S/SA were a few recognized names like Ed Miller and Joe Smith's Fenner-Tubbs car. Both classes were, as they had been at the Winternationals, made up entirely of '65 Plymouths and Dodges.

Miller won S/S in his '65 4-speed Plymouth at 11.82; while Smith showed the troops how it was done in S/SA, when he turned a terrific 11.40 against Mary Ann Foss' *Go-Hummer* '65 Plymouth for the title. A/Stock was a virtual dogfight between the Street Hemis and Bill Jenkins. Jenkins was very quick but Jere Stahl's Street Hemi was quicker — 11.96 to 12.25. Besides, Jenkins fouled on the trophy run. A/Stock Automatic class was also loaded with Street-Hemi cars, but the class win went to "Akron Arlen" Vanke when Al Olster fouled on the final go.

In B/Stock, the name of the game was the same as at the Winternationals, when Wiley Cossey's big black '66 Chevy won the class. However, a new name was coming onto the B/S scene: Wally Booth, whose '66 396 Chevelle was running right beside Cossey all day long. It took a hole shot for Cossey to beat Booth, as he turned a 12.69 to Booth's 12.62 on the trophy run. The GTOs finally got to run the Ram-Air package legally and the Royal Pontiac team made a big showing. Again, Akron Arlen showed them the way home when he won the class with a GTO. The Vanke team took home a third trophy when Bill Abraham beat all comers in B/Stock Automatic.

Adding insult to injury, the Vanke team took home all the marbles in Junior Stock Eliminator when Vanke's GTO defeated his teammate Bill Abraham for the title.

In the running for Top Stock Eliminator were the big names from S/S down to A/S, both stick and automatic cars, including the Street Hemis of Ken Heinemann (*Brand X Eliminator*), Don Grotheer, and of course Jere Stahl. The S/S cars of Mary Ann Foss, Joe Smith, Ed Miller, and the big Fords of Mike Schmitt, the Ulrey Brothers, and Joe Spears were waiting for anyone to make a mistake; and then there was that pesky little red and white Chevy II.

Round One saw Kenny Heinemann foul against Jenkins, Al Olster beat Grotheer, Joe Smith put Joe Spears' Ford out, Stahl shut down Mary Ann Foss, John Ulrey's Ford advanced by beating Gerry Fink, and Vanke and Schmitt both advanced. Round Two found Vanke losing to Jenkins, Smith downing the Ulrey Brothers' Ford, Stahl beat Olster's '63 Plymouth, and Schmitt and Miller both advanced.

In Round Three, Jenkins lost a close one to Joe Smith, and Schmitt's big white Ford beat Ed Miller. Stahl made a bye run. That left three cars: one S/SA Plymouth, an A/S Plymouth, and Schmitt's big '64 Ford A/SA. Stahl drew Smith for the race. Smith knew he had to cut a close light to beat the big white Plymouth. Stahl cruised to the win when Smith cut it a bit too close and left the big red eye glowing in his lane. Schmitt soloed to advance to the trophy run.

The trophy run matched the veteran old-timer in Mike Schmitt and his automatic '64 Ford against newcomer Jere Stahl and his '66 Plymouth Street Hemi equipped with a 4-speed transmission. (Mike had been here so often, it seemed like he just was automatically in the Top Stock trophy run.) With both cars running identical national records (11.66), there was no handicap start.

Stahl had been working on making the new low-pressure wrinkle wall tires work with a 4-speed car. They worked superb with the automatics, as evidenced by the domination of the S/SA Mopars and AA/SA Fords in Top Stock. However, the horsepower being delivered directly to the rear wheels through a manual transmission was more than the 7" tires (required by NHRA in Stock classes) could handle. Jere Stahl, working with Bill Jenkins, developed a low pressure driving technique using the 7" tires that ended the domination of the automatic cars in the 7" tire era. In 1967, NHRA allowed use of any size tire in the new Super Stock categories.

Stahl let the pressure down in the slicks a little more. At the Green, the big white Plymouth launched very hard and Stahl never looked back. It would've been difficult for Schmitt to catch the big Plymouth even if he had left at exactly the same time. Stahl's hole shot turned into an unreal 11.80 ET at 119.20 mph. Schmitt lost with a 12.15 and 117.95. Stahl and Jenkins would not only own A/S, but Top Stock wherever they ran throughout 1966.

The Springnationals saw the debut of a new stock class in NHRA — Experimental Stock. It was NHRA's answer to the AHRA classes for the match race stockers, i.e. Funny Cars. Tommy Grove's *Ford Charger* stretched Mustang, was the first winner in a Funny Car class, when he took the gold for A/XS over Ronnie Sox's altered wheelbase Barracuda. Grove turned an unreal 8.79 when he won Competition Eliminator. Lee Smith's AWB Plymouth beat Dave Koffel's AWB Plymouth to win in B/XS. Al Joniec's *Bat Car* Mustang beat Herb McCandless' AWB Plymouth to win C/XS. A.J. Lancaster won D/XS, with Tom Sneden taking E/XS. At least the match race guys wouldn't have to run against dragsters anymore.

Super Stock drag racing had gotten so big in 1965 that several events were totally devoted to the sport in 1966. There were the *Cars Magazine* Super Stock Internationals, the *Drag News* Super Stock Invitational, and the *Super Stock Magazine* Nationals. There were also super stock meets held at big name drag strips all around the nation, such as Lions Drag Strip in Southern California, and York US 30 Dragway in Pennsylvania.

However, by 1966, these meets were built around what had become universally known as the Funny Cars, those altered wheelbase, nitro-burning, supercharged vehicles that looked like a stocker at first glance. However, 1500 horsepower was a bit much to expect to find under the hood at your local dealer. What you could find were the 396 Chevelles, Dodge and Plymouth Street Hemis, GTOs and 4-4-2s, and in the late Spring of 1966, the 427 Fairlanes.

The '66 427 Fairlanes borrowed a lot from the original Fairlane Thunderbolt. Under the hood was a 427ci Ford wedge motor, topped with a pair of big Holley four barrels. It was basically the same engine, transmission, and rear end setup that had been used in the '64 T-Bolts. Except that it was now in a fully street-legal Fairlane with a full interior. It was Ford's answer to the new dominance of the Dodge and Plymouth Street Hemis in A/Stock. Even though there was a growing amount of interest in the big name legal stockers of Bill Jenkins, Jere Stahl, and others, it was still the Funny Cars that brought in the crowds.

The *Cars Magazine* meet was held at Cecil County Dragway in Maryland. Funny Car classes were set up by weight and fuel type; 2,000 lbs. being the low side and on fuel, with 3,000 lbs. being the high side and using pump gasoline only. The 2,000-lb. Fuel Class was the one that the new tube chassis, fuel-burning, injected SOHC Comets were in. The new ultra-light, tube chassied Darts and Barracudas also qualified in the 2,000-lb. Fuel Class. They were running ETs in the middle 8-second bracket, but there were very few of these cars built. At the *Cars* Meet, the class was made up of the Don Nicholson and Eddie Schartman Comets, and the Dodge

*Action in S/XS at the '66 Nationals pitted Don Gay's blown, injected GTO against the rebuilt Bob Ford match race Mustang, driven by Dick Brannan. Brannan's Mustang had been destroyed in a crash at US 131 Dragway in May, but was rebuilt for the Nationals. By the way, Brannan won when Gay exploded a transmission.* (Author's Collection)

*Bill "Grumpy" Jenkins wheels his second Grumpy's Toy '66 Chevy II at the AHRA Winternationals in 1967. The familiar red and white Chevy II had been destroyed in a towing accident in late 1966. Grumpy lost at the NHRA winter meet, but turned it around and won Middle Stock Eliminator at the AHRA Winternationals with a time of 11.70 seconds. The Chevy II was then retired and replaced with a new big-block Camaro. (Matchracemadness)*

Darts of Dick Landy and the Ramchargers, driven by Mike Buckel. Buckel won the class with an ET of 8.63.

Ronnie Sox won the 2,400-lb. Fuel Class when his Barracuda turned an 8.92 to beat Charlie Allen. The 2,700-lb. Fuel Class was won by Phil Bonner's SOHC Falcon. He narrowly defeated Pete Seaton in the Seaton's Shaker Chevelle, 9.39 to 9.41. Wayne Gapp won the 2,700-lb. Gas Class by beating Dave Koffel and the Maloney Plymouth, 10.08 to 9.99. A hole shot was the difference. The 3,000-lb. Gas Class, made up mostly of almost legal super stock and FX cars, was won by Melvin Yow and the O.B. Hewett 4-speed '65 Dodge with a time of 10.52.

Top Stock Eliminator was a battle between the AA, A, B, and C Stockers, both stick and automatic. "Big John" Valente's '64 GTO did in all the troops, including "Grumpy" Jenkins' Chevy II, for the win and $200.00! There simply was no fan base, thus no big money for the new breed of true stockers.

The 2nd Annual *Super Stock Magazine* Nationals was held over the first weekend in August at New York National Raceway. As with all the other big stocker meets, it was aimed at the Funny Car set and was staged quite similar to the *Cars Magazine* meet, with weight and fuel classes. ETs included a fantastic blast of 8.42 seconds for Dyno Don's *Eliminator I* Comet during the Sunday class eliminations. Yet even that was bested by his compatriot, Eddie Schartman, who recorded an unbelievable 8.41 and 172.74 mph!

Mr. Super Eliminator was Pete Gates driving Don Nicholson's old '65 AWB Comet Cyclone. Running in the 2,700-lb. Fuel Class, Gates got a handicap on the final against Eddie Schartman's new '66 Comet. When the lights went green, Gates was gone while Schartman waited. When his light went green, Schartman shot out of the hole and went sideways. Schartman had to take his foot out of the throttle, straighten it up, then hit it again. By that time Gates was almost into the traps. Pete Gates turned a 9.14 and 151.77 mph on the final.

As with the *Cars* meet, the Mr. Stock Eliminator title was between the top legal stocker classes, A/S through C/S. There were some big names at this meet for the Mr. Stock Eliminator runs. Tom Crutchfield had the Button Motors '63 Dodge wagon, Milt Schornack drove the Royal Pontiac GTO, Eddie Schartman had one of the new C/S Comets, and there was that little Chevy II driven by Bill Jenkins. The final run was between two Jenkins Competition cars, a blue B/S Chevelle driven by Tom Kerr, and Jenkins' own *Grumpy's Toy* A/S Chevy II. Jenkins had run as quick as 11.41 in the red and white Deuce coupe. Kerr would have to be perfect to beat Grumpy. He wasn't! At the Green, Kerr got the handicap start but cut the light too quick and fouled. Jenkins won the title and $1,000.00.

## 1966 NATIONALS

The 1966 NHRA Nationals was held at Indianapolis Raceway Park over Labor Day Weekend. As mentioned in Chapter One, it was the first NHRA Nationals that I had attended and I thought it was wild. My friend Brink was entered in G/Stock with his '56 Nomad. He made a few passes and then we hooked up and watched the rest of the races. Brink lost in G/S class, but we sure had a good time. That's the way it was in 1966, when drag racing was still a little guy's participation sport.

For 1966, NHRA created a new class for the match race stockers, that all the fans wanted to see: Experimental Stock, or XS. There were six XS classes, from Super/XS down to E/XS. To the fans, it was Funny Car class. Most of the old '65 altered wheelbase Mopars were in B/XS class. Vernon Rouley drove one of Sox's old AWB '65 Plymouths to victory, defeating Lee Smith's AWB Plymouth for the class win with a 10.11 ET at 136.98 mph.

The new stretched wheelbase Mustangs, including entries from Gas Ronda, Bill Lawton's Tasca Ford, Dick Brannan's Mustang driven by Hubert Platt, and Tommy Grove, as well as Ronnie Sox's stretched Barracuda were in A/XS. These cars were turning ETs in the high 8-second bracket. The trophy run for A/XS matched two of the best drivers in the east: Ronnie Sox and his fuel-injected Hemi-Barracuda against Bill Lawton's *Mystery 9* fuel-injected SOHC Mustang.

Sox had run as quick as 8.64 on previous runs, but Lawton's Mustang was equal to the task. At the Green, both cars shot out of the gate with Sox in front. Wait! There was a red light in Sox's lane. Lawton won with a time of 8.66. By the way, he did beat Sox in spite of the early jump by the Barracuda.

In S/XS were the really far-out entries: the tube-chassied funny Comets of Nicholson, Schartman, and Chrisman; plus wild creations like Landy's Dart, the Ramchargers Dart, Don Gay's supercharged GTO, Darrell Droke's supercharged Mustang, Larry Reyes and Tom McEwen with supercharged Barracudas, and a host of others. Most of the cars were running in the high 8-second bracket. Only two cars stood out — the previously-mentioned Comets, driven by Don Nicholson and Eddie Schartman. Nicholson came off the trailer at

*Hubert Platt and the '67 Georgia Shaker SS/B 427 Fairlane at the Super Stock Nationals held at Cecil County, Maryland in June 1967. The Shaker ran high 10s at Cecil County, but lost to Sox's Boss Street Hemi. Note that Platt's Fairlane has all the refinements, including a vinyl roof. (Joel Naprstek)*

8.31, with "Fast Eddie" right behind at 8.39. When the final call came for S/XS trophy, there were the two Comets, facing each other.

In the pit lane was the beautiful orange metalflake Comet of "Dyno Don." On the tower side was Schartman's Day-Glo yellow Comet. Nicholson's Comet engine was a little sick and ETs were slowing with every run. His semi-final victory over Darrell Droke's Mustang saw his ET slow to 8.58. At the Green, both cars came out even, but after that it was all Schartman. Fast Eddie charged through the win lights at 8.28 (a new low ET for Funny Car) and 174.41 mph. Nicholson's ET slipped to 9.29. Other winners in XS were Tom Tignanelli in C/XS with a '65 Plymouth; Richard Hankinson in D/XS in a '65 Dodge; and Jerry Harvey in E/XS, driving the Harvey Ford '65 Thunderbolt with SOHC Ford power.

The top Stock classes were next to the starting line. A/FX class was won by Ed Russell's '66 SOHC Mustang at 11.99. Mike Schmitt won B/FX in the Desert Motors SOHC '66 Galaxie. Ed Terry took the trophy for C/FX in a small-block '66 Galaxie sponsored by Desert Motors Ford. There were familiar names at the top of S/S and A/S, although not the winners everyone had predicted.

In S/S, the winner was Ed Miller and his '65 A-990 Plymouth, with a time of 11.99 and 117.64 mph. In A/S, the upset winner was Akron Arlen Vanke's Pontiac with a 12.43 winning ET. Both Stahl and Jenkins lost via the red light in class eliminations. In S/SA was another familiar car, the '65 Plymouth of Joe Smith running out of Fenner-Tubbs Plymouth in Lubbock, Texas. He turned an 11.38 on the trophy run. Clayton Wright drove his '63 Plymouth to victory in A/SA at 11.91.

On Monday the fastest 32 cars in S/S, S/SA, A/S, and A/SA vied for the title of Top Stock Eliminator. Besides the class winners mentioned above, Top Stock saw Shirley Shahan, Mike Schmitt, Mary Ann Foss, Jack Werst, Ken Heinemann, and Don Grotheer in Plymouth Street Hemis, and of course, both Bill Jenkins and Jere Stahl with their tremendous A/S cars. The ETs ranged from Ed Miller's 11.28 to Mary Ann Foss' 12.28.

As each round came to the starting line, it was obvious who the odds-on favorites were: Stahl's white Street-Hemi Belvedere sedan, and the little red and white Chevy II of Bill Jenkins. Both cars were running quite a bit quicker than their own national record, but at the '66 Nationals you ran off your best qualifying time.

Round after round, the white Plymouth and red Chevy II advanced, until they were the only two cars remaining in Top Stock. On the tower side was the little Chevy II, with Stahl's Plymouth in the pit lane. Both cars were running in the 11.70s throughout the eliminations. At the green light, the little Chevy II leaped out in front, as it had been doing to every opponent throughout the eliminations. The lead was a full two car lengths when both drivers went for second gear. The big white Plymouth started gaining ground in third gear, and had pulled even when both drivers went for fourth gear. Stahl's cubic inches really paid off in fourth gear and he pulled away for the win, but it really didn't matter as Jenkins had red-lighted at the start.

Jere Stahl was Top Stock Eliminator with an ET of 11.73 at 119.68 mph. Jenkins lost at 11.76 and 118.11 mph. In Junior Stock Eliminator, Dave Kempton waded through an endless stream of lower class stock cars for the title. Kempton's C/SA '62 383

On the West Coast, the "Drag-On-Lady", Shirley Shahan, continued with Chrysler but switched from Plymouth to Dodge. Her '67 426 Street-Hemi Coronet, again set up by her husband, was a consistent winner, with times in the high 10s. (Drag Racing Memories)

Plymouth turned a 13.08 and 108.17 mph, to defeat Ernie Musser's D/S '61 Chevy. Competition Eliminator was the '65 Dodge Dart Funny Car of Gene Snow, running in C/Fuel Dragster class, who beat Greg Gibson B/Dragster for the title, 9.04 to 9.62.

## 1967

The new year brought many changes in all aspects of life. It was called the Summer of Love and California was "where it's at." Young people flocked to college campuses and parks in the San Francisco area. They wore flowers in their hair, they danced and sang love songs. Their motto "Make Love, Not War!" was seen everywhere. This way of thinking spread throughout the country, many times ending in student protests over the military actions in Southeast Asia. In July, civil unrest again erupted, this time in Detroit. President Johnson ordered Army troops to quell the riots which ended with over 2,000 people injured and 45 dead.

Unfortunately, the motto of the young people was having little impact on the world's battles. Red China agreed not to enter the ongoing war in Vietnam if the United States would refrain from invading North Vietnam. However, some 300,000 Red Chinese "volunteers" entered the war anyway on the side of North Vietnam. Other conflicts arose in the Middle East, when Israel launched a pre-emptive air strike against Syria, Egypt, and Jordan 24 hours before those countries were set to invade Israel.

With all of its troubles and tribulations, 1967 was a year of new ideas and products. Amana marketed the first compact microwave oven, the Radar Range. Oxford biologists did the unthinkable when they cloned a frog in October. In December, the first complete heart transplant was performed.

Innovations were also taking place in the world of auto manufacturing. For the first time, seat belts were installed in cars for *every* passenger, along with other safety innovations like dual brake systems and collapsible steering columns.

Change was everywhere and drag racing was not untouched. In 1967, NHRA modified the rules in such a way as to bring some of the classes in line with AHRA rules, which were much more liberal than NHRA rules regarding what was and wasn't stock. It was the end of the true factory stocker. NHRA created an entirely new division called Super Stock. The cars were basically stockers except that they were now allowed to run any camshaft and lifter as long as the valves remained stock in size. All cars classified as Super Stock, could run any size wheel/tire combination that would fit in the original fenderwells. Five new classes were created: SS/A through SS/E. In addition, all Factory Experimental classes were eliminated from the rules.

A car owner now had the option to run a totally factory stock vehicle in any one of the classes from A/S through N/S; or in one of the five new Super Stock classes. All cars previously classed as Factory Experimental now fell into Modified Production class, as long as they retained the stock wheelbase. Thus none of the altered wheelbase cars, including the older 2% Mopars, could compete in

Modified Production. Match race cars that competed in Experimental Stock (XS) classes in 1966, now competed in the new Funny Car classes.

There were, of course, new models and engine combinations that manufacturers had dreamed up for the street. Chevrolet had done away with the '66 Chevy II with the 350 hp, 327ci 'Vette motor that had given Jenkins so much success. In 1967, Chevrolet unveiled the new Camaro "pony car" to compete with the Ford Mustang. The Camaro came with a variety of powerplants, eventually releasing a 375 hp version of the 396 Semi-Hemi, which put the car squarely in the top of C/Stock or Super Stock/C depending on the camshaft. However, at the '67 Winternationals, Chevrolet would again be represented by the '66 Chevy II, along with many new SS 396 Chevelles.

Chrysler stood pat with the 425 hp, 426ci Street Hemi, available in either Dodge or Plymouth, and running in B/Stock or SS/B. Chrysler also introduced the new 440ci wedge engine. (NHRA had dropped the 427 cubic inch displacement limit.) Equipped with dual quads, the new 440 was rated at 375 hp, which put it into the very top of E/Stock or SS/E, where it was virtually unbeatable. Seems the 375 hp rating was a bit understated. Dodge Darts and Plymouth Barracudas were also available with a variety of engines, although really big powerplants wouldn't be available until 1968.

Pontiac and Olds had the GTO and 4-4-2 respectively. Both types went to new 400ci powerplants and single four-barrel carburetion. Pontiac also introduced the Firebird pony car, which was built alongside the Camaro. The Firebirds had the 400ci GTO engine option available, and competed in D/Stock or SS/D classes. The GTOs and 4-4-2s were in E/Stock or SS/E, against the 440 Mopars, and were at a decided disadvantage in the class. Ford had the 427 Fairlanes for B/Stock and SS/B. Some were older '66 models, some were '66s with '67 parts to make them look like new models, and some were true '67s.

## 1967 WINTERNATIONALS

At the '67 Winter meets, many of the new car types were not yet available to the general public or the race teams. Chevrolet was represented by Bill Jenkins and several other '66 Chevy IIs. The Chrysler Street Hemi bunch was out in force, as were many of the remaining Mopar S/S cars from 1965, including Dick Landy, Akron Arlen Vanke, Don Grotheer, Ed Miller, and Joe Smith with the venerable Fenner-Tubbs S/SA '65 Plymouth, now running SS/AA.

In the new Super Stock classes, many of the winners were very familiar, and many would remain so throughout 1967. SS/A was won by Ed Miller and his 4-speed '65 Plymouth; SS/B had a familiar sight in Don Grotheer's Street Hemi; SS/C was the Chevy II of Eddie Vasquez! Who? Wasn't that Bill Jenkins class? SS/D belonged to Dick Arons and his 396 Chevelle; and Ron Garey's 4-4-2 Olds captured the gold in SS/E.

Over on the automatic side, Joe Smith and the Fenner-Tubbs car again captured SS/AA. SS/BA was won by Dick Charboneau and

*The King of Top Stock, Jere Stahl, returned in 1967 with this Belvedere hardtop running in SS/B against the likes of Ronnie Sox, Hubert Platt, and Dick Landy. Once again his car was equal to the task as he set low ET at the Super Stock Nationals with a time of 10.66. (Joel Naprstek)*

his very consistent '63 Plymouth. Akron Arlen Vanke turned back all comers in SS/CA with his '63 Max Wedge Plymouth. Dave Kempton, who had seemingly been campaigning his '62 Plymouth forever, won SS/EA. Joe Smith and the Fenner-Tubbs car were clearly the fastest of the Super Stock Division, running an 11.27 on the SS/AA trophy run.

Many of the times were inconsistent due to the fact that many were new classes with no national records. It was this fact that ultimately led to the winner of Super Stock Eliminator, when a car first set the record, then ran consistently right on that record throughout eliminations. During eliminations for SS/C, Eddie Vasquez won the class and set the record which would determine the handicap his car would get in the running for Super Stock Eliminator. Jenkins could and did run much quicker, but just not at the right time.

Thus Vasquez and Jenkins both, had a "dial-in time" of 12.72 seconds for the handicap starting system. Jenkins cut the lights too close in Round One and lost via the foul start. All Grumpy would've had to do was wait on the Green and he probably would have won the eliminator since he ran much quicker than anyone else in SS/C. However, he might have run too quick also! It was possible to lose in an eliminator race by beating the national record by too much. Jenkins was running in the very low 12s and high 11-second bracket throughout the meet, which would have been enough to be eliminated through the process of "breaking out", i.e. running too quick on the existing national record.

Vasquez, having set the record at 12.72, simply had to match his own record. He was masterful at doing this throughout the eliminations. His opponent in the trophy run was Ed Miller, who was also

*At the '67 NHRA Nationals, the old '65 – '66 A/FX SOHC Mustangs were running in C/XS. Jerry Harvey's Mustang, the only true 1966 A/FX Mustang built, lost the class to Tom Tignanelli's Plymouth that turned a 10.55 for the win. (Author's Collection)*

consistent, with his '65 Plymouth running between 11.43 and 11.69 all day. Yet, Miller had a problem: He had a "dial-in" of 11.18 which was the national record for SS/A. Thus, he had to give Vasquez's Chevy II over 1 1/2 seconds head start. Miller wasn't running anywhere near that record, which put him at another 3/10s disadvantage. The result was predictable. Eddie Vasquez's *Too Costly* SS/C Chevy II beat the big Plymouth easily for the Super Stock Eliminator honors. Vasquez ran a 12.74 on his 12.72 record, to beat Miller in the finals.

The Stock Eliminator race in previous years was called Junior Stock. This race was open to winning and runner-up cars running factory stock class from A/S through N/S, both stick and automatic. The winner was the old G/SA '60 Pontiac station wagon of Graham Douglas which ran right on the record, run after run.

At the AHRA Winternationals, it was another Chevy II that walked off with the Top Stock honors. This time it was Bill "Grumpy" Jenkins and his new *Grumpy's Toy*. This was a different

car than he'd campaigned throughout 1966, as the old red and white car had been wrecked in a towing accident. Bill's new *Toy* was all white, and ran even better than the old version. Bill ran 11.70 to win Middle Stock Eliminator (the equivalent to Top Stock at NHRA meets) at the AHRA meet in Phoenix. It would be one of the final times that "Grumpy" would run the little Chevy II.

## SPRINGNATIONALS 1967

By the time the Springnationals rolled around, Super Stock as a class unto itself was gone. The liberalized top stock classes under NHRA rules had replaced the top-of-the-line stocker class. No longer did anyone need to have the biggest and baddest to win the top stock award. An automatic Camaro with a 325 hp rat motor at the bottom of the performance scale could and eventually did win Super Stock Eliminator, but not at the '67 NHRA Springnationals.

As usual, the Springnationals were held the first weekend in June at Bristol International Raceway, which had become known as "Thunder Valley" because of the surrounding hills' effect on the noise level. All of the major players were in the lanes. Ronnie Sox had a new SS/B 4-speed '67 Plymouth Hemi car called *The Boss* (and it lived up to its name!). Bill Jenkins had a new 375 hp 396 Camaro, *Grumpy's Toy II*, that ran in SS/C. Jere Stahl, Jenkins' nemesis throughout 1966, had another big Plymouth in the staging lanes. This time he had a 2-door hardtop in SS/B, and it really shook up the troops with runs in the 10.60 range! Dick Landy had an SS/B Dodge. The new 427 Fairlanes were there, although they were still in the shakedown mode. Finally, there were the usual number of remaining SS/A and SS/AA '65 Plymouths, whose numbers were dwindling at an ever increasing rate.

The Super Stock class winners included: John Hagen in SS/A; Ronnie Sox and *The Boss* in SS/B; Bill Jenkins' Camaro in SS/C; Wally Booth's SS 396 Chevelle in SS/D; and Mike Frederick's Plymouth in SS/E. On the automatic side, the winners were: Paul Richardson's *Hustlin' Hemi* in SS/AA; Ron Mancini's *Zoom-O* '63 Plymouth in SS/BA; Akron Arlen Vanke's '63 Plymouth in SS/CA; Tommy Clise's Plymouth in SS/DA; and Dick Arons' maroon Camaro in SS/EA.

Super Stock Eliminator was open to any car that had won its class or was runner-up in the Super Stock Division. However, the lights (the red ones) and *The Boss* put away everybody in short order. Stahl fell via the red light, and all the Fords were gone after the first round. Sox calmly marched through Jenkins, Akron Arlen

*Action in SS/B at the '67 Super Stock Nationals, Cecil County, Maryland matches up "Dandy Dick" Landy's '67 Dodge Coronet against Hubert Platt's Georgia Shaker. Landy had the jump right at the starting line and went on to win with a time of 10.76. This would be an ongoing battle throughout the '67 season – Street Hemi against 427 Fairlanes in SS/B. (Joel Naprstek)*

Vanke, and Ron Mancini for the win, running an 11.34 and 123.45 mph. Stock Eliminator, which was open to winners and runners-up in the factory stock classes, was won by Jay Hamilton and his E/SA '58 Pontiac Bonneville, with a time of 13.85.

Later that summer *Super Stock Magazine* held its annual meet at Cecil County Drag-O-Way. From the moment the gates opened, the fans knew this was going to be something special because the Chrysler teams had come to the Super Stock Nationals with winning on their minds. They would go home very unhappy.

Through the gates came the Sox & Martin Mopar Clinic — a flatbed Dodge truck with a '67 Belvedere on it, pulling a trailer with another red, white, and blue Belvedere. Behind that trailer was still another Dodge truck and trailer with a third S&M Plymouth. Behind that was the Dick Landy caravan of Clinic cars. The question on people's minds was, how do you drive two and three cars at a meet when they could possibly race against one another at some point?

Landy had his son driving the SS/EA Dodge, while he handled the SS/BA. Sox & Martin had three cars, but they had their choice of a number of other factory drivers that were handling Funny Cars at the meet. Butch Leal handled the SS/D car, Lee Smith drove the SS/EA car, and Ronnie Sox handled the SS/B car. This was cubic factory money at its best, or worst, depending on whether you were just a fan or someone who had to contend with the Mopar Clinic teams.

There would be dual class eliminations on Friday and Saturday nights, which would make up the field for Sunday's Super Stock Eliminator. The Cecil County guys had taken some steps to alleviate the problem of so-called "brake-light racing", whereby a racer was

*Wiley Cossey had been the man to beat for Junior Stock throughout '66 with his 427 Chevrolet. For 1967, he switched to Plymouth with this 426 Street Hemi sponsored by Hooker Headers. Cossey's Belevedere ran SS/BA at the '67 Nationals, but Tom Myl's '67 Plymouth won the class with a time of 11.64. (Author's Collection)*

easily capable of running much quicker than his national record, but didn't. Many racers were standing on the brakes going through the traps to avoid a breakout from the record. Remember, you could lose by running too quick during an eliminator run-off.

On Friday night, Sox and *The Boss* whipped everyone in SS/B with an 11.83 time against a national record of 11.63. Dick Landy lost the Friday night race with a 12.08 but on Saturday, he shut down everyone with an 11.55. Everyone in the place could see the red taillights go on as the cars entered the timing traps. Was this cheating? People called it sandbagging or laying back. The true times would come out during the eliminator runs on Sunday.

It wasn't just the Mopar guys who were sandbagging. Dick Arons had one of the new 396 Camaros equipped with a 325 hp, 396ci Semi-Hemi and 3-speed Turbo Hydra-Matic transmission. He won SS/EA class with a time of 12.62. The national record for SS/EA was 12.38, but the Cecil County tech people changed the rules for the eliminator. Instead of running against the existing NHRA national record, everyone would run against the average time in class run-offs. Thus Sox would be running off the 11.83 he had recorded on Friday night, and Arons against a 12.38 time.

Arons had beaten the Landy Dodge in SS/EA, even though Landy had run an 11.92. There was something strange going on here. The last 427 Fairlane, Harold Dutton's SS/C car, was eliminated by Arons in Round Four. Next up was Landy's SS/B car. Arons got the handicap based on his 12.38 class average, Landy ran off his 11.55. The Camaro was out first and well gone by the time the silver Dodge got the green light. "Dandy Dick" posted an 11.11 losing time against Arons.

The final race matched the Camaro against *The Boss*. Again, the Camaro got a huge lead under the handicap start. At the Green, Sox leaped out of the hole giving chase but the Camaro was sandbagging every bit as much as *The Boss*. Sox crossed the finish line in a phenomenal 11.02 seconds, but lost badly to Arons and the Camaro, which turned an 11.63, almost a full second quicker than what he had turned in winning SS/EA class. The rules had been changed to eliminate sandbagging, but had resulted in even bigger problems. No one had an answer for the problem then, and no one has an answer for the exact same problem today. The racers of course, simply unplugged the tail lights.

## 1967 NATIONALS

By Labor Day weekend 1967, the pieces were all in place for a slam-bang super stock race at Indianapolis Raceway Park. The Fords, headed by the Paul Harvey Racing Team, were being handled by none other than "Dyno Don" Nicholson, Hubert Platt, Eddie Schartman, and Ed Terry. Being located in Indianapolis, the Ford gang had free use of the Paul Harvey Ford facility to plan and tune, and generally make life miserable for the Mopar Clinic boys. However, the fly in the ointment would be the Chevys of Dick Arons, Wally Booth, and Bill Jenkins.

Class winners, which were automatically entered in the Super Stock Eliminator, included Bob Brown's gorgeous lime green '65 Plymouth in SS/A and R.L. Williams' *Hillbilly* Street-Hemi Plymouth in SS/B (after Ed Terry's 427 Fairlane was disqualified). Bill Jenkins was the only car entered in SS/C. Wally Booth won

*Dick Landy showed up at the '67 Nationals with a pair of Dodge Coronets, one for SS/EA and this car in SS/B. Landy and the Sox & Martin team were touring the nation with the Chrysler Clinics, which went to dealers and talked with prospective buyers about high-performance Mopars. Both of Landy's Dodges were shut down in Round One of Super Stock Eliminator. (Author's Collection)*

*Action in Round One of Super Stock Eliminator at the '67 Nationals. Bill Allie drives the Fastbacks SS/BA '67 427 Fairlane against Howard Maseles and the veteran '62 Packer Pontiac. The Fairlane won this round. (Author's Collection)*

*Action in SS/B between Herb "Mr. 4 Speed" McCandless' Plymouth Street Hemi, and John Downing's* Respect, *one of the new 427 Ford Fairlanes. Obviously, with the type of gate job that McCandless did on Downing, he was the winner of the race. (Author's Collection)*

SS/D with his red and gold 396 Chevelle, and Ronnie Sox took home the gold with his 4-speed 440 Belvedere in SS/E. The automatic class winners were as follows: Leonard Hughes' '65 Dodge won SS/AA, Tom Myl's '67 Plymouth Street Hemi won SS/BA, Ron Mancini won SS/CA, Tommy Clise's '62 Plymouth was the winner in SS/DA, and the maroon Camaro of Dick Arons was again the winner in SS/EA.

There were 30 cars entered in Super Stock Eliminator. The Fords were bunched in SS/B and SS/C, both stick and automatic, with Dick Brannan, Hubert Platt, and Don Nicholson. There were Mopars throughout every class, including the clinic cars of "Dandy Dick" Landy (2 cars) and Ronnie Sox (3 cars). Other Mopars to watch were Mary Ann Foss' '65 SS/AA Dodge *Go-Hummer*, Herb "Mr. 4-Speed" McCandless' '67 Plymouth Street Hemi, and Jack Werst's *Mr. 5&50* Plymouth. The Chevys of Jenkins, Booth, and Arons dominated SS/C, SS/D, and SS/E.

By the end of Round Two in Super Stock Eliminator, it was Chevy vs. Mopar. Rounds Three and Four looked like an instant replay as Jenkins downed the Sox & Martin SS/B Hemi in Round Three, then turned around and beat the Sox & Martin 440 SS/EA car

in Round Four. That was the last of the Chrysler Clinic cars. Bob Brown pushed Ron Mancini so hard in the other half of Round Four, that Mancini ran too quick and was disqualified.

The final matched the grumpy one from Berwyn, Pennsylvania and his white SS/C Camaro, against the beautiful lime green and gold '65 Plymouth of Bob Brown. Jenkins got the handicap start and was gone at the first flicker of green. Brown waited patiently for his green, then gave chase to the little Camaro but to no avail. Jenkins crossed the finish line first turning an 11.55 and 115.97 mph. Brown lost with a time of 11.10 and 125.52 mph. Stock Eliminator went to Ben Wenzel's B/S 396 Camaro. Wenzel beat the light green Gunning Brothers '57 Chevy station wagon, *The Jolly Green Giant*, with a time of 12.33 and a speed of 113.92 mph.

At the NHRA World Finals meet in Tulsa, Oklahoma, there were a couple of big differences in the way NHRA handled the big super stockers. First off, NHRA started paying some big money to the winner — $10,000 to the winner of Top Stock, plus round money. The winner ended up taking more than $18,000 home! Second, an attempt was made to deal with sandbaggers. NHRA announced that anyone besting a national record, either in time trials or for class runoffs, that time would become the new national record, at least for the handicap start system at Tulsa. Also, NHRA cut the field down from 30 cars at the Nationals to 16 cars at the World Finals.

The field was made up of two Dodges, three Camaros, two 427 Fairlanes, and the rest were Plymouths. Pure numbers don't usually win in drag racing. Grumpy Jenkins had waded through a bigger field of Mopars at the Nationals to win Super Stock Eliminator, and so it would be at the World Finals. Round after round, the little white Camaro shut down all comers. The semi-finals matched Jenkins against Ed Miller's SS/AA '65 Plymouth, and Ron Mancini's '63 Plymouth against the other Camaro, Dick Arons' SS/EA car.

The first two at the starting line were Jenkins and Miller. Jenkins knew this would probably be his toughest competition. As the last yellow was blinking off in Jenkins' lane, he made his move. Red Light! Miller won! Next up was Arons against Mancini. Like Jenkins, Arons had the handicap lead. Green! The maroon Camaro flew. Mancini watched the yellow lights then made his move. Red light! Arons advanced.

The final matched Miller's SS/AA 426 Plymouth against Arons' SS/EA 396 Camaro, but the skies were growing ever darker as a rain-

*In Round Three of Super Stock Eliminator, Jenkins' Camaro beat* The Boss, *Ronnie Sox's SS/B Street Hemi.* The Boss *was the favored car at the Nationals based on Sox's wins at the Springnationals and* Super Stock Magazine *meet.* Grumpy's Toy *turned a time of 11.57 for the win. He also took Sox's SS/EA car out of eliminations.* (Author's Collection)

*Action in Stock Eliminator showing how much lead the handicap starting system could give. This round matched Ted Harbit's M/S Studebaker against Bill Morgan's A/SA '63 Plymouth 426 station wagon. Unbelievably, the Plymouth caught the Studebaker at the 1,310 foot mark to win.* (Author's Collection)

storm threatened to wipe out Super Stock Eliminator. The rain had actually begun during the Jenkins-Miller race, then stopped suddenly. NHRA told both drivers to immediately return to the starting line, no cool down period, no nothing.

Arons got the handicap lead and was gone with a good start. Either the Camaro was a little off due to lack of cooling, or perhaps the rain had made the strip a little wet. At any rate, the Camaro just wasn't up to its previous times. Miller calmly waited on the green before launching the big Plymouth. He didn't even spin the slicks, just let off the brakes a little, then nailed it. Miller easily caught the maroon Camaro and passed him at the 1000 foot mark, before letting off the gas and coasting through the lights. Miller turned an 11.19 against Arons 12.32 for the win. George Cureton's G/SA '56 Chevy sedan delivery was the winner in Stock Eliminator, when Wally Nisson red-lighted on the final run.

The 1967 race year ended with big news coming out of Detroit for 1968. There was a rumor that Chrysler would put the 426 cross-ram Super Stock Hemi into the Plymouth Barracuda and Dodge Dart. It proved to be true and set up some of the most ferocious battles in Super Stock history, both on and off the strip.

## 1968

The year started out promising with politicians and military strategists saying there was an end in sight for the conflict in South Vietnam. Hope quickly died when on January 30 the North Vietnamese and Viet Cong launched an all-out offensive during the Tet holiday. Although the Tet Offensive was a military defeat for the Communists, the U.S. populace was furious. A majority of the people were against the war, and it seemed protests grew in size and numbers literally overnight. The entire nation was shocked as television cameras showed thousands of young people being beaten and arrested for protesting a war that no one wanted.

During the year the civil rights agenda suffered horribly with the assassination of Martin Luther King, followed two months later by the killing of Robert Kennedy, another champion of civil rights.

Unrest was a common theme in world events in 1968, including drag racing. By the year's end, many drivers would call for changes in the rules for classes and eliminations. To say drivers were frustrated would be an understatement.

The drag racing year of 1968 started with a bang, got even hotter in the Spring, but then closed with a loud noise — Pro Stock. The rules were virtually unchanged from the previous year, with Super Stock classes from A through F in both stick and automatic. In S/S classes, you were allowed to use any intake manifold as long as it was the same configuration as the original. Thus, if the car ran a single four barrel, you could use one of the aftermarket manifolds such as Edelbrock. The only restriction was in height, which could not be more than 1" taller than the factory type.

While Stock class was still limited to a 7" tire no matter what the class, Super Stock cars could run any wheel/tire size and combina-

tion that would fit in the original wheel opening. Now S/S cars could use any cam, any intake, and any tire size. We were getting further and further from factory stock. Of course, you *could* still run in Stock class with all factory parts, which many drivers and teams chose to do. However, the money was in Super Stock racing and the factories knew it.

## THE COBRA JET MUSTANG

Just prior to the opening of the Winter drag meets, Ford released a new package aimed directly at the heart of the Super Stock classes, the Mustang Cobra Jet. Under the hood of a '68 Mustang 2+2 coupe was a new 428 Ford wedge engine with a solid lifter camshaft, adjustable rocker arms, big valve heads with 11.5:1 compression, and a big Holley four-barrel carburetor.

Ford built 50 of these Mustangs, enough to get NHRA to classify them as stock, complete with deep sump oil pan, Jardine Headers, dual electric fuel pumps, trunk mounted battery, hood scoop, and heavy-duty traction bar setups that were a direct result of Funny Car research vehicles. The Cobra Jet Mustangs weighed 3184 pounds, dropping them squarely in the top of C/Stock or Super Stock/E. The Cobra Jets were very quick, running 11.60s in tests just prior to the NHRA Winternationals.

The AHRA Winternationals were run a week prior to the Pomona meet and just across town at Lions Drag Strip. Hubert Platt had one of the new Cobra Jet Mustangs at the AHRA meet. Running out of Tasca Ford (the factory drivers were now switch-

*Al Joniec got out of his* Bat Car *funny Mustang and jumped right into this Cobra Jet Mustang, running in NHRA SS/E class. Ford built fifty of the Cobra Jet Mustangs with both 4-speed and Cruise-O-Matic transmissions in 1968. All were delivered from the factory in identical white paint jobs. In SS/E, the Cobra Jets were capable of running in the low 11-second bracket. (Images Unlimited)*

*Immediately prior to the '68 Winternationals, Ford unveiled the first of the Cobra Jet Mustangs, powered by the 428 Ford Wedge engine. With times approaching the 11s, the Mustangs owned the SS/E class, with Al Joniec beating out Hubert Platt for the trophy.* (Matchracemadness)

ing sponsors like changing socks) in C/SA, Hubie made a single run in the mid-12s to show the crowd what the new Mustangs were capable of even as a factory stocker.

In Super Stock Eliminator, which bore little resemblance to either a factory stocker or even an NHRA Super Stock car, there were only three cars entered led by the Mopar Clinic cars of Sox & Martin and Dick Landy, and Bill Hielscher. Both Sox and Landy had cars that were equipped with all fiberglass front ends, stripped interiors, hood scoops, and cross-ram super stock Hemi engines. Hielscher's big Camaro had a busted rod so he ran his 327 'Vette.

After Ronnie Sox disposed of the pesky Hielscher, a final between the two Clinic cars was set up. Sox had run a 10.53 against Hielscher, while Landy had just cruised in the bye run. As the light winked down for the final, Sox left just a bit early, leaving Landy the

winner with a time of 10.49 and 132.45 mph. Interestingly, during the post-race inspection and weigh-in, both Landy and Sox were underweight. The drivers and tech crews conferred and declared the race would stand with Landy as the winner.

In Top Stock Eliminations, Bill Jenkins had a new '68 Camaro that was running in the 10s all day long, but he lost — twice! In the third round, he was beaten but then reinstated when the race winner broke out, i.e. he ran faster than his existing record. In the next round, Grumpy actually beat Dick Smith's Ranchero but the clocks malfunctioned and AHRA officials re-ran the race. This time Jenkins fouled and lost, which made him even grumpier than usual.

Many of the big names went by the wayside before a winner was declared in Top Stock. Ed Miller drove his '65 Plymouth to victory in one of the early rounds, then lost the race when he broke out.

Platt's new Cobra Jet Mustang was a big threat until he red-lighted. The final matched Dick Smith's Ranchero against another of those little Chevy IIs. Ron Robles drove Bob Heinz's Formula 4, G/S Chevy II to victory with a time of 12.13 to beat Smith.

The following weekend, Pomona again hosted the NHRA Winternationals. When the gates opened, there were more than 100 cars waiting to compete in the Super Stock classes led by a fleet of new white Mustangs with "Cobra Jet" prominently written on the side in big letters. The Mopar Clinic boys, Sox & Martin and Dick Landy, were there with a fleet all their own. Bill Jenkins was there with his '68 Camaro. Hubert Platt not only had a Cobra Jet, but also competed head-to-head with Jenkins in SS/C with his '67 427 Fairlane.

The Fords, including all the new Cobra Jets, didn't fare too well in class run-offs. Platt's Fairlane, with Ed Terry driving, lost to "Grumpy" Jenkins in SS/C, and Gas Ronda lost the SS/EA class to Dick Landy. Only in SS/E did the Mustangs win out, when Al Joniec's Cobra Jet beat Hubert Platt's Cobra Jet for the trophy. Platt had a good chance in C/SA but didn't hear the call for class and was eliminated as a no-show.

Other class winners included: Ed Miller's veteran '65 Plymouth in SS/B, Ronnie Sox's new version of *The Boss*, a '68 Roadrunner in SS/F with Herb "Mr. 4 Speed" McCandless driving, and Sox driving his old *Boss* to victory in SS/D. Tom Crutchfield took all comers in SS/BA with his '65 Dodge, Bob Allie's SS/CA 427 Fairlane won with

a time of 11.49, Dave Wren's beautiful '64 Plymouth shut down Dick Landy in SS/DA, but Landy recovered to beat Ronda in SS/EA, and Tony Kneiper's Firebird won in SS/FA. So, all in all, the clinic cars won four of the ten S/S classes, and placed second in another.

Super Stock Eliminator was run on Sunday. The Sox & Martin team had so many cars in the teardown barns, that Jake King, head wrench for the Burlington, North Carolina gang, didn't get the last car put back together until four in the morning. Around noon the call went out for Super Stock Eliminator. The top 32 cars, including the 10 class winners, came to the staging area. There were 13 Plymouths, 6 Dodges, 7 Fords, and 6 from the GM camp headed by Jenkins. The Cobra Jets looked like a Ford all-star team with Gas Ronda, Don Nicholson, Hubert Platt, and Al Joniec behind the wheels.

Interestingly, many of the class run-off matches were again matched up in Super Stock Eliminator, and with very different results. Ed Terry, driving Platt's 427 Fairlane, pulled a hole shot on Jenkins in Round One, winning with a time of 11.16 to Grumpy's 11.04. Landy and Gas Ronda hooked up in a repeat of their SS/EA class run, with the results being the same — Landy 11.91 to Ronda's Cobra Jet 12.00. Dave Wren shut down Landy's new '68 Coronet with his '64 Plymouth, and the Sox & Martin gang just kept rolling.

Landy's SS/EA car put Ed Miller's SS/B Plymouth back on the trailer to begin Round Two with a surprise. The dark horse in the crowd was John Livingston out of Nashville. He had lost the SS/B

*Sox & Martin had so many cars at the Winternationals that the Chrysler reps at Pomona volunteered other Dodge and Plymouth drivers to handle some of the cars. Herb "Mr. 4 Speed" McCandless drove the SS/F version of* The Boss, *a 4 speed, 440-powered Belvedere hardtop, winning the class with a time of 12.17 and 105.81 mph. (Drag Racing Memories)*

title to Ed Miller in a very close race. However, in Round Two Livingston beat Herb McCandless in the other S&M car, then put it on Ed Terry in Platt's big 427 Fairlane. The semi-final run matched Landy's '68 Charger SS/EA car against Al Joniec's SS/E class winning Cobra Jet, and Livingston's '65 SS/B Plymouth against Dave Wren's SS/DA '64 Plymouth.

Wren beat Livingston with a close race highlighted by a masterful start by Wren using the handicap system. Wren turned 11.56 for the win. Next up was the silver and red Landy Charger against the white Mustang out of Rice-Holman Ford. Landy knew he had to have a perfect start to win and took a chance on the last yellow. RED! Joniec's Mustang advanced to the final and all the clinic cars were gone.

The final matched two cars that were running right on the record for each class. As the two cars staged, it was apparent that the Ford would get the handicap start, about a half second. Yellow, yellow, yellow, green and the white Ford is gone. Yellow, yellow, yellow, oops, red! Wren cut the light a little too close giving the win to Al Joniec's Cobra Jet Mustang. Ford had spent a lot of money on the Cobra Jet program, and even though it wasn't one of Ford's name drivers who won, the Cobra Jet won beating the Mopar Clinic in the process.

The Stock Eliminator title was up for grabs between every class winner from A/S through N/S. Within this maze of no-names were a couple of pretty familiar ones too. Sox & Martin had still another entry, this time a '68 Barracuda in E/SA. Bill Shrewsberry, formerly of the A/FX Comet ranks and now driving the *LA Dart* wheelstander, drove an E/S 340ci '68 Dodge Dart. Hubert Platt brought the factory-stock C/SA Cobra Jet Mustang that had made big noises at the AHRA Winter meet.

*The Strickler-Jenkins camp looked like a new car dealership. Dave had a new 396 Camaro to run in SS/C. Grumpy also had a Camaro in SS/C as well as a Nova in SS/D. Dave also had a new '68 Camaro Z-28 to run in SS/J. (Author's Collection)*

Big-block and small-block Chevrolets, with a few 409s thrown in, were the biggest winners with 16 class trophies to their credit. As usual, it was the most consistent driver and car that won Stock Eliminator. The winner, running on a 14.60 record, ran 14.63, 14.60, 14.50, 14.60, and 14.59 during Stock Eliminations. His name was John Barkley, who waded through a host of '55 - '57 Chevys, with a few old Oldsmobiles thrown in to make it to the final. His opponent was the red, white, and blue Sox & Martin '68 Barracuda driven by *Hot Rod Magazine* Editor John McFarland. Making a perfect start and a perfect run throughout, Barkley's '57 Chevy held on for the win at 14.59. The S&M 'Cuda ran 12.99 in a losing effort.

It was now time to start looking toward the Springnationals. Chrysler unleashed what would become the ultimate super stocker — the '68 Hemi-Barracuda and Hemi-Dart. In early '68, with the Ford Cobra Jets well into production and having success at the strips, Chrysler engineers started working out the details of installing the 426 Hemi engine into the lighter and shorter Dodge Dart and Plymouth Barracuda body styles. With the money available to a factory like Chrysler, this project should have been easy. The only thing easy about it was the availability of the engines and bodies.

### THE HEMI-DART AND HEMI-BARRACUDA

Chrysler wanted these vehicles to come off the assembly line and beat everything that was already in full race trim. The orders went out to pull 50 Darts and 50 Barracudas from the assembly line, minus engines, transmissions, radiators, hood assemblies, rear seats, win-

*One of the new Hemi-Darts went to Melvin Yow, who drove the O.B. Hewett '65 A/FX Dodge to many victories. Yow's Dart was one of the 4-speed cars. The national record for SS/B had been 10.75 but these new cars were demolishing it every time they ran, with times dipping into the 10.20s by Nationals time. (Marv Smith)*

dow crank assemblies, heaters, and of course, no sound deadener, not even paint. They were then trucked across town from the Hamtramk, Michigan assembly plant, to the Hurst Performance Research facility in Madison Heights, Michigan.

At Hurst, the cars were made ready for the conversion to Hemi power and competition drag racing. The front fenders were removed and replaced with lighter fiberglass units. The doors were pulled off and acid-dipped to the thinnest that was possible and still retain any kind of strength. Windows were replaced with plastic and no crank mechanisms were installed. The driver had a strap attached to each window that raised and lowered them. Front seats were replaced with lightweight Dodge van units, and the carpeting was rejected in favor of a single rubber mat.

Under the new fiberglass hood that had a huge air intake scoop was an engine compartment modified for Hemi installation. The brake master cylinder was installed slightly to the left and made so that it could be moved to allow quick access to the valve cover and head bolts. The right side of the engine compartment saw the shock tower reworked for valve cover clearance. The K member was reworked to accept the Hemi engine, which had been moved slightly to the right during the installation.

The engine itself was the 426 Hemi that had been blazing a path to glory at strips all over the nation since 1964. Based on the Street-Hemi version, it had many refinements, including use of the new aluminum crossram intake mounting a pair of big Holley four-barrel carbs, and 12.5:1 compression heads and pistons. A transistor ignition supplied the spark, and the exhaust was routed away through specially designed Hooker Headers.

Behind the engine was a choice of transmissions: 4-speed manual or 3-speed 727 Torqueflite automatic. Neither was your standard unit as supplied by Chrysler. The 4 speed was one of the new slick-shift transmissions equipped with a Hurst Competition Plus shifter. The cars also came with a stamped steel blow-proof bellhousing from the factory. The Torqueflites were supplied by B&M Automotive, a hot rod transmission specialist in Van Nuys, California. The B&M Torqueflites had high-stall speed converters and manual-shift valve bodies, and also were equipped with a Hurst Shifter.

Underneath, the power was transmitted to a heavy-duty rear axle assembly, fitted with a Sure-Grip limited-slip differential. The rear springs were the well-known super stock units designed specifically for racing. The production front disc brake units normally used to stop the standard street Dart and Barracuda, were discarded in favor of much larger units normally used on Belvederes and Coronets. You have to be able to stop the thing on those 130 mph jaunts! The initial order was for 50 Darts and 50 Barracudas, of which 60 were 4 speed and 40 had Torqueflites. Production was begun in late February 1968. As demand grew, the production was upped to around 75 of each body style, not counting the home-built versions.

The prototype or mule car, a red and yellow Barracuda, was built and trucked to the West Coast shortly after the end of the Winternationals where a test program was set up using the Irwindale

*Hubert Platt introduced the Cobra Jet at the AHRA Winternationals at Lions Drag Strip, California. The weight of the Cobra Jets put them in the top of C/S or SS/E. Platt ran an easy 12.60 in his brand new C/SA Cobra Jet. His* Georgia Shaker *is seen here at Southeastern International Dragway in July 1968. (Marv Smith)*

Drag Strip facilities. At Irwindale, the car was put through its paces resulting in some astounding numbers: mid-10s at 130+ mph right off the trailer! Weighing in at around 3020 lbs., the Darts and 'Cudas were originally built to compete in SS/B, but they instantly overwhelmed all competition in that class and NHRA re-classed them as SS/A.

## 1968 SPRINGNATIONALS

The NHRA Springnationals were held at Englishtown, New Jersey over the second weekend in June 1968. By that time, many of the new Hemi-Darts and Barracudas were ready for the competition. Among the many entrants were Dick Landy, "Wild Bill" Flynn, and Ron Mancini in Darts, with Akron Arlen Vanke, Don Grotheer, and of course, Sox & Martin in Barracudas. Ford was well represented with Cobra Jet Mustangs driven by Platt, Harvey, Joniec, and others. Chevrolet had the indomitable "Grumpy" Jenkins, Dick Arons, and Dave Strickler.

Sox came right off the trailer to run 10.30s, which were almost 6/10s of a second under the existing national record for SS/B! The other Hemi-Darts and 'Cudas weren't far behind, but what happened during actual competition was a battle of the sandbaggers. Rather than modify the handicap rules as had been done at other major meets in the past, and using the fastest qualifying or time trial elapsed time as the record, NHRA stood on its existing national record handicap rule.

Run after run produced the tell-tale brake lights and tire smoke in the lights to keep from breaking out and losing. There was tire

*Warming up the slicks in the resin at the* Cars Magazine *meet held at Cecil County, Maryland in the Summer of 1968, Ronnie Sox's Hemi-Barracuda, the* Lil Boss, *was one of a whole trailer full of vehicles campaigned by the Sox & Martin team in 1968. The Barracuda was easily capable of times in the very low 10s on every run, and competed in SS/A, SS/B, A/MP, and anything else the sanctioning bodies asked them to – and won!* (Matchracemadness)

smoke at the starting line and at the finish line on many runs. The new Hemi-Darts and 'Cudas systematically put down all the competition in Super Stock Eliminator. The final matched Sox against Don Grotheer's 'Cuda, but Sox wasn't in his Hemi-Barracuda. He had spun a slick almost off the rim on a previous run and was in his older Hemi-Belvedere *The Boss* with a SS/D handicap.

At the Green, Sox was out and gone, with Grotheer's 'Cuda in hot pursuit. The race was going to be very close since both cars were capable of running well under the existing records. When Sox went through the win lights his brakes were locked up so hard that smoke was rolling off the big M&H slicks. None of the spectators could tell who the winner was until the win light came on. Grotheer, maybe. A quick check of the times revealed that Grotheer had broken out. He

lost! But wait, so had Sox broken out. NHRA looked at the clocks, looked at the results, and looked at the crowd. Then declared Sox the winner because he had broken out by less than Grotheer! Sox was only .19 under the record, Grotheer was .23.

It didn't make any sense to anyone who witnessed the debacle. The original concept of drag racing was to run as hard as you could, and go as quick as you could, and hope it was enough to beat the other guy. In the old days, just 6 years prior, Top Stock Eliminator (equivalent to the '68 Super Stock Eliminator) matched up the top 50 cars in the top class. Handicap starts had ruined this by making it possible to lose two ways — by running too slow and by running too quick! A change was being called for by drivers, fans, manufacturers, everyone, but it wouldn't be this year.

The '68 *Super Stock Magazine* Nationals were held at New York National Speedway on Long Island. The first hint of the forthcoming pro stockers was exhibited at this meet. The New York National rules crew created a new class just for ultra-light super stockers like the Hemi-Darts and Hemi-Barracudas, Experimental Super Stock (X/SS), with its own eliminator. Whoever won the class also was the X/SS Eliminator. Entries were small in number but high in quality, but the results were the same as the Springnationals. Ronnie Sox put down Dick Landy's Hemi-Dart to win the title with a 10.34 ET and 134.35 mph speed. With no national record to run against, thus no handicap start, the races were all heads-up and no brake lights were seen. Everyone enjoyed the races, especially the drivers who didn't have to worry about breaking out no matter how fast they ran.

In Super Stock Eliminator, the races were run under the handicap start system, but with a difference. The New York National rules stated that you ran either on the existing NHRA national record, or used your own quickest ET, whichever was lowest. Thus you could run all-out, and simply run on your own ET from that point on. Again, the brake light brigade was closed down. There were 64 cars entered in the Eliminator, all legal NHRA super stockers.

As each round was run, more and more name stockers bit the dust. Jenkins, Werst, Nicholson, Lawton, Shahan all were gone in the early rounds. One of the most interesting races was between Bill Jenkins and his SS/D Nova, and his old friend Dave Strickler with a new Z-28 that Jenkins had built for SS/F. The little 302ci Z-28 beat the 396 Nova to advance. The quarter finals matched Dick Arons' Camaro convertible against Melvin Yow in the Sox & Martin wedge car. Arons defeated Yow. Hubert Platt drew Bill Stiles' SS/BA 'Cuda, with Stiles winning.

*The Chevrolet teams also brought several cars. This is the Dick Arons Berger Chevrolet team that had cars entered in SS/EA and SS/E. Interestingly, the near car is the SS/E car, but has 427 emblems on the front fender. How did that get into SS/E? (Tom Schiltz)*

The next race matched two of the sport's best: Dick Landy and Dave Strickler. Strickler was driving the *Old Reliable* SS/F Z-28. The orange Camaro screamed to an 11.94 victory over the 440 Dodge. The final two cars were Ronnie Sox and the quickest of the SS/B Barracudas and Darts, against Bill Miller's older SS/B '65 Plymouth. Sox won but then lost by breaking out. Miller won by default, then he too was eliminated for breaking out.

That left three cars: Strickler's little screaming 302ci Z-28 Camaro, Dick Arons' 396 Camaro convertible, and Bill Stiles' SS/BA Barracuda. Arons drew the bye run and cruised through to advance to the finals. Strickler and Stiles came to the line. The little orange Z-28 screamed off the line with an 11.90 handicap. Stiles left on the Green with a 10.75 handicap. At the lights it was close but Strickler pulled it off, beating the big white Barracuda with an 11.82 ET. Oops, he was too quick. Stiles won by running exactly what his handicap was, 10.75.

The final for Super Stock Eliminator matched Bill Stiles in one of the new SS/BA Hemi-Barracudas, against Dick Arons and his SS/F '68 Camaro convertible. Stiles had been running in the 10.60s throughout the meet, with a 10.75 dial-in on the handicap. Arons was running mid-11.60s with an 11.63 dial-in. At the lights, the Barracuda went by the Camaro for the win. Or did he? Stiles had run 10.69 for the victory, but his handicap had been 10.75! Arons was declared the winner with a time of 11.69.

Once again, the drivers had found two ways to lose, and the big names were becoming increasingly frustrated. It was time for a showdown at the upcoming national meets.

## 1968 NATIONALS

Over the Labor Day weekend in 1968, some of the most exciting and controversial races ever run, were decided at Indianapolis Raceway Park. It was the 14th Annual NHRA Nationals. As with every other meet in '68, all the big boys were there, usually with more than one entry. Some teams brought tractor trailers full of race cars to Indy in '68. Bill Jenkins and Dave Strickler brought a car carrier filled with super stock Chevy IIs and Camaros. The Mopar Clinics were set up at Indy, with multiple entries. Of course, the Cobra Jet Mustangs were there by the herd.

There were a couple of other things at Indy that would be the cause of much consternation by the NHRA officials, the drivers, and the fans — representatives of various manufacturers. Several times during the 14th Nationals, it was obvious that certain drivers were ordered not to win! Of course, the infamous NHRA handicap starting system saw the demise of more and more cars through the break-out.

Super Stock class run-offs on Saturday produced many a familiar face, plus several new ones. Super Stock/B was won by Wiley Cossey at 12.30 seconds even though Ronnie Sox was capable of running 10.30s. Gary Ostrich took SS/BA with a 12.67 in another Hemi Barracuda, when most of the drivers were in the mid-10s. The familiar white Camaro of Bill Jenkins took home the class gold in SS/C, with Rudy Schings winning SS/CA in a '67 Street-Hemi Plymouth. SS/D went to the equally familiar red, white, and blue '68 version of *The Boss*; while Jerry Maes' '63 Plymouth was the winner in SS/DA.

The Cobra Jets made a breakthrough in SS/E when Jerry Harvey pulled off a win; and Lance Hill's 396 Camaro won SS/EA. Ernie Musser won SS/F with a new Z-28 Camaro, while Edgar McClelland pushed his 396 Camaro to victory in SS/FA. Most of the times were way off what the class was capable of and the speeds were ridiculous: 67 mph for Cossey's SS/B 'Cuda, 77 mph for the Jerry Harvey Cobra Jet, 80 mph for the SS/BA winner. The factories were dictating who was supposed to win and what times they were going to run in so doing. NHRA was at a loss as to what to do about it.

On Monday, the fastest 32 cars made up the Super Stock Eliminator field: 10 class winners and the 22 quickest cars running nearest the respective national record. Of those 22 cars, ALL were running well under their respective national records. How far off were they? John Hagen held the SS/B national record at 10.75, and there were six cars running well below 10.40! Jerry Harvey's Cobra Jet Mustang was running 11.40s all day, with a dial-in of 11.64. Jenkins was running 10.98 on his own record of 11.16.

It was a well-known "unknown" who would ultimately win Super Stock Eliminator, and he would beat all the major players along the way. In Round One he beat Rudy Schings' SS/CA Street-Hemi Plymouth, then came back in the next round to get Sox's SS/D *Boss*. Next up was "Wild Bill" Flynn and his SS/B Dart. A close race but Akron Arlen got the job done. Then it was the master of super

stock, Bill "Grumpy" Jenkins and his SS/C Camaro. Grumpy got the jump and ran as hard as he could but lost to the big Barracuda due to a slick track in his lane.

The final was against another unknown who had suddenly come to life at the '68 Nationals — Wally Booth. Booth had been running a '66 Chevelle and had switched to a new Camaro in SS/E. Choosing the same lane that he had run when he beat Jenkins, Vanke beat Booth's Camaro in the final when the same slick track also slowed down the green Camaro. Akron Arlen Vanke pushed the SS/B Barracuda to a 10.62 to beat Booth for Super Stock Eliminator. Stock Eliminator was won by Larry Lombardo's '61 F/S Corvette over Dave Duell's B/SA '63 Dodge station wagon with 426 power. Although the sandbagging problem was also evident in the lower stock classes, it wasn't enough to change the results.

Following the end of the '68 Nationals, a number of drivers got together and demanded changes in the way the top stock classes and eliminators were being run. Bill Jenkins was a leader in this movement. What they called for was a heads-up racing category exclusively designed to pit all the big stockers against one another with no handicap start system. It would of course, require that some cars be allowed to enter with non-stock engine combinations, such as Camaros with 427 Chevrolet engines rather than the stock 396 version. These cars would be known as professional stockers, i.e. Pro Stock for short. The class was a huge success, but it rapidly led to development of one-off vehicles like Ford Mavericks with Shotgun Hemi engines, and Chevrolet Vegas with big V-8s.

*Bill "Grumpy" Jenkins and his new '69 SS/C Camaro,* Grumpy's Toy VI, *at York US 30 Dragway in September 1969. It's generally thought that all the cars had switched to Pro Stock by this date, but "Grumpy" still had one legal car for NHRA S/S racing. Note Lakewood Chassis Co. lift bars under the rear of the car. (Joel Naprstek)*

*Grumpy rolls down the window in his '69 SS/C Camaro,* Grumpy's Toy VI, *at the '70 Nationals. The car has been converted to Pro Stock with a 427 engine and tunnelram intake. Jenkins had two Pro Stock Camaros at the '70 Nationals, this car and a '70 Camaro driven by Dave Strickler. (Author's Collection)*

*Showing just how far things advanced with the creation of Pro Stock, we have "Fast Eddie" Schartman in a Ford Maverick powered by one of the new Boss 429 Shotgun Hemi engines, against Bill Stiles driving a Hemi-powered Plymouth Volare coupe. Neither car could be bought with that engine/transmission combination, making them Gassers at the very least. However, both were declared stockers by the sanctioning bodies.* (Images Unlimited)

## A LOOK BACK, AND LOOKING AHEAD

Although Super Stock as a class would continue beyond 1968, and indeed is still with us today, it would never be the same. All the big names like Nicholson, Jenkins, Sox, et al, would forsake the old Super Stock classes for the new Pro Stock, which bore little resemblance to a factory stocker. Today's Pro Stock class is dominated with front-wheel drive cars with rear wheel drives, and engines with cubic inches in excess of 500 and horsepower measured well over 700. Let's see you run down to your local dealer and order up one of those!

What started out in the mid-1950s as a class where every young man (or woman) could race at the local track in what usually was the family sedan, rapidly escalated to out of control manufacturers building one-off vehicles that were available only to a select few. The various associations did their best to keep the manufacturers under control, especially the NHRA. However, they were soon completely overwhelmed with cheater cams, cheater slicks, and just plain cheating. This would lead to rule changes which in turn led to the manufacturers coming up with something to go around the rules. It was inevitable that big name racing teams would design a new cam or head

or intake, have it built and tested on their cars, then apply to it a factory part number. Of course, they were the only ones that would have that part for many months, giving them a decided advantage.

When Super Stock class was created in 1957, it was designed so that only the top high-performance vehicles from each manufacturer would compete against each other in head-to-head racing. This of course led to the great horsepower race of the early 1960s, but, and this is a very big but, everything that you saw on the track was available at your local dealer. You just had to walk in, sit down, and order it. Six weeks later it was in your driveway.

That was the way it happened, at least through 1962. That was the last year that the average Joe could walk into a Chevrolet, Ford, Pontiac, Dodge, or Plymouth dealership and order up the same car that had won at the drag strip the previous weekend.

In fact, 1962 was the only year that all the major manufacturers competed against each other in heads-up racing. In 1963, the first special-built vehicles began coming off the assembly lines. Available to only a select few drivers were 426 Dodges and Plymouths with aluminum body parts, 427 Chevrolets that you needed a special license to buy, aluminum Pontiacs with swiss-cheese holes cut into

*A familiar name returned to Chevrolet in 1970 with this Pro Stock '70 Camaro. Butch "The California Flash" Leal ran a 409 Chevy in 1962, then switched first to Ford Thunderbolts, then Plymouth Hemis. (Author's Collection)*

the frame making them almost illegal for the street, and fiberglass body panels for Fords. This list doesn't include the one-off vehicles like the 421 Tempest, 413 Dart, and 427 Fairlane.

By 1964, Super Stock class had evolved into a class for only the manufacturers racing teams to compete in, much like NASCAR. Ford's 427 Thunderbolt Fairlanes were clearly dominant in standard shift Super Stock class. The Dodge and Plymouth Hemi's were unbeatable in any of the automatic classes as well as Top Stock Eliminator trophies. General Motors had given up on the entire racing scenario after 1963, withdrawing all factory support for the teams that had dominated in 1962 and 1963.

Even the legitimizing of the 1965 rules which outlawed all non-steel body parts did not help. Chrysler simply came up with the superb A-990 Mopars which actually weighed less than their aluminum-bodied counterparts from 1964. Ford seemed interested in only the extreme top of the so-called "stock" classes, i.e. the Factory Experimental classes. Super Stock class in 1965 was strictly a Chrysler event, as it had the only cars available that met the class rules. You had to be someone to even get one of these new super stockers. Not mentioned yet are the really wild handful of altered wheelbase cars that were unleashed on both the unwary public and the sanctioning bodies in 1965.

By 1967, the sanctioning bodies simply threw up their hands in dismay. They liberalized the rules, thus destroying what was left of the original Super *Stock* class. Now it was legal to run any camshaft and any intake manifold. Not one, but twelve classes were created within a Super Stock division. What had begun as a class for everyone to race the car they bought to go to the grocery store, had finally developed into a mega-horsepower, mega-dollar division that was outside the scope of the normal Joe to compete.

In turn, this was still not enough for the race promoters. They wanted everyone to compete against one another in a top class, instead of using the handicap start procedure that was prevalent in Super Stock Eliminator. *Voila*, Pro Stock, where all the rules for stock were thrown out the window. The car just had to look stock. That opened the door to V-8-powered Vegas and Pintos in the early 1970s. It was just a small step to the Pro Stockers of today with their tube chassis, tubed rear wheelwells to keep huge tires within the body lines, and monster motors of up to 600ci and beyond. *Stock?* Nothing could be further from the truth.

The stocker and especially the super stocker, had been the king of the drag strips in popularity. The King was dead — assassinated by greedy track officials, inept rules makers, and manufacturers bent on winning at all costs. Who was the winner? Actually, no one. The teams now have to spend hundreds of thousands of dollars to have a competitive Pro Stock car. The sanctioning bodies have seen their fan base erode year after year. Drag strips all over the nation have folded their tents and built apartment complexes on the old 1/4 mile. The reason? It cost too much money to have these new Pro teams make an appearance at the local track. With a declining fan base, they were not getting the good return to their investment. The fans? Few of the old gang want to go to the track to watch photocopies of a car powered by the same type of motor run each other for Pro Stock Eliminator. A person who loves Chevrolets wants to cheer for a Chevrolet, or Olds, or Pontiac, not a clone body shell with a clone motor that simply has a Chevy "Bow Tie" painted on the nose or a Ford "oval". It sure was great while it lasted.

*Dave Strickler leans on the front of the latest* Grumpy's Toy, *the '70 Camaro that he drove in Pro Stock, and listens to Ronnie Sox (in striped pants) as both await the call for Pro Stock at the 1970 Nationals. In 1970, the Pro Stock cars were still just built-up super stockers. The completely outrageous Pro cars came along the following year. (Author's Collection)*

The Sox & Martin Plymouth Superbird makes a pass at Suffolk County Raceway in May 1970, competing in SS/E with one of the 440 Magnum engines. Although the bodies were designed for NASCAR use, Plymouth and Dodge released them for the cruising crowd. Properly tuned, the Sox & Martin car was capable of times in the low 11s. The car has been completely restored and still makes runs at nostalgia races throughout the nation. (Matchracemadness)

Grumpy Jenkins pulls the wheels on his Camaro at the '69 Super Stock Nationals. The Camaro has been modified for the new Pro Stock class. The sanctioning bodies liberalized the rules for Top Stock cars beginning in 1969, allowing them 427-inch motors, any type of carburetion system on 427-cube motors, and any size tires that would fit. Most of the cars went to the new tunnel ram intake mounting a pair of big Holley four barrels and 10-inch slicks. The times quickly dropped into the low 10s/high 9s. (Matchracemadness)

# NHRA RULES AND CHANGES FOR S/S AND FX

## 1955–1956

All cars must be completely factory stock, with closed exhaust systems and production size and type tires. The class is determined by the shipping weight divided by the manufacturer's advertised horsepower. Four classes: A/Stock through D/Stock. Both manual and automatic transmission vehicles in the same class.

## 1957–1958

New class: Super Stock (S/S). All cars with a horsepower-to-weight ratio between 0 – 12.59 compete in S/S. Six total classes between S/S and E/S.

## 1959

NHRA adds a Stock Eliminator title to National Championships.

## 1960

One new class added bringing Stock classes to seven: S/S to F/S. Automatic transmission classes added as optional. Any complete engine built by a manufacturer allowed, even if it is NOT optional for a particular model. "Non-visible" changes allowed, including ignition modifications inside the distributor. Any jet size allowed in carburetor. No open exhausts. Traction devices permitted as a safety feature against rear wheel windup. Only next bigger size tires allowed, but includes use of cheater slicks with a minimum of 1/16" tread for the first time. No floor shift conversions allowed.

## 1961

Super Stock class weight break at 0 – 10.59 lbs./hp. Stock class expanded to eleven classes: S/S to K/S. Any battery-operated ignition system allowed for first time. Floor shift conversions allowed. Open exhaust bypasses allowed for first time, if full exhaust system is retained. Scattershields now required on all stick-shift cars between S/S and C/S. June 1961, NHRA creates new class for cars with optional equipment not necessarily available to the general public: Optional Super Stock, O/SS.

## 1962

Factory Experimental (FX) class created as a follow-on to the late 1961 O/SS class for vehicles with optional equipment not readily available to the general public. Three FX classes determined by cubic-inch-to-weight ratio: A/FX, 0 – 8.99; B/FX, 9.00 – 12.99; C/FX, 13.00 or more. All stock rules apply except any size tire allowed that will fit in wheel well.

Stock Class now must be factory assembly-line produced and showroom sales available. New class at top of stock: Super Super Stock (SS/S), with class break at 0 - 9.89. S/S class now between 9.90 and 10.59 lbs./hp. Fourteen total classes between SS/S and L/S, with classes specified for automatic transmission cars for the first time. Automatic classes between SS/SA to G/SA.

New rules include raising and/or lowering of front or rear of car limited to a maximum of 2 1/2 inches over stock. Engines can be overbored a maximum of .060 to make an adjustment for wear. Any heavy-duty clutch or explosion-proof clutch assembly allowed. Open exhaust headers allowed as long as the exhaust collector or outlet is not bigger than the original head pipe diameter. Scattershields are now required on all FX, SS/S, S/S, A/S classes, and on all 283ci Chevrolet engines through C/S. Seat belts now required in all classes. Any size tire allowed as long it is less than 7" wide and has 1/16" tread, and that will fit in the original wheel well opening. Any gears allowed that will fit inside the original transmission housing.

## 1963

Fifteen classes in Super Stock between S/S and N/S, with automatic classes between S/SA and I/SA. S/S and S/SA limits are 0 – 8.69 lbs./hp. Factory Experimental class includes both 1962 and 1963 models with optional equipment not available to the general public. The minimum number of cars built to be classified as stock is set at fifty.

First time there is a limit on cubic inches. NHRA sets it at 427.2 cubic inches maximum displacement. NHRA also sets limits on cylinder overbore size. Cylinders can be overbored .060 for 1962 and earlier engines; and .030 for 1963 engines IF the overbore does not exceed the 427.2ci maximum displacement limit.

Other changes include an increase in the size of the header collector opening at 3.5 inches. Safety helmets are required in all FX classes and recommended in stock class. Wheel/tire sizes remain the same for stock classes, but FX cars can use any size wheel/tire combination that will fit in the fenderwell.

## 1964

One new class in Stock: AA/Stock and AA/Stock Automatic, with the break being S/S 0 – 6.99 and AA/S from 7.00 – 8.69. This is done to allow some of the older A/S cars to compete against one another and not have to race against the new factory models that would dominate the class. NHRA moves the small stock sports car classes into stock classes, i.e. C/Sports to H/Sports are now entered in one of the regular stock car classes. For the first time, NHRA limits the Factory Experimental entries to only that year's model cars, i.e. only 1964 cars can enter FX classes. All previous years' FX class entries will now run in one of the new Modified Production classes. A new change in FX and S/S classes is the first real breakaway from a stock engine: any flat-tappet camshaft will be allowed in both FX and S/S classes.

## 1965

One change in FX is a new rule that allows the wheelbase to be relocated a maximum of 2%. Also, FX cars will be able to run ANY type camshaft, including one of the new design roller lifter cams. Other changes include altered fenders and wheelwells in FX classes. Roll bars are now required in all FX class vehicles.

The camshaft rules are again relaxed further in Stock as any flat-tappet camshaft is now allowed in S/S, S/SA, AA/S and AA/SA. Safety helmets are now required in all FX, S/S, and Sports car classes. NHRA changes the minimum number of units to be classed as stock from fifty to one hundred.

At the end of the 1964 model year, NHRA instituted a program of 'factoring' certain engine horsepower ratings. Factories were rating horsepower low to get around high insurance premiums. So NHRA began running dyno tests to determine what horsepower a certain engine really was putting out. It was this figure, not the manufacturers' rated horsepower, that was used to determine a car's classification.

## 1966

Stock classes expanded to twenty-seven between S/S and O/S, and S/SA and J/SA. Factory Experimental classes and rules remain the same as 1965. The only major rule revision is that any intake manifold, as long as it has the same basic configuration as the stock manifold, can be used on Stock vehicles.

This year brought the introduction of the first Experimental Stock classes — NHRA finally recognizes "funny cars" and classifies them as Experimental Stock, with five classes within the XS Division, A/XS to E/XS.

## 1967

NHRA creates a new division within the rules of Stock Class: Super Stock Division. There are ten classes within S/S – SS/A to SS/E and SS/AA to SS/EA. NHRA now has twenty-three classes within Stock – A/S to N/S and A/SA to I/SA.

Super Stock division cars use all the same rules as Stock class vehicles with the following exceptions: S/S vehicles can run any type of camshaft and valvetrain; can use any type of intake manifold that is of the same configuration as the original stock intake; and can run any size wheel/tire combination that fits in the wheel well. Stock Class vehicles still limited to a 7" wide tire having a 1/16" tread.

The NHRA eliminates all Factory Experimental classes from the program.

## 1968

Super Stock division is expanded to twelve classes, SS/A to SS/F and SS/AA to SS/FA. Stock Class is expanded to thirty-four classes, A/S to U/S and A/SA to N/SA. The engine size rules are modified so that the new Chrysler 440ci engines are allowed to compete. Only those engines in competition in SS/A and SS/AA are limited to the old 427.2 maximum cubic inch displacement. All clutch assemblies in S/S classes must be an explosion proof unit. No stock clutch assemblies are allowed in Super Stock division.

*Action in S/SA at the '63 Nationals between Bill Shirey and the Golden Commandos #1 Plymouth and Roger Lindamood in the* Color Me Gone *'63 Plymouth, with Shirey about 2 car lengths in front. In the next round, Shirey lost to Jim Thornton and the Ramchargers No. 1 car. (Jack Bleil)*

# *NHRA STOCK ELIMINATORS*

**1955 Nationals** at Great Bend, KS
Top Stock: Arnie Beswick, '54 Oldsmobile @ 80 mph (no ET)

**1956 Nationals** at Kansas City Drag Strip, Kansas City, KS
Top Stock: Arnie Beswick, '54 Oldsmobile

**1957 Nationals** at Oklahoma State Fairgrounds Drag Strip, OK
Top Stock: John Zink, '57 Pontiac @ 93.60 mph

**1958 Nationals** at Oklahoma State Fairgrounds Drag Strip, OK
Top Stock: No stock classes run

**1959 Nationals** at Detroit Dragway, Detroit, MI
Super Stock: Harold Ramsey, '57 Chevrolet @ 14.94 ET
Top Stock Eliminator: Harold Ramsey, '57 Chevrolet @ 14.94 ET

**1960 Winternationals** at Spruce Creek Drag Strip, Daytona Beach, FL
Top Stock: Arnie Beswick, '60 Pontiac

**1960 Nationals** at Detroit Dragway, Detroit, MI
Super Stock: Jim Wangers, '60 Pontiac
Super Stock Automatic: Al Eckstrand, '60 Plymouth
Top Stock Eliminator: Jim Wangers *Hot Chief #1*, '60 Pontiac @ 14.14 ET

**1961 Winternationals** at Los Angeles County Fairgrounds, Pomona, CA
Super Stock: Frank Sanders, '61 Chevrolet @ 13.63 ET
Top Stock: Don Nicholson, '61 Chevrolet @ 13.59 ET

**1961 Nationals** at Indianapolis Raceway Park, Indianapolis, IN
Optional/Super Stock: Hayden Proffitt, '61 Pontiac @ 12.55 ET
Super Stock: Arnie Beswick, '61 Pontiac
Top Stock: Don Nicholson, '61 Chevrolet

**1962 Winternationals** at Los Angeles County Fairgrounds, Pomona, CA
Super/Super Stock: Hayden Proffitt, '62 Pontiac @ 12.75 ET
Super/Super Stock Automatic: Lloyd Cox, '62 Pontiac @ 13.00 ET
A/FX: Hayden Proffitt, '62 421 Pontiac Tempest @ 12.37 ET
Top Stock: Don Nicholson, '62 Chevrolet @ 12.63 ET

**1962 Nationals** at Indianapolis Raceway Park, Indianapolis, IN
Super/Super Stock: Dave Strickler, '62 Chevrolet @ 12.97 ET
Super/Super Stock Automatic: Al Eckstrand, '62 Dodge @ 12.72 ET
A/Factory Experimental: Lloyd Cox, '62 421 Pontiac Tempest @ 12.66 ET
Top Stock: Hayden Proffitt, '62 Chevrolet @ 12.83 ET

**1963 Winternationals** at Los Angeles County Fairgrounds, Pomona, CA
Super Stock: Tom Grove, '63 Plymouth @ 12.37 ET
Super Stock Automatic: Bill Hanyon, '62 Plymouth @ 12.30 ET
Limited Production: Frank Sanders, '63 Chevrolet Z-11 @ 12.01 ET
A/Factory Experimental: Bill Shrewsberry, '63 Chevrolet Z-11 @ 12.04 ET
Top Stock: Al Eckstrand, '63 Dodge @ 12.44 ET

**1963 Nationals** at Indianapolis Raceway Park, Indianapolis, IN
Super Stock: John Barker, '62 Plymouth
Super Stock Automatic: Jim Thornton, '63 Dodge @ 12.23 ET
A/Factory Experimental: Dave Strickler, '63 Chevrolet Z-11 @ 12.17 ET
Top Stock: Herman Mozer, '63 Dodge @ 12.22 ET

**1964 Winternationals** at Los Angeles County Fairgrounds, Pomona, CA
Super Stock: Gas Ronda, '64 Thunderbolt @ 12.05 ET
Super Stock Automatic: John Rodgers, '64 Plymouth @ 11.83 ET
Factory Stock Eliminator: Ronnie Sox, '64 427 Comet @ 11.49 ET
Top Stock: Tommy Grove, '64 Plymouth @ 11.63 ET

**1964 Nationals** at Indianapolis, Raceway Park, Indianapolis, IN
Super Stock: Butch Leal, '64 Thunderbolt @ 11.76 ET
Super Stock Automatic: Jim Thornton, '64 Dodge @ 11.37 ET
A/Factory Experimental: Dave Strickler, '64 Dodge @ 11.04 ET
Top Stock: Roger Lindamood, '64 Dodge @ 11.31 ET

**1965 Winternationals** at Los Angeles County Fairgrounds, Pomona, CA
Super Stock: Bill Andress, '65 Plymouth
Super Stock Automatic: Bill Jenkins, '65 Plymouth
Factory Stock Eliminator: Bill Lawton, '65 SOHC Mustang @ 10.93 ET
Top Stock: Bill Jenkins, '65 Plymouth @ 11.39 ET

**1965 Springnationals** at Bristol International Raceway, Bristol, TN
A/Factory Experimental: Don Nicholson, '65 SOHC Comet @ 10.80 ET
Match Bash Champ: Dave Strickler, '65 AWB Dodge @ 10.64 ET
Top Stock: Mike Schmitt, AA/SA '64 427 Ford Galaxie @ 12.32 ET

**1965 Nationals** at Indianapolis Raceway Park, Indianapolis, IN
Super Stock: Butch Leal, '65 Plymouth @ 11.56 ET
Super Stock Automatic: Bob Harrop, '65 Dodge @ 11.39 ET
A/Factory Experimental: Les Ritchey, '65 427 SOHC Mustang @ 10.67 ET
Top Stock: Bud Shallenberger, AA/S '64 427 Ford Galaxie @ 12.16 ET

**1966 Winternationals** at Los Angeles County Fairgrounds, Pomona, CA
Super Stock: Butch Leal, '65 Plymouth @ 11.50 ET
Super Stock Automatic: Joe Smith, '65 Plymouth @ 11.33 ET
A/Factory Experimental: Jerry Harvey, '66 SOHC Mustang @ 10.62 ET
Top Stock: Shirley Shahan, S/SA '65 Plymouth @ 11.26 ET

**1966 Springnationals** at Bristol International Raceway, Bristol, TN
Super Stock: Ed Miller, '65 Plymouth @11.82 ET
Super Stock Automatic: Joe Smith, '65 Plymouth @ 11.40 ET
A/Factory Experimental: No entries
Top Stock: Jerry Stahl, '66 A/S Plymouth @ 11.80 ET

**1966 Nationals** at Indianapolis Raceway Park, Indianapolis, IN
Super Stock: Ed Miller, '65 Plymouth @ 12.12 ET
Super Stock Automatic: Joe Smith, '65 Plymouth @ 11.38 ET
A/Factory Experimental: Ed Russell, '66 Ford @ 11.99 ET
Top Stock: Jere Stahl, '66 A/S Plymouth @ 11.73 ET

**1967 Winternationals** at Los Angeles County Fairgrounds, Pomona, CA
Super Stock/A: Ed Miller, '65 Plymouth @ 11.66 ET
Super Stock/A Automatic: Joe Smith, '65 Plymouth @ 11.27 ET
Super Stock Eliminator: Eddie Vasquez, SS/C '66 Chevy II @ 12.74 ET
Stock Eliminator: Graham Douglas, G/SA '60 Pontiac @ 14.42 ET

**1967 Springnationals** at Bristol International Speedway, Bristol, TN
Super Stock Eliminator: Ronnie Sox, SS/B '67 Plymouth @ 111.34 mph
Stock Eliminator: Jay Hamilton, E/SA '58 Pontiac @ 13.85 ET

**1967 Nationals** at Indianapolis Raceway Park, Indianapolis, IN
Super Stock/A: Robert Brown, '65 Plymouth @ 11.01 ET
Super Stock/A Automatic: Leonard Hughes, '65 Dodge @ 11.71 ET
Super Stock Eliminator: Bill Jenkins, SS/C '67 Camaro @ 11.55 ET
Stock Eliminator: Ben Wenzil, B/S '67 Camaro @ 12.33 ET

**1968 Winternationals** at Los Angeles County Fairgrounds, Pomona, CA
Super Stock/B: Ed Miller, '65 Plymouth @ 11.08 ET
Super Stock/B Automatic: Tom Crutchfield, '65 Dodge @ 11.13 ET
Super Stock Eliminator: Al Joniec, SS/E '68 Mustang @ 12.50 ET
Stock Eliminator: John Barkley, M/SA '57 Chevrolet @ 14.59 ET

**1968 Springnationals** at Englishtown, NJ
Super Stock Eliminator: Ronnie Sox, SS/D '67 Plymouth @ 11.20 ET
Stock Eliminator: Ron Garey, E/S '68 Oldsmobile @ 12.78 ET

**1968 Nationals** at Indianapolis Raceway Park, Indianapolis, IN
Super Stock/B: Willey Cossey, '68 Hemi-Barracuda @ 12.30 ET
Super Stock/A Automatic: Gary Ostrich, '68 Hemi-Barracuda @ 12.67 ET
Super Stock Eliminator: Arlen Vanke, SS/B '68 Hemi-Barracuda @ 10.64
Stock Eliminator: Larry Lombardo, F/S '61 Corvette @ 12.73 ET

*Proving that the eyes can be deceived, this photo appears to show Bill Lawton with a healthy lead over Al Eckstrand's Lawman Dodge. However, the two cars are actually side-by-side heading for the finish line during the run-off for the '63 Top Stock Eliminator. Eckstrand's Dodge was the winner with a time of 12.30. Although Eckstrand had won S/SA class, he would lose the Top Stock final to the Ramchargers Dodge driven by Herman Mozer. (Jack Bleil)*

# TOP STOCK QUALIFIERS

**1957**  *(First year for Super Stock class)*

Chevrolet   all models with 283ci, 270 hp with 2 - 4s or 283 hp with fuel injection, 3-speed manual transmission only

Pontiac   all models with 347ci, 317 hp, either 3-speed manual or 4-speed Hydra-Matic

Ford   all models with 312ci, 300 hp V-8 supercharged, 3-speed manual transmission

Dodge   D-500 with 354ci, 340 hp hemi-head V-8, either 3-speed manual or Torqueflite 3-speed automatic

Plymouth   Fury with 350ci, 290 hp V-8, either 3-speed manual or Torqueflite automatic

**1958**

Chevrolet   all models with 348ci, 315 hp V-8 with 3 two barrels, either 3-speed or 4-speed manual only

Pontiac   all models with 370ci, 310 hp fuel injected V-8, either 3-speed manual or Hydra-Matic

Ford   all models with 352ci, 300 hp V-8, 3-speed manual or Ford-O-Matic

Dodge   D-500 with 361ci, 320 hp fuel injected V-8, either 3-speed manual or Torqueflite

Plymouth   Fury with 361ci, 305 hp V-8 with 2 four barrels, either 3-speed manual or Torqueflite

**1959**

Chevrolet   all models with 348ci, 335 hp V-8 with 3 two barrels, either 3- or 4-speed manual only

Pontiac   all models with 389ci, 345 hp with 3 two barrels, either 3-speed manual or Hydra-Matic

Ford   all models same as 1958, not competitive

Dodge/Plymouth   all models with 383ci, 345 hp with 2 four barrels, either 3-speed manual or Torqueflite

**1960**

Chevrolet   all models with the 348ci, 335 hp V-8 with 3 two barrels, either 3- or 4-speed manual transmission only

Pontiac   all models with the 389ci, 363 hp V-8 with 3 two barrels, 3- or 4-speed manual or Hydra-Matic

Ford   all models with the 390ci, 360 hp V-8 with 1 four barrel, 3-speed manual transmission only

Dodge/Plymouth   with 383ci, 330 hp with 2 four barrels and ram induction, either 3-speed manual or Torqueflite

**1961**

Chevrolet   all full-size models equipped with the 409ci, 360 hp V-8 with 1 four barrel, 4-speed manual transmission only

Pontiac   all full-size models equipped with the 389ci, 363 hp Super Duty V-8 with 3 two barrels, either 3- or 4-speed manual and/or Hydra-Matic transmission

Ford   all full-size models equipped with the 390ci, 401 hp V-8 with 3 two barrels, 3- or 4-speed manual only

Dodge/Plymouth   all full-size models equipped with the 383ci, 330 hp V-8 with 2 four barrels on ram induction intake, 3-speed manual or Torqueflite

**1962**

Chevrolet   all full-size models equipped with the 409ci, 409 hp V-8 with 2 four barrels, and either 3- or 4-speed manual transmission only

Pontiac   all full-size models equipped with the 421ci, 405 hp V-8 with 2 four barrels and aluminum body parts, either 3- or 4-speed manual

Ford   all full-size models equipped with the 406ci, 405 hp V-8 with 3 two barrels, 4-speed manual only

Dodge/Plymouth   all full-size models equipped with the 413ci, 420 hp V-8 with 2 four barrels and ram induction, 3-speed manual or Torqueflite

**1963**

Chevrolet   Z-11 Impala in A/FX, equipped with 427ci, 430 hp V-8 with 2 four barrels, 4-speed manual transmission only, and with aluminum body panels

Pontiac   Catalina in B/FX equipped with the 421ci, 405 hp V-8 with 2 four barrels, aluminum body panels, and swiss-cheese frame, 4-speed manual transmission only

Ford   all full-size models equipped with the 427ci, 425 hp V-8 with 2 four barrels, 4-speed manual or Cruise-A-Matic

Dodge/Plymouth   all full-size models equipped with the 426ci, 425 hp V-8 with 2 four barrels and ram induction, aluminum body panels, 3-speed manual or Torqueflite

**1964**

| | |
|---|---|
| General Motors | no entries from any General Motors brands |
| Ford | Fairlane 2-door sedan equipped with 427ci, 425 hp V-8 with 2 four barrels and fiberglass body panels, 4-speed manual or Cruise-A-Matic transmission |
| Dodge/Plymouth | all full-size models equipped with the 426ci, 425 hp V-8 with 2 four barrels and ram induction, aluminum body panels, and gutted interiors, 4-speed manual transmission or Torqueflite |
| | At mid-year Dodge/Plymouth released the 426ci Hemi engine rated at 425 hp, with 2 four barrels and aluminum body panels, 4-speed manual or Torqueflite transmission |

**1965**

| | |
|---|---|
| General Motors | no entries from any General Motors brands |
| Ford | FX classes only, either Comet or Mustang coupes equipped with 427ci, 425 hp V-8 with 2 four barrels and fiberglass body panels, 4-speed manual transmission only |
| Dodge/Plymouth | A-990 2-door, full-size sedans equipped with 426ci, 425 hp Hemi V-8 with 2 four barrels and ram induction, lightweight steel body parts, gutted interiors, and available with either 4-speed manual or Torqueflite transmission |

**1966**

| | |
|---|---|
| General Motors | no entries from any General Motors brands |
| Ford | at least two 1966 Mustangs constructed for A/FX class only |
| Dodge/Plymouth | no 1966 entries in S/S; class dominated by 1965 A-990 entrants |

**1967** *(Creation of Super Stock Division within NHRA Stock Classes and elimination of all FX classes)*

| | |
|---|---|
| SS/A | Dodge/Plymouth 1965 A-990 cars |
| SS/B | Dodge/Plymouth full-size models equipped with the 426ci, 425 hp Street Hemi V-8 with 2 four barrels on inline intake, either 4-speed manual or Torqueflite<br>Ford Fairlane equipped with 427ci, 425 hp V-8, either 4-speed manual or 3-speed Cruise-O-Matic transmission |
| SS/C | '67 Chevrolet Camaro coupe equipped with 396ci, 375 hp V-8 with 1 four barrel, 4-speed manual transmission only |
| SS/D | '67 Chevrolet Chevelle SS 396 coupe equipped with 396ci, 375 hp V-8 with 1 four barrel, 4-speed manual transmission only<br>Pontiac GTO and Firebird coupe equipped with 400ci, 360 hp V-8 with 1 four barrel, either 4-speed manual or 3-speed Turbo Hydra-Matic transmission |

| | |
|---|---|
| SS/E | Dodge/Plymouth full-size models equipped with 440ci, 375 hp V-8 with 2 four barrels, either 4-speed manual or Torqueflite transmission<br>Chevrolet Camaro coupe with 396ci, 325 hp V-8 with 1 four barrel, 4-speed manual or Turbo Hydra-Matic transmission |

**1968**

| | |
|---|---|
| SS/A | Dodge Dart 2-door hardtop equipped with 426ci, 425 hp Hemi V-8 with 2 four barrels and lightweight body panels, either 4-speed manual or Torqueflite<br>Plymouth Barracuda 2-door fastback coupe equipped with 426ci, 425 hp Hemi V-8 with 2 four barrels and lightweight body panels, either 4-speed manual or Torqueflite |
| SS/B | Dodge/Plymouth 1965 A-990 2-door sedans equipped with 426ci, 425 hp Hemi V-8 with lightweight steel body panels, either 4-speed manual or Torqueflite |
| SS/C | Ford Fairlane 2-door hardtop equipped with 427ci, 425 hp V-8 with 2 four barrels, either 4-speed manual or 3-speed Cruise-O-Matic<br>Chevrolet Camaro coupe equipped with 396ci, 375 hp V-8 with 1 four barrel, 4-speed manual transmission only |
| SS-D | Chevrolet Nova 2-door sedan equipped with 396ci, 375 hp V-8 with 1 four barrel, either 4-speed manual or 3-speed Turbo Hydra-Matic transmission<br>Dodge/Plymouth full-size models equipped with 426ci, 425 hp Hemi V-8 with either 4-speed manual or Torqueflite transmission |
| SS/E | Ford Cobrajet Mustang fastback coupe with 428ci, 335 hp V-8, with either 4-speed manual or Cruise-O-Matic transmission<br>Dodge Charger 2-door hardtop equipped with 440ci, 375 hp V-8 with 2 four barrels, either 4-speed manual or Torqueflite transmission |
| SS/F: | Chevrolet Camaro equipped with 396ci, 325 hp V-8 with 1 four barrel, either 4-speed manual or 3-speed Turbo Hydra-Matic transmission<br>Chevrolet Camaro Z-28 coupe equipped with 302ci, 290 hp V-8 with 2 four barrels and ram induction, 4-speed manual transmission only<br>Dodge/Plymouth 2-door hardtop equipped with 440ci, 375 hp V-8 with 2 four barrels, either 4-speed manual or Torqueflite transmission<br>Pontiac Firebird coupe equipped with 400ci, 340 hp V-8 with 1 four barrel, either 4-speed manual or Turbo Hydra-Matic transmission |

**1969** *(Creation of Pro Stock)*

# SUPER STOCK ENGINE DEVELOPMENT

**1957** *(Creation of Super Stock class in NHRA)*

Chevrolet 283ci, 283 hp V-8 with Rochester fuel injection, solid lifter camshaft, 10:1 compression ratio

Ford 312ci, 300 hp V-8 with supercharged Holley four-barrel intake, 9.60:1 compression, solid lifter cam

Pontiac 347ci, 317 hp V-8 with one Carter four barrel, 10:1 compression, hydraulic lifter cam

Oldsmobile 371ci, 312 hp V-8 with three Rochester two barrels, 9.5:1 compression, hydraulic lifters

Dodge 354ci, 340 hp Hemi V-8 with two Carter four barrels, 10:1 compression

Plymouth 350ci, 290 hp V-8 with two Carter four barrels, 10:1 compression

**1958**

Chevrolet 348ci, 315 hp V-8 with three Rochester two barrels, 9.5:1 compression, solid lifters, 4-speed transmission available

Ford 352ci, 300 hp V-8 with one Holley four barrel, 10.2:1 compression

Pontiac 370ci, 310 hp V-8 with Rochester fuel injection, 300 hp with three Rochester two barrels, 10:1 compression, hydraulic cam

Dodge/Plymouth 361ci, 320 hp V-8 with two Carter four barrels or 333 hp with Rochester fuel injection (Dodge only)

**1959**

Chevrolet 348ci, 335 hp V-8 with three Rochester two barrels, 11.25:1 compression, domed pistons, hotter solid lifter camshaft

Pontiac 389ci, 345 hp V-8 with three Rochester two barrels, 10:1 compression, hotter hydraulic lifter camshaft

Dodge 383ci, 345 hp V-8 with two Carter four barrels (new engine design), 10:1 compression, solid lifter camshaft

**1960**

Chevrolet 348ci, 350 hp V-8 with three Rochester two barrels, 11.25:1 compression, hotter solid lifter camshaft

Ford 352ci, 360 hp V-8 with one Holley four barrel, solid lifter camshaft, 10.6:1 compression heads with larger valves

Pontiac 389ci, 348 hp V-8 with three Rochester two barrels, hydraulic camshaft, 10.75:1 compression, 4-speed transmission available

Dodge/Plymouth 383ci, 330 hp V-8 with two Carter AFB four barrels on ram induction intake, solid lifter camshaft

**1961**

Chevrolet 409ci, 360 hp V-8 with one Carter AFB four barrel, hotter solid lifter camshaft, same cylinder heads as '60 350 hp engine

Ford 390ci, 401 hp V-8 with three Holley two barrels, same cam and cylinder heads as 360 hp '60 engine, 4-speed transmission available

Pontiac 389ci, 363 hp V-8 with three two barrels, solid lifter cam, 11.2:1 compression, bigger valves

Dodge/Plymouth same V-8 engine availability as 1960

**1962**

Chevrolet 409ci, 409 hp V-8 with two Carter AFB four barrels, 11.25:1 compression with high dome pistons, bigger valves, hotter solid lifter camshaft

Ford 406ci, 405 hp V-8 with three Holley two barrels, 11.4:1 compression, bigger exhaust valves in cylinder heads, same cam as '60 360 hp engine

Pontiac 421ci, 405 hp V-8 with two Carter AFB four barrels, 11:1 compression, .030 overbore at factory, hotter solid lifter camshaft

Dodge/Plymouth 413ci, 420 hp V-8 with two Carter AFB four barrels on ram induction intake and 13.5:1 compression (410 hp with 11:1 compression), new heads with bigger valves and hotter solid lifter camshaft

**1963**

Chevrolet A/FX Z-11 427ci, 430 hp V-8 with two Carter AFB four barrels on two-piece, high-rise intake manifold, 13.8:1 compression, hotter solid lifter camshaft

Ford 427ci, 425 hp V-8 with two Holley four barrels, 12:1 compression, new design cylinder heads with bigger valves and hotter solid lifter camshaft

Pontiac    B-FX Catalina, 421ci, 405 hp V-8 with two Carter AFB four barrels, domed pistons, 13:1 compression, new design cylinder heads with bigger valves, same camshaft as '62 405 hp engine

Dodge/Plymouth    Stage 1: 426ci, 425 hp V-8 with two Carter AFB four barrels on ram induction intake and 13.5:1 compression (415 hp with 11:1 compression), hotter solid lifter camshaft
Stage 2: 426ci, 425 hp with two Carter AFB four barrels on ram induction intake and 13.5:1 compression, hotter solid lifter camshaft and bigger Carter four-barrel carburetors

## 1964

General Motors    No new special high-performance engines due to GM anti-racing edict of 1963

Ford    427ci, 425 hp Mk.II V-8 with two Holley four barrels on high-rise intake manifold, 14:1 compression, hotter solid lifter camshaft, new design cylinder heads with bigger valves

Dodge/Plymouth    Stage 3 426ci, 425 hp V-8 with two Carter AFB four barrels on ram induction intake, new design cylinder heads with bigger valves, 12.5:1 compression, hotter solid lifter camshaft, 4-speed transmission available

Dodge/Plymouth    (late): 426ci, 425 hp Hemi V-8 with two Carter AFB four barrels on ram induction, hemispherical compression chamber with 12.5:1 compression, much bigger valves, same camshaft as Stage 3 V-8

## 1965

Dodge/Plymouth    A-990: used same 426ci Hemi V-8 as 1964 model but with lightweight sheet metal

## 1966

Chevrolet    Chevy II A/S: 327ci, 350 hp V-8 with one Holley four barrel, 11:1 compression, hot hydraulic lifter camshaft, big valves in new design cylinder heads
Chevelle B/S: 396ci, 375 hp V-8 with one Holley four barrel, 11:1 compression, solid lifter camshaft, big valves in new cylinder heads
Full size B/S: 427ci, 425 hp V-8 with one Holley four barrel, 11:1 compression, cylinder heads and solid lifter camshaft same as 375 hp 396 engine

Ford    Fairlane A/S: 427ci, 425 hp Mk.II V-8 with two Holley four barrels, solid lifter camshaft, same heads as '64 Mk.II engine

Pontiac    GTO C/S: 389ci, 360 hp with three Rochester two barrels, 10.5:1 compression, hydraulic lifter camshaft

Dodge/Plymouth    A/S: 426ci, 425 hp Street hemi V-8 with two Carter AFB four barrels on inline intake manifold, solid lifter camshaft, 11:1 compression

## 1967

Chevrolet    Camaro SS/C: 396ci, 375 hp V-8 same as used in '66 Chevelle 375 hp engine
Camaro SS/E: 396ci, 325 hp V-8 with one Rochester four barrel, hydraulic lifter camshaft, 10.5:1 compression

Pontiac    SS/E GTO: 400ci, 360 hp V-8 with one Rochester four barrel, hydraulic camshaft

Pontiac    Firebird SS/D: same engine as '67 GTO

Ford    Fairlane SS/B: 427ci, 425 hp Mk.II V-8 as in '66 Fairlane

Dodge/Plymouth    SS/B: 426ci, 425 hp Street hemi V-8 as found in '66 Dodge/Plymouth
Dodge Charger SS/D: 440ci, 375 hp V-8 with two Carter four barrels
Dodge/Plymouth SS/E: same engine as SS/D Charger in heavier body

## 1968

Chevrolet    Camaro SS/C: 386ci, 375 hp V-8 as found in '66 Chevelle
Nova SS/D: same engine as in '66 Chevelle
Camaro Z-28 SS/F: 302ci, 290 hp V-8 with two Holley four barrels on ram induction intake, solid lifter camshaft, bigger valve cylinder heads, 11:1 compression
Camaro convertible SS/F: 396ci, 325 hp V-8 as found in '67 Camaro

Pontiac    GTO SS/F: same engine as '67 GTO

Ford    Mustang Cobrajet SS/E: 428ci, 335 hp with one Holley four barrel, solid lifter camshaft, bigger valves

Dodge/Plymouth    Dart or Barracuda SS/A: 426ci, 425 hp Hemi V-8 with two Carter four barrels on ram induction, 12.5:1 compression, solid lifter camshaft, same heads as competition Hemi engine of 1965
Plymouth Roadrunner SS/D: 440ci, 375 hp V-8 with two Carter four barrels on inline intake, solid lifters, same heads as '67 440 engine
Dodge/Plymouth SS/C: 426ci, 425 hp Street Hemi V-8, same engine as '66 Strect hemi

# CAR NAMES AND ASSOCIATED DRIVERS

| | |
|---|---|
| *Big Ma Mau* | '62 Ford driven by Phil Bonner |
| *Big Red* | '64 Plymouth driven by Tom "Smoker" Smith |
| *Black Arrow* | '65 Plymouth driven by Bill Jenkins |
| *The Boss* | series of Plymouths driven by Ronnie Sox in 1967-68 |
| *Bounty Hunters* | series of Dodges driven by Bob Banning |
| *Bronco* | '65 Match Bash Mustang driven by Dick Brannan |
| *The California Flash* | series of Fords, Plymouths, and Chevrolets driven by Larry "Butch" Leal |
| *Candymatic & Candymatic Too* | series of '63 – '64 Dodges campaigned by The Ramchargers |
| *Carolina Thunder* | '62 Chevrolet 409 driven by Ronnie Sox |
| *The Challenger* | '62 406 Fairlane driven by John Healy |
| *Color Me Gone* | series of Plymouths and Dodges driven by Roger Lindamood |
| *Color Me Kwik* | '63 Corvette driven by Jim Thompson |
| *Comet A-Go-Go* | '65 A/FX Comet driven by Eddie Schartman |
| *Dixie Twister* | series of Chevrolets driven by Huston Platt |
| *The Dodge Boys* | Dodge S/S and A/FX cars driven by Dave Strickler in 1964-65 |
| *Drag-On-Lady* | series of Plymouths and Dodges driven by Shirley Shahan |
| *Dyno Don* | nickname for Don Nicholson carried on many of his cars beginning with the '65 Comet |
| *Eliminator I* | '66 Comet funny car driven by Dyno Don Nicholson |
| *The Farmer* | nickname of Arnie Beswick and name of '63 Pontiac FX Catalina |
| *Flintstone Flying Commando* | '66 AWB Plymouth driven by Dave Koffel |

| | |
|---|---|
| *Flying Carpet Dodge* | series of Dodges driven by Bob Harrop |
| *The Fugitive* | '64 Thunderbolt driven by Skip Wilson |
| *Georgia Shaker* | series of Chevrolets and Fords campaigned by Hubert Platt between 1963 and 1970 |
| *The Goat Herder* | '64 Thunderbolt driven by Duke Burn |
| *The Go-Getter* | '63 Ford driven by Bill Lawton |
| *Go Hummer* | '65 Dodge S/S driven by Mary Ann Foss |
| *Golden Commandos* | series of Plymouth S/S and FX cars campaigned by Plymouth engineers and driven by Al Eckstrand, John Dallifior, and others |
| *Golden Lancer* | '62 413 Dodge Lancer campaigned by Dragmaster team of Jim Nelson & Dode Martin |
| *Goldenrod* | '62 Chevrolet 409 driven by Ron Nemeth |
| *Goldfinger* | '65 A/FX SOHC Mustang driven by Dick Brannan |
| *Goldfish* | '65 G/S Barracuda campaigned by the Golden Commandos |
| *Grumpy's Toy* | series of Chevrolets driven by Bill Jenkins 1966–1975 |
| *Hemi-Honker* | '64 Dodge driven by Bud Faubel |
| *The High & The Mighty* | '64 Dodge driven by Jim Fisk |
| *The Honker* | series of Dodges driven by Bud Faubel |
| *Hot Chief* | series of Pontiacs driven by Jim Wangers in 1960-61 |
| *Jerry G* | '62 Chevrolet 409 driven by Jerry Gribbons |
| *Landy's Dodge* | series of Dodge S/S and FX cars driven by "Dandy" Dick Landy |
| *Lawman* | '63 Dodge and '64-'66 Plymouths driven by Al Eckstrand |
| *'Lil Boss* | '68 Hemi-Barracuda driven by Ronnie Sox |
| *Little Pilgrim* | '64 Plymouth driven by Billy West |

| | | | |
|---|---|---|---|
| Little Red Wagon | 1965 Dodge A-100 pickup truck driven by Bill "Maverick" Golden and equipped with 426 Hemi engine | Retribution | series of '64 – '65 Chevrolets driven by Dick Harrell |
| The Lively One | '63 Ford driven by Dick Brannen | The Roadrunner | '65 B/FX Dodge driven by Fred Cutler |
| Maverick | series of Dodges driven by Bill Golden in 1962-64 | Running Bear | '63 421 Tempest coupe driven by Arlen Vanke |
| Melrose Missile | series of Plymouths driven by Tommy Grove and Cecil Yother in 1962-1966 | Seaton's Shaker | series of Chevrolet funny cars driven by Pete Seaton |
| Mr. 427 | '63 Z-11 Chevrolet driven by Ronnie Sox | Smoker | '63 Plymouth driven by Tom Smith |
| Mr. 4 Speed | series of Plymouths driven by Herb McCandless | Stampede | '64 A/FX Mustang driven by Dick Loehr |
| Mr. 5 and 50 | series of S/S and FX Plymouths driven by Jack Werst | The Steel Ram | '62 Dodge driven by John Barker |
| Mr. Bee | '65 AWB Plymouth driven by Vernon Rowley | Stinger I | '64 Thunderbolt driven by Kenny Vogt |
| Mr. B's Runabout | '63 421 Tempest coupe driven by Arnie Beswick | Strip Blazer | series of Chevrolet race cars driven by Malcolm Durham |
| Mrs. B's Grocery Getter | '63 421 Tempest station wagon driven by Arnie Beswick | Suction II | '63 Plymouth driven by Dick Lawrence |
| Mr. Ford | '62 Ford driven by Bruce Larson | Suddenly | '62 and '63 Chevrolets driven by Larry "Butch" Leal |
| Mr. Unswitchable | '65 AWB GTO driven by Dick Jesse | Suddenly III | '64 Dodge driven by "Doc" Dixon |
| Mystery 7 and 8 | Mustang funny cars driven by Bill Lawton | Super Cyclone | '64 S/FX Comet driven by Jack Chrisman |
| Mystery Tornado | '64 S/FX GTO driven by Arnie Beswick | Tension | '65 Dodge driven by Shirl Greer |
| New York Shaker | '63 Z-11 Chevrolet driven by Wally Bell | Tension II | '65 Chevy II driven by Bud Richter |
| Northwind | '62 Chevrolet 409 driven by Joe Gardner and Joe Tryson | Thumper | '61 B/S Chevrolet driven Gene Carter |
| The Old Reliable | Chevrolets driven by Dave Strickler between 1961 and 1963, and 1966 and 1975 | Tiger Tamer | '66 Oldsmobile C/S 4-4-2 driven by Ronnie Broadhead |
| The Old Goat | '64 Dodge hardtop driven by Dave Strickler | Tin Indian | series of Pontiac S/S cars driven by Arlen Vanke |
| The Original Dependable | '63 – '64 Dodges driven by Wes Koogle | Tip Toe | '62 Dodge driven by Bud Faubel |
| Paper Tiger | 1965 AWB Plymouth driven by Ronnie Sox | Too Costly | '66 SS/C Chevy II driven by Eddie Vasquez |
| Passionate Poncho | '61 and '63 Pontiac Catalina S/S cars driven by Arnie Beswick | The Ugly Dickling | '62 327ci B/FX Chevy II station wagon driven by Don Nicholson |
| The Professor | series of '64 – '65 Plymouths driven by Bill Shirey | Ugly Duckling II | '64 A/FX Comet station wagon driven by Ed Schartman |
| The Quiet One | series of Fords driven by Jerry Harvey | The Virginian | '65 Plymouth driven by Pee Wee Wallace |
| The Ramchargers | series of Dodge S/S and FX cars campaigned by Dodge engineers, and driven by Al Eckstrand, Herman Mozer, and Jim Thornton | Yankee Peddler | '65 AWB Dodge driven by "Wild Bill" Flynn |
| | | Warbucks | series of Ford S/S and FX cars driven by Phil Bonner |
| Res Ipsa Loquitur | '62 Dodge driven by Al Eckstrand | Zimmy | '63 and '64 Fairlane S/S cars driven by Bill Lawton |
| | | Zimmy II | '64 Fairlane S/S cars driven by Bill Lawton |

# MAJOR U.S. DRAG STRIPS IN THE 1960S

Alamo Dragway, San Antonio, Texas

Alton Dragway, Alton, Illinois

Amarillo Dragway, Amarillo, Texas

Aquasco Speedway, Aquasco, Maryland

Atco Dragway, Atco, New Jersey

Ardmore Dragway, Ardmore, Oklahoma

Arlington Drag Strip, Arlington, Washington

Atlanta Speed Shop Dragway, Atlanta, Georgia

Beechmont Dragway, Cincinnati, Ohio

Bonneville Dragway, Bonneville, Utah

Bristol International Raceway, Bristol, Tennessee

Caddo Mills Dragway, Caddo Mills, Texas

Capitol Raceway Park, Millersville, Maryland

Carlisle Drag-O-Way, Little Rock, Arkansas

Carlsbad Raceway, Carlsbad, California

Cecil County Dragway, Cecil County, Maryland

Cherokee Dragway, Frederick, Oklahoma

Childress Dragstrip, Childress, Texas

Connecticut Dragway, East Haddam, Connecticut

Continental Divide Raceway, Castle Rock, Colorado

Davie Drags, Davie, Florida

Deer Valley Dragway, Phoenix, Arizona

Detroit Dragway, Detroit, Michigan

Dragway 42, West Salem, Ohio

Dover Drag Strip, Wingdale, New York

Eastern Dragway, Petersburg, Virginia

Empire Dragway, Leicester, New York

Emporia Drag Strip, Emporia, Virginia

Erie Dragway, Presque Isle, Pennsylvania

Esta Safety Park, Cicero, New York

Evansville Raceway, Evansville, Indiana

Fayetteville Drag Strip, Fayetteville, North Carolina

Fontana Drag Raceway (aka Drag City), Fontana, California

Fremont Raceway, Fremont, California

George Ray's Wildcat Dragstrip, Paragould, Arkansas

Grand Island Jaycee Dragstrip, Grand Island, Nebraska

Green Valley Drag Strip, Gadsen, Mississippi

Green Valley Race City, Smithfield, Texas

Half Moon Bay Drag Strip, Half Moon Bay, California

Hub City Dragway, Biloxi, Mississippi

Indianapolis Raceway Park, Indianapolis, Indiana

Inyokern Drag Strip, Death Valley, California

Island Dragway, Great Meadows, New Jersey

Jaycee Dragway, Oklahoma City, Oklahoma

Lancaster Speedway, Lancaster, New York

La Place Dragway, La Place, Louisiana

Lassiter Mountain, Coalburg, Alabama

Lawton Dragway, Faxon, Oklahoma

Lions Drag Strip, Long Beach, California

Los Angeles County Fairgrounds, Pomona, California

Magnolia Drag Strip, Magnolia, Ohio

Mason-Dixon Drag Strip, Hagerstown, Maryland

McMinnville Dragstrip, McMinnville, Oregon

Miami, Florida (Masters Field or Amelia Earhart Field)

Minnesota Dragway, Anoka, Minnesota

Muncie Dragway, Muncie, Indiana

Nashville Dragway, Nashville, Tennessee

National Trail Raceway, Columbus, Ohio

New London Drag Strip, Lynchburg, Virginia

Newton County Drag Strip, Covington, Georgia

New York National Speedway, Center Moriches, Long Island, New York

Niagara Raceway Park, Niagara Falls, New York

Oklahoma State Fairgrounds Drag Strip, Oklahoma City, Oklahoma

Old Dominion Speedway, Manassas, Virginia

Omaha Dragway, Omaha, Nebraska

Osceola Dragway, Elkhart, Indiana

Pacific Raceway, Kent, Washington

Piedmont Drag Strip, Greensboro, North Carolina

Pittsburgh International Drag Strip, Pittsburgh, Pennsylvania

Pocatello Drag Strip, Pocatello, Idaho

Quad City Dragway, Cordova, Illinois

Quaker City Drag Strip, Salem, Ohio

Red River Drag Strip, Wichita Falls, Texas

Richmond Dragway, Richmond, Virginia

Riverside Raceway, Riverside, California

Rockford Dragway, Byron, Illinois

75-80 Dragway, Monrovia, Maryland

Spruce Creek Drag Strip, Daytona Beach, Florida

Sturgis Drag Strip, Sturgis, Kentucky

Southwest Raceway, Tulsa, Oklahoma

Tampa Dragway, Tampa, Florida

Texoma Dragstrip, Whitesboro, Texas

Thompson Drag Raceway, Thompson, Ohio

Tulsa International Raceway, Tulsa, Oklahoma

US 30 Dragway, Gary, Indiana

US 131 Dragway, Martin, Michigan

Valkaria Dragway, Valkaria, Florida

Victory Field, Vernon, Texas

Vineland Speedway, Vineland, New Jersey

Walker AFB Strip, Roswell, New Mexico

Yellow River Drag Strip, Yellow River, Georgia

York US 30 Drag-O-Way, York, Pennsylvania

*Clayton Wright goes off against the Coble & Bolland lightweight Galaxie in the AA/SA trophy run at York in October 1966. Wright's Slo Motion '63 Plymouth won the class at the '66 Nationals. Note the front fender logo, "It's Not a Hemi!" (Lee Menszak)*

*The old Ramchargers Candymatic was sold to Ray Christian in Columbus, Ohio who painted the car a light blue overall, but kept the custom "500" trim around the taillights. Christian continued to race the car into 1965, and is seen here at the '65 NHRA Regional Meet, held at Dragway 42 in May where he set a new record for A/SA. (Author's collection)*

# WHAT IT ALL MEANS

**2% AWB.** Maximum allowable wheelbase alteration per NHRA in 1964

**6V Package.** Six ventures — i.e. 3 two-barrel carburetors.

**AWB.** Altered Wheelbase.

**butt.** Slang for rear axle differential.

**cheater slicks.** Soft, wide tires with multiple grooves cut in them to simulate tread.

**Christmas Tree.** A starting line system consisting of a tall pole with several sets of yellow, green, and red lights, used for the start of a drag race.

**closed exhaust.** A complete exhaust system with mufflers and/or resonators

**Clutch-Flite.** Automatic transmission with a clutch for use when starting the car.

**Cruise-O-Matic.** Ford three-speed automatic transmission.

**dump tubes.** Exhaust header collector pipes.

**dual quads.** Two four-barrel carburetors.

**eliminator.** Final winner in a competition category.

**EquaLok.** A limited slip differential assembly used with Ford high-performance cars.

**exhaust cutout.** Open pipes that routed exhaust gasses out of the engine before the mufflers.

**factored horsepower.** NHRA took dynamometer horsepower readings for certain engines and used them to classify certain Stock class engines.

**flag man.** Drag race starter that used a flag to signal Go!

**Flathead.** A cylinder-head design which featured the intake and exhaust valves in the block, which were activated directly by the camshaft.

**Flathead in-line 6.** A Chevrolet engine with all six cylinders in a line and having a single, flat cylinder-head design.

**Ford-O-Matic.** A two-speed Ford automatic transmission.

**funny car.** Slang term for an altered wheelbase automobile, i.e. "looks funny huh?"

**gold dust.** Slang term for powdered resin used to increase traction on any surface.

**headers.** Competition exhaust system that featured individual tubes from each exhaust port joining together in a common "collector" to allow exhaust gas the easiest route out of the engine.

**Hemi.** Short slang term for an engine with hemispherical heads.

**hemispherical head.** Cylinder-head design in which the combustion chamber was a dome shape, usually with a valve on opposite sides of the dome and the spark plug in the center.

**Hydra-Matic.** A four-speed GM automatic transmission used in Pontiac and Oldsmobile vehicles

**lakes pipes.** Open exhaust pipes originally used on the Bonneville Lakes cars.

**mags.** Originally short for "magnesium wheels", but later used to signify any custom wheel that looked like a magnesium wheel.

**Match Bash car.** Car built specifically for professional match racing.

**open rear end.** A nonlimited-slip rear differential.

**out of the chute.** To leave the starting line quick.

**overhead.** Cylinder-head design wherein the intake and exhaust valves are located in the head and actuated by a "valve train," i.e. valve lifter, valve push rod, and rocker arm assembly.

**pipe rails.** Slang term for the early all-out dragsters.

**plumber's pipes.** Term for cheap open exhaust cutouts using galvanized plumbers pipe.

**Positraction.** A Chevrolet limited-slip differential assembly.

**Powerflite.** 1950s two-speed Chrysler automatic transmission .

**Powerglide.** A two-speed Chevrolet automatic transmission.

**punkin'.** Slang term for the rear differential, aka "butt."

**Saf-T-Track.** A Pontiac limited-slip differential assembly.

**slicks.** Soft, wide tires having no tread, i.e. they were slick all the way across the surface.

**SOHC.** Single Overhead Camshaft.

**Sonoramic.** Chrysler term for description of the ram induction intake system used on 1960-62 Chrysler high-performance vehicles.

**Sure-Grip.** A Chrysler limited-slip differential assembly.

**swiss-cheese frame.** A vehicle frame that has had holes cut in the walls for lightening.

**three on a tree.** Three-speed manual transmission shifter on the steering column.

**Torqueflite.** A Chrysler three-speed automatic transmission.

**Turbo Hydra-Matic.** A GM three-speed automatic transmission first used in 1965.

**Turboglide.** A three-speed automatic transmission used on Chevrolets from 1957 through 1961.

**typewriter drive.** Chrysler automatic transmission with push buttons instead of a gear shift handle.

**wedge head.** Cylinder-head design with a small wedge-shape depression or combustion chamber.